UNION MAN

UNION MAN

The Autobiography of

JACK JONES

COLLINS
8 Grafton Street London W1
1986

William Collins Sons and Co. Ltd
London · Glasgow · Sydney · Auckland
Toronto · Johannesburg

BRITISH LIBRARY CATALOGUING IN PUBLICATION DATA

Jones, Jack, *1913–*
Union man: the autobiography of Jack
Jones.
1. Jones, Jack, *1913–* 2. Transport and
General Workers' Union—Biography
I. Title
331.88′113805′0924   HD6665.J6

ISBN 0 00 217172 4

First published 1986
Copyright © 1986 by Jack Jones
Photoset in Monophoto Ehrhardt by Ace Filmsetting Limited, Frome, Somerset
Made and printed in Great Britain by
William Collins Sons and Co. Ltd, Glasgow

To Evelyn
whose continuous encouragement
is responsible for this book,
although its shortcomings
are very much my own.

FOREWORD

Jack Jones holds a special place in the hearts and minds of workers not only across the wide trade union movement but well beyond.

Union Man takes us on an interesting and fascinating journey through the life of a man clearly dedicated to the struggle for the betterment of workers' lives. From his childhood in his native Liverpool and through his early involvement in trade union organization to his experiences in opposing Fascism when he served in the International Brigade in Spain, Jack's dedication and commitment are clearly demonstrated.

That period of his life as a full-time trade union official in the Midlands and his promotion and development of trade unionism is reflected in the organization that exists today. As General Secretary of the country's largest union and in his relationships with the governments of the day he displayed the qualities of a great trade union leader and statesman.

Jack's autobiography is not only a chronicle of one man's dedication to the ideals that inspired his life, it is also a significant chapter in the history of the Transport and General Workers Union's industrial and political development based on participative democracy, which Jack has strived for from the moment he took trade union membership nearly three decades ago.

Over that wide span of years, from childhood to his current role as the champion for the rights of pensioners, this autobiography is a testament to a real 'union man'.

RON TODD
General Secretary
Transport and General Workers Union

ILLUSTRATIONS

ABBREVIATIONS USED IN TEXT

ACAS   Advisory Conciliation and Arbitration Service.
AEF   Amalgamated Engineering and Foundry Union.
AEU   Amalgamated Engineering Union.
AFL/CIO   American Federation of Labour and Congress of Industrial Organizations.
ARP   Air Raid Precautions.
ASLEF   Associated Society of Locomotive Engineers and Firemen.
AUEW   Amalgamated Union of Engineering Workers.
BMC   British Motor Corporation.
CBI   Confederation of British Industry.
CGT   Confédération Générale du Travail.
CNT   Conferación Nacional De Trabajo.
CPR   Canadian Pacific Railways.
DGB   Deutscher Gewerkshaftsbund.
EC   Executive Council.
EEC   European Economic Community.
EFTA   European Free Trade Area.
ETU   Electrical Trade Union.
ETUC   European Trade Union Confederation.
GEC   General Executive Council.
GKN   Guest Keen and Nettlefold.
ICFTU   International Confederation of Free Trade Unions.
ICI   Imperial Chemical Industries.
ILD   International Labour Defence.
ILO   International Labour Organization.
ILP   Independent Labour Party.
IMF   International Monetary Fund.
IRC   Industrial Reorganization Corporation.
ITF   International Transport Workers Federation.
MAP   Ministry of Aircraft Production.
NASD   National Amalgamated Stevedores and Dockers (Union).
NCLC   National Council of Labour Colleges.
NEB   National Enterprise Board.
NEC   National Executive Committee (of the Labour Party).
NEDC   National Economic Development Council.
NIRC   National Industrial Relations Court.
NJC   National Joint Council.
NJIC   National Joint Industrial Council.

NS&FU	National Seamen and Firemen's Union.
NUM	National Union of Mineworkers.
NUS	National Union of Seamen.
NUVB	National Union of Vehicle Builders.
PAC	Public Assistance Committee.
PTA	Passenger Transport Authority.
PTE	Passenger Transport Executive.
TGWU	Transport and General Workers Union.
TUC	Trades Union Congress.
TUCSA	Trade Union Council of South Africa.
UAW	United Automobile Workers.
UCS	Upper Clyde Shipbuilders.
UGT	Unión General de Trabajadores.
USDAW	Union of Distributive and Allied Workers.
WEA	Workers' Educational Association.

ACKNOWLEDGEMENTS

I am grateful to the following for permission to reproduce copyright material: David Higham Associates Ltd for extracts from works by Dylan Thomas; Roger Woddis for a poem first published in the *New Statesman*; and the *Daily Mail*, the *Daily Telegraph*, Mr Gerald Scarfe and the *Sunday Times*, and Trog and *The Observer* for the cartoons that illustrate the text.

Chapter One

And where is your table laid?
And where is your Sunday suit?
Tell me, where's your fireside warmth?
Say, where is your sword's sharp tooth?

GEORG HERWEGH

'Rain, rain, go away, come back on mother's washing day.' As we sang my mate and I spat on the wall and watched the spittle trickle downwards. It was a race, the one whose spittle went the fastest and furthest won. On rainy days we played inside the passage which opened on to the street. The walls were rough and the plaster was cracked and broken. There was no lino covering the bare boards, and the passage was dark and ugly. It typified the slum dwelling that was our house. Yet it was home and a refuge from the street when the weather was bad. Now the house where I was born and bred, and all the houses around it, are no more. They have been demolished, and not before time, for they were condemned as unfit for human habitation in 1913 – the year I was born.

My home was in York Street, Garston, in the south end of Liverpool – a long street of poor and mean terraced houses. They had two rooms up and two rooms down, generally in a decaying state. They had been built some time in the last century – obviously with the minimum of cost – to house labour for the nearby factories and docks. The houses were infested by rats, mice, cockroaches and bugs. Our rent was five shillings a week, and even that was exorbitant!

From a child's point of view the street had one advantage: out of the maze of working-class streets it was the nearest to the Mersey river. We walked past the copper works, the tannery, Grayson's shipyard, the bobbin works (making wooden bobbins for the textile industry), a derelict glass works and King's ship-breaking yard and there we were on the shore, a wonderful if muddy playground when we tired of playing our games in the the street. The proximity of the various industries attracted me. When I was a little boy I wandered into the local shipyard, somehow escaping the attentions of the gatekeeper, and got lost. That experience did not stop me from going again and again, if I got half a chance, to wonder at everything around me: the noise of riveting, hammering; the fumes and the flashes; the movement of the cranes; the red-hot rivets. . .

At times my friends and I would attempt an invasion of the shipyard or the copper works, only to be pushed back to the gates. There we would stand, until the men came out at the end of the afternoon shift. We would call out, 'Any bread left, mister?' and occasionally we would be rewarded with a sandwich or two, left over from a man's packed dinner. The corned beef sandwiches were the best, and if we were especially hungry a fight might start over their possession.

I had three brothers and a sister, all older than me. Because my early childhood was spent during the First World War, life was a little extra-ordinary. My sister (the eldest) went to live with an aunt and my father was in the army in France. My mother had to eke out a living for us and since the miserly army allotment was not enough we had lodgers in the front room. First it was an old man who had been estranged from his family. His name was Pearce and we called him 'P.P.'; he could play the tin whistle very well and often did so, sitting on the front doorstep. Later the room was occupied by an Italian, Tony, and his young wife, Sally, whom my mother 'took in' so that she could have her baby. I liked Tony, he romped around with me on his back and played with me and the other kids in the street. He had a job in the local shipyard and I remember he sometimes took me down to the docks to visit Italian ships. One of his friends was a skipper and once I was present at a party in the skipper's cabin and sat up to the table to eat a piece of cake. Oh! that cake was marvellous. Tony ended up a gangster in the United States and was killed in a gang war in Chicago.

My mother was no stranger to poverty but she had a resilient spirit. She had first been married to a seaman who became a customs officer. They had three children (my sister and two elder brothers – I never thought of them as 'half') but her husband died early, leaving my mother without anything. She determined to keep her little family together, to scrat and scrape and do everything in her power to avoid going into the workhouse – the evil prospect which then faced poor people in such circumstances. First she did washing for neighbours in the street, then she opened a little shop in the front room of her house. She kept going in her battle against adversity by the aid of a poor Jewish pack-man, Mr Tumarkin. When nobody else would help her, this stranger let her have goods on extended credit. He had fled from the pogroms in Poland and must have suffered further privation to help my mother keep her business going.

Her stories of those difficult days used to make me sad, but then she would say, as if drawing a moral: 'There are more good than bad people in the world, always remember that.'

When I was a little boy my mother bought something every week from a modest shop owned by an elderly Jew, who had been a friend of Tumarkin when he was alive. Even if it was only a penny tin soldier for me, the purchase was a mark of respect to her old benefactor. She would never visit the shop without mentioning Tumarkin's name. I am sure that her attitude helped form my opposition to Nazi Fascism and my hatred of all kinds of racialism.

In her struggle to make ends meet, Mother took in lodgers, including my father who later married her. He was a hard-working man but he liked a drink. It was always a happy occasion when he came home, more than a little merry, and would sing 'I'll Take You Home Again, Kathleen', or some such song and scatter what coppers he had left in his trouser pockets. We would scramble about picking up the coppers as though it was Christmas. My father had started work at eleven years of age in the brickyards. At thirteen he was driving a crane at the docks. While unloading a ship one day he inadvertently caused some damage and was fined five shillings and told it would be deducted from his meagre wages. He refused to accept the penalty and went to sea. Some time afterwards he returned to the docks and worked as a docker until he was seventy.

Father was a kindly man, loyal to his family, his workmates and his union. He believed in the union because he had lived through the changes achieved by it, especially in the docks where conditions had been atrocious. He often told how men had fought physically for a job, and of the times when he had worked days and nights continuously on iron ore ships until the vessel had been completely discharged. This was hard work indeed, especially for undernourished men as they so often were. Occasionally he would describe the difficulties men had faced in building the union. It was then I first heard the names Jim Larkin and Tom Mann, and developed a healthy dislike for knobsticks or scabs, people who had been used by the employers to break strikes, who had betrayed their own class. (Larkin and Mann were legendary union leaders with strong Liverpool connections. Mann had led the big Liverpool transport strike of 1911, and my father had known

Larkin on the docks before he achieved fame as an Irish trade union leader.)

Being kind didn't prevent Dad being firm and giving me a hefty smack if I misbehaved. This was nothing to the treatment other boys in the street received from their fathers. Some men used the belt unmercifully on their children, as became apparent when we played together in the river with our clothes off. The unlucky ones would have big red weals on their backs.

A few of the women suffered similar treatment. It was a rough street. One man living near to us used to come home on Saturdays from the pub and beat up his wife. He would then put their few sticks of furniture out into the street and there would be a hell of a row. The woman usually appealed to my mother, who would put her shawl on and go and reason with the man. She was a natural peacemaker, and managed to get respect even from the half-drunken man.

Life in the neighbourhood reflected the harsh conditions of living in overcrowded and squalid housing; of heavy work on the docks, in the shipyards and local factories; of casual employment or, even worse, unemployment; of low wages and in some cases 'parish relief'. Not a house in the street had an inside lavatory or a bathroom. There was no gas or electricity in the houses. We had a paraffin lamp downstairs, otherwise we used candles. We bathed in a tin bath once a week, and even that wasn't easy, for the water had to be heated on the one coal fire. My three brothers and I slept in one of the two bedrooms, in the early days in one bed. Every morning a lad would trundle a metal barrel on wheels round the street shouting 'lant', which meant urine for use in the pickling process in the local copper works. The women would empty the contents of their chamber pots into the barrel. As a kid I didn't question these things, I just accepted them as the natural order of living.

It used to be said in Liverpool, 'It's the poor who help the poor,' and there was plenty of evidence of that in our neighbourhood. Knock-knock at the door, and someone would want to borrow half a cup of sugar or a bit of marge (always margarine, we didn't know anything about butter then, not in our street). Perhaps some tea would be requested, or half a loaf of bread. People helped each other, even if the loan couldn't be repaid for a long time – if ever.

If a young woman had trouble bringing her baby into the world there would always be older women on hand to help, supplying advice, maybe a bit of clothing, and not least comfort. Usually old Meg

Stanton would act as the midwife. Almost like a character out of Dickens, with her grey shawl and bonnet, Meg was also the woman who 'laid out' the dead in our street. If she got paid at all for her services it wouldn't be much, just a few coppers. But she performed many tasks, including the important one of taking bundles to the local pawn shop. On Mondays people would wrap up anything of value, perhaps the old man's suit, the one suit of a lifetime, and the bundle would be taken to the pawn shop and redeemed on the Friday. Meg would take it and redeem it – in that case for a fixed charge of a penny or twopence.

Things were so bad that many people didn't have a 'Sunday suit' or anything else of value to pawn at 'Uncle Edward's', the local name for the pawnbroker. In the house next door the children didn't even have a bed to sleep in, nor did their parents. They slept on the bare boards of the floor with old overcoats and other clothing to cover them. The father was a ship's fireman, but the seagoing fraternity was paid atrociously low wages at that time. It was no wonder that many youngsters died from scarlet fever, diphtheria or tuberculosis. Tuberculosis was a disease of poverty, a working-class plague that swept through Liverpool. We knew the disease as 'consumption' then. We would hear that Mrs 'so and so' was sick with galloping consumption and within a month or two she would be dead. Then there would be a collection in the street to help pay for the coffin and the hearse. Usually it would just be a hearse without any following carriages. Neighbours and friends walked behind. In the case of children sometimes there would not even be a hearse; the father and relatives or friends would carry the coffin to the graveyard, through the streets.

Despite its harshness, life for me was not all gloom. The street was a community and I had a lot of mates. Even at night, when we were exhausted from active games like 'rally-vo' and wrestling, we would huddle together in gangs, telling each other stories of the banshee and other ghosts. Any unusual cry would be translated into the lonely croon of the banshee. For the rest, the films we had seen at Saturday matinées in the local picture house for a ha'penny plus a jam jar (or a penny without the jar) would be re-enacted. Buffalo Bill, Tom Mix and Pearl White would live again. I was well known for my imitation of Charlie Chaplin, twiddling a little cane found for me by my grandfather.

My paternal grandfather lived a little way down our street. He was a boilermaker by trade. Red-faced, with white hair and white beard, he had a big red nose which he claimed had been caused by a hammer blow in the shipyard. Another view was that it had developed from drinking beer. He was the source of my only pocket money at the time and gave rise to my first negotiations for extra pay. I got a penny a week, which was quite generous, and I shared it with three friends in buying tiger nuts, locust beans, liquorice and sometimes a carrot or two. Sweets were costly and generally out of our range. One day I took my mates with me to see grandad and asked him if he would give them a penny a week also. Well, he wouldn't go that far but he agreed to give them a ha'penny each, and the same to me. So we did well out of that. I had been spending a penny a week on the four of us, now we got twice as much, a lesson in the redistribution of wealth!

One of my trio, my companion of the 'spit race', died shortly afterwards, a victim of tuberculosis. I remember crying my heart out. It must have had a dramatic effect on me, for the memory of that little boy and his early death has remained with me over all these years.

From my grandfather I learned much, usually while munching a fat bacon sandwich which he had made for me. He cooked the bacon on a Dutch oven in front of the open fire. The old man would tell me about the ships he had worked on. He was proud of the jobs he had done, and yet he had been dismissed, along with some other men, for leading a strike at a local shipyard. I listened to him closely as he told me how, after months of being out of work, he had tramped from Liverpool to Edinburgh to work on the railway bridge there. He had not started out intending to go that far, but had walked from town to town seeking work by contacting the local lodge of the Boilermakers' Society. As a 'tramp boilermaker' he got one shilling and sixpence or thereabouts for food and a bed provided by the local lodge. It was an example of mutual aid, workers helping each other through their union in the time of adversity.

At five I started going to school at the nearest elementary school. It was no worse – or better – than most of the schools in Liverpool. We were all children from the working-class streets around. Our fathers were dockers, seamen, workers at the local shipyards of factories. Some fathers were unemployed, other children had only their mother or a relative to look after them. The worst-off kids who came to school in rags and tatters and bare feet were sent with a note to the local police station. The police administered a welfare fund which provided corduroy trousers and a jersey for the boys and something similar for the girls. The trouble was that these clothes emphasized their poverty and the corduroys smelt terribly. The rest of us were not much better off. Outside school we played in our bare feet (oh, the pain when we ran across a piece of glass and cut our feet!). We were lucky if we had pumps or clogs to go to school in.

I was a typical youngster of the area, with no more than average educational ability. The teachers appeared to give much more attention to the brighter children (often the children of foremen or local shopkeepers) who might qualify for scholarships. There weren't many of these. I don't remember knowing anybody who got to university. Extended education was obtained only by great sacrifice on the part of parents, who generally were anxious to see their kids at work and supplementing the family income. Basically, for us, school was something you had to 'go through'. The teachers who helped most were those who made education close to real life. In general I did not get much stimulation. We were taught history with emphasis on 'kings and queens, lords and ladies'. This had some colour to it, but it never came alive for me until a neighbour, when I was ill and home from school, lent me a copy of a book entitled *Our Old Nobility*, which gave the origins of the 'great' noble families. Imagine my interest in discovering that one of the Liverpool noble families had its beginnings in cattle robbery and land thieving.

In our school little was taught of industrial history or the background to the lives of ordinary people – or if there was it was not taught in such a way that I remember it. If there were no formal civics courses at school, there was plenty of practical instruction outside. I remember hearing Tom Mann and Mary Bamber (the mother of Bessie Braddock who became Liverpool's best known MP and City Councillor) address open-air meetings, and as children we got to know what strikes were about and what a terrible person a 'scab' was. Even getting soup from the local soup kitchen (in a nearby chapel) during the 1924 dock strike was a lesson in itself. I don't think we were aware of being educationally under-privileged, but we were. In a cramped slum house you can't do well at homework, which reinforced the deficiencies of the school itself.

Discipline couldn't have been easy to maintain in our school. One of our teachers was named Miss Shufflebottom; her fellow teachers always referred to her as 'Miss Shuff' and expected the children to buy that one, but of course we insisted on calling the lady Miss Shuffle-*bottom*. Another teacher whose name was Westlake earned the title of 'Jenny Wet-legs', because if she got into trouble with the class she would go behind the blackboard and cry. The men were made of tougher stuff but in the main they didn't do any caning in class. That was reserved for the headmaster. Outside his office each day there would be a big queue of boys waiting to be caned. We believed that if we rubbed our hands with a piece of resin it would take the sting out. I don't know about the others, but it didn't work for me.

Liverpool had its fair share of 'do-gooding' charities, but some were closer to the ground than others. Such was the case with the Liverpool City Mission in Mill Street. The mission was run by a Mr Tom Hughes, who was devoted to the welfare of youngsters from the poorer areas to the south of the city. He had raised funds to buy a cottage in the Isle of Man and during the summer groups of children were taken there for a free holiday. My father was able to arrange for my nearest brother and me to go on one of the holidays, and when he told us about it excitement wasn't the word. I was eight years old and it was my first (and only) holiday away from home during the whole of my childhood.

We travelled across on one of the Isle of Man steamships, a wonder in itself, and then on to the country cottage at Surby. Some of us slept in one big bed, top and tail. I was a little frightened by the new experiences: washing under the water pump, scrambling around the fields. But I was most amazed by the vivid colours of the island, the various shades of green and gold in the patchwork of fields around us. It contrasted sharply with the drabness of my home. My greatest pleasure was carrying back a pair of red herrings, which all the children were given before we left, and handing them over as a present to my dad.

Very occasionally we would glimpse the joys of the seaside on a day trip to New Brighton. A penny on the tram and twopence on the ferry boat took us there. The problem was to find the pennies!

Outside school our great interest was football. We played it in the street and the school yard. We were supporters of Liverpool or Everton, but as children we couldn't afford to go to their games, although we knew the names of the players by heart. The local (semi-professional) team was Garston Gasworks and we gave them every support, either paying a penny to get in or slipping under the fence. One of the most popular players was Bill 'Stonewall' Jackson who later, when I went to work in the docks, proved to be a solid companion in fighting corruption and bureaucracy on the job and in the union.

When twelve years old I developed rheumatic fever and was away from school for about twelve months. During this time, when I wasn't in hospital, a schoolteacher friend of the family, Madge Noonan, helped me greatly with my education. Her individual tuition made sure I didn't fall too far behind and in some ways helped me to achieve a wider vision.

My three brothers were in the Boy Scouts and I was encouraged to join too. My second eldest brother, who carried all his life the nickname 'Gogo', was the more glamorous. He was a leading Sea Scout, and had saved a man from drowning in the Mersey; he also played soccer so well that he had had trials for Everton. I accompanied him to the Sea Scouts until he went to sea. 'Biff', the brother nearest to me in age, was ready for a scrap at any time. I recall his intervention when I was involved in a fight with another boy. First, he pushed the other boy away and then he bashed me. I took a poor view of that . . . after all he was *my* brother!

The most marked influence on me and, indeed, on the rest of the family, was that of my eldest brother Syd. It was he who taught my father to ride a bicycle when Dad was well over fifty years old, braving the cursing and swearing when he fell off the bike. Even later it was Syd who persuaded my father occasionally to wear a collar and tie instead of the usual muffler.

Syd became a scoutmaster and I joined his troop, which was linked up with a chapel in the area. He enticed me to take an interest in the Sunday School and for a time I had the temerity to teach there. But my interests turned in a more political direction and later, when I became active in the Labour Party, I sometimes performed the role of teacher in a socialist Sunday school. The movement, now almost defunct, gave children an ethical outlook on life without involving them in religious creeds.

Ten commandments were taught in the socialist Sunday schools, but not those one heard in church. I remember particularly:

> Honour good men and women, be courteous to all, bow down to none.
>
> Do not hate or speak evil of anyone; do not be revengeful, but stand up for your rights and resist oppression.
>
> Do not be cowardly. Be a friend to the weak and love justice.
>
> Remember that the good things of the earth are produced by labour. Whoever enjoys them without working for them is stealing the bread of the workers.
>
> Observe and think in order to discover the truth. Do not believe what is contrary to reason, and never deceive yourself or others.
>
> Do not think that they who love their own country must hate

19

and despise other nations, or wish for war, which is a remnant of barbarism.

Look forward to the day when all men and women will be free citizens of one community and live together as equals in peace and righteousness.

I have reflected on those ideas throughout my life and have tried to be guided by them. But life ahead was going to test some of those lofty ideals. . . .

Chapter Two

Everything indicates – the smallest does, and
the largest does;
A necessary film envelops all, and envelops the
Soul for a proper time.

WALT WHITMAN

I had just gone back to school when the General Strike of 1926 occurred. For a long time the dire position of the miners was discussed in our home and, although I couldn't really visualize their work, I felt strong sympathy for them. This attitude was strengthened when one of my uncles took me to a miners' meeting in the Wigan area. The main speaker was A. J. Cook. I was enthralled. The miners responded to him as a great hero. He shouted out his defiance of the mine-owners, he stooped, he gestured. I remember one phrase he used: 'Figures can lie and liars can figure.' He was attacking the statistics being used against the miners but the phrase stayed with me, and often came back into my mind, when later in life, I saw figures unscrupulously manipulated.

During this period too I remember Ernie Bevin addressing a big meeting in one of the Liverpool parks. My father had taken me along to the meeting and when Bevin came off the platform I was one of a few boys who shook his hand. I'm afraid his speech did not impress me; I just thought he was a big, fat man. Of course I knew his name, because frequently he was referred to as the 'Dockers' KC' in our house, especially by my father. When the General Strike broke out life seemed to change completely. I read anything I could lay my hands on, especially the *British Worker*, and listened avidly to the radio. My father and brothers were on strike but I sensed no anxiety in the family, only a desire for the strike to succeed.

My elder brother, a railwayman and member of the ASLEF (Associated Society of Locomotive Engineers and Firemen), was actively involved with the local Council of Action and I used to help him by running messages on my bicycle. I felt I was part of a great army, particularly so when I was noticed by one of the local leaders, Bill Bewley. A powerful personality and vigorous speaker, red-haired and burly, he took an interest in me and it was reciprocated on my part. Years after, as a young trade unionist, I turned to him often for advice and he it was who persuaded me to read *The Ragged Trousered Philanthropists*. The book is a realistic description of the building trade in the early years of this century and a powerful exposition of socialist ideas, written by a working-man, Bob Noonan, under the pen-name of Robert Tressell. In my youth it was passed from hand to hand among people in the Labour movement and had a remarkable effect on our thinking. The atmosphere of the strike entered into my being and, with the strikers, I loathed the scabs and blacklegs.

After the high enthusiasm generated during the strike, the bewilderment and disillusion when it was called off were intense. Bill Bewley and others spoke at a hurriedly called mass meeting of the strikers in Garston. Angrily Bewley accused the leadership of betrayal and his cry 'We have been let down!' was bitterly applauded. The trust of working people is not easily won, it needs to be nurtured and sustained by sincerity and dedication; to brush it aside damages confidence for a long time. This is what happened when the General Strike was brought to an end. There was a feeling that the leaders had acted like the grand old Duke of York, who 'had ten thousand men, he marched them up to the top of the hill and marched them down again'. By leaving the miners to struggle on their own, the leadership of the TUC had not only let them down, but had stained the honour of those who had been on strike. The leader most reviled was J. H. (Jimmy) Thomas. He had had a bad record on the railways, according to my two brothers, and the General Strike confirmed the strong feeling against him. The bitterness continued for some time, for with the end of the General Strike came victimization. At some places of work, including the railways, there was no automatic return to employment. Men were taken back in dribs and drabs and many active trade unionists were pushed out of a job altogether.

The experiences of the time had a powerful impact on my thinking. I followed closely the events which came after the General Strike. Newspaper accounts of the efforts of Baldwin, the Prime Minister, and his cohorts to weaken organized labour, consolidated my sympathies for working people and the unions. I read my father's TGWU (Transport and General Workers Union) *Record* and my brothers' ASLEF *Journal*; so much so that my brothers began to object to a· youngster, still at school, commenting on 'their' union affairs! There was no doubt the unions were under attack. Sir John Simon introduced his Trades Disputes and Trade Union Act, and came to be regarded as the hatchet man of the Government. (The Act made general strikes and sympathetic strikes illegal. It drastically altered the law on picketing and provided a procedure for legal injunctions against 'illegal strikes' and for trade union funds to be attacked on the lines of the Taff Vale case. It also introduced 'contracting in' in place of 'contracting out', in trade union political funds.) Unions, anyway, were having difficulties in keeping their members, because of the slump in trade and the imposition of wage reductions in some industries. The miners' continuing struggle against wage reductions and an extension of the working day, emphasized the depth of despondency which faced the Labour movement.

It was in that period that I left school and went to work. It wasn't easy to get a job at that time in Liverpool. There is nothing worse than the feeling of being unwanted. I wrote lots of letters and traipsed around factories until finally I found a vacancy and later an apprenticeship. The firm was in general engineering, making components for Graysons and Harland and Wolff, the shipbuilding and ship-repairing firms. As was the custom, my father signed indentures for me. The apprenticeship was supposed to last for five years. My first pay was five shillings a week, and as I had to take sandwiches and travel by tram and overhead railway to get to work, my contribution to the household income wasn't very great.

The term 'apprenticeship' was something of a myth. It implied systematic training, but that certainly wasn't forthcoming. The training depended upon the goodwill of the older men. I was moved around the fitting and machine shops and got some experience of filing, milling, drilling and other work and a strong impression that we apprentices were being used as cheap labour. Even the older men benefited from our exploitation, because we became the tea boys. We were also used as messengers. Often we were the butt of men who would tell us to go for a couple of sky-hooks or to ask the stores if they had got a tin of rainbow paint in stock. There were no women on the shop floor and the language was uninhibited. The facts of life quickly became apparent, causing many blushes in my youthful years.

Some of the machine tools were rackety, they were belt-driven and the lighting was poor. The shops were oily and dirty. It was no wonder that minor accidents occurred frequently and it was this which directed my thoughts towards joining a union. Some of the men were in the AEU (Amalgamated Engineering Union) and in various craft unions, but general apathy prevailed, linked with an understandable fear of getting dismissed. Men were often sacked on the spot for the slightest misdemeanour. I began to urge older workmates to join up, but apprentices weren't welcome in the AEU. Despite my recruiting efforts for his union, I was told to wait until I grew older by Jack Clark, the District Secretary. Eventually I joined the Power Group of the TGWU (Transport and General Workers Union) and I persuaded a few of the semi-skilled workers and labourers to do the same. The District Secretary, Albert Ellis, became anxious to help, at least with advice, once he knew that my father was a member of the TGWU.

Some of the men were on individual piecework and invariably complained about the 'lousy rates'. I managed to get information about piecework agreements in the industry and was satisfied that the men were getting a raw deal. There were no proper negotiations, and where earnings began to increase, the management would find ways to cut the rates. In some cases they would simply change the drawing number and claim it as a new job, so that the rate could be 're-arranged'. I urged a few of the men to make a stand and not just accept any old price. They clearly didn't like taking advice from a young lad, but it had some effect, and occasionally a man would sidle up to me to ask about the agreements. The trouble was that they had little or no confidence in appealing to the union.

I regularly attended my union branch meeting and was always amazed and concerned at the small number of members present. Usually about twenty attended out of a branch of some hundreds. There is a myth that small attendances at union meetings is a present-day phenomenon but this is not the case. At the second branch meeting I attended I was elected branch delegate to the Liverpool Trades Council and Labour Party. I must have been the youngest delegate by far. It was a most august body, well attended and conducted with firm chairmanship. The authority of the chair was always well sustained with the aid of a couple of burly doorkeepers who moved in quickly if anyone attempted to defy a ruling. I suppose my youth must have aroused the interest of the Trades Council Secretary, an old-style Marxist named W. H. (Bill) Barton, because he often sought a chat with me and at his suggestion I became active in the Liverpool Labour College, the local arm of the National Council of Labour Colleges. This body ran evening and weekend classes for trade unionists.

I was already a member of the Labour Party and secretary of my local ward organization, so as well as going to the soccer match on Saturdays (or in the summer rambling on the Wirral with other youngsters) and attending evening classes at the technical school, my spare time was rapidly filled up by trade union activity. Many exciting times were spent at the Trades Council meetings. They certainly provided a striking example of animated humanity; a couple of hundred working people concentrating their minds in fierce debates on the problems of the day.

Perhaps the most memorable meeting for me was at the time of the 1931 crisis. The Labour Government had collapsed, with MacDonald, Snowden and Thomas going over to form the so-called 'National Government'. Most delegates denounced them as traitors and were determined to support all efforts to keep the trade unions and the Labour Party together. A few of the old school expressed their sadness at such defections. I recollect a man named Chadwick, who had been an official of the Electrical Union for many years, movingly describing the love and respect which he had had for MacDonald. He reflected the bewilderment and dismay of a number like himself, but most of the active people in the Labour movement were bitter at the betrayal. Britain came off the gold standard. Large numbers of jobs were lost. Savage cuts were made in unemployment benefits, in workers' wages and the pay of the armed forces. There was even a mutiny in the Navy. My youthful interest in trade unionism and the wider world of economics and politics sharpened considerably.

There was no canteen at the works, only a cramped and not very clean messroom, so I used to take my sandwiches to the Cocoa Rooms (one of the working men's cafés with that title peculiar to the Liverpool docks area) on the dock road. There I would buy a mug of strong tea, or occasionally, a bowl of soup. Its attractions didn't end there, for it became a debating centre. One of my older workmates was renowned for his turn of phrase. By repute an old communist, he was a rough-hewn character and his castigation of some Labour leaders was vitriolic: 'James Keir Hardie, James Ramsay MacDonald, James H. Thomas . . . Jesus Christ!' But he astounded all of us once with his declaration: 'Russia's gone red, Germany's going red, China will go red, the whole bloody world will go red . . . and we'll all be in hell!' And Hitler and Mao weren't exactly on the world stage then.

Among groups of working men there is a strong sense of companionship, and that was the case with us; only for it to be disrupted when we turned up one day to find the works closed. We were told that the firm had gone bankrupt. To see the look of bewilderment and despair on the faces of most of the men was a terribly sad experience. It seemed that nothing could be done; the unions were powerless. All we could do was to look for other jobs against the background of massive unemployment in Liverpool. One in three men in the area were unemployed and the situation was rapidly getting worse. I was attending evening classes in the technical college at the time, studying, among other subjects, machine drawing. That helped a little in my getting work but some time was to elapse before I did so. I signed on at the Labour Exchange and joined the large numbers of seekers for work. The 'dole queues', as they were referred to, contained much hope and yet a great deal of human misery, accentuated by the behaviour of hard-hearted clerks behind the counters. These seemed impervious to the needs of those who sought their aid, and all too often appeared to take pleasure in applying petty restrictions and rejecting claims to benefit. I was enraged by such treatment, and when I looked back at that period in later years I recalled those lines from Shakespeare: 'Man, proud man, Drest in a little brief authority, Most ignorant of what he's most assur'd. . .'

I managed eventually to obtain employment with a firm of sign-makers and painters and settled in quickly. My knowledge of draughtmanship and an artistic interest helped me. I liked the work and became reasonably proficient. It was diverse and interesting, from painting commercial vans and outside signs to the design and painting of advertising posters. Unfortunately the pay was poor and work became irregular. I was desperate to find other and, I hoped, better employment so I moved off to London. I spent a few months in Poplar and Stepney, obtaining odd jobs, but generally failing to earn enough to live on. I kept going with the help of a poor Jewish family in Stepney who provided me with bed and breakfast for ten shillings a week, and the friendship of good people which I have never forgotten.

Moving back to Liverpool I found that the dole queues were bigger than ever and that unemployment benefit still spelt hunger. I managed to get the occasional day's work here and there, including a couple of trips on a hopper, a vessel taking dredgings from the entrance of Garston docks, at the south end of the River Mersey, to the mouth of the river. Unfortunately I could not get a regular job there. I would have liked to have gone to sea but there was no prospect of that, either. I had pinned my hopes of a job on my brother, Gogo, who was a ship's engineer with the White Star Line. Unfortunately he was discharged, along with hundreds of other men, including many ship's officers and engineers, when the Cunard Company took over the White Star Line. It would be called 'redundancy' today and substantial severance payments would be made, but at that time no compensation was provided. For a period my brother took up work at Cammell Laird, the shipbuilders, and then left for a job as a marine engineer in the United States. Unemployment forced him out of his own country and he became a US citizen, remaining there until he died a few years ago. It was a sign of the times. Ship's officers and engineers were glad to get a job selling Kleen-E-Ze brushes on the doorsteps, and I began to look towards the docks.

During this period I was approached by a group of youngsters who were employed at a mass-production woodworking factory. They were clearly being exploited, and their already meagre wages had been cut arbitrarily by management. They had reacted by walking out from the job, but they had no idea what to do next. Approaches to union offices brought a rebuff. Unions were not inclined to accept responsibility for such spontaneous strikes and the youngsters were on their own. I accompanied a few of the lads to the Labour Exchange to enquire about the possibilities of unemployment pay, but nothing was forthcoming. The visit, however, led to the involvement of a Ministry of Labour man, the first indication I had had that the Ministry might play a conciliatory role. Although I did not meet the man, I helped the lads to prepare their case. It came as a shock to me to realize the limitations of trade unions at the time. For the life of me I could not understand why the unions were not playing a more active role and organizing the many women and youths in Liverpool who worked for extremely low wages, scarcely above the level of unemployment benefit.

My mind was full of questions, but the main consideration was to find work myself.

Chapter Three

A Day's Work at the Docks

Before the great world's noises break
The stillness overhead,
For toiling life begins the strife –
The day's grim fight for bread.
Where Mersey's mighty greyhounds speak
The wealth of England's stocks,
Stand, mute and meek,   he men that seek
A day's work at the docks.

Behold them now – a motley throng,
Men drawn from every grade:
Pale, florid, puny – weak and strong,
All by one impulse swayed.
One impulse – bread: one impulse – work!
How hope at each heart knocks
As mute and meek, they crush to seek
A day's work at the docks.

'Stand back! Stand back!' a hoarse voice storms,
With curses muttered lower,
The straining ring of human forms
But closes in the more.
Well fed, you foremen scarce can know
How Want the judgment mocks,
When, mute and meek, men eager seek
A day's work at the docks.

GEORGE MILLIGAN

(George Milligan, himself a Liverpool docker and later a
leader of the Liverpool Dockers' Union, published his verses
in 1910 but they were still relevant during the 1930s.)

I combed the waterfront for work in Liverpool's south end, and
because I was a member of the union I occasionally got picked for a
job after the more regular hands had been engaged. Standing about
waiting for work in the early morning near the river was bad enough,

then to be subjected to the 'you, you and you!' calls of the foreman stretched tolerance to the limit, but it had to be accepted because of the urgent need for work. Many of the men with me had wives and children and their misery when they couldn't get a job was heart-rending. Way back in 1920 the Report of Lord. Shaw's Inquiry into Dock Labour had declared:

> The court is of the opinion that labour frequently or constantly under-employed is injurious to the interests of the workers, the ports and the public, and that it is discreditable to society. . . .
> In one sense it is a convenience to authorities and employers, whose requirements are at the mercy of storms and tides and unforeseen casualties, to have a reservoir of unemployment which can be readily tapped as the need emerges for a labour supply. If men were merely the spare parts of an industrial machine, this callous reckoning might be appropriate: but society will not tolerate much longer the continuance of the employment of human beings on these lines. . . .

I can see in my mind now the grey, drawn faces of the men who were turned away. Despite Lord Shaw's fine words and a lifetime of endeavour by Ernie Bevin, we did not finally put the axe to the root of casual employment in the docks until 1972. Then I was able at last to initiate the elimination of the 'temporary unattached register' in the docks industry.

My experiences in the south-end docks led me to try to follow my father in working at Garston Docks. These were railway-owned docks even further south of the river, operated separately from the main port of Liverpool. My father had worked there for many years, which helped me in becoming a member of that docks branch of the union. New membership of this branch was almost entirely confined to dockers' sons, a qualification which had grown out of the bitter past, when men had been set against men in the fight for work. Restricting the number available for work, and ensuring a degree of loyalty through family connections, was regarded as essential protection against the job being swamped and a defence against the use of scabs by employers.

Improvements had been secured in wages and working conditions but I found that complacency had set in. Full time trade union officials on the docks were inclined to become tin-pot dictators, supporting the decisions of management and resenting any queries or complaints from the men. Men were reluctant to speak up for themselves. Because of this I was pushed into the limelight at an early stage.

One of my early clashes with authority (both management and union) was over the rate of pay on ships discharging bananas. These banana-boats came into a special berth, at regular intervals, and their unloading employed a large number of men. The fruit had to be man-handled, although mechanical elevators were used in the discharge. There was much disgruntlement because only the bare national mini-mum rate (11s 2d – 56p a day) was paid for most of the work. I raised the matter at the union branch meeting and secured unanimous sup-port in pressing for increased payment. Delay after delay ensued and finally a negative response from management was reported by the officials, who had resented the issue being raised in the first place. In view of their attitude there was no prospect of getting support for an official strike, although the men had a genuine grievance. I therefore decided to lead some action when the next banana-boat came into the docks.

I had many friends working at various points on the ship and the quay; some acquaintances were from my childhood, others, workmates whom I met occasionally in the pub, the club or at the soccer match. I called them together and persuaded them to pass the word along for all work to stop at a certain time and for the men to walk to the end of the quay where I would hold a meeting. There was a 100 per cent response. I had a great reception from the men and a unanimous vote to stay out until we got some satisfaction – remarkable, I suppose, considering that I was one of the youngest of the hundreds of men involved. It was a total stoppage in the middle of discharging a valuable and perishable cargo. There was pandemonium in the ranks of author-ity, but the strike concentrated their minds no end, leading to a settle-ment after two days. This was one of a few strikes I led in those years. The advice I continually gave my fellow workers was, 'Let's make the union work for us.' Union branch meetings increasingly became packed, with hundreds of men attending, compared to the relative handful which had attended the first meetings of the branch I had gone to.

But my main concern was to earn a living. I applied myself steadily for a number of years, working in various capacities on general cargo, mineral ores and timber ships. Garston Docks had huge timber storage estates and I worked on those too. It was hard work, requiring physical strength, versatility, quickness of mind and an ability to work in con-cert with your workmates. The idea that dock work is unskilled is a nonsense, although I perhaps would not go so far as Jimmy Sexton's description of a docker as 'requiring the intelligence of a cabinet minister, the mechanical knowledge and resource of a skilled engineer, and, in addition, the agility and quick-wittedness of a ring-tailed monkey'. (James Sexton was General Secretary of the National Union of Dock and Riverside Workers – the Liverpool dockers' union prior to the TGWU amalgamation.) Most of the work was paid for on a piecework or tonnage basis and the men worked in gangs, each member sharing the piecework earnings according to the hours he had worked. The advantage of working in a gang was that each man got to know the ways of his fellow members and there was considerable *esprit de corps*. The gang became something like a family.

Because it was piecework, men worked fast and sometimes dangerously. Accidents occurred, partly because of this but mainly because safety arrangements were inadequate. In the case of serious accidents the methods applied were primitive. Some of our number trained in first-aid and received some privileges because of it. I recall one man being terribly injured (in fact he died) when a baulk of timber fell out of a sling and struck his head. When the first-aid man arrived he could do little. We had to fetch the handcart, used in that set of docks as an ambulance, put the man on it, and haul him for half a mile or more to the local cottage hospital. A similar situation arose when five men were gassed while working in the bilges of a ship where I was working.

Incidents like this impelled me to study closely the Docks Regulations (under the Factories Acts) and the safety rules of the company. I found a number of instances of infringement and I persuaded workmates to become vigilant in checking cranes, winches, slings, ropes, chains, and working gear generally (I worked at times as a crane-driver). In the case of timber piling and stacking, I led a campaign to restrict the height of the stacks. There was a clear need for port rules and agreed safety arrangements to be published and improved where necessary. I devoted a lot of my spare time to this and my reputation must have spread, for I was invited to assist union members in drawing up revised port working rules in Liverpool, Glasgow and Preston.

My interest in safety conditions led me also to study workmen's compensation laws and the laws on employers' liability. I borrowed books from the local library and took a correspondence course with Ruskin College. I was worried that injured workmates were not getting the help they should have had from the union. There were many delays in getting compensation and in some cases the settlement seemed to me to be inadequate. At the time a finance clerk at the union's area office dealt with such claims. I pestered him quite a bit and finally managed to get some cases handled by sympathetic lawyers.

The trouble was that injured members began to come to my home instead of going to the union office, possibly because I listened more sympathetically, took a keener interest in what they had to say, and understood from my own practical experience the conditions under which they had been working. This meant that my home (my parents' home, rather, since I was still living there) became the equivalent of a surgery. Often I would fill out forms for members or reply to letters. This sort of task is the bane of many workers and they were greatly relieved to have it done for them.

I had already been elected as a shop steward, and to the branch and area committees of the TGWU, as well as delegate for the ports of Garston and Preston on the National Docks Group Committee of the union. This meant that I came into contact with Ernie Bevin, the General Secretary of the union, who took a keen interest in the Docks Group and was present at all the national meetings. He had been the driving force in building the union and he let everybody know it. On occasions we had to listen to Ernie orating about the financial problems of the world. My impression was that few, if any, members of the committee took in what he was saying. He spoke over their heads, certainly over mine although I was attending classes on economics and finance organized by the Labour College in Liverpool. No wonder Bevin took a poor view of the Labour College movement! But I wondered sometimes whether he was clear in his own mind or was simply trying to unravel his thoughts aloud to a sympathetic audience. He may not have been the clearest exponent of complicated issues but he achieved remarkable results by his driving power.

Bevin did not take a narrow view of trade unionism or his duties as General Secretary. Evidence of this was his involvement in the abdication crisis. Bevin considered that Edward VIII was letting down the country and to offset any adverse reaction from members he undertook a tour of the union. In Liverpool he addressed a conference of branch committees and was scathing in his attack. He suggested that Edward was profligate and implied that he was an alcoholic too – he quoted the old musical hall song 'You won't find many pimples on a pound of pickled pork'. Bevin had no need to worry in Liverpool, we couldn't have cared less what happened to Edward VIII or Mrs Simpson. I noticed, however, that Bevin and Harry Pugh, the Area Secretary of the union, had a bottle of whisky between them on the platform while the rest of us had to make do with jugs of ale!

Earlier I had been active in a campaign to make good the wage reductions in the docks industry that had been applied in 1931. At a meeting attended by Bevin I had the audacity of youth and asked why he had ever agreed to a pay reduction. His argument was that other industries had fared worse and he had done a good job by escaping with a smaller reduction. I urged early restoration of the cuts, which he resented. Others took stronger action and in Salford an overtime ban was applied. At Bevin's instigation, the three leaders of the ban were expelled from the union and lost their employment. It was an example of his ruthlessness. He brooked no opposition. I, and others, got our branches to send in resolutions asking for the reinstatement of the men, but without avail. Bevin was not prepared to show mercy even to men whose crime was opposing wage reductions. I am sure that his attitude derived from a jealous loyalty to the union; if he was criticized or opposed he seemed to feel that 'the union was being stabbed in the back,' but I would have preferred a little more humanity.

As a shop steward and branch committee-man I was continually in danger of victimization. To demand the circulation of agreements or port working rules meant you became suspect by management and trade unions officials alike. To query piecework or tonnage payments brought down the wrath of the establishment. Where I worked, the Marine Superintendent, with whom we negotiated from time to time, claimed to be a little deaf, and when I was putting the case for the men he insisted that I should stand up and speak down his ear trumpet! Trade union officials present would give little encouragement to the men's case, but if they made some disparaging remarks about the workers, he heard all right without the use of the ear trumpet. Management claimed the right to manage, and the role of full-time trade union officials was, all too often, to secure acceptance of management policies.

Because of the piecework system earnings were good at Garston Docks. Problems arose, however, with abnormal cargoes which slowed down the pace of work and reduced earnings. Attempts would be made to negotiate special rates but these were not always successful. Another problem was the delay in any negotiations. Although we had a Local Joint Committee consisting of management and union represntatives, the powers of the local management to make concessions were limited.

The London office of the company had overall control and only when a dispute was on the cards or in progress would a headquarters representative appear on the scene. It was understandable therefore that we began to have strikes when the men's impatience could be contained no longer. Invariably I would be to the forefront in putting the men's case. Union officials told me to 'watch my step'.

Once I was off work for some weeks due to a severe accident to my foot. I was receiving workmen's compensation, which was paid at the docks office. During that period I attended a meeting of the National Docks Committee of the union, for which payment was made by the union. I advised the docks office that this was the case and compensation was deducted for the days in question. Not knowing this, the Area Secretary of the union, Harry Pugh, made a special visit from Liverpool to the docks office to find out if I had drawn payment at the same time as attending the union meeting. My friends in the docks office told me that he appeared to be disappointed when he found I was in the clear. Had I slipped up he would have sought my removal from union posts. The incident did not enhance my respect for union bureaucracy. Pugh, who had had a militant record from earlier days for his work in building up union organization on the docks, was very much the trade union boss. Bowler-hatted, with a cigar in his mouth and flower in his buttonhole, he aped the get-rich-quick businessmen who were his *confrères* and confidants. Using his position to secure personal favours, he ensured that his daughter and son-in-law became employees of the union and his brother was pushed forward above others on the docks. I became a firm opponent of nepotism.

Trade unionism was in my blood and I tried to encourage the same enthusiasm among workmates. On days when we were not working I organized visits to timber berths along the Manchester Ship Canal and at nearby Widnes, to recruit the workers there into the union and at the same time to help them in pressing for similar rates of pay to those we were getting at Garston. We felt it to be in their interests, but also in ours in resisting the undercutting of rates of pay and preventing the diversion of work from the Port of Garston. We succeeded in some measure, and I became the proud possessor of the TUC Tolpuddle Medal for union recruitment – an award initiated by the TUC to commemorate the Tolpuddle martyrs of 1834.

Our efforts were not confined to timber yards but extended also to a metallurgical works where conditions were atrocious. At the request of Ernie Bevin I helped to check long-distance lorry drivers coming into the port, to see if they had union cards and, if not, to recruit them.

I began to question whether the members themselves were being encouraged to play a big enough part in the work of the union. Surely, I argued, the union shouldn't be seen as just another insurance company. There should be more meetings of members in addition to the so-called 'statutory' branch meetings held every three months. My efforts were opposed by officialdon. I determined to arouse more interest in union affairs by initiating educational activity in the branch. I pressed my case for a WEA (Workers' Educational Association) class to be held each Sunday evening. It was something almost unheard of, and perhaps because of that I gained the support of influential people in the WEA, a much more respectable body than the Liverpool Labour College. Our dockers' class met on a Sunday evening in a room above the bar in one of our local pubs. It was well attended and popular. We always finished in good time to allow at least an hour's drinking in the bar below.

There was still suspicion on the part of friend Pugh. After a while he declared in the middle of an Area Committee meeting: 'That class of yours, young Jones, is nothing but a rank-and-file movement: I'm sending an official in to watch it!' Maybe he was worried because we were studying workmen's compensation laws and the constitution and structure of trade unions. Even worse, our lecturer was a young Liverpool lawyer named Papworth – no relation to but with the same name as a prominent communist busman in London who was causing some headaches for the union leadership. To speak your mind in the union then was like walking on glass!

Chapter Four

Stanzas on Freedom

Men! whose boast it is that ye
Come of fathers brave and free,
If there breathe on earth a slave,
Are ye truly free and brave?
If ye do not feel the chain
When it works a brother's pain,
Are ye not base slaves indeed,
Slaves unworthy to be freed?

Is true Freedom but to break
Fetters, for our own dear sake,
And, with leathern hearts, forget
That we owe mankind a debt?
No! true Freedom is to share
All the chains our brothers wear,
And, with heart and hand, to be
Earnest to make others free!

They are slaves who fear to speak
For the fallen and the weak;
They are slaves who will not choose
Hatred, scoffing and abuse,
Rather than in silence shrink
From the truth they needs must think;
They are slaves who dare not be
In the right with two or three.

JAMES RUSSELL LOWELL

'We shall not starve in silence': the shout of the unemployed in a
Liverpool demonstration in the early thirties rang in my ears for years
afterwards. It might not have much meaning today but it was very
relevant then. Want prevailed amongst the unemployed in Liverpool.
Suicides were common and large numbers of children suffered from
malnutrition, rickets and other such diseases. The poverty caused by
unemployment and low wages was made worse by the shocking housing

36

conditions in the slum areas of the city. The Labour Party was in a minority on the Liverpool City Council and although it fought hard it was frustrated at every turn.

On odd days off work from the docks I often took part in meetings and demonstrations and I listened, with increasing sympathy, to speeches by Leo McGree, the communist leader in Liverpool and chief spokesman for the unemployed. He impressed me greatly with his vigorous exposition of the facts, laced with sharp Liverpool wit. He became a thorn in the side of authority and even of my own friends in the Labour Party like Jack and Bessie Braddock. While they were experts in dealing with the bureaucrats, Leo McGree on the other hand advocated direct action against housing evictions. The massive demonstrations he organized gained the support of thousands of the unemployed. For his pains Leo landed up with twenty months in gaol. The police authorities panicked, even at one stage arresting Jack Braddock for leading an unemployed action at which he was not even present!

Within the union and the local Labour Party I was continually pressing for action against unemployment. I felt deeply that more should be done. When early in 1934 a national 'hunger' march was being organized I offered to join the Liverpool contingent to march to London. My union branch endorsed the idea and I had the sympathy and support of fellow Labour Party members, although the main organizers of the march were members of the Communist Party. The Independent Labour Party (ILP) was also active in getting recruits for the march. In my youthful enthusiasm I could never understand why the different socialist groups could not work together, and here was evidence of that ambition being, in part at least, fulfilled.

I knew a number of young men who had suffered under the means test, being deprived of benefit and doomed to leave home in a futile search for jobs in other towns. I felt that some means must be found to provide work for the unemployed of Liverpool. In this I must have been influenced by the speeches made by Ernie Bevin which put forward a strong case for work or maintenance for the unemployed.

It was cold and the skies were grey as the forty or so marchers set out from Liverpool early in February. We had been joined by a group of unemployed men from Belfast and luckily a couple of them possessed concertinas and kept up our spirits by playing marching tunes. It was no holiday jaunt. Our clothes were not of the quality to keep out the cold. For some, years of unemployment meant that they attempted the march in rags and tatters, and but for gifts of second-hand boots provided by the march organizers, they would not have been able to participate at all. In Wigan and other places we slept in the workhouse, lying on the bare boards with just a rough blanket around us. Our food consisted of rounds of bread and a hunk of cheese. We were treated no more favourably than the usual workhouse habitué, except that we were not required to do work. Our spirits were good, so we survived the experience. I found the workhouse atmosphere little worse than the Salvation Army hostels I had stayed in in London at fourpence a night for a dormitory bed, or the 'common lodging-house' I had slept in in Dublin for a shilling a night. In any case the company was more friendly!

In Manchester accommodation for the night was provided in All Saints Church where the vicar was the Rev. Etienne Watts, a very left-wing Church of England clergyman. By this time we had been joined by many more marchers from various parts of Lancashire and Manchester itself. After a meal in a nearby hall the marchers scrambled into the church. We lay down in the pews and slept the best we could, only to be awakened in the early morning by the noise of a small congregation celebrating mass. A number of marchers, not realizing the cause of the disturbance, shouted abuse and used some pretty rough language. I'm sure it caused some consternation among the devout, but they did not protest. Soon afterwards we were on our way to London, having been seen off by a group of Labour councillors and Trades Council men.

After leaving Manchester our first intended stop-over was Congleton, but it was there we had our first clash with authority. The local bigwigs were not prepared to offer accommodation and told the march leaders that we would have to stay in the nearest workhouse about sixteen miles away. We lay down in the main road, and our action brought a quick reversal of attitude. Arrangements were made to transport us to the workhouse by bus. The police helped on that occasion, but throughout our march they appeared generally hostile. It may have been a reaction to the resentment displayed by many of the marchers and the view taken by the Government and some newspapers that the march was a nuisance and a 'red plot'.

In the main the marchers aroused sympathy in the public. Consciences were touched, gifts of food and clothing were made and collections well supported. At Birmingham the workers employed at the Co-operative Society boot factory repaired our boots. At Oxford we slept in the Corn Exchange and were looked after by the students. I was given a pair of Oxford bags (grey flannel trousers with wide bottoms) by one student, and I'm sure my comrades did equally well. A football match was arranged between the marchers and students but our team (I was one of them) was outclassed. A day off from the march was allowed for this relaxation and we also had meetings at various factory gates. I spoke outside the Pressed Steel factory at Cowley and was well received. Trade unionism was weak at the plant but the movement was beginning and a strike took place later that year. It was suggested that I might stay behind and try to get work there but I decided to continue on the march.

Refreshed by our welcome in Oxford, we soon received a knock-back at the Bicester workhouse. Soup was handed out but it was almost inedible, consisting mainly of potato peelings. The crowd erupted and the workhouse master was quickly surrounded by angry men. Once again attitudes changed and we succeeded in obtaining a supply of corned beef, margarine and bread. I was learning the hard way that in unity authority's hard face could be challenged successfully.

In London, I was involved in a number of spectacular activities designed to bring public attention to the plight of the unemployed. The critics had to admit that the marchers had undergone the hardships of a long march in bitterly cold weather, ill equipped with the minimum of clothing. It was evidence of desperate determination which made a deep impression on decent folk. In the first lobby of Parliament I had ever been in I led a group of the Liverpool men. Large groups of police, mounted and on foot, patrolled the queue. Presumably the show of strength was designed to cow the marchers, but cold and dishevelled as we were, we demonstrated defiance by shouting slogans like 'Down with the means test!' 'Down with the baby-starving national government!'

Only a few hundred of the two thousand managed to gain admission to the Central Lobby. I was amongst them, and led a group of the Liverpool men in seeking to make contact with Liverpool Members of Parliament. One of those who met us was David Logan, the ex-pawnbroker and Labour member for the Scotland Division of Liverpool. He wasn't the brightest of men and he offered little by way of action, but he showed his sympathy by handing me a ten shilling note which he asked me to share 'amongst the lads'. The Central Lobby was packed but in the middle of the throng I saw a distinguished-looking man, who, I was told, was Dingle Foot, then a Liberal MP.

I took my group over and we surrounded him, urging our point of view. He was visibly shaken by the examples we cited of hardship caused by the means test and the poverty represented by the low rates of unemployment benefit. 'How the hell can a family live on 15s 3d a week for the man, 8s for the wife and 2s for a child?' we asked him. He agreed to do all he could to press our case and to urge the leader of the Liberal Party, Sir Herbert Samuel, to do the same. He created a better impression than some of the Labour MPs, but Clem Attlee, the leader of the Labour Party, came up trumps. He led the fight in the House for a deputation to be received by the Prime Minister, Ramsay MacDonald, and the Cabinet. 'The marchers,' he said:

> are fair representatives of the great masses of unemployed. The injustice from which these men and women are suffering is very widely known in all parts of the House and the feeling in the country is now tremendous. There is an ever increasing volume of opinion that the unemployment problem should be grappled with. There is no reason why these men should be refused a hearing by the Cabinet.

I was pleased with Attlee's efforts and the way he had met us. I said to my mates: 'He is a small man and he doesn't look very strong but you must admit he's got guts!' He strengthened my faith in the Labour Party at a time when circumstances were inclining me to move further towards the left.

During our remaining days in London the agitation continued. On one occasion the marchers assembled in twos and threes around Buckingham Palace. It was in the early evening and the mist added to the remarkable spectacle of a couple of thousand ill-dressed men in front of the Palace. The guards were brought out and mounted police appeared but the marchers dispersed in little groups just as quickly as we had assembled. It did not end there, for we then made for the best restaurants in the West End and once at the tables took out packets of sandwiches. The waiters and the management were flummoxed. They tried to get us out but couldn't. Finally the manager pleaded with us to go to the back of the restaurant where he would provide us with a warm meal. With the others I enjoyed a good plate of nicely cooked fish and chips and plenty of tea. I had learned another lesson in the university of life.

The Hunger March stirred public opinion. The Archbishop of York and other church leaders supported the demands for restoration of the cuts in unemployment benefit which had been imposed in 1931. Even the Chambers of Commerce urged the Government to provide public work for the unemployed. Demonstrations took place all over the country and on Budget Day (April 17) the Chancellor, Neville Chamberlain, announced that the 1931 cuts would be restored. It was a total reversal of the Government's previous attitude and meant that all claimants would receive a 10 per cent increase in their benefit scale. The Government also announced that special investigators were to be appointed to inquire into conditions in those parts of the country which were suffering from acute industrial depression.

I had been back at the docks for some weeks when the Budget announcements were made and I was able to point out to my workmates that the Hunger March had been worth while. The fact that the Government had decided to restore the 1931 cuts, I argued, justified a stronger effort by the unions to press the port employers to restore the wage reductions which had been applied in the industry at the same time. Overtime bans were in operation in Salford and Birkenhead and feelings were running high. A special Docks Delegate Conference insisted that our claim for full restoration of the 1931 cuts be pressed to a satisfactory conclusion. Delays ensued and many dockers felt that Ernie Bevin was dragging his feet.

This was the view of a prominent rank-and-filer working at the Birkenhead docks, named Alf Brammell. I got to know him well. Brammell had a good reputation for it was he who had given evidence in the Inquiry conducted by Lord Shaw in 1920. Ernie Bevin had made his name as the 'Dockers' KC' at that Inquiry, during which he had called Brammell to testify that dockers couldn't live properly and work efficiently on the wages then paid.

With the backing of men like Brammell the Docks Delegate Conference called for notice of strike action to be served on the port employers. This was used to great effect by Bevin and a settlement was reached. Bevin was able to claim that this was an example of the success of peaceful negotiations which had not cost the union a penny except for the cost of committees and conferences. I'm afraid I shared the sense of frustration felt by the older men, who drew attention to the years which had elapsed since the cuts were imposed, and the fact that there was no retrospective payment.

Day after day at the docks I tried to draw the attention of my mates to what was happening in the world. It wasn't easy, for the order of debate was: sport, sex, beer and, of course, the job! But Hitler had come to power, the trade union movement in Germany was in tatters, and trade unionists, socialists and communists were being pushed into concentration camps along with the Jews. Early in 1934 the Austrian trade unionists had been brutally suppressed by Dolfuss. Older trade unionists on the Trades Council were apprehensive and conveyed their fears to me, but to my workmates Germany and Austria were far-off countries. True, I could express my worries in the Ward Labour Party, and we carried many resolutions denouncing Fascism and especially Mosley and his Blackshirts. This seemed very near to us, because it had not been long since we had listened to Mosley and his wife Cynthia speaking on Labour Party platforms in Liverpool. Mosley was regarded as both mad and a traitor, and those who had been associated with him around the period of his defection were still suspect in our ranks.

Around this time I joined the Territorial Army, not so much out of patriotism as because some of my mates from the docks had joined and persuaded me to follow suit. It was good fun and I learned to handle a rifle and later an eighteen-pounder gun. I became a bombadier. The comradeship amongst the men was splendid, the beer in the canteen was good too, and we got free heavy boots (useful on the docks) and overalls. The officers were young, middle-class business types and didn't impress me much. To my amazement, when I went along to a Mosley meeting to protest against his Fascist policies I found some of our TA officers among the Blackshirts. Needless to say I watched them closely afterwards and warned the men about them. We mocked them behind their backs, and any standing they had diminished to nought.

Within the Trades Council we formed an anti-Fascist group, giving out leaflets to people attending the Blackshirt meetings and protesting inside the meetings. It was not official Labour Party policy to protest in this way; the leadership felt we should 'ignore' the Blackshirts, but that didn't seem much of a policy to me. I led groups of young Labour, ILP and Communist members in trying to speak out at Fascist meetings and was forcibly ejected at each meeting. Burly Blackshirts (they seemed to be paid thugs to me – the officer types weren't involved) would jump on you and lash out with knuckle-dusters on their hands. On more than one occasion I was thrown out of the building and left almost unconscious, with a bloody nose and a black eye. The police would be standing by but took no action.

My anti-Fascist feelings hardened when a number of Jewish refugees from Germany came to Liverpool and told us of their terrifying experiences. News was coming through from the union and the International Transport Workers Federation (ITF) detailing the arrest, imprisonment, torture and in some cases execution of trade unionists. Occasionally, when I worked on a German ship, I would make contact with a friendly German who would tell something of the situation in his country. Polish and Danish seamen, too, expressed their fears to me. As dockers we got to know many seamen from foreign countries. If any of them got into difficulty they were referred to me, because my mates knew I would help them if I could.

Any anti-Fascist leaflets or stickers printed in German which came into my possession, I quickly distributed. Leaflets would be left lying about in parts of the ship where they were likely to be picked up; stickers were placed on the hatch coamings, on cabin doors, indeed in any place where they might be seen. The ITF produced useful material of this kind. Of course it was much better to pass copies of the leaflets directly to sympathetic seamen. On one occasion I invited two young German seamen to visit my house for a chat. I wanted to exchange ideas and information in rather more detail than was possible over a pint of beer in a pub. We had a cup of tea together but my sister Winnie left abruptly, and my mother told me afterwards that she wouldn't stay in the same house because I had brought two foreign 'reds' home. She was a devout Catholic and inclined to regard anyone on the left as anti-Christ. I learned later that one of my two friends had been arrested and put in a concentration camp.

Chapter Five

My respect for Ernie Bevin increased each time he denounced Fascism and I began to appreciate the thinking behind the formation of the TGWU as a practical means of meeting the needs of ordinary workers over a range of industries. It was, and is, a great conception, but my experience in the docks underlined for me that any trade union has also to be a living, democratic reality at the place of work. Otherwise it can suffer from the same bureaucratic insensitivity as any other large organization. I saw too the danger of trade union officials forming an informal alliance with the employers, and forgetting their role as representatives of their members. With workmates on the docks I tried to guard against these dangers by persuading fellow workers to use the machinery of the union, by bringing deputations to the Branch Committee meetings and by attending the full Branch meetings.

When I first attended the Branch meetings it was usual for a dozen or so members to be present, so I reckoned we were successful when we pushed attendance up to hundreds. The full-time officials were not so enthusiastic about this, nor about the view I continually advanced that Branch membership meetings should be held every month rather than at three-monthly intervals. When issues boiled up to crisis point I would requisition a Special Branch Meeting, by collecting the signatures of fifty members. The officials did not like this approach either, although it avoided a strike on more than one occasion.

One development that concerned me in particular was the increased use of mechanical equipment, larger grabs, electric cranes which could displace anything up to twenty men on one job, and the many other labour-saving devices which were making their appearance. It seemed to me that the union should do more to retain jobs, and I applauded Bevin's declaration about the need for a cut in working hours. I followed closely the proceedings of the union's Biennial Conference (the main policy-making authority of the union) which in 1935 was held in the Isle of Man. I urged that maximum publicity should be given to one of the Conference resolutions which read:

> In view of the rapid growth of mechanisation and rationalisation, with its consequent displacement of labour, this Conference welcomes the acceptance of a general convention of principle by the International Labour Conference at Geneva for the limitation of hours to a maximum of forty a week, as a contributing factor to the amelioration of the unemployment problem, and urges the Government to take every possible step to bring the respective industries within this limit, without lowering the workers' standard of living.

Among my many friends in the Docks Branches I tried to arrange checks on new equipment and pressure for the retention of jobs. This was an outlook shared throughout the union, so much so that port employers complained: 'The union maintains that the advantages from the introduction of machinery should be labour aiding, not labour saving, and this attitude has to an extent limited the benefits derived from the installation of such machinery.' The argument continued over the years and is still going on.

My friend George Gibbins had been appointed a Docks District Organizer in Liverpool around this time, and had promised me that he would try to clean up the petty corruption which abounded. But he told me that often his efforts were hampered by the friendly relations which the union's chief official, Harry Pugh, had established with some port employers. Instances of violations of the port working rules were drawn to the attention of union officials but then ignored. The view I took was that, unsatisfactory as the port working rules were, the best means of improvement was to ensure that the minimum rights laid down should be strictly adhered to. A cosy relationship between union officialdom and employers had led to slackness in observing agreements and the emergence of non-unionism in some parts of the port. Combined with ugly, indeed alarming, evidence of bullying and dictatorialness in union affairs, the atmosphere was not encouraging to an earnest young trade unionist like me.

I determined to fight on and encouraged others to do the same. Branches which elected critics of the union establishment by show of hands were told to hold ballots for new elections. All too often when ballots took place officials interfered to make sure that the preferred candidate was 'elected'. In the case of one ballot, for the election of an Executive Councillor, voting was recorded as having taken place at particular union offices yet in the case of the port of Fleetwood the union office had been closed during the period of the ballot. Furthermore, the members of the branch had not been notified that there was to be a ballot, nor given the opportunity to nominate a candidate. Despite this, the branch returns for the election recorded a number of votes from the Fleetwood branch for the candidate favoured by the union establishment. I challenged the return and encouraged members of the Fleetwood branch to make an official protest. This reaction clearly touched a sensitive nerve.

The successful candidate, a man named Hadley, was a crony of Pugh and rumoured to be a fellow freemason. He had previously been an official of the Municipal and General Workers Union and had left that union's service rather hurriedly. Later he appeared on the docks and was shown considerable preference in employment as a checker; then, almost out of the blue, he had been nominated for membership of the union's Executive Council.

Together with one of the candidates, Tom Gutcher, a well-respected docker from the Liverpool north-end docks, I pressed for an investigation and a sub-committee was set up to look into the matter. In the face of all the evidence this sub-committee found that the ballot *had* taken place in the Fleetwood branch. They admitted that 'notice had not been given about the ballot at a meeting of the branch', but claimed that there was nothing in the union rules which 'charged Branch secretaries with the duty of giving notice'.

The report of the sub-committee was accepted by the union's General Executive Council, but the latter also decided, on the advice of Ernest Bevin, that the Liverpool Area Committee should take all steps necessary to ensure that in future branches should 'be afforded a proper opportunity to make a nomination' and that Branch Secretaries should notify their branches about the dates and arrangements for ballots. This decision implied that something needed to be corrected, but in the future. It was of little consolation to those of us who had protested. Gutcher and I believed that a fresh ballot was justified and we said so. In response it was put to us in unmistakable terms that we would be subject to physical attack and our jobs would be in danger if we continued to press the issue. Similar threats were made to a man from Fleetwood named Langley and he was 'persuaded' to ship out of the port on a trawler, which meant we had lost out main witness.

I was shocked and dismayed, and shared my suspicions about the conduct of union ballots with other members. No wonder Ernest Bevin was to tell the union Conference in 1937 that union ballots did not reach the standards of Parliamentary elections. I certainly learnt the need for vigilance in ballots in which I was personally involved.

Worries about the way the union machine operated as well as about working conditions in dockland led me to suggest to a number of my friends that we should publish a news-sheet for circulation along the line of docks. The idea took on and we formed a committee, all of us working dockers, to run the show. First, we published a duplicated affair called *The Mersey Docker*. I was able to secure the unofficial assistance of one or two sympathetic full-time officials in the union. Our paper quickly attracted support, because we dealt with essentially practical matters. For about eighteen months we had to make do with amateurish and ill-prepared duplicated sheets, but thanks to the support we were getting we were able to launch a printed paper called the *Ship and Dock News*. The printing was made possible by the help of a friendly horse-race tipster who owned a printing machine. His support meant that we were able to have the printing done 'at cost' and our circulation plus a few advertisements enabled us to meet the bill.

The adverts were interesting. M. Davis of 61 Park Lane, 'Seamen's Outfitter', offered 'new and second-hand overcoats for 5/- each'. John Olswang of Bootle, 'Ladies and Gents Tailors', advertised suits from £2 and costumes from 30s, 'all clothes made by Trade Union Workers'. Although the paper was selling well among union members, we did not dare ask the union to advertise in it, because it was regarded as 'an unofficial organ'. The union leadership, including Ernie Bevin, opposed any activity of this kind, regarding it as a challenge to their authority. We recognized the need for caution, in not offering evidence to the union which might lead to disciplinary action.

As the (very unprofessional) editor of the paper, another slice of my spare time was being taken up, but this was a period of intensive education for me. I was 'learning by doing'. I taught myself to write with a purpose, directly and simply about issues all of us were involved in. The first issue of the *Ship and Dock News* coincided with the loss of a number of ships at sea and a lot of seamen were anxious about the situation. Under the heading 'Death of British seamen must end! Wipe out the scandal of Coffin ships', I wrote:

> The first issue of the *Ship and Dock News* coincides with the Inquiry into the loss of the s/s *La Cresenta* and at a time when disasters at sea are increasing in number due to winter gales and the sending to sea of overloaded, undermanned and un-seaworthy ships. British seamen, in face of this terrible loss of life of our fellow workers, must now get into the fight against those responsible – the profit grabbing ship owners, and for such changes being made as will ensure that no unseeaworthy overloaded or undermanned ship leaves port. By a united protest we can secure these changes, we can make the House of Commons face up to the situation, and we can force our trade union leaders to conduct a great public crusade that will finally wipe out the terrible scandal of the 'Coffin Ships'.

Details were given of the ownership of the vessel and readers were urged to press for more stringent inspection of ships by the Board of Trade and the union before sailing was permitted.

I found myself reading more. I had discovered secondhand book-shops and the local public library, where I drew heavily on books dealing with politics and economic subjects. H. G. Well's *Outline of History* impressed me, and I traversed a range of books by Marx, Engels, MacDonald, Blatchford, James Connolly and others. I also read Darwin and Huxley. For a lad who left school at fourteen none of this was easy. Luckily I was able to avail myself of educational opportunities provided by the union and the National Council of Labour Colleges. I was drawn to the latter because its economics and economic geography classes provided the clearest approach to the subjects that a young working–class mind could absorb. I took Ruskin College correspondence courses on Industrial Law and Workmen's Compensation. With little assistance from the union's full-time delegates I tended to become the 'oracle', advising on what damages might be claimed, what working methods were wrong and how they could be improved.

I had been elected honorary secretary of the Liverpool Labour College when I was eighteen and was helped by the organizer and principal tutor, Jack Hamilton. A stonemason by trade, Jack combined much practical wisdom with deep socialist conviction. The labour college movement took the 'learning by doing' method to heart, and active students like me rapidly become voluntary tutors. I am not sure about the effect on the students (mostly middle-aged, hard-bitten working men) but I certainly learned a lot.

The collective method of education suited us down to the ground in Liverpool. Sometimes formal tutoring would be abandoned and we would read a page from books like the *Ragged Trousered Philanthropists* and then discuss it. Weekend schools and dockers' educational outings (with hot-pot suppers a frequent event) became popular local forums in which I involved many of my workmates and other friends from the different dock branches on Merseyside. Classes which I organized were as much practical as academic. I remember a class on world economics, where the discussions were wide ranging, reaching a crescendo with the declaration of one member, 'Fisty' Byrnes, that 'There'll be no peace in the world until the Chinese have bacon and eggs for their breakfast, like the rest of us.'

Occasionally the fact that I had friends throughout dockland proved useful. One incident sticks in my memory. One weekend Sydney Silverman, the Liverpool Labour lawyer, sought us out. He said that a prominent unemployed leader, Tom Cacic, was being deported from Canada, where he had already served a long gaol sentence. Cacic had been put aboard a CPR liner and was being kept in chains. Because he was a Yugoslav national, the intention of the authorities was to deport him to Yugoslavia. It was feared that as soon as the ship docked, the British police would take over and try to move him quickly through Britain. It was the period of the White Terror in the Balkans and it was likely that if Cacic got to Yugoslavia he would be executed, or at best imprisoned and tortured. Silverman, who was acting with the International Labour Defence (ILD), asked if I could make contact with Cacic when the ship docked and help, with some other men, to check where the police took him. I agreed to co-operate in every way possible. On the arrival of the ship I was able to get aboard, and as Cacic was being taken from the ship in handcuffs I called out: 'Hello, Tom. Ask for Silverman, the lawyer.' I then signalled to the men on the quay to follow the police car. My friends had a car waiting. Cacic was taken to the Liverpool Bridewell in Dale Street. Within a short time Silverman was there and demanded to see Cacic and for a hearing of the case against deportation. The delay which resulted enabled Eleanor Rathbone MP to make representations to the Home Office and to thwart the plan to send Cacic to Yugoslavia. He was allowed to proceed to France and I believe later went on to the Soviet Union. Some years afterwards, he fought and died with the International Brigade in the Spanish Civil War.

Not all my fellow dockers were politically progressive. Working men's Conservative Clubs throve in various parts of Liverpool, attracting support by offers of cheap beer and facilities for billiards. Some of the men who supported these clubs worried me by their readiness to back the management, often in the most aggressive manner. We had the other type, of course, who paid their union contributions reluctantly and preferred to 'keep themselves to themselves'. Such men invariably voted Tory because their fathers had done so in the past. They were meat and drink to the bullying boss and the wily politicians.

These were not the only difficult characters we had to contend with. There were some who would buy drinks for particular foremen to curry favour. These creepers were even known to pass money to foremen to obtain preference when men were selected for work. Foremen had enormous power in hiring and firing men and in allocating work. I recall that one of the senior foremen was a teetotaller and religious, and to our surprise we discovered that some men suddenly became chapel-goers. Others cultivated allotments and passed gifts of vegetables and eggs to the boss. All too often this type of man would put up with dangerous methods of working rather than complain. In contrast to the subservient and compliant, other men breathed defiance. Two men I knew well were dismissed for insulting a foreman and refusing to carry out his instructions. I was satisfied that they had been provoked, but it took me nearly three months to secure their reinstatement. It was another feather in my cap as a spokesman for the men, but of more importance to me it demonstrated that injustice could be corrected by persistence.

For the most part there was a grand sense of comradeship among the men on the docks. You got to know fellow workers very well, their home life, their background, their hopes and dreams. There was general acceptance of the special position of the elderly worker. We tried to make sure that the easy corner, the lighter jobs, were given to the older men. Through the union branch we organized an annual Christmas dinner and social evening for the men who had retired, 'too old to work, too young to die'. Collections were well supported and committee members canvassed the local pubs and shops for gifts (bottles of whisky, turkeys, hams, etc.) which were then raffled. I enjoyed this activity and especially the Christmas 'do' – the happiness of the 'old boys' transmitted itself to me. I never lost my respect for the veteran workers. Within the local Labour Party I urged national pressure for better old-age pensions, but we were not to see any major improvement until the end of the Second World War.

When work was not available in the daytime I would go into the 'pen' where men were selected for the night shift. The foreman was an obnoxious bully who delighted in exercising his power. I felt humiliated on these occasions and finally initiated a move to negotiate rota schemes so that the work would be fairly shared. We succeeded in this, but my prominence as a spokesman often meant I lost work myself. As a single man I could just about manage, but I understood the fear of victimization which prevailed among the married. Luckily there were some who displayed great courage. I could rely on those men to turn up at union meetings, help canvass for the Labour Party and participate in educational classes. There was plenty of sacrifice but even more goodwill.

International links, it seemed to me, were very important. We tried to expose the conditions of the Indian seamen, whom we then called Lascars. They were getting about £1 a month, compared to £9 a month paid to British seamen, and their living conditions were atrocious. If Indian seamen died on a voyage it was not unusual for their bodies to be simply thrown overboard and no record made or report given. Seamen, white or black, had little redress when at sea because the laws regulating shipping were obsolete and vague. We ran a campaign to revise the Merchant Shipping Act.

I wrote an article which was published in local Labour Party newssheets, in which I said: 'Overwork, undermanning, insanitary and verminous quarters, are commonplace on British ships . . . and there is no democracy at sea! Once away from port and immune from Government inspection, all power is vested in the Captain, his word is law, and protest can be treated as mutiny.' I pointed out that seamen might be expected to perform the work of dockers in the event of our being on strike. There was therefore every reason for unity between the dockers and seamen to get rid of the antiquated legislation.

As part of this campaign, and to support the development of the Seamen and Dockers Club, I helped organize a smoking concert. To make it a success I took the audacious step of inviting the veteran trade union leaders Tom Mann, Ben Tillett and Liverpool's Jimmy Sexton. To my surprise, they accepted. It was marvellous to see them together, each a character of world-wide renown. Tom and Ben were in their element, striding the little platform and holding everybody present spellbound by their oratory. To be in their company was an inspiration. One thing that worries me still is that I can't remember if we paid their expenses. I'm fairly sure we didn't, for the club was on its beam ends. In any case Sexton could not have been badly off. The former General Secretary of the Liverpool Dockers' Union, he had been an MP for many years. Known as 'Snuffy Jimmy' because of his speech, which had been affected by a bad accident to his face in his old days as a docker, he was one of the older Liverpool Labour movement characters whom I got to know, and provided, for me, a vivid link with the past.

There is nothing like learning history through the eyes of a partici-pant, even if the lily is gilded a little at times! The knowledge of past struggles and personal sacrifices encouraged me to further efforts for my workmates.

Chapter Six

The one method

You are inspired to hardihood –
Ah, that is good!
Yet inspiration's not sufficient;
Remember, evil is omniscient.

The foe, I grant you, does not fight
For light or right.
But he is armed whatever happens;
His always are the heavier weapons.

So arm yourself, steady your hand,
And take your stand.
Aim well; and if the shot should carry,
Rejoice and let your heart make merry

HEINRICH HEINE

Labour politics in Liverpool were different to those in the rest of the country in the 1930s. What was called 'religion' had a big influence because of the mixed nature of the population. There was a separate Protestant party represented in the City Council, known as the 'Protestant Reform Party', and a Catholic party to balance it called the 'Centre Party'. If that wasn't enough, the Labour Party itself was pretty well divided. Sections of the party were strongly influenced by the Catholic hierarchy, especially on issues affecting Catholic schools. For years the Scotland Road area of Liverpool was represented in Parliament by an Irish Nationalist MP, T. P. O'Connor, and when he died and was replaced in 1932 by a Labour MP, David Logan, there didn't seem much difference in outlook.

In my early twenties I was selected to stand for the Labour Party as the candidate for Breckfield Ward in the elections for the City Council. Part of the ward was in the centre of a militant Protestant area, where the King was 'King Billy' and the man to follow was 'Pastor' Long-bottom, the Liverpool equivalent in his time of the present day Pastor

Paisley. Since the area was one of serious poverty (like most of Liverpool) I launched my campaign with an attempt at an open-air meeting. Friends told me it was the quickest way to learn public speaking, but it was my knowledge of bad language that was enhanced that evening. After I had been speaking for about five minutes, a number of the women present, in the traditional black shawls of my home town, were screaming out 'Go home, you Fenian bastard' and other less polite messages. Then stones and bottles began to fly and we retreated fast.

I really had no political ambitions in mind when I had the temerity to accept nomination for the City Council. The union's Area Committee badly wanted a union man on the Council and the old 'shellbacks' who were my fellow committee members pushed me into the deep end. It would be called 'community politics' today and that is how the Labour Party played it then. There was plenty to fight for; we wanted more houses, more jobs through council projects, better roads, new schools.

I didn't win that election but we conducted a rip-roaring campaign. The local party workers were supplemented by teams of my mates from the docks. Most of them hadn't canvassed before but they took happily to the task. Night after night we held meetings, we canvassed, we distributed leaflets and put up fly-posters. The streets were white with chalked slogans. At the count I refused to shake hands with the Tory victor and declared that, 'We of the Labour Party have every right to celebrate a moral victory. Every vote for us was one for reason against reaction. A vote for truth against Tory lies.' But we had lost just the same and we adjourned to the nearest pub to celebrate the occasion in the best traditions of a wake.

I was getting in more practice as a speaker at open-air meetings of seamen and dockers on the dock road. It was a means of selling our paper *Ship and Dock News*, and part of our campaign to make the TGWU and the NUS more effective in pressing the members' issues. The meetings were often turbulent. I recall one speaker who had been criticizing the Seamen's Union, then known as the National Sailors' and Firemen's Union, with the initials NS&FU. The speaker emphasized the last two initials, until a seaman standing in front of him shouted back, 'And fuck you too!' – naturally a fight ensued.

World events provided provocation enough for sectarian Liverpool, with the news of the revolt against the Spanish Republican Government. A wave of sympathy for the Spanish Government and people swept through the Labour movement. Many meetings took place and resolutions were passed urging support.

I held meetings with Spanish seamen and with members of the Spanish community in Liverpool. They were worried, but proud of their Government, and urged me to do all I could to ensure solidarity. Spanish Aid Committees were set up and the National Council of Labour called for support for the International Solidarity Fund for the relief of distress amongst the Spanish workers. News came through that the TGWU Executive Council had made a grant of £1000 to the Fund and was calling upon areas and branches to make donations also.

In August 1936 Ernest Bevin praised 'the heroic struggle being carried on by the workers of Spain to save their democratic regime'. The *Daily Mail* and other right-wing newspapers took a different view and poured out attacks upon the constitutional Government. The Catholic Church, for the most part, was equally tendentious. In some churches Franco was proclaimed as the defender of Christianity against atheistic materialism, church burning, outrages against nuns and other things too horrible to relate. A few Catholic Labour City Councillors swallowed the propaganda and declared their support for Franco, but they were the exceptions. The Catholic leader of the Party, Luke Hogan, supported the Loyalist Government from the start and encouraged me in my endeavours.

Luke Hogan was a powerful leader and a remarkable speaker but his reputation suffered from the stories which circulated about his drinking, which went on late into the night. One journalist gave him the title of 'three-cigar Hogan', and that didn't help. I was a little sceptical when I went to seek his support for an 'Aid Spain' meeting, but he soon settled my doubts. While I was in his office he urged me to continue to try to gain a seat on the City Council. 'We need young men from the Unions like you,' he said. 'I'm not afraid of a left-wing view, I expect young men to be on the left.' He was scathing in his criticism of some of the older Labour councillors and at the same time questioned the loyalty of Jack and Bessie Braddock. I queried this attack for I was friendly with the Braddocks and I had a youthful wish for unity in the movement, but a doubt remained with me after that interview.

The Braddocks were controversial figures. Together with Bessie's mother, Mrs Mary Bamber, they had been founders and leaders of the Communist Party in Liverpool but had then left it. Although they continued to advocate left-wing policies, they were attacked as traitors by the communists yet were looked upon with a suspicious eye by most of the other Labour Councillors. Differences in the movement were not helpful to the 'Aid Spain' movement. I recall one meeting, when Mrs Bamber was speaking. Someone interrupted with a shout of 'Who stole the Russian banner?' and the meeting collapsed in argument. Mrs Bamber years earlier had been to Russia, had been presented with a banner by one of the Red Army groups and had retained it as a personal memento. Some of the older communists felt that she should have handed it over to the movement. Political controversies can run for a long time!

Franco and his insurgents, backed by Hitler and Mussolini, made considerable advances in the early months of the civil war and the Spanish Government was under great pressure. Non-intervention became a cruel masquerade, preventing the legitimate Government from getting the supplies it needed from Britain and France. Strong feelings of frustration led to a flow of volunteers going to fight on the Government's side.

I had no doubts as to where I should be, and offered my services at the 'Aid Spain' office in the Haymarket at Liverpool. After all, I had some territorial training and was young and fit. My hopes were soon dashed. I was told I would be of greater service to the Republic by continuing to play an active role in the TGWU and carrying on my activities among the dockers and seamen. Because of my many contacts I was asked to assist in recruiting specialists for the Republican Navy and for the International Brigade. This I did, but always with the feeling that I should be going as well.

Joe Cummings, a man of sparkling wit and friendly character, was the co-ordinator of 'Aid Spain' activities in Liverpool, and he asked for urgent help when the crew of the SS *Linaria* landed in Liverpool. The men had been arrested for refusing to sail the ship from Norfolk, Virginia, with a cargo of nitrates bound for Franco Spain. The men believed, correctly, that the nitrates were intended for use as explosives. They were brought over on another vessel to Liverpool and charged with 'impeding the progress of the vessel', i.e. civilian mutiny. I quickly arranged for legal defence, through Sydney Silverman MP, the Liverpool solicitor, and got a small committee together to make a financial appeal.

The case was first heard before the Liverpool Stipendiary. About twenty-five people were involved and all were arraigned before the bench. They got restive with the proceedings; none more so than the old bosun who, from time to time, made his way ostensibly to the toilet, but in fact nipped out for a quick pint of beer. At the end of the initial hearing they were committed for trial at the subsequent Quarter Sessions. This meant two or three months' wait and meantime we had to arrange to meet the travel costs to get them to South Shields, their home town. Bail had been allowed and the men would have to be accommodated when they returned to Liverpool for trial. We raised money for this and appealed successfully for people to put up the men in their homes during the trial.

Counsel was obtained and a good case was presented before the Recorder, E. G. Hemmerde, KC. The defendants were lucky because Hemmerde had strong socialist sympathies. They went free. In summing up the Recorder ridiculed the prosecution argument that the cargo was simple fertilizer. He indicated that the nitrates more likely were intended to 'fertilize' the fields of Spain with human blood.

Shortly after the *Linaria* case, I was asked to stand as the candidate for the Croxteth Ward in Liverpool. There was strong Labour support in the area, which consisted mainly of new housing estates providing homes for people who had been moved out of the slums. I entered into a gruelling campaign. There was plenty of support in the ward and from my workmates but I wanted to spread the message far and wide. I spoke at meetings galore, at street corners or in the local schools. It was hard work, putting in a full day on the docks and then spending nights and weekends on the campaign. I needed to acquire a lot of knowledge to answer the many questions and give advice to troubled housewives, unemployed fathers and youngsters needing a home of their own.

In my meetings and leaflets I concentrated on the need for more council housing, because I knew there was overcrowding in many of the houses in the ward, and there were still terrible slums in Liverpool. At the time there were sixty thousand citizens on the City Council's waiting list for houses. A lot of human misery was involved in that. Even worse was the poverty. Thousands were in receipt of Public Assistance and close to starvation. In spite of this the Tories trundled out as a candidate a middle-class young woman, the daughter of a Church of England vicar, who was notorious for her right-wing views.

It was meat and drink to me to have such an opponent. To demonstrate her outlook I quoted from a pamphlet she had written called 'Red Flag, Rome and Shamrock'. She referred, for example to 'the lavish expenditure of Public Assistance' (2s a week for a child and 15s for a sick man were examples of her 'lavish expenditure'). Describing the unemployed as 'professional scroungers', she wrote: 'one remedy would be to require all recipients to sign a register twice daily'. My pleasure in winning the election was reinforced by the knowledge that I had defeated such a reactionary. Among the Council Committees I sought to gain a seat on was the Public Assistance Committee. I wanted to use what influence I could to help the poorest of the poor. My wish was granted and I joined forces with Bessie Braddock, who was the Deputy Chairman of the Committee.

Bessie fought like a tiger to get any advantage she could for the poor devils on Public Assistance and I tried to emulate her. I successfully challenged the idea that men could be forced to leave home and move away in search of work, without the prospect of a decent house the other end. The 'other end' usually meant the West Midlands. New industries were springing up rapidly in the Birmingham and Coventry areas and many factories there got a reputation for non-unionism, low wages and poor working conditions. I argued that men should not be forced to go to 'non-union hell-holes'. I began to take an interest in the Midlands, visiting the area occasionally to talk to fellow trade unionists, and I could see that there was vast scope for union development. It was something I had in ·mind when I finally decided to move out of Liverpool.

I developed an affinity with the Braddocks because they were prepared to fight. Bessie in particular was audacious. I admired the way she would walk into a hospital, pick up a plate from one of the patients, and if the meal looked inadequate or inedible, march into the House Surgeon's office demanding something better. But although she did much good, sometimes she let down her deservedly high reputation.

I recall on one occasion she asked my support for Dave Nixon, a Labour councillor, who was unemployed and a particular friend of the Braddocks. A vacancy existed on the Mental Asylums Board for the County of Lancashire. The job meant travelling to Preston for the meetings and involved the payment of expenses, which in those days was regarded as a perk. When the day came to elect our nominee, to the surprise of everybody present, a right-winger in the Labour Group, Mrs Sarah Demain, nominated Bessie Braddock herself. She accepted and won the vote. I was flabbergasted. A few of us questioned Bessie afterwards and she explained that even if she had not stood, Nixon wouldn't have got the nomination. That didn't wash with me, but I remained close to the Braddocks.

Spain continued to involve me. News of reverses suffered by

Government forces threw a black shadow across my life. A number of Liverpool lads had gone to join the International Brigade and I took a keen personal interest in their progress. Early in 1937 many Britishers were killed at the battle of Jarama, including about twelve from Liverpool. Some I knew well and I grieved for them. With my friend Joe Cummings I visited relatives. To carry the message of the death of a loved one is distressing at any time, but when the details are unknown and the death has occurred in battle in a foreign land it is doubly difficult. Most widows and dependents were suffering dire poverty and the help we could give was small.

I repeated my request to be allowed to join the International Brigade and was told that in principle it was accepted, but I was still needed to work in the union and the Labour Party to gain as much support as possible for the Spanish Government. I spent a lot of my spare time organizing collections and arranging meetings of every size and shape. I told Bill Barton, the Secretary of the Liverpool Trades Council, 'More, much more must be done to save the Spanish Republic.' He agreed, but like so many of the old school didn't seem to know what to do except to forward a resolution to the TUC and the Labour Party.

Some of the big meetings were wonderful: well-attended, enthusiastic and generous. There was no doubt that many working people and large sections of liberal-minded opinion sympathized with the Republic. The Government and many Labour leaders, however, dithered and dallied with their policy of 'non-intervention'. The Duchess of Atholl spoke at the meetings and encouraged many to rebuff the views of the *Daily Mail* and other pro-Franco influences. The Liberal MP Wilfred Roberts and the courageous Eleanor Rathbone MP also helped widen the appeal. At such meetings Paul Robeson was a big attraction. The absence of mainstream Labour and trade union speakers, however, worried me and provided ammunition for left-wing critics and the Communist Party.

I was disappointed by the efforts of my own union and the TUC. Financial support from that quarter was negligible. I had the feeling that people in high places were washing their hands of the whole business. I began to wonder how our leaders would have reacted under Hitler had they been leaders in the German Labour movement.

On the docks I was still busy with tonnage and piecework disputes, and I was elected to the union's Biennial Delegate Conference. The conference lasted five days, though half a day was spent on a 'conference outing'. I objected to this waste of conference time but found little support for my view. Most of the time was spent debating proposals for changes in the union rules. Ernest Bevin, whose standing was very high in the union and among the delegates, was able to win the support of Conference on most issues, but he suffered defeat on a proposal to tighten up the qualifications required to become a Docks Officer of the union. Bevin argued against the proposal but most delegates stubbornly refused to be convinced.

I personally felt strongly about the matter because of my experience in my own branch, where the son-in-law of a senior union official had been foisted on the membership although he had no experience of the docks. It had been claimed at the time that the man had been working 'in connection with the industry' as a union clerk. It was this type of incident which influenced the docks delegates. Left, right and centre, they were for the change, and we managed to persuade most of the other delegates to support our view.

Although the youngest of the team, I enjoyed the company of the Liverpool dockers who were co-delegates with me. We stayed together in the same 'digs'. About ten of us managed to sleep in a basement room, on camp beds, couches and one or two of us on the floor. The accommodation was cheap and the entertainment superb. There is some truth in the claim that to have been born and bred in Liverpool is to be a comic, and that is especially the case in dockland.

Immediately after breakfast we all made for the local Trades Council club, where rules were bent and we managed to drink a couple of glasses of Guinness before the Conference started. I found little interest among my friends in the wider issues, but I had come particularly to get support for a resolution on workmen's compensation and I found ready encouragement on this. The experience was heart-warming. I felt that the older men saw me as a hope for the future and I was anxious not to disappoint them. They gave me all sorts of advice, on sex and booze and living life itself; we stowed and discharged a few ships too over the drinks!

A resolution which originated from my branch, indeed from me, called for increases in workmen's compensation and the extension of the schedule of industrial diseases to cover all diseases resulting from employment. It was, of course, carried unanimously by the Conference. It was a very practical issue for me: I had in mind mates who had been struck down at work being made to suffer poverty as well as the pain and suffering of their injuries.

Shortly after the conference I told the union branch committee and a meeting of the members that I intended to go to Spain. Many members urged me to stay because they seemed genuinely to feel that a lot of rank-and-file influence in the union would be lost with my departure. The branch chairman, a moderate man, was very upset and urged me to remain. I stood firm and tried to explain in simple terms just what was involved. For many present I truly believe that Spain and the terrible problems facing its people became a living reality at last. My closest friends on the docks promised me that they would continue to work hard in the union while I was away.

In this period I met again Evelyn, whose husband, George Brown from Manchester, had been killed in Spain at the battle of Brunette. She had been working abroad, in the underground movement against Fascism, and had taken many risks in doing so. The death of George was a deep personal wound which only time could repair, yet her mood was not to grieve but to fight on. My admiration for her spirit was more than matched by my growing love for her. We both knew, without putting it into words, that if I returned from Spain we would marry.

My impending departure was mentioned to a big financial backer of the Aid Spain movement, Jimmy Shand, owner of the Liverpool greyhound track. Among other good causes he gave a lot of help to needy dependants of International Brigaders. His own son was already in Spain. Jimmy wanted my departure to be marked with guns on the station platform and a mass meeting to emphasize the need for arms for the Republic. But I slipped away quietly. . . .

Luke Hogan and other leaders of the Labour Party and the Trades Council gave me a message to take to Spain expressing their support for the Spanish Government and my action in going to fight. I called on Ernest Bevin at Transport House. He had told the union's Area Secretary that he would like to see me. The General Secretary's office then was small – he seemed to fill the room. He asked me why I was going to Spain and listened with great attention. 'Have the communists been after you?' he asked. 'No,' I replied, 'the issue affects a lot more people than the communists.' He nodded assent, but I got the impression he was pessimistic about Spain and probably felt that my going was just another youthful indiscretion. At one stage he growled: 'Britain must stand up to these dictators, but we need to be stronger.' He said that he hoped everything would go well for me, and that when I got there I should meet the Spanish unions, who might help me. He then dictated a letter to the UGT (*Union General de Trabajadores*). While the letter was being typed he talked about the Spaniards he had met in the International Transport Workers Federation. I departed with the letter, mightily pleased that Bevin had been so friendly but still disappointed that he had not done more for Spain.

Before leaving London I again met Tom Mann and Ben Tillett, both of whom greeted me warmly. They said they would like to go to Spain and despite their age I'm sure they would have made a success of it had they done so. In their time they were marvellous propagandists. But even at their best, in the Spanish setting they could not have equalled 'La Passionaria'. When I heard her later the effect of her speaking was truly electric. I went on my way encouraged by Tom Mann's hug and message, 'Good luck, owd lad!'

Chapter Seven

To the Living

It is not seemly for you to
Mourn,
It is not seemly for you to
Delay;
You have received a legacy
Soaked
In the heart's blood of your brothers.
The pregnant deed
Waits
For you.

The time,
Burdensome,
Presses upon your necks.
Wide burst
The gates
Of bright morning!

ERNST TOLLER

The focal point for the mobilization of the International Brigades was in Paris; understandably so, because underground activities against Fascism had been concentrated there for some years. I led a group of volunteers to the headquarters there, proceeding with the greatest caution because of the laws against recruitment in foreign armies and the non-intervention policies of both Britain and France. From London onwards it was a clandestine operation until we arrived on Spanish soil.

While in Paris we were housed in workers' homes in one of the poorest quarters of the city. But it wasn't long before we were on our way, by train, to a town near the Pyrenees. From there we travelled by coach to a rambling old farmhouse in the foothills of the Pyrenees. After a rough country meal in a barn we met our guide who led us through the mountain passes into Spain. My comrades accepted *alpargatas* (rope-soled canvas shoes) for the long climb, but I kept my

Territorial Army boots. I felt they would provide better protection against the rough terrain, and I certainly escaped the blisters and cuts which others seemed to suffer. It was an arduous journey through the dark night. For about nine hours or more we were climbing, one walking in front of the other, with occasional short spells of rest. It was a bit like a commando course.

In the light of the morning we could see Spanish territory. After five hours or so, stumbling down the mountainside (I found it almost as hard going down as climbing up), we came to an outpost and from there were taken by truck to a fortress at Figueras. This was a reception centre for the volunteers. The atmosphere of old Spain was very apparent in the ancient castle. For the first day or so we felt exhausted after the long climb. The food was pretty awful. We ate it because we were hungry but without relish.

For some the first lessons about the use of a rifle were given before we moved off to the base. I at least could dismantle and assemble a rifle bolt and knew something about firing and the care of a weapon. But my first shock came when I was told of the shortage of weapons and the fact that the rifles (let alone other weapons) were in many cases antiquated and inaccurate.

Training at the base was quick, elementary but effective. For me life was hectic, meeting good companions and experiencing a genuine international atmosphere. There were no conscripts or paid mercenaries. I got to know a German Jew who had escaped the clutches of Hitler's hordes and was then a captain in the XII Brigade. He had hopes of going on ultimately to Palestine and striving for a free state of Israel. He was not only a good soldier but a brave one too. That was also true of a smart young Mexican whom I met. He had been an officer in the Mexican Army and was a member of the National Revolutionary Party of his country.

As the days passed I became more and more impatient to meet members of the Spanish trade union movement. It was important to me to find out what their situation was and to deliver the letters I carried from Ernest Bevin and the Liverpool Labour movement. After persistent pressure, I was allowed to proceed to Barcelona to meet the UGT leaders. The UGT, primarily a socialist trade union federation, also included the communist trade unionists. I especially wanted to meet leaders of the Transport, Docks and Seafaring Unions and to renew contacts I had made earlier.

I was not disappointed, for my first meeting was with leaders of the

Before the Battle of the Ebro, Spain, 1938, with comrades in the International Brigade.

Facing the future with Evelyn after my return from Spain.

Don't be bluffed by Tory Lies——
MAKE NO MISTAKE:
VOTE THUS:—

JONES, J.L.	X
WHITTINGHAM-JONES, BARBARA	

Continue Mrs. Hamilton's good work. Elect a man who understands your needs and will

GET THINGS DONE!

Give your support to the Party who fight for the Poor. Vote Labour on Thursday. Show your Strength and Might.

Vote for J. L. JONES

[P.T.O

Part of my campaign leaflet for the 1936 City Council election in Liverpool.

With fellow members of the union after a visit to a Midlands factory by the Mayor of Coventry in the early 1950s.

Transport Union and the dockers' leaders of the UGT. At the door of the union building were armed guards, and the union officials had revolvers attached to their belts. I remember thinking how different it was to the British trade union scene, and wondering how the average British trade union leader would react in a similar situation.

The UGT leaders explained the current situation and told me about the difficulties caused by the shortage of vehicles. At the outset of the civil war the army had largely depended on horse transport. A fleet of motorized vehicles had been built up with great difficulty but it was still inadequate. We discussed the attitude of the CNT (the syndicalist trade union federation) to the Republican Government and to the war. My friends were sharply critical. They claimed that the CNT was not pulling its weight and was restricting the war effort by persisting in its traditional attitudes. An example mentioned was its resistance to the employment of women, even in cases where the men employed were needed at the front.

The UGT officials I met were socialists but supported a united war effort with strong central control, a view shared by the communists. The CNT still tended to support de-centralization policies and this, it was also alleged, was exploited by the POUM (the ultra-left *Partido Obrera de Unificacion Marxista*). It was suggested that they had disrupted the war effort and caused a lot of trouble in Barcelona. When I mentioned Goerge Orwell I was met with derision because of his association with the POUM.

I had hoped to meet Largo Caballero, for whom I had formed a high regard and even today still retain a measure of admiration. He has been called the Spanish Lenin. I would have thought he was more like the Spanish Bevin, but perhaps there was a bit of the two about him. He had been a genuine working man who led a revolution in his country and became Prime Minister. Anyway, I didn't meet him; he had resigned as Prime Minister and had lost his post in the UGT – sadly he was in virtual isolation. I did meet, fleetingly, Gonzalez Péna, his successor as UGT leader, who was then in the Government.

I delivered the letters I carried to the new General Secretary of the UGT, Rodriguez Vega, an able but worried man. The letter from Bevin seemed to irritate him. In his conversation with me he scorned the way the British Labour movement had failed the Spanish socialists and trade unionists. 'Why have they not forced your Government to support us? Why have they not done more to demonstrate solidarity with us in action?' I had no answers, I felt ashamed. In my reply I spoke about the many rank-and-file activities in Britain and told him, 'I have come to fight.' He raised his eyebrows: 'One young man, well. . .'

At the end of my visit to the UGT I was persuaded to join a group of UGT men, Spanish workers (including some ex-seamen), going into action at the front. Permission was obtained. I was given a rifle, a revolver and ammunition for both. The rifle I knew how to use, the revolver I was not sure about, and I handed it back. (I learned to use one later.) One action I became involved in was a defensive one in the Lérida area, towards the Aragón.

I was helped by two of the men I was with, who spoke English pretty well, but communication wasn't easy in an entirely Spanish force. If I had any doubts about the spirit and strength of feeling in favour of the Republic, they were soon dispelled. The soldiers were firm in their determination under conditions of intense adversity, knowing that their women, old people and children back home were suffering bombing, strafing, shortages and near starvation.

My character was hardened by many experiences at that time but one incident stands out vividly in my memory. '*Yo lucha para libertad!*' ('I fight for liberty') shouted the old Spaniard, digging in alongside me. The ground was hard and stony and with the aid of a trenching tool it was possible to dig only a shallow strip and use what natural cover was available. Laying his trenching tool on the ground, he picked up his rifle to fire at the opposing force. We faced a hail of rifle and machine-gun fire and shells came flying over at the same time. I looked at the unlikely soldier by my side and marvelled at his courage. He had a gnarled bronze face, a heavy body, and was wearing the cap and overalls of a working man. He was afraid of nothing. It turned out that he was an anarchist, but he typified for me the resolve of so many Spaniards who hated the idea of a Fascist take-over. In his courage he was reckless, a recklessness which did for him, for he was killed within minutes of his picking up his rifle and firing a few shots.

He was shot in the head and died quickly. Others around me dragged him away and later buried him in a rough, shallow grave. I kept on firing, and it was only luck that saved me from the same fate as my anarchist friend. I must have been as reckless as he was, because I foolishly insisted on wearing a black leather jacket, which wasn't the best camouflage. The jacket had been given me by friends at home and I couldn't bear the thought of not having it with me.

People have asked me: 'Did you kill anyone in Spain'? Frankly, I do not know, but it is possible. In that engagement I didn't think of death, yet people were being killed and wounded by my side. In battle, one experiences a numbness that is difficult to describe; one's first impulse is to protect oneself as much as possible and then to fire in the direction of the enemy. One tries to pinpoint a target, but almost in a frenzy. To keep cool and calm in such circumstances is an ideal not easily achieved. Nor did I have great confidence in the accuracy of my rifle. It was a Remington-type rifle, Russian made, and after firing a few rounds the bolt got very hot. All I do know is that some of my comrades were killed and wounded and men on the other side suffered the same fate. That is war.

After a time I returned to the British Battalion and was asked by Sam Wild, the commander, and Bob Cooney, the Battalion commissar, to act as a commissar with the Major Attlee Company. They pointed out the need for the men to feel that the movement was supporting them, and my links with the Labour Party and trade union movement were important in this respect. One was not expected to refuse an assignment and so I accepted and proceeded to study the duties of a *comisario de guerra*. In practice the job was a combination of welfare officer and political adviser, but the official instructions handed to me were awe-inspiring. I was expected to 'watch carefully over the prestige of the command'. In my hands were placed 'political and moral education and vigilance'. I was to concern myself with 'the mental and physical well-being of the combatants'.

The commander of the Major Attlee Company was Paddy O'Daire, who held the rank of captain and some time previously had distinguished himself by taking over the leadership of the Battalion when the commander, Peter Daly, had been killed in action. It was my job to work closely with him and I quickly found this a pleasure. Quiet, nonchalant and friendly, Paddy impressed me greatly with his deep knowledge of military matters and his experience of life.

As a teenager, he had joined the Irish Free State Army and had become a sergeant. Afterwards he emigrated to Canada, where he tried to develop a farm and did some trapping. It was during the depression, however, and he became involved in the unemployed movement – an activity which landed him in jail for fifteen months and deportation to Britain. From there he had joined the International Brigade. He was admired and trusted by the men of the Company. Paddy and I became firm friends and our friendship lasted until his death in 1981.

I was continually struck by the working-class nature of most of the

British and Irish who were fighting in Spain. They reminded me of stories from the First World War about 'Tommy Atkins'. Politics were not that much talked of and yet they all knew why they were there. The basic loyalty to the Spanish Republic was self-evident, and relations with the Spaniards in the Battalion were close and friendly. The use of basic Spanish became second nature in communications between all of us.

At this time the Battalion was located in a valley close to the town of Falset and we began intensive training for what proved to be the re-crossing of the Ebro. In our spare time there were a variety of activities, from football matches to language classes. Our Battalion paymaster (there was little pay and it was doled out infrequently), took a class in Spanish. From time to time I gave a talk to the assembled company, squatting on the ground and under the shade of the olive trees. Most of the men would be smoking whatever they could get hold of, usually dried onion or almond leaves. I gave 'mini-lectures' on the Labour movement or on the fight against unemployment, and I dealt with the contemporary war situation, outlining the policy of the Negrin Government at that time.

The educational work became easier when we knew that an offensive was in prospect and the lads became enthusiastic. At one time I fell foul of the establishment when the idea of an 'activist movement' was being pushed. The proposal was that a drive should be made to improve morale and secure more understanding and commitment, by getting some of the men to sign up as 'activists' and become an example to the others in courage, discipline, hygiene, etc. Personally I saw the danger of elitism in this policy, and instead of making individual approaches I called a meeting of the whole Company. I outlined the reasons for the activist movement, and at the end of my talk asked who was prepared to sign the activist declaration. *All* hands went up. We didn't have enough forms for individuals to sign so I arranged for a number of men to sign on one form. When I took the forms in to Battalion headquarters there was hell to pay – 'You haven't understood!' 'This is ridiculous!' and so on – but we weren't bothered about 'individual activists' in the Major Attlee Company after that.

Life wasn't easy but a good spirit prevailed in the ranks. Food was short, our main meals consisted of beans, lentils and chick peas, sometimes beans with *bacaloa* (dried cod fish) in a stew, or beans with mule meat or old goat in a stew topped off with rough (very rough) red wine. Some of the lads visited an old chap in a nearby village who (allegedly) made stew with mice but nobody would admit to having tasted it. Needless to say, there were no cats and dogs around.

Occasionally problems would arise, I remember two men fighting, and in the course of the fight one calling the other (a Jew from Manchester) 'a Jewish-nosed bastard'. The International Brigade discipline was strongly against racialism; a complaint was registered and we had to deal with it. The offender, an Irish lad, was arrested and brought before the equivalent of a court martial, presided over by Sam Wild. I represented the Irish lad and argued that he was a good soldier and there was no evidence of him using racialist expressions previously. On his behalf I expressed regret for the lapse and urged leniency. I thought I had made a good case, but those adjudicating seemed determined to make an example and my 'client' was given a stretch in the labour battalion. I thought the sentence too severe, but there was nothing I could do about it.

Justice in the Battalion was not always so heavy-handed. While in Barcelona to make a broadcast I visited the docks to contact my UGT friends. Looking across to the dockside I caught sight of Taffy Foulkes, a well-known character in the Battalion who had been 'absent' for some time, in fact he was thought to have deserted. I had little doubt that he had been living (and probably sleeping) on the ships and hoped eventually to stow away on one of them. I persuaded him to come back to the Battalion with me and thought there would be another 'trial' – but Taffy was lucky, Sam Wild simply told him not to be a bloody fool again. I was pleased about this because Taffy was the proverbial jester, and very popular.

Important visitors came now and then, following the example of Clem Attlee and Harry Pollitt (the popular communist leader and a frequent visitor to the Battalion). They included Nehru, Alvarez del Vayo, and Jack Little, the AEU President (whom I got to know quite well during the Second World War). We also received a visit from a delegation of university students from Britain, one of whom was Ted Heath. He was then Chairman of the Federation of University Conservative Associations and was to the right of the five-man delegation. I suppose he reflected a strand of Conservative thinking which had some sympathy with the Republic, a line more prominently followed by the Duchess of Atholl and even occasionally by Winston Churchill. 'They were tough, hardened soldiers, burned by the Spanish sun to a dark tan,' Ted Heath later wrote. 'Their morale was high and they still genuinely believed that they were going to throw back

General Franco's troops.

'As we drove back into Barcelona one could not but admire these men, civilians at heart, who had had to learn everything of a military nature as they went along. They would go on fighting as long as they could, that was clear. . .'

When we stood around chatting that day we little thought that our paths would cross in later years in Downing Street and other prestigious places, very different to the Ebro front.

During the visit I entrusted one of Ted Heath's left-wing colleagues with the 'Book of the 15th International Brigade' signed by all members of the Major Attlee Company, with a short message from Paddy O'Daire as commander and myself as *comisario*. It was an act of respect to our patron, and we asked that the book should be delivered personally to him.

One of the exceptional personalities in the Battalion was Lewis Clive, a tall, smart, young man, who was a Labour councillor from the Royal Borough of Kensington. A lieutenant in the Brigade, he commanded the respect of his men by his obvious sincerity and devotion to duty, although he was clearly of a different background to most of us. Lewis had been an Oxford blue and had been educated at Eton and Christ Church, Oxford. He was a direct descendant of Clive of India into the bargain. He was never condescending (mind you, it wouldn't have done him any good if he had been), and always friendly. We had many conversations and undertook broadcasting missions together.

One day Lewis Clive and I were called upon to go to meet André Marty (the founder of the International Brigade). He was a sharp, imperious-looking man, and looked capable of performing all the actions Hemingway and others have written about. Yet to me there was a touch of the Tom Mann about him; he appeared to be vigorous, thrusting and bore evidence of long years of struggle. He wanted us to use our influence with the Labour Party to oppose all efforts at mediation. He claimed that talk of mediation was rife and that the British and French Governments could be involved, resulting in a weakening of the Republic's defences. I had received information from the UGT along the same lines and I knew from them that they had written to the TUC in Britain and the CGT in France. We readily agreed to send a letter to the Labour Party and to ask two other colleagues in the Battalion, who were also Labour Councillors, to join us in signing the letter.

Lewis and I drafted the letter. We had no difficulty about the contents, but did have quite an argument on how we should address Jim Middleton, the then Secretary of the Labour Party. I was all for 'Dear comrade Middleton,' but Lewis would have none of it and insisted on 'Dear Middleton,' which I thought snobbish and upper-class. He won! The sentiments expressed in our letter were very much from the heart:

> While it is difficult for us fighting in Spain to keep in the closest touch with the International situation, we could not fail to notice certain proposals now afoot for the liquidation of the Spanish war by 'mediation'. There are signs that the Labour Party might be influenced by these, and it is for this reason that we, four members of the Party and Councillors, are writing you this letter which we would be grateful if you would bring to the notice of the National Executive Committee. In our opinion, to accept any such proposals for 'mediation' would be to play straight into the hands of the Fascist invaders.
>
> The four of us writers of this letter are in each case proud to have the whole-hearted approval by our local Labour Parties of our presence here in Spain.

Urging support for the UGT appeal to the TUC, we concluded:

> We believe that there can be no compromise between Fascism and Democratic ideals for which we ourselves have come here to fight. We feel ourselves wholly at one with the determination of the Spanish people to drive out the invaders of their country, and as members of the Labour Party we urge that our leaders turn a deaf ear to talk of compromise, and continue to press ever more vigorously the Party's declared policy; namely, the demand that the British Government's support of 'non-intervention' be reversed and that the right be restored to the Spanish Republic freely to purchase arms.
>
> Nothing could be more encouraging to the work of those of us fighting with the British Battalion than to feel that we are being supported by the vigorous efforts of all the Democratic forces of Britain led by the Labour Party. In that struggle we are proud to act in the advance guard, and pledge ourselves to do all in our power to maintain the high reputation already gained by the Battalion in Spain.

The letter was dated 9 July 1938. We entrusted its despatch to the

International Brigade machinery and for some reason there was considerable delay, so that our letter was not posted in Paris until 10 August. By that time Lewis Clive was dead and I had been wounded and was in hospital – casualties in the battle for Hill 481.

I received Jim Middleton's reply to our letter (dated 11 August 1938) lying in my hospital bed in Mataro near Barcelona. I quote it because of its historical interest and to show the leisurely way the fight was being conducted back home. It read:

> Dear Comrade Jones,
>
> I am replying right away to assure you that so far as the Labour Party is concerned, either at Transport House, in the House of Commons, or anywhere in the country so far as I am aware there has not been the slightest support for mediation proposals. . .
>
> We are continuing our activities, although, as you will realise, August is not the most suitable month for propaganda, and Parliament has risen.
>
> The work on behalf of the International Solidarity Fund and the Milk for Spain Fund is continuing. We should be deceiving ourselves, however, if we have any indication whatever that there is any sign of a break in the Non-Intervention front so far as the Chamberlain Government is concerned.
>
> The National Executive Committee will not be meeting again until the first week in September, when we meet in Blackpool during the period of the Trades Union Congress.
>
> In view of this delay, however, I am immediately having your letter copied and circulated to all National Executive Committee members for their information.
>
> The fact that Comrade Clive's signature is appended to it makes the appeal all the more poignant.
>
> With comradely greetings. . .

When our letter was sent off early in July preparations for the 'fightback' were proceeding at great pace. Numerous reconnaissance activities took place. Weapons and ammunition were checked and re-checked. Military training was intensified and efforts increased to ensure political awareness. On 21 July our battalion moved off from the camp at Marsa and was on its way to the great Ebro offensive. We marched by night and rested in the daytime to avoid alerting the Fascist forces.

Towards the latter part of July the tide seemed to be turning for the Republic as our forces advanced into areas on the other side of the River Ebro, with the aim ultimately of reopening land communications with the south. The generals may have planned recklessly and in desperation, but the men were not aware of the considerations which influenced decisions at the top and we were glad to advance.

There was a spring in our step as we marched towards the river but it was past midnight before we came within reach of it. The men were grouped together in their sections. There had to be no smoking or talking, for we were within metres of enemy territory. Throughout the night the XIII Brigade crossed the river in small boats, and shell burst and machine-gun fire could be heard.

At dawn our battalion was on the move. The quartermaster had arrived with a lorryload of food, but we couldn't stop for breakfast. An artillery barrage was landing shells not far away, close enough to warm our ears. As we moved through the trees on the river bank enemy planes appeared in the sky above us bombing and then strafing the area. The bullets crackled but luckily there were few casualties. An old mule got the worst of it and died as a result.

Pushing our way through the trees to the edge of the river, a remarkable spectacle presented itself. The river was like a lake at one of the holiday resorts back home, full of little rowing boats crossing and re-crossing. Our lads got into the boats, about half a dozen at a time, and were quickly rowed across. On our right the labour battalion was erecting a pontoon bridge.

The elation at landing on what had been Fascist territory less than a day earlier was considerable. The boats were landing at scattered points along the bank and I had the responsibility of getting the men of our company together. We assembled quickly and had just time to break into our iron rations before we were off on our trek south-westward.

It wasn't long before we saw the first prisoners, Italians captured by the XIII Brigade at Corbera. In the main they seemed glad to be getting out of the war. Everywhere advances had been made and the news from all sections of the front encouraged our men to keep moving, despite the terrific heat of the day, and the incessant strafing and bombardment. Our company was quickly involved in fighting in the hills where Moorish troops were strongly established. The terrain provided natural cover for snipers and we suffered many casualties. It was exhausting work climbing the hills under the heat of the Spanish

73

sun in clothes that were often only rags and with little to drink. Some-times we went for a day without water, which we badly needed to moisten burning lips and parched throats.

We were spread out in small groups, in skirmishing order, and from time to time were confronted by fanatical Moorish soldiers who thought nothing of stringing together a number of grenades, pulling the pins out quickly and hurling the lot at us. It was a special skill they exercised at no small risk to themselves. We had an understandable fear of the Moors, who had a reputation for vicious treatment of their enemies, so it was a relief when we got control of the situation and secured a large number of Moorish prisoners. They were a fierce-looking lot but we treated them well, much to their surprise. A number were selected for questioning, but the information obtained was not all that helpful.

In this period I conducted my first burial. A young man from Lon-don, Ken Band, had been killed and a shallow grave prepared. As we gathered round the grave, on the rough hillside, there were no tears and little emotion – time was short and the ceremony was taking place under fire. But there was respect and determination shown as I spoke a few words: 'We shall remember him – Ken died for the cause of the people of Spain – *Viva la Republica Espana*!'

We tried at least to bury our dead but as casualties increased this became more difficult. We grew hardened and impersonal. I recall coming across a dead comrade, and before I thought of burial I looked over his gear for any food he might have and found to my pleasure a tin of corned beef. I shared this find with a good friend, Syd Booth from Manchester. We ate together, savouring the delicacy, under heavy fire.

The battles were hotting up as we climbed the hills leading to the 'Pimple' – a high hill heavily fortified by the Fascists – officially known as Hill 481. German and Italian planes were bombing and strafing, while anti-aircraft opposition from our side hardly existed. Here and there a horse or mule had been killed; after a day or so in the heat they swelled up and the smell pervaded the countryside for miles.

Day after day we made attacks on Hill 481 to try to gain the summit, an almost impossible task without artillery and air support. The Fascists had placed concrete pill-boxes and machine guns in key posi-tions commanding every approach to the summit. Mines had been tied to bushes; if you touched one you were blown to pieces. Above all they had plentiful artillery and a considerable force in reserve, plus German and Italian planes in abundance.

In action after action we faced snipers' bullets and machine-gun fire while shells were bursting all around us. As we moved up closer to the enemy hand-grenades were thrown at us – while on our side we had all too few hand-grenades to throw back. With more grenades and machine guns, combined with artillery support, Hill 481 could have been taken, thus making almost certain the recapture of Gandesa.

During a lull in the fighting, but while still under heavy fire, I was amazed to see my commander, Paddy O'Daire, reading a French military manual – an outstanding example of sang-froid! Somehow a letter reached me. When I opened it I found it was from Ernest Bevin, saying that he thought I would like to have a copy of the union's annual report and accounts. Out tumbled the document! I did not have the detachment of my friend Paddy, so I refrained from studying the report under fire.

The number of dead and wounded mounted rapidly. The British Battalion took a heavy battering. Among those killed was Lewis Clive. The news was a shock to all of us. It was difficult to believe that such a fine, upstanding man was no longer alive. Many harrowing stories could be told of those days. So many good men died, believing to the end in the cause of democracy. Win or lose, the world needs sincerity. In Spain it was demonstrated by so many in full measure – even unto death.

I was the recipient of confidences shared in a few minutes of respite, and one I often think about was the dream Paddy Sullivan had for the future. When the war was over, he said, he planned to go to Mexico with his sister, to travel the country and see what work was going. He had vague ideas of joining the revolutionary movement in the area. Paddy, a lieutenant, always looked smart and clean, whatever he did was done with great precision. He looked and acted like a Guards officer; yet when you broke through his natural reserve he was a great one to talk to. I felt that he was a young man who would go far in the world . . . but hours after our talk he was killed, leading his men courageously forward towards the summit.

There were many casualties and I became one of them. Once more I had clambered up the hill with my comrades, taking cover where we could and firing at the enemy wherever he appeared. The bullets of the snipers whizzed over, grenades and shells were striking the ground, throwing up earth and dust and showering us with shrapnel. Suddenly my shoulder and right arm went numb. Blood gushed from my shoulder and I couldn't lift my rifle. I could do nothing but lie where I was. Near me a comrade had been killed and I could hear the cries of others, complaining of their wounds. While I was lying there, to make things worse, a spray of shrapnel hit my right arm. The stretcher bearers were doing their best but could hardly keep up with the number of casualties. As night fell I made my own way, crawling to the bottom of the hill. I was taken with other wounded men down the line to an emergency field hospital at Mora del Ebro where I was given an anti-tetanus injection. The place was like an abbatoir; there was blood and the smell of blood everywhere.

I was taken by ambulance to a hospital at Mataro near Barcelona, where the bullet and bits of shrapnel were extracted. My arm was out of action for quite some time and although moved to hospitals at Barcelona and Santa Colomba, my wounds didn't heal easily. It was decided that I should go back to Britain.

Chapter Eight

We who are left, how shall we look again
Happily on the sun or feel the rain
Without remembering how they who went
Ungrudgingly and spent
Their lives for us loved, too, the sun and rain?
A bird among the rain-wet lilac sings –
But we, how shall we turn to little things
And listen to the birds and winds and streams
Made holy by their dreams,
Nor feel the heart-break in the heart of things?

WILFRED WILSON GIBSON

When I was fit enough to move around I secured permission from the doctors to go to Barcelona to meet my friends from the UGT. It was agreed that one of my fellow patients, Dusty Miller, should accompany me. Dusty was a bit of a humorist, and I knew him well from the Battalion, so I was happy to have someone with me who would be agreeable company. Later he acknowledged that he had learned more that day about trade unionism and the Spanish worker than he had gathered in his whole life previously.

My friend Vidal, the General Secretary of the Federation of Transport, Fishing and Maritime Industries of the UGT, greeted me most warmly with a great hug. He enquired about our wounds and events on the Ebro front and told us about the grave situation facing the Government and industry. Material shortages had severely affected production in the factories, dock cranes and transport vehicles badly needed replacements. Above all, the food shortage was causing great problems, children were suffering terribly and workers couldn't work properly. There were many instances of workers fainting at work due to lack of food. He knew that we would shortly be going back to Britain and he urged me to press with all my power for the embargo on arms to be lifted and for the British Labour movement to ensure the shipment of food supplies.

I maintained contact with Vidal and others of the UGT through the difficult years that followed. Under Franco's rule some went to prison, others into exile, and one man I knew was executed. One friend survived the years of dictatorship and was playing an active part in the revived UGT Transport Union when I saw him in Madrid on recent visits there.

As we made our way through the streets to get our transport back to hospital we passed little children calling out *poco pan* ('a little bread'). There were tears in the children's eyes; they were no ordinary beggars, just desperate for a little to eat. With their stomachs swollen, they bore all the signs of approaching starvation. The misery of the children was made worse by the widespread bombing of civilian areas in Barcelona.

A week or two afterwards I was on my way by train to Paris *en route* to London. There were many wounded men on the train, of various nationalities, but travelling with me were Paddy O'Daire and Alan Foot, both of whom had served the Republic in Spain for nearly two years. Once over the border and into France our first stop was Cerbère where we quickly sought the station restaurant. The meal was decidedly different to the food we had been used to; it was like a banquet. Then we got the bill and for a minute or two there was consternation, for none of us had any French currency. Then I remembered that I had three English pounds which I had carefully kept inside my passport during my time in Spain. I was able to change the pounds into francs and pay the bill. Then Alan Foot produced some Canadian dollars so we were all right for drinks too. Later he told us that Malcolm Dunbar (an aristocratic Englishman and Chief of Staff of the 15th Brigade) had asked him to take the dollars to a relative in England, so they weren't Alan's to buy the drinks with! But he did, and we felt no great remorse.

Our stay in Paris was short. We spent the time searching for beer, and for Paddy's benefit journeyed around the restaurants seeking boiled eggs. We were offered omelettes of all descriptions but no boiled eggs. We had to wait until we arrived in London before Paddy could satisfy his craving.

Naturally I wanted to get back home to Liverpool as quickly as I could to see my friends and family, especially Evelyn, my wife to be, but I was asked to lead a small delegation to Clement Attlee to solicit his support for the inauguration of a National Memorial Fund. The purpose was to raise £50,000 'to meet the future needs of the wounded and the families of the men who have fallen'.

'Munich' was in the air and when we met Clem Attlee he told us of his fears. He seemed to be a frightened man, more nervous than I had noticed when I had seen him on previous occasions. Our meeting took place at Transport House, in the Labour Party offices, and he was accompanied by Jim Middleton, the Secretary of the Party. Both were friendly and courteous. After a brief chat our request was agreed and Clem became a patron and signatory of the appeal. It included the words: 'These men, true to the great tradition of the freedom-loving people of Britain, have suffered heavily in the cause. Four hundred and thirty-two have•made the supreme sacrifice. . . .' The success of this approach to Attlee encouraged other well-known people to lend their names to the appeal.

A great welcome awaited us at Liverpool. The entrance to Lime Street Station was packed with a teeming mass of people. From the crowd the Consul of the Spanish Republic, a number of Labour Councillors including Jack and Bessie Braddock, officials of the TGWU and many other friends came forward to give a personal welcome. But for me the best moment was my reunion with Evelyn.

The Liverpool Trades Council and Labour Party had decided to raise funds to provide an ambulance for Spain and I was told about this when I met the Executive shortly after my return. I gave a résumé of events in Spain and explained the dangers facing the people there. 'The people of Spain are hungry,' I said. 'Children are dying of malnu-trition and men and women at the front and in the factories are on the verge of starvation.' I went on, 'It is criminal that our Government maintains the embargo on arms supplies to the constitutional Govern-ment but we can only keep up and intensify the campaign on that. The urgent need we can directly help to meet is the provision of food.' I then urged that a big effort should be made to send a food-ship, which I suggested was more urgently required even than ambulances. My colleagues were a little incredulous and seemed to doubt whether the sort of money needed could be raised. They were clearly in no mood to run a campaign themselves and they decided to leave it to me.

To raise a large sum of money in Liverpool, in 1938, was not going to be easy and I wanted to make progress quickly. I realized that to achieve any reasonable target required the support of wealthy people and I didn't move in that circle. I decided to make the effort anyway and first approached a Liverpool doctor, Dr Tumarkin, who was known to be sympathetic to Spanish Aid appeals and at the same time, as a throat specialist of high repute, knew many of Liverpool's rich fraternity. He agreed to help.

Between us we worked out a list of possible sponsors for a food-ship campaign to whom he might make an initial approach. Through him we managed to get together an *ad hoc* committee, including George Holt, a member of the shipping family, who had known Lewis Clive at university, as well as one of the young Rathbones, a relative of Eleanor Rathbone, MP. Harold Bibby, chairman of Bibby's Oil Cake Mills, was persuaded to be chairman, and Mr Phillips, the Registrar of Liverpool University, agreed to act as treasurer. It was decided that I should be secretary and organizer of the campaign.

We were on our way. An appeal was drafted and I was able to get the signatures of the Anglican Bishop of Liverpool, a leading Roman Catholic priest (it was felt inadvisable to make an approach to Archbishop Downey), Alderman Luke Hogan, the leader of the Labour Party, Sydney Jones and Professor Lyon Blease, leading Liberals, and other prominent citizens. The appeal was put in the hands of the printers, who agreed to do the work without charge.

I knew that simply sending out an appeal in the usual way would not be sufficient. We had to have an organization, supporting groups and an office with people to help with the work. My friends in Liverpool's Spanish community drew my attention to the vacant premises of the Spanish Bank, which were ideally situated in the centre of the city.

I approached the Spanish Consul and with his help obtained the use of the Spanish Bank. The office space was considerable and there was room to store some goods. But an empty office wasn't much use, I needed helpers and equipment. The business contacts I had made speeded this along. Typewriters, a duplicator, typing paper and all the other essentials were made available. The local office of the League of Nations Union seconded their shorthand typist to work full time with us and Evelyn became the general factotum and copy typist. To round it off two returned International Brigaders who had been badly wounded in Spain, Jimmy Allen and Paddy Brady, turned up every day at the office to help in any way required.

We built up an address list and the appeal was printed and posted. It was well received (except for a little resentment from the Braddocks whom I had not asked to sign – I thought their signature might put off some of the wealthy people!) and donations began to roll in. I knew that more was required, much more, so I persuaded Harold Bibby to list his business and other friends with money and influence. More importantly, he agreed to write a personal letter which we then typed on his personal notepaper. Each letter was typed individually and he then topped and tailed it himself. The results were marvellous.

I tried to publicize our appeal in every way possible: leaflets, meetings, special approaches to the churches, chapels, and the Jewish community. I went all over Merseyside addressing meetings, especially trade union branches, Labour Party wards, Co-operative guilds and religious groups. The office became a hive of activity and more and more voluntary workers joined us.

A flag day throughout Liverpool was organized. Canon Raven preached a special sermon to a packed congregation in the Liverpool Anglican Cathedral. Not least, we got the press on our side. Women and children responded to the call, and collections of tinned food were organized at the schools, house to house in the streets and in the Co-operative stores and some other shops.

Farmers in the surrounding area sent in large quantities of potatoes. The press called me Councillor 'Potato' Jones, after the brave ship's captain who broke through Franco's blockade. By this time Evelyn and I were married and one newspaper suggested that we would spend our honeymoon on the food-ship. It wasn't true, but it was a good story. The press coverage brought in many individual donations and letters of support. Within four to five weeks well over £6000 had been raised. Two big companies, Lever and Bibby, gave half a ton of soap each. Crawfords gave half a ton of biscuits. Other companies offered tinned meats and milk, sugar and other goods that would stand the sea voyage. The workers at Bibby's worked overtime without payment, packing the firm's consignment of soap. The women put goodwill messages in the boxes. I went round the works and then addressed an enthusiastic meeting on the shop floor.

Masses of good quality new and second-hand clothes and shoes came in. The Mersey Dock and Harbour Board waived their dock dues. The ship was loaded free. With support from the Spanish Aid Organization and the Co-operative movement, enough cargo was secured for the ship to sail. It wasn't the largest ship afloat but it was a real cargo of goodwill. An obligation to the brave Spanish people had been discharged and none appreciated our efforts more than the Spanish community in Liverpool.

With the end of the campaign, my wounds having healed, I returned to the docks and my own community. I was quickly back in the world of ships and cargoes and the human problems of the waterfront. Piecework issues meant that there was no lack of involvement in union affairs and members welcomed me back as a mate and, for many, as a spokesman in adversity.

My old adversary in the union – Harry Pugh, the Area Secretary – was not so pleased. While I had been away he had connived at attempts to secure my removal from membership of the National Docks Group Committee and the Area Committee of the union. His attempts had been obstructed, but shortly after I returned elections were due and lo and behold a candidate was nominated against me out of the blue, a dock checker by the name of 'J. W. Jones'. Although it seemed his candidacy owed more to his name than to his qualities, and was intended to cause confusion in the ballot, the attempt failed and I was re-elected. The members were vigilant enough to see through tricks like that.

Mr Pugh was not satisfied and persuaded the Area Committee to set up a sub-committee to inquire into my conduct in relation to 'unofficial activities'. No specific charges were made and I was able to demonstrate that this was contrary to the union's rules. I had also taken some workmates with me to the inquiry, two of whom had been members longer than Mr Pugh himself. I called them as witnesses to the work I had done to build up the union and strengthen its influence in the docks. Pugh realized he was on weak ground but he tried one last trick. 'Haven't you been in Preston organizing unofficial meetings there?' he asked. 'I have been in Preston to report to the branch meeting,' I replied, 'because, as you know, I represent the membership in that port as well as my own. That I regard as official business. I have also been in Preston to speak at a meeting of the Labour Party.' He was nonplussed and asked no further questions. That was the end of that.

I learned later that Bell, a member in the Preston docks branch, had been the subject of a similar inquiry on the previous day, charged with unofficial activities. He was asked if he had been at meetings with me and replied, 'No.' Mr Pugh then pulled out an envelope from his breast pocket and said: 'I have the evidence here!' Bell agreed that he had been at a meeting with me, but his attempts to explain were brushed aside. The fact that he had inadvertently told an untruth was used against him and he was removed from membership of the branch committee and banned from holding any office in the union for two years.

This was typical of the atmosphere of fear built up against men who dared to speak out for their mates. The union in the Liverpool area (which included the Preston docks membership) had become a disciplinary arm acting on behalf of the employer. Membership was retained by fear rather than conviction. Yet at committee meetings Pugh would often sneer about the membership being 'conscript trade unionists'.

My experience of Ernest Bevin was quite different, even if I disagreed with some of his views, and he with mine. He was vigorous and able, and there was no doubt that he really did want to look after the interests of the membership, as he saw it. There were times when some of us felt that he was responding to the overtures of big business and the establishment rather more than was good for the union, but he was in absolute control of the administration, the 'machine' which is the key to authority in a trade union.

I had been immensely impressed by Bevin as a negotiator. I understood why the older dockers referred to him as the 'dockers' KC'. Time had eroded the image and he had plenty of critics among the younger dockers but he appeared impervious to attacks from left or right, including those in newspapers which he delighted in calling the 'yellow press'.

Another doughty fighter for the union was the national organizer, Dan Hillman. Dan had been a strong syndicalist as a young man and had done much pioneering work in Bristol and the south-west. He had been largely instrumental in persuading Bevin to be active in the Dock, Wharf, Riverside and General Workers' Union, which later took the lead in forming the TGWU in 1922. Without Hillman we might not have had Bevin.

Because I knew that Dan Hillman was close to Bevin I put a question to him which had worried me for a long time: 'Why don't we force the Government to lift the arms embargo on the Spanish Government by industrial action?' Dan's reply was revealing. 'You know,' he said, 'we always give the impression that we are stronger than we really are. The truth is that we were and are too weak industrially to try any fanciful ideas like that, even if we had the disposition to do anything. . . .'

The war in Spain came to an end early in 1939. The Franco regime was recognized by the big powers, including Britain but excluding Russia. Republican merchant ships in British ports were arrested by the British Government and handed over to Franco, but the crews in the main said they would not serve under the new regime. When a ship was arrested in my own port of Garston the crew made contact with me. Workmates and other friends helped to supply the men with food. A local shopkeeper who was sympathetic gave a great deal of assistance, but he fell foul of the local Catholic church. The shopkeeper had a news-stand at the local church where he sold Catholic periodicals. This was now in danger, as hostility to the Spanish Republicans still lingered in sections of the Church. I was able to convince the priest of the humanitarian aspect of the operation, and my friend retained his news-stand.

After that, groups of Spanish seamen seemed to pop up from every-where. Ships were arrested in Liverpool and Preston and the crews made contact with me. They were being harassed by the police and had nowhere to go. The British Government was determined to hand over the Republican ships without delay. I rushed down to the office of the National Union of Seamen and insisted on seeing the District Secretary, Mr Boalase. I put it to him that the men needed accommoda-tion and other help while we tried to obtain sea-going jobs for them. My request was agreed and the men were housed in the Seamen's Home in Canning Place, Liverpool, where their accommodation was paid for by the National Union of Seamen.

With the help of donations from trade union branches, Co-op guilds and the remnants of the Spanish Aid movement I was able to organize financial help for the men sufficient to provide little extras like cigarettes and tobacco, soap and clothing. During their stay in Liverpool I kept in regular contact with them. A group of them knitted a tea cosy in the Spanish Republican colours and gave it to me for my wife.

News came through that employment opportunities for Republican refugees might exist in Argentina and Mexico. Some of the Spanish seamen established that if they could get to Argentina they would be looked after. The problem was, how could they get to that far-distant country? Here those two stalwarts of the food-ship campaign, George Holt and his friend Rathbone, came to the aid of the Spaniards, through their shipping connections, and were able to arrange one-way trips for all the men to Argentina. I felt then and still feel deep gratitude to these two men, from a different class and background to my own, who responded so splendidly to the call.

As a Labour city councillor I became increasingly frustrated. We were in a minority and the Conservative majority rode roughshod over our attempts to secure a little humanity in the administration of Liver-pool's affairs. I was more a trade unionist than a politician, and couldn't stomach the niceties of political debating. For example, when Coun-cillor Moore referred to unemployed people as 'scroungers' I wanted the whole Labour Group to demonstrate against him. I was active in pressing for work schemes at trade union rates to be developed for the unemployed and appalled at the lethargy or downright inhumanity of the well-heeled Tory councillors, in rejecting or holding up any real progress. Repeatedly I questioned Labour's feeble opposition to the scandalous way Conservative councillors used their position to advance business interests. Public houses would be built in the middle of a field and later a council housing estate would be built around it. Exposure of such chicanery was needed, but always caution was counselled and prevailed.

When air-raid precautions were discussed, against the background of the bombings of open cities in Spain and the increasing fear of war, a Tory dignitary gave it as his opinion that the best protection against bombing was to walk out into the open fields. I sought to ridicule him, because I knew from my direct experience of mass bombing that the only protection was deep shelters. To talk of lying down in the open fields, when for many citizens the nearest field to their home would anyway be three or four miles away, was nonsense, but it was difficult to arouse enthusiasm even in Labour's ranks on this issue.

If progress was difficult on the political scene it was even more so in the docks. I kept banging my head against the brick wall of union officialdom. The members had little influence within the union, which led to cynicism. As a shop steward and committee-man my efforts were circumscribed. Some of my workmates had moved down to the Midlands and taken up employment in the aircraft and motor industries and I was inclined to do the same. At that moment an opportunity came along that interested me greatly. The Executive of the union had invited applications nationally for the post of District Organizer in the Coventry District. I applied as I knew I had the practical experience and ideas to do the job.

Meantime our eldest son, Jack, was born. Evelyn was in the Mill Road Hospital and as our son was born, Mrs Bamber, that indefatigable old fighter, was dying in a nearby ward. I was at a meeting of the National Docks Committee of the union when the news came through. Two telegrams, one following the other, were delivered to me while Ernie Bevin was addressing the meeting. At the first he said nothing but when the second arrived he asked what all the fuss was about. 'All right, young Jones,' he observed, 'you'll want to get home as quickly as you can when the meeting is finished.'

Shortly afterwards I was appointed to the post of Coventry District Organizer. Bevin congratulated me and asked me to take up the job in August. Amongst the disappointed applicants were Bob Mellish, later to become an MP and Government Minister, and Tom Birkett, who became a National Officer of the union. I had been confident in the examination because I did know the engineering collective agreements and the nature of the industry as well as having clear ideas and experience of organizing workers into the union. Here, I felt, was my opportunity to prove that the union really could work for its members.

Evelyn and I had been living in a two-room apartment, but with the baby coming I had been able to secure a new flat which had pleased Evelyn very much. She and baby Jack were well settled in our new home when I broke the news about my new job. She was sad to leave but her natural enthusiasm soon surfaced. 'So long as we are together it will be all right,' she said. My first weeks in Coventry were spent in digs while I anxiously searched for a place for my little family to live. This was easier said than done, because the salary for my new job was less than my dock earnings, and the cost of living seemed higher in Coventry.

With the help of the Midlands Area Secretary of the union, Joe Blewitt, a good old trade unionist, a house was found at eighteen shillings a week. But my experience of household needs was limited and when Evelyn appeared it was pronounced unsuitable. The rooms were small and the walls thin, so much so that when I sang to our baby, the neighbours next door made loud objections! Within two weeks we had moved to the centre of the town, Evelyn having found a roomy flat at twenty-one shillings a week.

My workmates wished me well in the new venture, although they were sorry to lose my help. My friends on the docks who were active in the union maintained contact with me and I was able to help with a little unofficial advice from time to time. Some made the journey to Coventry and occasionally stayed with us, becoming as interested in my new activities as I was by news of the waterfront.

I was quickly aware that Coventry presented the trade union challenge I was looking for.

Chapter Nine

We are entering upon a new era to do
work worthy of the cause to which we
are attached.

JIM LARKIN

Coventry in 1939 was a highly industrialized town with a population
of nearly a quarter of a million. Outwardly, it was successful and
bustling, but conditions in many of its factories presented a less happy
picture. The motor-car industry suffered from seasonal fluctuation in
demand. To my amazement I learned that management regarded it as
their prerogative to lay off workers and then re-engage them when
trade improved, with no opportunity allowed for argument or complaints of victimization. This, it was explained, had a lot to do with
the low level of trade union organization in the factories and foundries.

This dismal view was given to me on the day I reported to the small
TGWU office in Bishop Street, Coventry, by the two full-time officials
who operated there, one of whom I was to replace. George Geobey
had opted to retire at sixty. In his time he had been a leading force in
the old Workers' Union, which had merged with the TGWU in 1929,
but he had seen the remnants of the old union decline and in Coventry
total membership in 1939 had slumped to 2000 or so. The membership
of the Amalgamated Engineering Union was not much better. The
overwhelming majority of workers in the area belonged to no union
at all.

Within the first few days of taking up my job I was urging the need
for a massive organizing campaign, but my two colleagues were not so
thrilled with the idea. They told me that 'it had all been tried before'.
The motor industry in particular, they said, was largely unorganized
everywhere. I found their view pretty complacent, but I knew in any
case that the key to developing organization was to find and cultivate
the enthusiastic shop steward and the odd individual who had a
grievance.

87

Geobey was persuaded to accompany me on an organizaing expedition. It was his idea to go to Fisher and Ludlow, a plant on the outskirts of the city. 'They all come into the local pub at dinner time, we'll catch them there,' he said. We duly called at the pub, drank and waited, drank and waited, but no one seemed to arrive. 'Don't the lads from Fishers come in here?' I asked the landlord. 'Not now,' he replied. 'The bloody works has been closed for three weeks. They're re-tooling for war work and it won't be re-opened for a couple of months yet.'

At that time union members paid their subscriptions directly at a branch meeting or to collectors in the factory they worked in. The collectors were the main point of contact. Often they had to carry out their work for the union surreptitiously; if they were caught collecting they risked dismissal. The union had few shop stewards then, for they too ran the risk of losing their jobs. The member with a problem would bring it to the branch meeting, or attend at the union office to see the trade union official.

I made it my business to meet as many of the collectors and shop stewards as I could, to help them in their activities and gain information which might aid my plans to strengthen the membership. It meant attending all the branch meetings of the six or seven branches operating in Coventry and the half dozen branches in the outlying areas of Rugby, Warwick, Nuneaton and Warwickshire generally. Sometimes there were two meetings in one night. I regarded that sort of thing as my duty, for now I was being paid for my work. In the past I had spent most of my spare time on trade union activities or City Council work without any remuneration.

Most of the active members would gather in a Branch Representation Committee, a relic of the old Workers' Union. It was known locally as the 'District Committee', but was not officially recognized by that title within the TGWU. Early on I suggested that we should ask such shop stewards as we had to meet with the committee, and this helped to provide a sense of moving forward together. An old friend of the Hunger March Days, Jock Gibson, was the chairman of the committee and became my loyal lieutenant in many activities. The secretary, Norman Edwards, was an electrician by trade, one of the few skilled men the TGWU had among its members in the area. It was my view that all workers should be organized in unity, and that meant skilled, semi-skilled and non-skilled workers acting together. I saw the TGWU as the 'one big union', rather more comprehensive in nature than Ernie Bevin originally intended.

The obstacles which confronted us were enormous. In factory after factory I found that it was difficult to arouse the workers' interest. Meetings at the gates and the distribution of leaflets as men and women went to work, seemed doomed to failure. I made what contact I could in the pubs and the workmen's clubs but most people seemed afraid of joining the union. Even those who were members were worried lest their workmates found out, because if they did they might pass on their knowledge to the 'boss', the foreman or chargehand.

The industry was busiest from September to April. Workers were anxious to keep their jobs during this period, working as much overtime as possible and driving themselves flat out on piecework. It was in individual piecework that the law of the survival of the fittest most starkly prevailed. In the slack periods many workers were laid off and even the lucky ones worked short time. It was as casual as the old days on the docks. In such circumstances victimization could be and was practised with impunity. The picture was disheartening but the few valiant men and women who were prepared to stand by the union encouraged me to keep trying. I knew that one way or another I had to develop confidence and a strong sense of solidarity among the workers.

My determination to improve the atrocious conditions in many of the firms operating in the area became known almost overnight. Workers in the paintshop at the Carbodies plant (a company still well known as the producer of London taxi bodies) asked to meet me because the management was imposing cuts in their piecework prices. Most of the men were not in a trade union and I invited them to join. This they did. I asked the owner, Mr Bobby Jones, to meet me, only to receive a blank refusal. There was no possibility of official support from the union, because the men had only just joined. The men therefore had to face up to the alternatives of submitting to the cut or taking action on their own. On my advice they decided to strike and I assisted in planning their action. Efforts were made to raise funds from the TGWU branches but time was not on our side. For myself I said I would go without my wages, and share with the men whatever help we could get. I knew I had Evelyn behind me in such a sacrifice. To the men it was unheard of to have such support from a trade union official. The action lasted about two weeks. It was not totally successful but none of the men was sacked and Bobby Jones eventually met me. He agreed in future to abide by agreements between the unions and the Engineering Employers Federation, even though the firm was not affiliated to the Federation. We had many difficulties afterwards in trying to keep the firm to the understanding reached but it was a breakthrough all the same.

After all the trials and tribulations of the strike, an old gentleman appeared at my office and introduced himself as the Branch Secretary of the National Union of Vehicle Builders. 'You know that most of the men you had on strike at Carbodies are members of my union,' he said, 'but they haven't paid their dues for about twelve months. They've been in and out – here is the record [and he produced a copy of his branch register written in old-fashioned well-shaped writing]. I call it my unfinished symphony.'

I said I was sorry but they appeared to me as non-unionists needing help. I felt that they would not return to the NUVB. Whether it was my youth or my sincerity I do not know, but he accepted my position and agreed that he would leave the membership to me to do my best with. This NUVB official, Ted Buckle, had a reputation for straight speaking as befits a Yorkshireman. I got to know him well and liked him. On one occasion he caused a commotion when, in the middle of a Conference with the Coventry Engineering Employers Association, he pulled his watch from his waistcoat pocket and said: 'Well, it's half past twelve and I'm going home for my dinner.' Thereupon he left, leaving the rest of us to carry on.

They were busy days, getting to know the industrial areas and attending endless meetings. The strike at Carbodies was followed by a strike of paintshop workers at the Humber motor-car works. But most workers looked for solutions short of strike action. There were many individual grievances which people brought to me and I listened, advised and took action. As members related their problems I tried always to put myself in their place. If they had been injured at work I suffered with them and articulated their worries and fears. Sometimes only a searching conversation revealed that there had been some defect in a machine or other circumstance which established the employer's negligence. It was part of my job to negotiate with insurance companies, representing the employers, on damage claims arising out of workers' accidents. So I tried hard to master the law, the factory regulations and other aspects which might help.

If a letter had to be written, or there was a form to be filled in, I didn't think it good enough to give a little advice and send the member away. I helped write what was necessary or did the writing myself. Many a bureaucrat or employer's agent has got away without meeting his obligations because workers have been ignorant or afraid. I was trying to make my small contribution towards correcting the balance.

Some of the older trade unionists harked back to the militant days of the First World War in Coventry and blamed the extent of non-unionism on the defeat of the engineering unions in the big lock-out of 1922. Following that débâcle the employers had asserted their right to exercise managerial functions without restriction. Union footholds had been retained only in isolated occupations such as toolmaking and sheet metal work. The employers had used their powerful position to enforce tight supervision and to apply piecework with unilateral control over the prices paid.

Yet there was no shortage of labour. From the masses of unemployed came an unending flow of hands eager for work, especially young people. They came from Wales, Scotland, the north-east and Ireland. New methods of production, including the assembly line, made it possible for employers to use such labour easily. Much of the labour force in the new aero-engine 'shadow' factories (state built and equipped units operated by private firms) was made up of this labour, unorganized and generally inexperienced. The employers were operating these factories on the basis of fat cost-plus contracts, and sought to prevent the growth of trade unionism lest it rebounded on their parent factories. I saw it as my major task to break down the solid phalanx of non-unionism in these factories.

Some of my loyal members who appeared to have more enthusiasm and daring than others, were in poor jobs in the older factories. I persuaded them to leave and to seek work in the shadow factories. I had made useful contacts at the Labour Exchange and was able to help in the process of getting new jobs. My plan was that these activists would organize the workers around them and become shop stewards. The plan succeeded.

Membership began to increase, the numbers of shop stewards of the TGWU grew rapidly and there was a keener interest in trade union activities. Firms which were members of the Engineering Employers Federation accepted the principle of shop stewards and conceded to the unions the right to apply for conferences with management within the agreed procedure – a facility I used extensively, even on issues affecting only small groups of workers. Although our success rate was minimal the approach caught on. My insistence to members that they should 'not take "no" for an answer' was welcomed.

Management resented my assertiveness. On one occasion in the first few weeks of my new job I sought an increase in the rate paid to a member on a particular machine. The issue was disputed at a works conference. I pressed the case but the response of management was negative. I then asked that we should go down to the shop to inspect the machine. The reply of the works manager was, 'I'm not letting *you* loose on the shop floor!'

Our efforts were not confined to the factories. With new workers being housed in industrial hostels around the city, we held meetings at the hostels and in some cases succeeded in recruiting representatives there to hand out forms and leaflets. With groups of our active members (not too many, I'm afraid) we also met trains on which we knew workers were coming in for employment.

Some of the worst conditions were to be found in the smaller factories where bullying by the foreman or the employer himself was rife. Wages were generally low and the Factories Acts and regulations were usually honoured 'in the breach'. I held many meetings outside these plants. Once we had succeeded in building up our membership, the only way to get talks going, invariably, was to threaten strike action. I had no authority for this but the workers were impatient and their enthusiasm and interest was often short-lived. Once a decision to strike was made I would invoke the aid of the Ministry of Labour concilation officer, telling him, in the language of the law, that 'a dispute was apprehended'. This usually broke the ice and a conference would be arranged. I believe that the Ministry of Labour records for that time state that I was making 'the TGWU more prone than they had been to threaten strike action and be aggressive'. I plead guilty!

The TGWU was not exactly geared to my endeavours. Demands for more and more recruiting leaflets and membership forms from the area office in Birmingham were reluctantly met, and I was asked: 'Are they being used in the toilet?' The membership had trebled within weeks and was continuing to soar, but the duplication of leaflets or announcements of meetings had to be arranged through the area office eighteen miles away. The area secretary was a good man, but he erred on the restrictive side when it came to even small items of expenditure. I agreed with his frequently expressed view that the expenditure of workers' money was a 'sacred trust', but there were limits. My insistence on having a duplicating machine at the Coventry office was met by his purchase of a very old Gestetner machine for ten shillings (50p). It was difficult to operate and turned out work that was hardly readable but we made do until I persuaded the local branches to raise funds to buy a new machine.

In September war was declared. This had no immediate effect on the industrial scene in Coventry. There were still thousands of unemployed and conditions left a lot to be desired. People could be dismissed without notice and for no good reason. In many factories, if pieceworkers failed to earn their time-rate one week, they would receive a make-up payment but the 'debt' would be carried forward and deducted from piecework earnings in a subsequent week. Belt-driven machinery in badly lit, inadequately heated shops was operated with little regard to the health and safety of the operatives.

In many of the small firms there were no shop stewards and members' grievances had to be dealt with directly. I became very much the full-time convenor, co-ordinator or just steward, dashing from one workplace to the next, to negotiate piecework prices, check a machine tool, draw attention to a breach of the Factories Acts (the factories' inspectors weren't easily available, there were too few of them and if they paid a visit the employer seemed always to know about it in advance) or simply claim the correct overtime pay. Where progress was made I tried always to persuade interested members to become shop stewards, and management to accept them as spokesmen for their mates. In the larger firms we already had stewards and I encouraged the election of more of them. With this growing interest came demands for information, advice and guidance and I was hard put to respond quickly enough.

Drawing upon my Liverpool experiences I knew that I had to develop a collective approach to problems. I began to organize classes, in addition to special meetings of shop stewards. The union office became a workshop for the exchange of information and training of shop stewards. Teach-ins, mock negotiating sessions and educational courses were developed. By involving an increasing number of members I found that not only did we gain strength but we got an informed approach to practical industrial problems too. This groundwork incidentally played an important part in our success in maintaining production and keeping the union working effectively during the terrible air-raids on Coventry.

Our home became an extension of the office. Members found their way there after working hours and shop stewards were frequent callers, many becoming personal friends. In that atmosphere even our baby son demonstrated a trade union approach. A friend held out a half-crown and a penny to see which he would take. Young Jack grabbed both! Air-raids were occurring frequently and we often played cards with our friends at home rather than visiting the cinema or the pub. The card-playing went on long after the air-raid alarms had sounded – we somehow didn't take seriously the idea of going into the cellar although the war had started with a vengeance in Coventry ... 234 people were killed in the raids on the town prior to the big blitz of November 1940.·

The best organized labour in the area was in the Armstrong-Whitworth Aircraft factory at Baginton. The Amalgamated Engineering Union had a strong membership there, the TGWU had over four hundred members, and the 'craft' unions – vehicle builders, sheet metal workers and coppersmiths – were also well represented. The shop stewards of the various unions worked through a joint Shop Stewards' Committee which tended to take a strongly independent stance. I built up a good personal relationship with most of the stewards, once they realized that my view of trade unionism was close to theirs.

Full-time officials were anathema to the stewards of the AEU and the craft unions at this factory because of the officials' insistence on keeping tightly to the 'procedure agreement', although the inbuilt delays in this system often made protests meaningless. I overcame this prejudice early on with Bill Tattersall, the AEU convenor and chairman of the Shop Stewards' Committee. He and other stewards had been under attack at a works conference called by the Employers Association to protest at a strike which had taken place. The leader of the employers, a local solicitor called John Varley, gave a long harangue against what he called 'unofficial and irresponsible action'. I intervened to say that we had not come to listen to a lecture and that it would be in the best interest of everyone if we dealt with the issue at stake, the grievances which had led to the strike.

Despite his 'hail fellow well met' manner, Varley could never quite understand the wit of the workshop. He complained that when men had gone on strike they had marched down the drive singing 'Roll Out the Barrel'. What else could he expect? And he was most annoyed to find that a rumour had circulated throughout the works that the works manager was a German spy and had been arrested! Shortly after my arrival he told me 'in confidence' that a CID officer had warned him that I was a dangerous left-wing agitator from Liverpool. I thanked him for telling me but said I wasn't sure whether it was a complaint or a compliment. We clashed many times but a degree of mutual respect existed between us.

Differences began to grow with the officials of the Amalgamated

Engineering Union, who claimed superiority in the industry. Their dominance in the tool-rooms led them frequently to conclude agreements with employers without reference to other unions. It was an attitude I found insufferable. My response was to insist on the equal right of TGWU stewards to elect a chief shop steward or convenor. But that in itself was not enough to develop the spirit of solidarity that I felt was so necessary.

The Confederation of Shipbuilding and Engineering Unions was in existence and operated as a joint movement of all the unions in the industry, with the exception of the AEU and the Foundryworkers. I had had some experience of its district committee system in Liverpool, and although the emphasis there had been on shipbuilding and repair I felt it could be adapted effectively to the motor-car and aircraft industries. Sounding out the local officials of the vehicle builders, the sheet metal workers and the brassworkers, I found favour for the idea and a meeting was convened and a district committee was formed. I was elected District Secretary. This happened on 19 March 1940 . . . it was to prove a momentous year.

In May 1940 Ernest Bevin joined the Government at the suggestion of Clem Attlee and became Minister of Labour. Although it was still the 'phoney war', in the factories things began to hum. The Essential Work Order and the Conditions of Employment and National Arbitration Order (Order 1305) were introduced under Bevin's influence and in consultation with the national trade union leaders. They had a profound effect upon the lives of people in industry. I made it my business to master the various clauses in the Orders and pass on the information in understandable terms to the shop stewards and branches, so that they would be aware of the advantages and disadvantages of the new legislation. Restrictions on the right to strike were offset by increased use of conciliation officers, and Ministry of Labour prosecution of employers who were not applying the 'recognized terms and conditions'. For the first time trade unionism began to operate in the smaller engineering firms.

I recall one foundry castings company where the management literally refused to talk to me. I brought in the conciliations officer, but again they stubbornly refused to acknowledge my presence. I had no alternative but to submit the case to arbitration and won. The terms of the decision were legally enforceable and the firm had to pay up. In most cases, however, firms conceded the 'recognized terms and conditions' without reference to arbitration, the mere existence of the

Order did the trick. Of course there were protest stoppages and they had an effect, but because of the new law and the demands of the war they were usually short – a few hours, half a day or a day.

In some respects the industrial world was turned upside down by the Essential Work Order, for it curtailed the power of the foreman to hire and fire and with it a lot of malpractice and corruption. If in a firm engaged on essential war work a worker was suspended or dismissed, the action could be challenged, and if it could be established that the management had acted unfairly, the firm could be made to pay for the period of suspension or reinstate the man in the case of dismissal. I took many such cases to the Appeal Board under the Order, and with careful presentation and preparation my success rate was high. Managements were forced to think twice before penalizing workers. Firms employed personnel officers and labour officers as a necessary precaution. The enormous growth in these professional areas is undoubtedly due to the wartime orders and the use of them by people like myself.

Yet another revolutionary aspect of Bevin's Orders – and there is no doubt that they owed a great deal to Bevin – was the introduction of the guaranteed week in all firms covered by the Order. This meant that time-workers would be assured of their week's wage each week while pieceworkers had a similar guarantee. 'Debts' were not carried forward any more. Prior to the Order being introduced most manual workers were in effect casually employed. If the employer had no work for them he could send them home without notice and without pay. Bevin was acutely aware of this, and he had an eye to the future in many of the things he did. If workers were to be tied to their jobs under the Essential Work Order they were also entitled to a guaranteed wage every week, something which he felt should be carried over into the post-war period.

Addressing the 1943 Trades Union Congress Bevin asked: 'Does anybody want to go back to the hourly payment? This standing on and standing off, this going to the factory door in the morning and "Nothing doing, Tom, go home!" Surely nobody ever wants to go back to that again.' That message was from the heart, it was one I shared.

As the process of changing from peace to war production proceeded, the new powers for the direction of labour caused problems. Many workers, uprooted from their family and friends, didn't like the changes. I had a multitude of personal problems to try to iron out. The urgent need was for toolmakers, designers, experimental workers:

Signing Standard Motors' wages agreement, November 1948.

At the 1964 Labour Party Conference with Frank Cousins.

Canvassing for Labour in a street near my birthplace in Garston, Liverpool.

Talking to striking dockers outside Transport House, August 1972.

skill, skill skill – but in Coventry some of the most skilled men earned good wages on production piecework. Others had left the trade because of the bad conditions and were reluctant to go back when the call was made.

In those early days I was sending urgent messages to officials of the Ministry of Labour and to Ernest Bevin himself, explaining that if skilled men were to be attracted to toolmaking and similar work they would have to be certain of earnings equal to those of pieceworkers. A response came in June 1940 when the Engineering Employers concluded a national agreement providing the assurance I wanted. Bevin had undoubtedly pushed things along. The national agreement was used in Coventry some months later, to establish a district agreement under which toolmakers received the *district* average earnings of production workers. I was kept busy with the complaints of skilled men, not members of the AEU, who had been moved off production but were not favoured by similar terms to those of the tool-room agreement. By acting jointly, through the Confederation, we were able to make the employers see sense in some cases. With the exception of the sheet-metal workers who had great strength on their own and were the most powerfully organized trade in the district, the other unions and their members tended to seek the umbrella of protection from the Confederation and myself. I was the District Secretary, but I regarded every trade unionist as my brother or sister unless they acted in an unco-operative way.

'I'm fed up, tired out, buggered up!' That is how one of our old members greeted me at one of the branch meetings. Men were working twelve hours a day, seven days a week, going home in the black-out, and often the wife was working too. Life was grim and made worse by nightly air-raids. The Germans made fifty-seven air-raids on Coventry before the major blitz in November 1940, and even before that terrible event, Coventry – a major munitions centre – seemed undefended, an open target to the enemy. Bombs, land-mines dropped by parachute and incendiaries rained down on the city.

Most of the top managers and employers lived well outside Coventry and, as conditions of life worsened, criticism of the 'gaffers' increased, much of it justified, with rumours that first-class cars were being stored at their big houses so that they could make a killing at the end of the war. Servants from butlers to chauffeurs, it was said, were being given 'check numbers' and placed on the books of the company. Food, wines and spirits and other material comforts were being bought on the firm as essential supplies and conveyed to the mansions of the bosses. But none of this slowed up the war effort; we didn't need politicians or servicemen to lecture us. The workers in Coventry just hated Hitler and the Nazis!

I was for the war from the very beginning. For me it was a continuation of the war in Spain, the war against Fascism. Support for the war in Coventry was virtually universal, and any doubts were removed by the bombing. The decision of the Communist Party to oppose the war in its early stages had no impact in Coventry.

Employers varied in their reactions to the new situation. I remember one day being sent for by Bill Lyons (later Sir William Lyons) of Jaguar. The firm was then known as SS Cars. He asked why I was pressing for higher piecework rates on a particular job. It was obvious he had checked every detail with his rate-fixer and I had a devil of a job convincing him that our members had a case. It was (and is) most unusual for a managing director to get involved in detail like that. Whenever I was involved in negotiations with members of his management afterwards I was always conscious that they were reflecting the gaffer's point of view.

Lyons had difficulty in accepting the idea of unions in his early days at Coventry and refused to deal with the sheet-metal workers' unions. On more than one occasion he dismissed active union men of other unions and once paid a TGWU steward full wages for a long time providing he stayed at home. Despite my entreaties Lyons would not allow him in the works, although labour was needed for the war effort.

Early in the war some managers resented the growing independence of working people. One senior shop steward (an AEU man) was actually fired for calling the manager by his surname. The latter had sent for the steward and referred to him throughout the interview as 'Wilcocks'; when the steward responded, 'Look here, Salter,' he was dismissed. It took a bitter strike to secure the man's reinstatement. I was able to organize support for the action by other unions, which helped to speed up the settlement.

It is a sad reflection on the state of our industrial relations that it took a war to provide the basis for much needed changes.

Chapter Ten

What though the field be lost?
All is not lost; th' unconquerable will,
And study of revenge, immortal hate,
And courage never to submit or yield;
And what is else not to be overcome?

JOHN MILTON

Thursday, 14 November 1940. In the afternoon I attended a conference with the management of Humber-Hillman at their Stoke works in Coventry. Officials of other unions and a number of shop stewards were present. The atmosphere was serious, there was somehow a sense of foreboding. We discussed the question of keeping the factory working after the air-raid siren had sounded. An experiment had been in operation by which the men worked up to an 'imminent danger' warning. The results were checked in detail. I argued that caution should be exercised, because a lot of people's lives were at stake. In response to an appeal from management we agreed to meet again at another date to give further consideration to the question. Meanwhile the experiment would continue.

In the early evening I was due to attend a meeting of the Coventry Trades Council Executive. Harold Taylor, the union's chief steward at Armstrong-Whitworth Aircraft, called at my home to take me to the meeting. I didn't have my own car, indeed few trade union officials did at that time. Before we could set off the air-raid sirens sounded. My wife brought Jack from his cot into the living-room. We heard the scream of a bomb close to our house. Windows and doors rattled. We could hear the sound of anti-aircraft guns. Incendiaries fell around the house, on the roof, in the garden and street. We rushed Evelyn and young Jack into the cellar, to join tenants from the other flats.

Harold and I went to see what help we could give in the street. There were fires everywhere, and high explosives were falling all around us. Houses came crashing down. There was a shortage of water, but we put out many fires with buckets of sand. In retrospect it was ironical to

99

discover that the cases of the incendiary bombs that were dropped on us in that horrific raid had been manufactured before the war by a Coventry firm.

At eight o'clock that night Harold Taylor left. We knew that it was no use attempting to go to the Trades Council meeting. He had a wife and a week-old baby at home, which was about a mile away from our flat. His trip home took a long time, he finally arrived at 3 a.m. after many adventures. Bombs fell around his car. Houses collapsed into the road. In a back court fires were raging. He called out for sand. A woman dashed down the court with a bucketful and threw it on the fire – as she was doing so she was killed.

Our eighteen-month-old son and Evelyn were in the cellar and as the bombing got worse I moved them under a stone arch which seemed the strongest part of the area. The baby slept on through the night. I was busy trying to put out a fire in the roof of our flats caused by incendiaries. I had just gone back to the cellar when a bomb struck the back of the house with a terrible crash. We heard the sound of bricks and stone falling and of shattering glass. For eleven hours the zoom of the German planes and the crashing of bombs dominated everything. At 4 a.m. a passing air-raid warden told me that the street in which the union office was situated was ablaze.

Throughout the night we were terribly worried for the safety of Evelyn's sister, who had come down from Liverpool to get work and was staying with us. She had gone out in the early evening to the cinema with her boyfriend. She came back to our flat half an hour or so after the 'all-clear' had sounded, at 6 a.m. They had taken shelter, but Anne was shattered by the effects of the bombing she had seen on her way back. Of our flat only one room was habitable, the rest was a heap of rubble. The whole city was a shambles. Devastation and death were everywhere.

The moon had shone brilliantly throughout the night and our anti-aircraft guns had given up for lack of ammunition early on in the raid. I heard later that the raid had been carried out by five hundred German aircraft and that nearly six hundred people had been killed, with more than a thousand seriously injured. The centre of the city had been almost totally destroyed. Few houses escaped serious damage. The tramway system and much of the railway network were destroyed. Coventry Cathedral was destroyed. The city was left without gas, water and electricity. For weeks all water had to be boiled and water was brought round in water carts.

Early in the morning a friend arrived with his wife and three children. Their house was down and all they possessed was gone. Could we help? We did what we could. The union office was wrecked but I saved whatever I could and rescued a lot of the records. I tried to make contact with City Council officials but part of the council buildings was destroyed and burning and no one was about. People were going around in a daze; some were still looking wearily, hopelessly, for relatives.

Later in the day we managed to assemble a 'Council of Action', in which my old colleague Bill Nelson and I were joined by Joe Blewitt, the Area Secretary from Birmingham. It was too early to assess the effect on the membership. I arranged with my colleagues to contact our branch secretaries and our principal shop stewards. We found that all our branch secretaries were alive, although some had lost their homes. Arrangements were made for an emergency meeting of everyone we could contact with influence among the membership. Meantime Joe Blewitt took Evelyn, our son and Anne, her sister, to the railway station at Birmingham to help them to get to their parents' home at Knutsford. Coventry was no place for distraught women and a baby!

I needed to find digs quickly and my friend Jim Startin, a building-trade worker, came to my aid and offered me a temporary home with his family at Nuneaton. No transport was moving so we walked the nine miles to his house that night. I was just one of thousands who were without a home.

Next day I had to make temporary arrangements for an office at the building-trades' club and then did my best to assess the industrial position. Although most of the larger factories on the outskirts had escaped, twenty-one factories were badly damaged by direct hits or by fire. A large number of members were out of work, in fact the number of unemployed in the city went up to thirteen thousand. Many in work were engaged in clearing debris, placing tarpaulins over damaged areas or co-operating in other recovery measures. Some were transferred to other factories. It was a period of dislocation and difficulty.

Trade union branch life was totally disorganized. With the problems of having to deal with damaged homes, working long hours, getting home in the black-out, branch secretaries found it difficult to settle down to their administrative work. People didn't relish going out again at night and the normal branch meetings had to be abandoned. Meetings were arranged on Sunday mornings and were relatively successful but we were unable to cater for the many members who were called upon to work on Sundays.

The idea of trade union meetings on works premises was strongly resisted by management, so there was hardly any possibility of getting approval for our branches to meet there. Shop stewards were no more than tolerated and strict measures were taken by management to confine them to their own sections. The courage of a number of our shop stewards in those difficult circumstances was outstanding, and I depended upon them as the most effective means of communication with the members. The efforts we had made earlier to train shop stewards paid off during this period. Management continued to give no quarter, trade unions were still regarded as an 'alien force'. What we were doing was challenging the divine right of management, and they didn't like it. Shop stewards used their training to challenge unreasonable decisions, to question bad conditions. The 'divine right of management' we countered with the 'divine right of discontent'.

Shortly after the blitz the General Manager of Singer Motors, a pompous, rotund gentleman sporting a gold watch-chain across his expansive stomach, invited me to see the effect of the bombing on his factory. We had met at a conference and his invitation was given on the spur of the moment, for we had not a lot in common. The place was in a mess. Whole areas of the factory were covered by tarpaulins to keep out the rain and the wind and the only heating in the shops was provided by coke-burning open braziers. Parts of the place looked like Dante's inferno. Yet he still kept up the pretence of a director's dining-room, a small room set apart in broken-down surroundings but with a white tablecloth on the table. We had sausage, chips and beans and I listened to his tale of woe. A day or so afterwards I presented the case for three of his employees at the Local Appeal Board and established that they had been wrongfully suspended for three days. A little later our shop steward came to see me. 'Mr Hunt [the General Manager] played hell with me,' he said. 'He told me he gave you a free lunch and then you went and opposed the company and won the case for these three men. He won't have anything to do with you again.'

Coventry was virtually in a state of emergency. Bread, water and other essential supplies were being brought in daily. People were bewildered, but most carried on despite the privations and worries. Living conditions for many were as bad as those in the factories. Whole streets were a shambles, especially those houses which had been jerry-built for quick sale to workers. They were shoddily constructed and a damn disgrace. I heard it said that 'Jerry put them up – and Jerry put them down.'

Dignitaries came to the city in swarms. One of the first was King George VI. Just before the big blitz Ernie Bevin toured the factories. He singled me out for a talk and I told him of our endeavours to keep the unions alive and the need for meeting facilities and better support for the shop stewards.

Bevin insisted on meeting the workers and addressed mass meetings in the bombed Humber and Daimler factories. His main themes were 'We are all in this together' and 'The trade unions are fighting for the country and every factory is part of the battlefront.' He appealed to management to treat the unions as equal partners and urged the workers to stick it through to the end. This was the first occasion I had met Sir Bernard Docker, top man in the Daimler and BSA companies, and I formed the impression that Bevin's appeal had not had much effect on him. At one stage in his visit Captain Black (later Sir John Black) of Standard Motors offered to drive Bevin in one of the small cars being used by all the top people at the time. Huffing and puffing, Bevin struggled into the car, remarking: 'You need a can opener to get into one of these sardine tins.'

At a meeting of the Confederation District Committee held some days before the blitz, on 10 November, I had reported on the subject of air-raid precautions. It was agreed to present the following proposals to the Minister of Labour at a conference to be held with him the following day:

(1) Improved shelters of the deep or 'Haldane' type should be provided in or adjacent to works;

(2) Listening posts should be established and linked with the factories;

(3) Control of warnings should be localized;

(4) There should be spotters at all factories, and they should not be interfered with by management in giving warnings.

It was an indication of industry's lack of preparedness that we were having to make proposals of that kind when there had been many raids on Coventry and only three days before the 'coventration' of the city.

It says much for the loyalty and stubbornness of the workers that most stuck at their jobs under the very adverse conditions. We played our part in rallying the people, and even those who had left the city after the big raid began to return. Productivity was accepted as a major responsibility of the trade unions. I saw the workforce as the soldiers at the rear, a major factor in winning the war against Fascism, and I spent all the time and effort I humanly could in keeping up their spirits.

At the outset of the war I had been told by Bevin, as General Secretary, that I must stick on the job in Coventry and I was placed on the schedule of reserved occupations. My strong objections were over-ridden by Bevin, who stressed the vital importance of Coventry in the war effort. I determined to work as hard as anyone at the front. For me this meant securing the unity of the workers and ensuring that their working and living conditions were as good as we could get them. If our members were called upon to work seven days a week and twelve hours a day or more, I would equal them in my response to the call of duty, and indeed would try to do more.

When Standard Motors changed over to aircraft production they looked for experienced men. The most likely source was Armstrong Whitworth Aircraft, which was in a position to allow the transference of about a hundred men. I was much involved in the discussions and was able to play a part in the transfer of some of our most active stewards and members. By ensuring a big TGWU influence in the move, two objectives were achieved. One was to develop the union's membership in what had been traditionally a non-union factory; the other to take the collective system of piecework into a new sphere, helping to achieve high levels of both output and earnings. Considerable success was achieved in both directions.

Not all employers appreciated our efforts. I ran up against trouble when I started to organize the Coventry Gauge and Tool Company. This was a high-precision engineering company, but despite the claims of my friends in the Amalgamated Engineering Union many of the skilled men were not in a trade union. The owner of the company was a peppery engineer, Harry Harley, who, in the pre-war period, had brought down many young men from the textile and other industries in the North and had trained them to a high degree of engineering skill.

Up to then he had successfully resisted the incursion of trade unionism. I had, however, established membership in the Standards Room of the company among men who were highly skilled and important to the company in ensuring high quality control. I wrote to the owner, seeking a meeting. I was received curtly and asked what my business was. I put a case for increased rates of pay for our members in the Standards Room, and drew attention to the quality of the work being done. Harley accused me of being in possession of official secrets and said that he would have me arrested. On the desk in front of him he had two revolvers which he proceeded to pick up and wave at me, rather excitedly.

I was amused but somewhat surprised at his attitude. I insisted that I had every right to have the information in order to put the case and seek to negotiate. He said it was bloody nonsense and he would send for the police. Didn't I know it was a protected establishment? After much argument we agreed that the National Service Officer should be sent for. Harley did not take kindly to the fact that the manager of the local Labour Exchange was also the National Service Officer, but the dignitary was duly sent for and arrived in haste, only to confirm that my approach was perfectly legitimate.

Women rallied to the union and grew in confidence, electing their own shop stewards (and in some cases chief shop stewards) in many factories. In the early years of the war the TGWU in Coventry faced no opposition from other unions in the recruitment of female workers; other unions regarded their entry into the factories as temporary and AEU officials would be heard to say, 'They'll be chucked out at the end of the war!' That attitude was foolish in the extreme, and experience proved that as women organized they strengthened unionization amongst the men.

Repeatedly I found that old-fashioned ideas and sectionalism stood in the way of workers' advance. The traditional attitudes of the many separate trade unions, the jealousies, the resistance to encroachment on old preserves, often led to bitter differences. Dilution policies fed this flame because of the insistence that workers transferred to skilled jobs should be labelled as strictly temporary. It was clear that the indiscriminate operation of dilution registration schemes, in a district where most men receiving the skilled rate had not served an apprenticeship, would cause division instead of creating the much needed unity.

I plead guilty to leading a campaign against registration. The campaign was successful because it made sense and for the most part we had the goodwill of AEU shop stewards and those of other unions. I felt I had been stabbed in the back, however, when I received a circular from Arthur Deakin, the acting General Secretary of the TGWU, requiring the operation of an agreement entered into by the union with the AEU; it required members of the TGWU who were upgraded and registered under the dilution scheme to take out a temporary card membership in the AEU, while retaining their membership of the TGWU. The same conditions were to apply also to members of the TGWU 'who have served their time in the Engineering Industry and who are released from their present occupations in order to return to the Engineering Industry for war purposes. . . .'

My first and sustained reaction to reading the agreement was 'What sort of trade unionism is this? Are our members to be treated like numbers on a sheet?' I saw no good reason for our members to pay contributions to another union. My anger was shared by all our active members in Coventry. There had been no consultation with the membership or with officials like me. I was astounded, but although resolutions of protest went up to headquarters by the dozen, Deakin remained impervious. I suppose it was that attitude which later, when I became General Secretary, led me to do all in my power to ensure that no agreement was concluded without the knowledge and approval of the membership.

Meanwhile I risked dismissal from my post by refusing to allow the agreement to operate throughout my district. Stokes and Taylor, the District officials of the AEU, knew I had the ability to arouse most of their members against them on that issue. Deakin and other senior officials did not seriously challenge me, for by this time our membership was moving up to the twenty thousand mark. But doubtless a black mark was recorded against me.

The common dangers and difficulties being faced were the best arguments for the collective unity which I preached. Skilled and semi-skilled workers, who had been unorganized, rallied round in the membership drive. Our campaign to organize the unorganized stimulated other unions too, and as we grew they grew. That was particularly the case with the AEU.

Social life wasn't easy, but Bevin's insistence on the provision of works canteens helped. They weren't only used for eating, but also for sing-songs and concerts. Where I could, I slipped in a few minutes of briefing about union affairs and recruitment appeals. The pubs and clubs were still open, even if they were confined to selling weak beer. The most daring would use them for an hour or two at night or at the weekend. Closing times varied, according to stock and the whims of the publican. I recall on one occasion a number of young men had come over from Birmingham and the landlady decided they had had enough of the precious liquid. She called 'time' and urged her regulars, who were all *Scotsmen*, to 'get these out-of-towners out!'

In 1941 difficulties were being experienced by the shop stewards in the bigger factories in getting together outside working hours. The Confederation Committee decided to press the Employers Association for facilities to hold meetings during the hours of work. The response was favourable. It was a step forward in the recognition of shop stewards. With it came an increasing acceptance by management that shop stewards could be elected on the shop floor. Instead of the hole-and-corner methods which people had had to adopt to elect their stewards in the past, the process was now out in the open. The new-found freedom created a deeper sense of unity.

It was difficult to segregate the members of one union from another when they worked together, and increasingly joint elections took place. This meant, in practice, that members of two or three unions, working on the same assembly line or machine section, would get together and elect the person they felt would be their best advocate. I strongly favoured this approach, which had the effect of breaking down barriers and reducing the hostility which some officials of other unions felt towards me and the TGWU. Officials of the AEU especially resented my activities and increasing influence in the ranks of the shop stewards.

The early 1940s in the Coventry area saw a remarkable transformation in attitudes on the shop floor. At the start managements had done everything possible to prevent people from recruiting for the unions. They had been suspicious of any moves to organize labour and made it almost impossible for union activists to operate on the shop floor. I was busy telling managements and Government officials to let up. 'If we are supposed to be engaged in a united war effort, withdraw your restrictions on shop stewards,' I said many times over. Step by step we inched forward until it became commonplace for shop stewards to be elected at shop-floor meetings, to hold committee meetings during working hours, and to report back, after meetings with management or the works committee, to members on the shop floor. This encroachment on managerial control over the workplace had considerable repercussions over the years. In my experience it prevented many disputes and strengthened trade union participation in the war effort.

Chapter Eleven

Who is the worst paid man today?
With haggard looks and hair turned grey,
Who's blamed when things do not go right,
Who gets no rest by day or night?
Though never having been to college
He must possess the widest knowledge,
On rates of pay and hours of labour
And how to keep peace with one's neighbour,
Of income tax and how to pay it,
What's best to say and when to say it,
The how and why and which and when
Of all the problems known to men.
If with the foremen he's agreed,
He's sold the men, or been weak-kneed.
When for the men he tries to cater,
He's called a blinking agitator.
Who is this chap? What, don't you know him?
Or how much you really owe him?
This chap, whose torment is assured,
Is no one else but your SHOP STEWARD.

(A workshop 'ditty' quoted a lot in trade union
circles during the Second World War, author
unknown.)

During 1941 criticism of management for inefficiency and mismanage-
ment was widespread and at shop stewards' meetings questions were
continually being raised about the management of this or that factory
which refused to discuss production matters with the stewards. Hitler's
attack on the Soviet Union in June 1941 gave an urgent turn to demands
for a greater war effort, and in Coventry memories of the blitz gave us
our own particular reasons for wanting to intensify the fight against
Fascism. It was against that background that there were increasing
demands for the setting up of what we then called 'Production Inquiry
Committees'. The Coventry employers strongly opposed the proposal.
The District Committee of the Confederation nevertheless decided at
its meeting in November 1941 that officers should take all steps in their

power to secure the setting-up of such committees. Jointly with the AEU we called a conference of all shop stewards in the district, under my chairmanship, to press the case. Leading employers were invited to attend as observers.

The meeting was held in the concert hall of a workmen's club and lasted over three hours. Speaker after speaker came up from the body of the hall to the platform with their complaints. At one factory, for instance, the design of a new and secret piece of equipment essential for the war effort was being held up for lack of draughtsmen and drawing-office equipment, while a fully staffed and equipped drawing office in the same works was engaged on designing and drawing post-war motor buses. In another, four thousand men were engaged on day-shift, while only 150 worked at night, when the plant lay practically idle. Fifty aeroplane engines had been waiting for carburettors at an aircraft factory. 'No one told us why and no one intends to,' said the shop steward bitterly.

Concluding the conference, I urged that men should not be thrown out of factories until other *suitable* employment had been found for them. Workers felt a sense of frustration which it was essential to remove. The proposal to set up inquiry committees of shop stewards had no ulterior motive, but was made with the object of pressing forward with maximum production. The conference unanimously backed the demand to set up such committees without delay and insisted that workers' representatives be elected from trade union members only.

Our campaign coincided with national efforts led by Jack Tanner, the President of the AEU, and in March 1942 the Engineering Employers Federation concluded an agreement with the unions for the setting up of 'Joint Production Consultative and Advisory Committees'. The title reveals the cautious nature of the approach and there is no doubt that most employers were sceptical about the new committees. The agreement specified that all adult workers could vote for Joint Production Committee representatives but only 'organized workers', i.e. trade union members, could stand for election.

Among the 'reluctant' employers was the Dunlop Rim and Wheel Company (the engineering division of the big Dunlop organization). They preferred to retain their Works Council, on which the majority of employee representatives were non-unionists. Trade union membership was weak but with the few shop stewards who existed I helped to plan a campaign. Conferences were held with top managers and the Employers Association and finally we gained approval for a ballot to be held on the issue. The result was 1300 for the production committee against 171 in favour of retaining the Works Council. It was a rebuff for management but a feather in our cap; we went on to unionize the factory.

Co-operation between the shop stewards and the new production committees kept management on its toes on production and supply matters, and the more competent and committed managers also felt the benefit of the committees. At the Armstrong Whitworth Aircraft Baginton works, for instance, all parties combined to meet high officials of the Ministry of Aircraft Production and the Ministry of Labour in order to discuss material shortages and labour displacement. The Joint Production Committee at this works consistently tried to keep the employees informed of their activities. In other plants lack of communications and general inactivity led to failure of the scheme. On the whole I learnt much from the experiment, with all its deficiencies. It was the first time that the principle of consultative rights on matters relating to planning and organizing production had been conceded to workers. On the whole the trade union response to this new opportunity was constructive and effective. Ideas emerging from the shop floor started to be taken into account in quite a new way, even if the successes were not spectacular. The system laid the basis for a new era of trade unionism and to my mind provided strong reasons for the expansion of industrial democracy.

I have often been asked 'Why were there so few strikes during the war in such a concentrated industrial area as Coventry?', a question usually followed by: 'Was it because the Communist Party supported the war?' My answer is that the shop stewards, with the rest of the trade union movement, were the key to success on the production front. There were Communist shop stewards and Labour Party shop stewards and non-party shop stewards (the latter being in the majority) and 99 per cent of them did a remarkable job. The irritations, the numerous queries, the piecework prices to be negotiated, the works rotas to be arranged: all these things, and countless more, called for tact, judgement and understanding. I know, because I experienced it all. I was with the shop stewards in victories and defeats, I attended their meetings, I was often their spokesman in conferences. For large numbers of members in the smaller plants I was, indeed, their shop steward!

Most of the strikes in Coventry were due to piecework issues: 30 per cent in 1941, 40 per cent in 1942; 67 per cent in 1943; 71 per cent in 1944. Victimization and disciplinary issues accounted for 26 per cent of strikes in 1941 and 19 per cent in 1944. In the main these strikes were short, sharp affairs, necessary explosions in a tense situation.

Sometimes recourse was had to the traditional 'procedure for the avoidance of disputes'. The AEU officials seemed particularly attached to this, but I was a reluctant participant. I shared the view of the old lad who said that over the entrance to the Royal Hotel at York, where monthly conferences were held between the leaders of the Employers Federation and the unions as the last stage in the negotiating procedure, there should have been a banner erected to read: 'Abandon hope all ye who enter here.' The 'procedure' in the engineering industry was long-winded, with inbuilt delays calculated to cause frustration. It could last two or three months before it was exhausted. The culmination of the 'procedure' was the monthly Central Conference.

Local representatives, whether of the workers or the employers, were not allowed to take part in the Central Conference, so that the people who knew the facts and the local circumstances had no place in the proceedings. They might be appealed to from time to time to check a point, but they were isolated from the debate. Not surprisingly, the most common outcome was 'a failure to agree' or to 'refer the issue back to the locality for settlement'.

When I embarked on the journey to York some shop steward or member would often say: 'Remember, Jack, *illigitimus nils carburundum*,' which was workshop Latin for 'Don't let the bastards grind you down'! I knew what they meant all right. In subsequent years I repeated that piece of advice to many a shop steward and new trade union official.

Trade unionism grew rapidly in Coventry but without detriment to the production effort. Unity was the key to progress. Here and there owners of factories made a last stand. The Conservative Member of Parliament for Coventry, Captain Strickland, was a director of Cornercrofts, a firm making aero parts. I do not know whether it was his influence which led the firm to seek an all-out battle, but on Christmas Eve 1941, when a number of employees asked if they could leave one hour earlier than finishing time in order to go shopping, permission was refused. The workers, thinking this unreasonable, took time off all the same. Over the Christmas holidays some 172 workers received dismissal notices for 'deficient timekeeping'. The remainder of the shop-floor employees went on strike, while those dismissed, on my advice, appealed *en masse* to the National Service Officer. A quick reference to the Local Appeal Board was arranged, just a few test cases being taken. Although most of the discharged men were members of the sheet-metal workers' unions, a few members of other unions, including the TGWU, were involved and I was asked to present the case as District Secretary of the Confederation. Our appeal succeeded and the men were directed back to work, but when they returned the 108 sheet-metal workers found there was nothing to do and were told by the firm that they were redundant. Without waiting to hear the result of the appeal the company had removed jigs and tools from the sheet-metal department to another area.

I ascertained, through the Ministry of Aircraft Production, that the removal of the tools had not been on the instructions or with the approval of the Ministry. I protested strongly that each day since Christmas Even over a thousand skilled man-hours had been lost to the nation's war effort due to the action of the management. My protest was reinforced by a delegation of shop stewards, which went off to London to contact MPs. As a result of the protests the men were reinstated.

In this instance and in many others I had worked closely with the skilled unions of sheet-metal workers, vehicle builders, coppersmiths, pattern-makers and others. I learned a great deal from their methods and traditions and formed a close friendship with them. I was proud to share their confidence and to be treated as 'one of them' and in return was always ready to give them such service and help as I could. Often this meant acting as their spokesman in conference with management.

Always I was encouraging greater involvement of members in the work of the union. Democracy in that sense was not strong in the TGWU. Attendance at branch meetings was low and most members knew little about national leaders and the policies they pursued. I felt I could improve things by urging shop stewards to keep members informed and draw them into the decision-making process. When new union branches were opened I tried to ensure that they were based on the plant or a section of it. As shop stewards grew more experienced so confidence developed and workers emerged from subservience. I urged audacity on them providing always it was combined with a sense of responsibility. My advice to shop stewards was straightforward: 'When you reach an agreement, make sure that you keep your word, but only give that word when you have got the approval of your members.'

Engels in his *Condition of the Working Class in 1848* wrote: 'The history of unions is a series of defeats of the working men, interrupted by a few isolated victories.' Well, in Coventry during the war years the unions had a long series of victories. This progress was linked with the expansion of trade-union membership among the semi-skilled and skilled workers in particular.

Women and girls figured prominently in this expansion. They joined in large numbers and showed their mettle quickly. Employers would occasionally play on the inexperience of women representatives. I remember one occasion when, on behalf of the TGWU, I had argued at a local conference for a uniform rate for female inspectors to apply throughout the district. The employers' spokesman (John Varley, the local solicitor whom I have mentioned earlier) at one stage in the proceedings remarked across the table to one of the women present: 'But, my dear, you wouldn't agree that all the other inspectors on your section were as good and as experienced as you, would you?' Before I could intervene she proudly replied: 'A lot of them are *not* as skilled as I am.' That defeated my case, at least on that day.

From the employers' side we met with strong resistance to claims that the man's rate should be paid to women. In this attitude they were helped by the somewhat ambiguous terms of the national agreement, which laid down, in effect, that where the work was 'commonly performed' by women in the engineering industry before the war the man's rate would not apply. Employers seemed often to be able to find some out-of-the-way district where the work being discussed had been done by women, and such evidence was used to defeat the claim.

I have to admit that there was latent and sometimes very open opposition from working men to women receiving higher rates. At one stage during the war an increase in basic rates for women was negotiated nationally. That was fine until the women also claimed a higher proportion of the 'gang' earnings (this was at Standard Motors, where the piecework earnings of the gang were divided between the workers according to the basic rate of each workers). The men in the gangs said that the new women's rate should have no effect on piecework earnings and the shop stewards supported them. Generally progressive though they might be, the stewards took the line of least resistance when confronted by the avarice of the men.

Evelyn, my wife, who was working in the factory at the time as a part-time worker, was asked to put the women's case to the convenor, Len Brindley. This she did and was told to 'piss off'. I wouldn't have known of this if Len hadn't had second thoughts; he came to see me at the union office and apologized for the expression he had used to my wife. This gave me the opportunity to persuade Len to stand up to the men on the issue and I promised that I would help. My promise meant my addressing many meetings on the shop floor to convince the men to agree to the women's increase, a much more difficult job than the normal round of negotiations. Trade union principle is not always acceptable when it runs contrary to personal greed.

In 1941 the Trades Union Congress and the Ministry of Labour provided permits for certain trade union officers to have access to the management of all firms engaged on Government work. I was one of the officials who received such a permit. I used it to advantage, visiting the smaller factories which were not organized or where we had just a few members. In some cases, instead of calling on the management, I would go and talk to the workers on the benches. Often I would get thrown out in consequence, but at least it enabled me to make contact, do a bit of organizing, and see what was being done in the smaller firms that had turned over to war work.

It certainly helped me in trying to organize the Imperial Foundry at Leamington. This was a Ford subsidiary, and Ford notoriously did not like unions. It was a dirty and chaotic undertaking, and conditions were bad, but I did manage to recruit a few people to assist in the organization. That didn't prevent me being physically thrown out of the foundry by the works police on two occasions.

The foundry was on my mind when a nephew of Stafford Cripps turned up at my office and told me he was going into the Commandos. He had just left university and wanted my help in finding him a job to toughen him up. I explained the sort of work he would have to do at the Imperial Foundry and he agreed to do it if I could get him in. In turn I sought his aid in persuading fellow workers to join the union. Ford would not have accepted him with my recommendation, but I enlisted the co-operation of the Labour Exchange at Leamington and in he went. I doubt if his commando training was any harder, if as hard, as the job he did at Ford.

At home the family was plunged into sorrow by the death of my brother-in-law, Maurice Solomon. A flight engineer, he had been killed over Hamburg. It was he who had accompanied Evelyn's sister Anne on the night of the November blitz on Coventry. Later they had married and had a little son, Lee, with whom I have retained a close affinity.

With the opening of a nursery nearby, Evelyn determined to do her bit in war production. She was not required to do so, because our son was still young, but she sat on a committee which heard appeals from women who had been directed to war work. She felt it right to do her bit as much as those whom she had helped direct to munitions production. Our home at that time was reasonably close to the factory so that she could manage part-time work. By combining with a neighbour, Evelyn doing the morning shift and the neighbour working in the afternoon, a full-time job on the Bristol Beaufighter was kept going.

Bevin's support of wartime nurseries greatly helped in that instance, and I am sure in many others. Our son Jack got fond of his nursery and at times did not like coming away. Evelyn's shift started at 7.30 a.m., so I would give Jackie his breakfast and take him to the nursery on my way to work. Evelyn would then collect him on her way home.

Social life tended to be limited to the odd game of cards, a visit to a pub or club, or sometimes visiting friends in their homes. A pleasant exception was the celebration arranged to honour my old friend of Spanish civil war days, Paddy O'Daire, on his attaining a commission in the Army. In response to my urgent pleas, shop stewards scrounged food and a limited quantity of spirits. This wasn't easy, for the only people who seemed to possess whisky at the time were American troops. A friendly landlord found enough beer to last us for a few hours, the entertainment was self-provided, and about 150 friends, mainly shop stewards, had a 'reet good do'.

Evelyn's father, a former Regimental Sergeant-Major, enjoyed the proceedings no end because of its slightly military aspect, and the whisky, which we made sure went his way, helped to raise his spirits. After the party about a dozen of us went back to my office to finish up what was left in the bottles and we seated the old chap at my desk. Almost immediately he picked up an agreement I had recently signed, providing for a payment of 15s per hour for certain classes of men. The amount astonished him and he declared it to be a 'damn disgrace' that men should be paid that sort of money. Rather than argue the matter we all stood up and sang 'God Save the King', which brought father-in-law to attention – and the agreement was forgotten.

Late in 1942 my father, in Liverpool, wrote to say that No. 11 York Street, Garston, where my grandparents had lived when they were alive, had been destroyed in an air-raid. The only person living in it at the time was my Uncle Bill, an old bachelor. Somehow he had managed to survive. He climbed out of the rubble, wearing only the shirt he had been sleeping in. Everybody thought he was a ghost and indeed while he had been lying in the midst of the destruction he had heard the ARP wardens shouting: 'There's no one alive in there!' When he emerged a neighbour took him across to the pub where, to his annoyance, he was given one solitary drop of brandy. He complained for a long time afterwards about the 'stingy landlord' (the grandfather, incidentally, of the subsequently famous Rita Tushingham). My grandfather, father and uncles had all been strong supporters of the pub but not of the landlord's politics; he was a Tory. Bill's entire fortune of seventy pounds was contained in a wallet lying somewhere in the rubble. When told about this, my father went down to the former dwelling and, despite barriers and police warnings, went in and salvaged it. Seventy pounds was a lot to a working man at that time.

Soon afterwards a land-mine landed close to my parents' home. The police and ARP wardens immediately set out to clear the street and take the local people to the local church hall for the night. My mother was in no hurry – when the ARP warden knocked at her door she insisted he come in for a cup of tea and told him not to worry, everything would be all right. He couldn't move her until he had complied with her request!

Many people were sustained by the speeches of Winston Churchill but they were also worried about the conduct of the war. Demands began to intensify for the opening of a second front. Underlying the concern was the question: 'How long is the war going to drag on?' There was also a feeling that 'Russia is being let down'. The District Committee of the Confederation rarely strayed from strictly industrial business but on 12 May 1942, after much discussion, it unanimously resolved 'That this Committee congratulates the Prime Minister on his recent speech and urges upon him the advisability of opening a land offensive against Germany as soon as possible this year.'

In October 1942 the District Committee joined forces with the Coventry Trades Council in organizing a mass meeting in the Opera House to discuss the need for a second front. The meeting, held on a Sunday morning, was packed to overflowing, with Harry Pollitt, the Communist leader, as the main speaker. I spoke for the Confederation and although I got a good reception it was nothing to the enthusiasm which greeted Pollitt. He made an oustandingly brilliant speech and as I listened I thought to myself, 'If only Harry had gone into the Labour Party, what a marvellous impact he would have had on the nation.' I always found Pollitt to be a sincere and able man, a fine trade unionist, and certainly a credit to the Communist Party which he led for so many years.

A number of visitors from the Soviet Union came to Coventry at this time, looking at our industries and speaking at meetings. The most prominent was Madame Nicolaeva, a leader of the Soviet trade unions. With white hair and a black dress, she looked like a typical Russian grandmother. One of the factories she toured was the big Rootes aero-engine plant at Ryton near Coventry. She took a keen intetest in everything she saw. I remember the occasion well because I had sprained my ankle badly and was walking with a stick. When she was taken into lunch, 'Billie' Rootes, later Lord Rootes, was buzzing about with other dignitaries including Lord Dudley, the Regional Commissioner. She asked who Lord Dudley was, and being told of his hereditary position and estates she declared that she would not sit down with such an enemy of the working class. It took a famous Coventry character and socialist, Pearl Hyde, a big, bouncing and friendly woman, to persuade Madame Nicolaeva to sit down. It was explained that shop stewards would be at the meal. Finally she agreed to take her place alongside me, as the representative of the workers, and not with the establishment dignitaries.

Later I was involved in another incident with her. The Ministry of Information had arranged a lunch for her at the local British Restaurant and my friend Alderman George Hodgkinson, the leader of the Coventry Labour Party, had invited me and other trade unionists along. But there were no seats for us. Madame Nicolaeva noticed this and demanded that we should be seated before she would sit down. Mind you, she didn't need to bother, for the British Restaurant was my regular eating place when I had time for a meal. With rations tight the B.R. was a godsend, as were the factory canteens.

In my work at this time I increasingly found myself at odds with W. H. Stokes, Divisional Organizer of the AEU, largely because I was continually challenging the traditional superiority of the AEU. This competitive aspect worked to the advantage of the trade union members generally, for we each tried to excel the other in our advocacy of the workers' claims. Our abilities were put to the test when determined attempts were made to reduce piecework earnings on aircraft production in Coventry. There was no doubt that earnings in Coventry were higher than anywhere else in the country during the war years, and employers and Government departments didn't like it. There was much discussion, but we were able to prove that costs of production were less in Coventry than elsewhere. High productivity accompanied high earnings.

I found that most employers applied a system of individual merit awards to workers on time-work. The foreman or shop superintendent would make the assessment and then the individual would be told 'privately'. They were advised not to tell their workmates, but eventually truth would out and the system created much jealousy and ill feeling. Often the 'blue-eyed boy' was favoured, without regard to skill and ability. I considered the system despicable and campaigned against it, winning support from the majority of the rank and file and negotiating it out of existence.

Straightening out such anomalies, resisting the worst features of bureacracy, trying to ensure unity and goodwill in the factories, guiding and encouraging the shop stewards: there was no lack of demand for my services.

Chapter Twelve

We will speak out, we will be heard,
Though all earth's systems crack,
We will not bate a single word,
Nor take a letter back.

Let liars, let cowards shrink,
Let traitors turn away;
Whatever we have dared to think
That dare we also say.

We speak the truth and what care we
For hissing and for scorn,
While some faint gleamings we can see
Of Freedom's coming morn?

JAMES RUSSELL LOWELL

Our younger son, Michael, was born on 6 June 1944, as the planes were flying over the Midlands down to the south coast in readiness for D-Day. Evelyn had been evacuated from Coventry with other mothers-to-be; first to the splendid country home of Henry Johnson, the managing director of Courtaulds, at Offchurch, near Leamington, and then, for the birth, to the home of Raymond Brookes (later Lord Brookes, chairman of the large engineering company Guest Keen and Nettlefold) at Bidford-on-Avon. Coventry City Council were responsible for these arrangements and expectant mothers could not have had nicer places to stay in. As a negotiator I got to know the owners, in subsequent years, when they had reoccupied their splendid properties. In each case I was invited to re-visit their home but I did not accept.

My old colleague, Bill Nelson, had retired from his union post and I had been joined by an able young man, George Massey, who had worked as an inspector at Humber-Rootes during the war years and had led a strike there. Between us we set about trying to improve the lot of workers in the cement and brick-making industries throughout Warwickshire and to strengthen trade union organization at the big

Courtauld factories and among manual workers in local government. The end of the war seemed in sight and workers became increasingly restive as changes were introduced in the plants. Transfers and redundancies were more strongly challenged. On the part of management, abrasive attitudes became more common.

At the main Humber-Rootes factory the bubble of wartime harmony burst with a vengeance. The workers came out on strike, protesting against the attitude of the works manager, Mr Pryor. A highly qualified engineer, with a good record in the AEU, Pryor had taken over his management post some time previously. His predecessor, Bill Hancock, had got on well with the workpeople and the shop stewards and had made a practice of having an open session with the senior shop stewards for a couple of hours every week. There had been some disagreement with the directors, however, and he had departed to another job at Wolverhampton.

Pryor was a meticulous man. He started changing procedures as soon as he took over. He stopped the weekly meeting with senior stewards. At one conference he said he was not interested in custom and practice at that works. When I queried his interpretation of an agreement he said: 'I never make an incorrect statement.' Then he looked up at the clock on the wall and said: 'If I read the time as being twenty-two and a half minutes past eleven, that will be it!' Needless to say we disagreed, not about the time, but about the issue involved. To our senior steward, Pat Brogan, who had dared to argue with him, his comment was: 'Take it or leave it – if you don't accept my decision you can kiss the north side of my arse!' He was determined that workers should have their rights under national agreements, and no more: an attitude which reflected his background in the Lancashire engineering industry and one that I knew well from my own experience. He padlocked the tea urns, so that workers could not have tea except during the official breaks; he dismissed an old man for leaving work a few minutes early, even though that privilege had been operating for some time.

The factory was soon seething with discontent and all the five thousand workers came out on strike. Strictly this was contrary to the law under Order 1305, but nobody made much of that, the main thing was to find a solution. After a few days with no movement from management, the stewards got jittery. Earlier in the war a strike of a day or two days at most had achieved results, now a change in the attitude of management was apparent, presaging the end of the war. The last thing I wanted to see was a fragmented return to work which would have been damaging to the unity of the trade union organization in the plant. I urged the stewards to organize social events to keep the members together, and we called meetings to instil confidence in the ranks. The result was that the employers agreed that Pryor would not be involved in further negotiations with the workers, at least until a local conference had taken place. At a mass meeting Bill Stokes of the AEU and I assured the strikers that we would pull no punches in the case against Pryor and they returned to work in good heart.

For the local conference the employers' association fielded a team of high-level management men from other factories, as well as a senior director of the firm, Mr Botwood. The number of detailed complaints that we put forward undoubtedly made an impression and it was agreed that Botwood himself would in future attend all major negotiations at the works. Pryor concentrated for some years after that on the technical side and did a very competent job. I got to know him well and his relations with the union and the stewards mellowed considerably. The real face of Humber-Rootes boardroom policy emerged a year later, meanwhile much of my energy was directed towards the coming General Election.

Due to the growth of Coventry's population, the city had been allocated a second parliamentary seat. Dick Crossman, who had been the adopted Labour candidate for the single seat, was selected to fight Coventry East. This was regarded as the safer of the two, and we felt that Labour did not have to worry too much there. Coventry West was the new seat and when applicants were invited for the Labour candidature nominations came in thick and fast. I was Chairman of the Coventry Labour Party and as I lived in the new constituency I suppose I was a natural choice to preside at the selection conference.

The front-runner, with a lot of local support, was Alderman Syd Stringer, a long time socialist of the old school and leader of the Coventry Labour Party. Looking at the assembled delegates I thought: 'Well, the majority are middle-aged ladies, the core of the Party here. They are bound to vote for Syd.' I was to have a shock.

First of the candidates to speak was a civil engineer from Nottingham wearing military uniform. He gave a strong and competent left-wing speech. Syd Stringer followed, with a plodding, pedestrian speech dealing with local questions, but it was easy to follow and he got a good reception. There were other speakers, but none reached the eloquence of Maurice Edelman. Maurice was in the uniform of the army press corps. Young, handsome, he delivered a socialist message which caught the mood of everyone present. It was brilliantly done. The ladies fell for him, as I could see while he was delivering his oration. In the voting he won hands down.

Although I had no shortage of work as a union official I devoted as much time as I could to the election. Attlee came down on a whistle-stop tour and I spoke alongside him and the candidates. In Coventry West funds were low and I raised what money I could from union branches. Almost single-handed I organized the publicity for Edelman and amongst the multifarious jobs I did was painting a number of huge signs reading: 'Vote Edelman – Vote Labour'. I drew on my recollection of my work as a sign painter, and though I say it myself, they were very effective. I spoke at meetings and helped to organize the canvass. Evelyn helped too in every possible way and our home was the committee room. Even my father-in-law the ex-RSM, who had hitherto been a Tory, put up a Labour bill in the window of his house. On election day the shop stewards in many factories organized marches of workers to the polling booths. I marched at the head of a big procession from Standard Motors. The atmosphere was enthusiastic, electric and determined.

The election of the Labour Government had little effect on management. Not long after the election Humber-Rootes had a major strike. The firm announced that all new piecework jobs (they were changing back to motor-car production) would be based on the national agreement's figure of $27\frac{1}{2}$ per cent above basic rates. This entailed a huge drop in earnings, piecework rates during the war years having been calculated on a much more generous scale. This unilateral attack on standards evoked a huge protest, which spontaneously developed into a 'go slow' throughout the three Humber-Rootes factories in Coventry. In response the management declared 1300 redundancies and stated that four to five thousand more would follow. This aggressive attitude caused resentment among the workers. An all-out strike followed.

Support came from all the other federated firms in Coventry, the shop stewards seeing the Humber-Rootes move as the beginning of a general offensive. The national executive of the AEU and the TGWU were not so enthusiastic and seemed to think that the workers should go back to work. Arthur Deakin, by this time General Secretary of the union, phoned me and said as much. He told me that he was sending down Harry Nicholas, the new Engineering Group National Secretary, to 'put things in order'.

I met Harry at the station. His first words were: 'You know, these fellows must be got back to work.' I had to explain that if we were going to keep a strong union in Coventry that attitude would not work. I was the confidant and adviser not only of the TGWU stewards but of most of the leading stewards of the various unions in the city. I persuaded Harry to meet them in a local pub instead of organizing what would have undoubtedly proved an abortive meeting to convey 'instructions' to them from Arthur Deakin.

The get-together with the leading stewards was a success. Harry Nicholas was truly put in the picture and could see the justice of the workers' case. But he had to buy a round of drinks, a number of us having done the same. Later he told me that when he reported to Deakin he mentioned the cost of the drinks, hoping for reimbursement. Deakin rounded on him, saying that it was not his place to be drinking with shop stewards, let alone buying the drinks! In fact the strike was brought to an end by the intervention of the sheet-metal workers' union. They decided to call a district-wide strike of their members unless the Humber-Rootes management arrived at a settlement. The firm agreed to reconsider the piecework prices and to arrange a phased reinstatement of the workers they had declared redundant.

I wasn't happy about the element of 'phasing', because I knew that the feeling of comradeship would be broken if some workers were not able to go through the gates at the same time as others. We agreed to put the management's offer to the people on strike, however, and the majority decided to return to work. On the piecework issue a victory was scored which was to reverberate over the years in Coventry. One of the most difficult firms to deal with had conceded to the principle of high wages for high output. Most firms were more open to our views. The best response came from Standard Motors. In trade union terms it was the most highly organized firm in the district and our relationship with the managing director, Sir John Black, was extremely good. A dashing, debonair man with a touch of the dynamic, he stood out in sharp contrast to many of his contemporaries in management. He enjoyed walking around the shop floor, chatting to the work-people and sensing the feeling which existed between line managers and the workers.

With the change-over of his factories to motor-car and tractor production he agreed, towards the end of 1945, that piecework rates would be based on those which had applied during wartime. Coming at a time when the employers collectively appeared to be planning to bring wages down, this agreement was a real smack in the eye for the reactionaries. The engineering employers in Coventry and elsewhere were most annoyed. Shortly after our agreement was concluded, Black came, unannounced, into my office. He was fuming with indignation. He told me that he had just left the offices of the Coventry Engineering Employers Association where a 'blow up' had taken place. 'I am not having those bloody fools dictate to me,' he went on. 'I gave my word to you and I'll keep it. It's up to you to help *me* now!'

In the Coventry area there was much anxiety about the prospect of massive unemployment. There had been a sharp rise in the numbers out of work, although at that time precise figures were kept secret. A large aircraft establishment had announced plans to dispense with about a thousand people and many other firms were declaring redundancies as Government orders finished and the scale of post-war industrial development remained unclear. There was stagnation in most of the motor-car factories due to difficulties in ensuring outside supplies of accessories and component parts and a shortage of certain materials.

Even though I believed the difficulties were temporary, I was very concerned about what would happen during the next twelve months. I warned Government departments and employers that, if work of some kind wasn't found, many workers with skill and specialized experience would be lost to the engineering industry, although they could be needed again in a year's time. I joined with the AEU District Secretary in seeking a meeting with Stafford Cripps, President of the Board of Trade, and John Wilmot, the Minister of Supply and Aircraft Production, to urge efforts to overcome Coventry's problems. Sometimes I wondered whether the years of assured wartime orders were responsible for the lethargy which most employers were displaying. They seemed to need somebody to take them by the hand.

In mid 1946 we secured a major breakthrough with an agreement with the Standard Motor Company to introduce a five-day week of $42\frac{1}{2}$ hours. This was the first five-day week agreement in the engineering industry and, with a reduction of $4\frac{1}{2}$ hours in one fell swoop, was more than most members had thought we would achieve. There is no doubt that it accelerated the negotiations for a national five-day week which came into force in January 1947. Despite this I got another black mark from Arthur Deakin for supporting efforts to enable night-shift workers to work reduced hours over 4 or $4\frac{1}{2}$ nights so that they could enjoy a long weekend. Having had some experience of night-shift working myself, I thought this would be good for their health. The employers, for the most part, agreed to operate the idea, although it was strongly opposed by Arthur Deakin and Executive Council members of the AEU.

This improvement in the working week, humdrum as it sounds, changed the lives of working people in Britain. Leisure activities increased remarkably as working people realized the value of two full days' holiday each week. 'Do It Yourself' hobbies were among the innovations which sprang from this change. A lot of critics said workers would not know what to do with their leisure, but they were proved wrong. I also saw the adoption of a shorter working week as a partial answer to unemployment.

Despite the shortages in fuel and other materials, the Government had launched a productivity drive. I questioned some aspects of this, both in the Midland Regional Production Board and publicly. The *Midland Evening Telegraph*, in October 1946, quoted me as saying:

> It is not 'pep' talks but materials that are needed. And machinery to enable management and workers to get down to factory problems rather than conferences. Production would not be increased by maligning the workers. At one factory recently workers were told to produce more, although they were held up because of an acute shortage of materials. The important task is the setting up of machinery in the works to enable management and workers jointly to examine factory problems. That means a renewal of the Joint Production Committees, which are now practically non-existent in Coventry. Such committees could and would function effectively if the workers' representatives were given a wider range of authority and opportunities to learn all the facts and offer constructive criticism.

I echoed some of these views years later when presenting the case for industrial democracy and applied them in firms which would listen, such as the Standard Motor Company.

An opportunity to initiate what was later called 'productivity bargaining' presented itself at this company. It was a comprehensive deal and took a long time to work out. For years people had talked about the chaotic wage structure in the engineering industry; well here, I thought, was a chance to try to put things right in one firm at least. The firm was manufacturing Vanguard and Triumph cars and Ferguson tractors and employed over twelve thousand people, so it was a big challenge.

While the company was drawing up its own proposals, we on the trade union side put our ideas together. It was hard work, involving much intricate detail and the marrying of the different craft and other interests. It was remarkable how officials and senior stewards, coming from different unions and with a variety of backgrounds, co-operated so well. This convinced me that trade unionists of different unions could plan together constructively and that closer association was both desirable and possible. In my mind's eye I could envisage the merger of some of the unions with the TGWU, especially the Vehicle Builders. But the prospect of using my influence in that direction was far off.

After prolonged endeavour agreement was reached; ninety-two different basic rates were wiped out and replaced by eight, much higher, rates, with production workers grouped in large gangs so as to ease the problem of transferring work-people from one job to another. This was to make a big contribution to higher productivity, while maintaining high wages. A guaranteed minimum wage was established for the standard week – skilled, semi-skilled and unskilled were guaranteed the same amount. Not only were production workers assured of high-paying bonus schemes but all the other members of the workforce were to be paid bonuses which allowed them to benefit from the productivity achieved by the production workers.

A major concession was given on overtime. Both sides were committed to eliminate overtime as far as possible but where it was regarded as necessary it was to be worked on a rota in agreement with the shop stewards. This represented a departure from the attitude of the engineering employers generally. In 1922 the employers had indulged in a long and bitter lock-out to establish the right of management to determine when overtime was to be worked and by whom. Our new approach not only reversed that stance but helped to cut down overtime and create more jobs. Another breakthrough was a big increase in holiday pay with two weeks' paid holiday in 1951; a concession well ahead of that allowed by other firms in the industry.

The only snag was that while most Standard workers would be gaining under the new arrangements, a small number were expected to accept a reduction. This I knew could create trouble. The challenge had to be met, for the overall benefits to members were enormous. As leader of the negotiating team I insisted on two things; first, that I should be allowed to explain the proposals to mass meetings of all the employees concerned, at the works and in works time; and second that after the meetings the members should decide whether they accepted the proposed agreement or not, by ballot vote.

Employers in those days, and all too often trade union leaders too, used to take the line: 'OK, if you think the agreement is all right and you are prepared to accept it as representatives of the workers . . . just sign.' I would have none of that. What we were doing would influence the lives and livelihood of lots of people, they should make the decision. It was a point of view I preached and practised throughout my trade union life, but it wasn't easy to put into operation.

My insistence on consultation meant that I faced thousands of workers, among whom the most vociferous were not surprisingly those who stood to lose by the agreement. But there were others who objected to the idea of any agreement just because it was an agreement. I was astounded, for instance, when one chap got up from a section which stood to gain over £5 a week, and said: 'This is diabolical; we are being sold down the river!' Luckily not many took as unthinking a line as that, but there was keen questioning and some criticism. After a few days the ballot was taken, each person being given a printed outline of the agreement. The result was as anticipated, a sizeable majority for acceptance.

Chapter Thirteen

It is not so much that it means a power to attack, as a power to negotiate, and that power to negotiate is the most valuable thing that we can have.

ERNEST BEVIN

Though we made a lot of progress over the years there were quite a few places in the district where trade unionism remained weak. At one hell-hole of a small jobbing foundry a member was being paid under the rate for overtime work. The owner was credited with being a tear-away boss but I braved the storm and sought an interview with him. He couldn't very well ignore me for I went inside the foundry to talk to him. Because of the noise we bawled at each other. He used a dictionary of expletives, telling me where to get off and refusing to make any concessions. I was in no position to threaten a strike, we did not have enough members for that sort of action, but I did invoke the name of the Ministry of Labour. That made him even angrier and he shouted: 'Before I'll give in to you I'll bloody well turn this place into an ice-cream factory.' Nothing could have been more incongruous, and I burst out laughing. That broke the ice. He listened to me, and having satisfied himself that I wasn't asking for the moon he agreed to my requests.

One large factory in Coventry which remained largely unorganized for most of the war was Morris Engines. This was chiefly due to the paternalism of Lord Nuffield, who had introduced a form of profit sharing called 'integers' which impressed the old hands very much. Many of them feared they would lose these benefits if they joined a union. My first managerial encounter there was with the father of the late Sir George Harriman (Chairman of the British Motor Corporation). Then a machine shop superintendent, he had been a militant shop steward in his early days and a well-known agitator on behalf of the unemployed. He displayed none of his past sympathies in 1946. The labourers in the machine shop were paid very low wages indeed compared to most labourers in the district and I put the case for an improvement strongly, seeking his sympathy. His attitude was: 'These men are ten a penny. They make no contribution to production and they can please themselves whether they leave or not. We can replace them if we want to.'

I knew that against such an attitude only trade union strength in the key areas would count, and I redoubled my efforts to organize the production workers in the machine shops and elsewhere. With the help of some of the younger ex-service men, and growing enthusiasm on the shop floor, Morris Engines joined the league of organized plants. A lively shop stewards' leadership emerged and many advances took place until, in 1953, an announcement was made that a thousand workers were to be discharged. This was one of the results of the rationalization of the newly created British Motor Corporation, which merged the Austin Company with the Morris organization.

Alarm spread throughout the plant. The management had been adamant in refusing to discuss the matter with the shop stewards and the latter came to me. I led a deputation of officials of the different unions to see the General Manager, Mr Clark. When we walked into his room his greeting was: 'What the fucking hell have you come for?' He made it clear that sacking a thousand people was the absolute prerogative of management. I advised the stewards that we would need to threaten strike action if we were to secure a change in attitude, and that we should insist on short-time working throughout the plant as an alternative to the dismissals. A mass meeting of the workforce endorsed this course, although I knew there was weakness in the ranks, especially among the old hands who were worried about their 'integers'.

To have consulted the General Secretary of the union would have been to invite a rebuke. Arthur Deakin appeared in those days to be always on the side of management. I decided to go it alone and publicly threatened strike action. The trade union officials dealing with both Austin and Morris factories then sought a meeting with the Chairman of the new Corporation, Leonard Lord.

The meeting took place at the Austin works in Longbridge near Birmingham. Lord finally agreed to reply in detail to my case at a conference to be held at Coventry. Our threat paid off. It was agreed that redundancies would be cut by half and that plans would be made to re-employ those laid off as trade picked up. It was also agreed that the lay-off would be spread over six weeks rather than on one date as originally intended. I put the terms to a mass meeting of the workers and they were accepted.

I got increasing support and encouragement from young men returning from the forces. They brought a feeling of audacity into the workshops and stimulated further recruitment. Many of them had reinstatement rights from their prewar employment and we helped them to get resettled. They expected changes in the industrial conditions they had known before the war and quickly picked up the idea of collective organization and of speaking up for themselves and their fellow workers. Their extra strength was needed, because a spate of what I felt to be unfair dismissals occurred in the postwar years. Employers went to great lengths to justify the removal of people they found to be irritant. All sorts of spurious reasons were advanced. Sometimes too employees were demoted on some excuse or other or transferred to a less favourable job. Victimization is a dirty business and an employer can hardly do worse than strike at a person's livelihood because he has the courage to speak up on behalf of his fellow workers. Wherever I could I acted strongly on such issues.

I had known discrimination in Liverpool myself, so my views were understandable. Maybe because my enthusiasm had occasionally ruffled the feathers of Arthur Deakin, I now ran into some more discrimination, this time from the General Secretary. In April 1948 applications were invited for the vacant position of Assistant General Secretary. I was persuaded to apply and, to my surprise, was placed on the short list of eight to appear before the Finance and General Purposes Committee. I was the only district officer among the eight; the others were prominent national officers of the union, including Bill Tudor and Frank Cousins. At thirty-five I was by many years the youngest. Arthur Deakin conducted the questioning, which ranged from detailed administrative and industrial matters to labour law and the economic situation. He seemed disappointed when he could not fault my responses.

A few days afterwards I was advised that Jock Tiffin, of the London Region, and I had been selected to appear before the full General Executive Council for a final decision. Privately I was told that I had been outstanding in the examination and that Tiffin was the only other candidate who had given a comparable performance. Deakin, I was told, had pulled out all the stops to persuade the committee to recommend Jock, on the grounds of age and experience, but they all agreed we should both appear before the Executive.

At the meeting of the Council I naturally expected to be heard before the decision was made. Instead a most unusual procedure was followed:

the decision was taken before I entered the room! The affair was curious indeed. Tiffin and I sat in the waiting-room. Tiffin was called in, then after twenty minutes or so I was asked to follow him. I expected to speak and to answer questions – not a bit of it. Deakin simply informed me that Tiffin had been appointed. The Executive had voted without even seeing me. I found it difficult to conceal my anger at what I knew to be manipulation by the General Secretary, but protest would have served little purpose. I felt no ill feelings towards Jock Tiffin, so I simply congratulated him and left the meeting.

Deakin did not like my support of the shop steward system. He disagreed with my ideas about consultation with the membership, reference back of employers' offers, local negotiations. He was less than enthusiastic about Joint Production Committees and industrial democracy. Although I felt resentful I determined not to allow it to deter me and, if anything, I intensified my efforts to achieve maximum membership in my neck of the woods.

Shortly afterwards the full-time officers of the Midlands Region were called on to elect a nominee to participate in the ballot for the Officers National Negotiating Committee. The Area Secretary, Joe Blewitt, presided over the meeting and did everything possible to see that I was not elected. Although I was nominated first, he put my name to the vote last and spoke strongly in favour of my opponent. Despite all this I was elected by an overwhelming vote. Afterwards, Joe told me in confidence that Deakin had asked him to make sure that I lost. He had told Deakin that I was his most efficient officer, but had reluctantly tried to carry out the General Secretary's request.

The idea of TGWU full-time officers having a Negotiating Committee was something entirely new – and Deakin did not like that either. It had been forced upon him by a decision of the Executive Council in a debate led by the communist members Bert Papworth and Bill Jones. They had argued that the six hundred officers employed by the union should themselves enjoy the benefits of a shop stewards' system. At the first meeting of the Negotiating Committee I was elected as secretary and chief spokesman. Our negotiating sessions were a little hectic. Meetings were with Arthur Deakin, representing the Executive. He was accompanied only by Alf Chandler, the union's chief clerk, ostensibly there to take the minutes. In fact I made an arrangement with Alf that I would prepare the minutes and send them to him, and he would accept responsibility for them. In that way I could make sure that our arguments were properly recorded.

For our first meeting I prepared a detailed case in support of the officials' claim for higher salaries. Evidence of salaries paid by other trade unions and for a variety of jobs of similar responsibility was assembled, and an analysis of the union's financial position was included. Half-way through my presentation Deakin exploded. 'Do you mean to say I don't know what's going on in industry?' he demanded. 'I don't have to listen to a lot of details like you're telling me. I'm the General Secretary of the union and I know the position very well, thank you. You've no need to bother me with that sort of thing. . .'

On the next occasion I avoided a detailed submission and argued simply that there should be an increase for the officers related to increases secured for members of the union in certain well-known industries. I reminded Deakin of recent negotiations he himself had undertaken for the dockers shortly before our meeting. His response was: 'You have brought people here from all over the country, from as far away as Scotland and Belfast, and you have not prepared a case! My time is too valuable for just a pleasant conversation. . .'

This was the sort of situation one had to face in dealing with Arthur Deakin. He was an awkward, intolerant man. Undoubtedly the pressures upon him were heavy and his health was poor. But he did not accept change easily. For example, I clashed with him when I pressed for the introduction of incentive payment schemes in Courtauld's factories. He did not like the idea, largely, I think, because he preferred the orderly approach of straight time rates, even if this meant low pay. In running the union Deakin resembled a small businessman in outlook, rather than the leader of hundreds of thousands of industrial workers. Yet deep down there was a gentleness which occasionally revealed itself. I formed the impression that he was a shy man who put on bluff and bluster as a front, although any liberal tendencies he may have had in his early years he brutally suppressed.

In the early post-war years he was active in the formation of the World Federation of Trade Unions and even more active in its break-up. With the increasing tension between East and West he began to look on the union and the TUC as battlegrounds and he set out to bludgeon any opposition, whether from Labour's left wing or from members of the Communist Party. He became highly suspicious of anything smelling of the Left. In my experience those who claimed that he suffered from a 'reds under the beds' complex were correct. His paranoia impeded anything he may have tried to do to make the union a stronger force.

When the Confederation of Shipbuilding and Engineering Unions produced a 'Plan for Engineering' which contained a substantial element of public ownership, he denounced it as 'the worst abortion ever conceived in the mind of man' (I remember wondering whether an abortion could be the subject of conception). It wasn't that he entirely opposed nationalization, he just couldn't accept the idea of a plan. He held firmly to the view that workers should get no special advantage from nationalization, which should be seen only as 'serving the nation'. This was the attitude he expressed to me when I pressed for higher wages for workers in the electricity supply industry. The fact was workers in that and other publicly-owned industries were suffering badly in comparison with their counterparts in manufacturing industry. But he seemed to ignore that.

Despite his attitude I pressed the case for an increase above the national rate in the electricity supply industry in the Coventry district. Eventually I secured a ten-shilling-a-week increase, which was quite an improvement at that time. The decision shocked the 'establishment', including the trade union leaders from left to right, who had nailed their colours to the mast of 'national fixation of rates of pay' irrespective of differing costs of living. This breakthrough had widespread repercussions in the Coventry area and the ten-shilling 'Coventry Plus Rate' was extended to all local government staff in the area. On my advice even the magistrates' clerks' department applied for and got it. I was then a Coventry magistrate and accepted as the industrial expert in magisterial circles, especially on Factory Act cases. Finally the Lord Chancellor's Department ruled that, as I was a trade union official, I should not sit on Factory Act cases!

Generally what happened in London had little impact on the Coventry district. We had built a substantial membership and day-to-day activities in the plants, where trade unionism is properly judged, were going well. National events passed most people by. Nevertheless the decision of the union's national conference in 1949 to ban communists holding office in the TGWU caused a commotion in the ranks of the active members. I shared their view that the decision smelled of McCarthyism. Since a number of shop stewards in my district were communists I felt that the union could only be harmed by the decision. Some members did, in fact, leave the TGWU and join the ETU. Determined to be no party to victimization, I managed to protect the shop stewards and they continued to function in my district.

Without making overt demands for 'closed shops', more and more sections of factories were insisting that only union members should work with them. A foolish act by management at Standard Motors, the 'flagship of our trade union fleet', opened up a major advance.

In the early fifties a large scale lay-off of labour caused massive concern. Compensation was unheard of; all we could do was mitigate the damage by slowing up the process and trying to ensure it was carried out as fairly as possible. This usually meant the preparation of lists by shop stewards and management, based on length of service and in some cases age or other special circumstances. This latter method had been adopted at the Standard Motor Company's large Banner Lane works when trade difficulties had resulted in a big surplus of labour.

I had been involved in the initial negotiations, so I was fully aware of the position. I thought all would proceed smoothly but to my surprise the leading shop stewards came to see me in a panic. They said that Mr Lord, the Works Manager at the plant, had interfered with the lists which had been agreed and well-known management favourites had been kept on, without regard to service or other grounds. Others, who had a proper claim to be retained, had been dismissed.

It was clear that I must act quickly. I phoned Sir John Black, the managing director. 'Lord has played ducks and drakes with our agreement at Banner Lane,' I said. 'It's not the first time he's caused trouble with the men, but this is the last straw.' Realizing the seriousness of the situation, Black agreed that a full conference of all union officials and senior stewards with management should take place the following morning. Everybody was tense as I presented our case. As I gave instance after instance of abuse and breach of our agreement I looked over to the other side of the table and could see Mr Lord smirking as though he could not care less. But his smile faded as I concluded my case for the reinstatement of the men unfairly 'sacked' and then said: 'For all these reasons and the many other complaints we have against him we ask for the dismissal of Mr Lord. Neither the trade union officials nor the shop stewards have any confidence in him. If you want peace in the factory, Sir John, then you should agree with our request.' There was a long silence. Then we moved into a recess.

After some time Sir John sent for me personally. He wanted to satisfy himself as to all the facts. Finally he told me he would remove Lord and correct the position over the dismissals. We then resumed the full conference and Black confirmed what he had said to me.

The drama was not quite complete. Within hours of the conference ending Black rang me and said: 'Look, we've removed our man. Now

I want a quid pro quo. I want you to remove your convenor, Gillan.'
He complained that Gillan was uncooperative and had caused many
problems for management. I had patiently to explain the difference
between an appointed manager and an elected senior shop steward.
Still he was not satisfied, and I had to jump in my car and go to see him
personally before he accepted the position. I promised to talk with
Gillan, but it was agreed that he should keep his post.

Seizing the opportunity, I was able to persuade Sir John that
vacancies in the company for manual workers should be filled from
the trade unions. I pointed out that the workers who had been dismissed as redundant should, in fairness, be reinstated in order of
seniority when work picked up again. I realized there would be a
problem in matching workers to particular vacancies in a number of
cases, and suggested that the best plan would be for the unions to
make the selection. Putting it this way, I won Black's support.

The news that the highest-paying company in the district was insisting on the employment of trade union labour spread throughout
the district. It spurred on the campaign for 100 per cent membership,
not only at the Standard Motor Company but in many other firms as
well. Nothing appeared in the signed agreements between the unions
and the firms about a 'closed shop', but the groundswell of shop-floor
opinion ensured that the non-unionist became a rare specimen.

I like to believe that, by such developments, we helped to make
management more enlightened over the need to treat labour with
respect rather than regarding them just as 'numbers on a sheet'.

Although Sir John Black was a bold man in many respects he would
never face his employees at mass meetings. If reports of negotiations
were to be made, or unpalatable news of lay-offs conveyed to his employees, he would gladly provide the facilities for meetings, but leave
it to me to do the speaking. This was true even if the news was good
news. I'm bound to say that Sir John was not unique in this; a reluctance to face the work-people applied to most industrialists with whom
I had dealings.

I had a bone to pick with Black when I found that he had been
secretly listening in to my reports at mass meetings of the workers. It
came to light when he saw me at the works and said: 'That was a
splendid speech you made last night.' He disclosed that he had been
using a new listening device. I was angry and showed it. Shortly afterwards he invited me to his home and offered me the post of Labour
Director for his firm. I was equally angry and made it clear that I

would never leave the ranks of the trade union movement. I had similar offers in later years from large companies and public corporations but always gave the same response. There is no finer cause than serving working people, the satisfaction of doing so far outweighed any rewards that might have come my way otherwise. Even in my retirement it is always a pleasure to hear an old trade unionist say: 'You never left us, Jack. You never tried to feather your own nest. You were true to our class.'

Some of the agreements arrived at nationally caused me a great deal of concern. That was particularly the case with the early agreements concluded with the Ford Motor Company. A national agreement had been concluded with the company, mainly to cover the big Dagenham works but then extended to the Leamington works, known as the Imperial Foundry. I was elected secretary of the Joint Trade Union Committee covering the plant, but soon found that we had little local leeway. The national agreement had been tightly drawn by Marsden Jones, a friend of Arthur Deakin's, who prior to working at Ford's had held senior positions at Courtaulds and ICI. Arthur Deakin had undoubtedly collaborated with him, but from all accounts Victor Feather, who was then a junior official of the TUC but had been deputed to act for Walter Citrine, the TUC General Secretary, had enthusiastically joined in.

Because of their deep hostility towards left-wing shop stewards, they had designed an agreement which put all power at the centre and virtually ruled out membership participation. A limited number of shop stewards were allowed, but their activities were tightly controlled and shop-floor bargaining was virtually outlawed. The management could exercise a veto on the nomination of shop stewards and altogether trade union activity was effectively circumscribed.

We would have gained few members at Ford's had we not made efforts to change the rules. Eventually we succeeded but it took many years. Meantime the loyalty of the valiant few, who had joined the union and remained firm in their trade union conviction despite rebuffs from the company and rebukes from national union leaders, was outstanding. Our most devoted steward at Leamington was a man from the nearby countryside who had a great reputation as a poacher. He put his wits at the service of his fellow workers and the union and we certainly needed them.

My meetings with the Ford membership frequently took place on Sunday mornings. When it was known that I would be going to

Leamington, or somewhere else in the Warwickshire area, my two children and nephew would recruit other children in the street and a carload would accompany Evelyn and me. Usually we would drop in at the open-air swimming pool at Kenilworth, and then I would leave them all at Warwick Park, while I went to my meeting. I suppose it could be called combining business with pleasure, and such occasions made up for some of the lost time in cementing family happiness.

On one occasion there was nearly a tragedy. The boys, all of them quite little at the time, were playing on the canal bank. It was the middle of winter and the canal was iced over. Jack, the elder boy, more adventurous than the others, stepped on to the ice to reach a piece of wood and fell in. Although I was watching the other boys I caught sight of young Jack in the corner of my eye and acted quickly. Almost as soon as he was in the water I was pulling him out. I rushed him to the car, stripped him and wiped him dry as best I could; then I took off my vest and trunks and put them on my son, wrapping him in my raincoat. We all got home safely, none the worse for wear. It was a trifling incident, but at such times feeling for one's family is very real.

In the midst of my daily activities came an opportunity to visit Yugoslavia. The Coventry District Committee of the Confederation of Engineering and Shipbuilding Unions had been invited to send a delegate to the Yugoslav Metal Workers Congress at Zagreb, who would then tour the engineering industry in that country. I was selected to make the trip. In 1952 Yugoslavia was still a 'far-away country' and I was intrigued by the chance to explore this new world.

Bill Carron of the Amalgamated Engineering Union was the only other trade union representative from Britain. After attending the Congress we toured many engineering plants. Yugoslavia was very much on its own and industrially backward. It was not unusual to come across a heap of horse manure in the centre of a machine shop or witness some other evidence of the close link between industry and agriculture. Horses and carts were used to transport materials to and from the factories. Former peasants were being trained slowly and painfully to acquire engineering skills.

I was impressed by the early attempts at workers' self-management and from that time onwards have watched the experiments with keen interest. Bill Carron, a very devout Catholic, was critical of the attitude of the Yugoslav communists to the Catholic Church and to meet his wishes we checked on the operations of the Church and I accompanied him to mass. His fears were allayed by the visit.

The need of Yugoslavia for transport vehicles at that time was considerable and the City of Coventry did in fact supply some steamrollers and used buses to the City of Belgrade. Rootes also provided some cars on a barter basis exchange for timber. I thought the British trade union movement very unimaginative in not pressing for more developments of that kind.

It was impatience with the lack of national action which led me to join forces with Maurice Edelman, one of the Coventry MPs, to create a Midlands motor industry lobby of Labour MPs. We were concerned to expand exports and restrict imports while at the same time trying to remove restrictions on the development of the home market. The Confederation Committees of Coventry and Birmingham joined forces with the Labour MPs of the West Midlands, among them Roy Jenkins, Woodrow Wyatt, Dick Crossman and others. In Parliament the most active was Edelman himself, who welcomed the opportunity to exercise his undoubted talents in the field of publicity.

The importance of parliamentary action for trade unionists is not always appreciated and this new initiative enabled us to expand the members' appreciation of the wider issues affecting the motor manufacturing industry. The 'Coventry MPs Maurice Edelman, Dick Crossman and later Elaine Burton were invited to address shop stewards' meetings in the district, but I'm afraid that Dick and Elaine never felt quite at home with the shop stewards.

I had the feeling that the education was coming from the shop floor rather than from the Members of Parliament, who were clearly not conversant with the intricacies of the industry. In our parliamentary system, then and now, an enormous weakness is apparent – the lack of representation from the shop floors of our industries. It has been a continual wonder to me that we have not been able to overcome this problem within the ranks of the Labour Party. Until we do, workers' interests will not be understood or properly advanced in Parliament.

This remoteness from the shop floor can occur in the trade union movement too, when leaders consider they know all the answers. For years the TUC General Council operated that way. Then somebody arranged for Regional Advisory Committees to be set up, composed of full-time officials of the unions in the regions. This was a small step forward. When the first meeting of the West Midlands committee took place I was elected chairman, and used my new position to publicize issues affecting the workers in the area. At the annual meeting in 1951 I drew attention to the serious material shortages affecting the engineering industry and at the same time replied to critics from right and left who wanted to end all ideas of joint consultation.

We made some progress with this new committee and began to secure some understanding of our fears on the part of the TUC staff, particularly George Woodcock. But a section of the hierarchy decided that Jack Jones should not be chairman, and on their advice the General Council decided to exercise its prerogative and appoint the chairman themselves, in the person of Harold Hewitt, the General Secretary of the Pottery Workers Union. There was a furore but the mandarins had made up their minds. Their decision was almost a joke, and in effect I had to continue to do the job. Later, in fact, I was reinstated as chairman. Years afterwards George Woodcock, who was no party to the manoeuvrings, apologized to me. George always displayed a scholarly attitude which contrasted with the rough earthiness, some of it put on, of a number of members of the General Council. He welcomed a discussion with me about unemployment in the Midlands and openly criticized General Council members for their lack of attention to such problems. 'I wish these buggers would read the papers we give them,' he said. 'They come to meetings with their papers unopened.' I'm afraid the same criticism could have been made of some of my colleagues when I became a member of the General Council years later.

Chapter Fourteen

But yet I'll make assurance
double sure,
And take a bond of fate.

WILLIAM SHAKESPEARE

Early in 1955 I was appointed Engineering Group Secretary for the whole of the Midlands Region of the union. It was an important post and I applied for it in the hope that I could help to organize areas of the Midlands which had remained centres of non-unionism. I wanted to extend the ideas we had applied successfully in Coventry to the big industrial centre of Birmingham and the other more 'backward areas' – an expression I had used when addressing a May Day rally in Coventry, alongside Dick Crossman who for once heartily agreed with me. My new job meant leaving Coventry and going to live in the Birmingham area, not too far away but nevertheless a vast change.

My primary concern was the degree of non-unionism in the vast industrial concentrations of Birmingham, Wolverhampton, Walsall and the Black Country area generally. Despite relative full employment in 1955, our membership was small and scattered over a range of firms. This inevitably reduced our negotiating strength because our membership was so limited. I found little disposition among many of the full-time officials of the union to recruit members. While from some I had a heartening response, as though they had been 'waiting for the call', from others there was cynicism. They relished the friendship of managers and personnel officers and were happy to enjoy the fruits of office without working for them. I reminded them that they were like generals without an army and urged them to earn their title to leadership by showing that they could organize.

Example is the best teacher and I prepared recruiting literature and issued it in large quantities. Using what contacts I could, I arranged meetings in pubs and clubs near the factories. Often the best results were obtained by small gatherings in people's homes. Enthusiasm grew and as gains were made we publicized them. Booklets about the engineering agreements were printed and circulated to meet the queries of active members and to demonstrate the role of the TGWU in the industry. It was like Coventry all over again.

Changes were taking place in my domestic life at this time. Our eldest son Jack, having got his O levels, wanted to go to sea. I made some contacts for him. When I was a lad I would have loved to have had similar opportunities to become a navigating officer. Jack was a strongly built lad, with a wonderfully happy nature. He had a quick brain, too; for years, while still at school, he had delivered milk and could calculate the change to give to the housewives quicker than the proverbial bookie.

His going to sea coincided with my new appointment, and Evelyn hit upon the idea of exchanging council houses so that we could live nearer my new office. We looked around the Solihull area and came across a street bounded on one side by a farm (adjacent to the Rover Company's works) and on the other by a row of well-kept prefabricated houses. They were ideal from our point of view. We did not have to go beyond the first house to find a man who worked at a factory near our Coventry home and had been hoping for the opportunity to exchange. So all was arranged in quick time and we lived for eight happy years on the borders of salubrious Solihull but in a council prefab.

Snooty Solihull did not go down well with our younger son, Mick, who scholastically was extremely good but had an understandable socialist streak. This got him into a few scrapes when he was transferred from the grammar school at Coventry (our two sons had won scholarships to the school) to Solihull School. Within days of his entering that grammar-cum-public school he came home and said, 'I don't like that school. The teacher said: "Button your coat, Jones, we are not *that* lot at Lode Lane [the local secondary modern school]." '
It took Evelyn and me all our time to persuade him to remain at the school. The difference sharpened and he made few friends there; his mates were the local lads in the neighbourhood who were very much part of 'that lot'. Mick became the best shot in the school but for the rest there was a long saga of opposition to authority.

Shortly after we set up our home in Solihull, Evelyn was elected to the Warwickshire County Council as a Labour representative and later served as a magistrate. We made many friends in the local Labour Party. I formed the impression that in challenging Tory ideas in adverse circumstances – and Solihull could hardly have provided more of these! – socialists draw closer together and develop a strong sense of comradeship.

In my new role I became involved in a number of negotiating bodies, meeting officers of various unions including my own. The experience was not encouraging. I was frequently infuriated by the light-hearted way members' claims were dealt with and by the close affinity between trade union officials and management. Settlements were made, usually most inadequate, without any reference back to the membership. Although numerous agreements left a lot to be desired, if unofficial strikes took place the local union officials were simply told: 'Get those men back to work!' I knew we would never build strong unions while such attitudes prevailed.

I recall the Divisional Manager of Esso sending for me and Harry Lett, the senior official of the TGWU Commercial Transport Group in the Midlands, and advising us rather pompously that there was an unofficial strike of electricians at a certain depot. Would we get them back to work? Lett was for rushing down there right away but I told the manager: 'These men haven't sent for us. . . . If they are our members we are their servants not yours.' I knew that trade union membership within Esso was very weak and it was likely that the men concerned were non-unionists. This proved to be the case. Union officials had drifted into becoming messengers for management: I did not see trade unionism that way.

Within twelve months of my moving to Birmingham, Arthur Deakin died. Jock Tiffin was elected General Secretary. In my dealings with Jock, from the very first time we met at the examinations for the Assistant General Secretaryship, I found him to be very critical of Deakin's dictatorial character. Tiffin wanted changes in the union, especially freer exchanges of opinion and more attention to union education. Politically a 'middle of the road' man and a traditionalist, whose attitude had, I think, been shaped by the fact that he gained an army commission in the First World War, Tiffin nevertheless sensed that the union was too bureaucratic, with a wide gap between the leaders and the membership. Unfortunately he did not know quite what to do about it, nor did he live long enough to effect many alterations.

Automation was casting a shadow of doubt across the trade union scene and in Tiffin's brief period of leadership he expressed an interest in the subject. I arranged for him to see the new transfer machines being introduced in the manufacture of engines for motor cars and tractors and drew his attention to the displacement of men which had already taken place. Although we had been able to avoid redundancy by absorbing the men into other sections, to me the implications were clear. Automation must lead to big savings in manpower. Tiffin did not live long enough to respond to my plea that the TGWU should take the lead in a campaign designed to retain jobs whilst accepting the technological changes involved. The policy of sharing the leisure was very much in my mind, together with plans for the re-training of workers displaced so that they could be moved to other jobs within the same firm. But time was not on our side, for within twelve months the motor industry was to face bitter so-called 'automation strikes'.

I had met the well-known American trade union leader, Walter Reuther, on a visit to Britain and had discussed with him the response to automation of his United Automobile Workers Union. It is a matter of much regret to me that we did not adopt some of the policies he expounded, seeking bigger pensions, earlier retirement and acceptance of the principal of the 'guaranteed annual wage'. Better treatment for the elderly was a crusade which had attracted my support from my early days on the docks. When the National Pensioners Federation was formed I spoke on its platforms in the Coventry area, but attempts to gain support from the trade union membership fell on deaf ears. The response was no better when it was suggested that we should claim pensions for manual workers as part of our collective bargaining. Employees in government and local government services and some of the national industries enjoyed such benefits, but we could inspire little interest among the workers in private companies, who preferred a 'cash in hand' high-wage policy.

Jock Tiffin died before he had been in office much more than six months and Frank Cousins became leader of the TGWU. It was a sign of the times. Rank-and-file members wanted changes. The union's policies did not switch from left to right overnight with his election. Many of the officers and branches remained faithful to the traditional right-wing policies of the union. But looking back at that period, the change at the top of the TGWU was a watershed in the history of the Labour movement.

The fertile brain of Ernest Bevin produced many ideas and one of them had been the system of examinations for the appointment of full-time officials within the union. In the dockers' unions, prior to the amalagamation, officials were directly elected by the membership, which occasionally resulted in illiterate men securing office. A couple of the Liverpool dock officials whom I knew as a young man had in fact been elected in the old way. They were colourful and popular with the older fraternity, but they did not always show the respect expected of them by the 'establishment'.

With his system of examinations Bevin tried to secure a more capable and sophisticated type of official. I'm not sure that he succeeded, but that is another story. Posts like that of Regional Secretary and National Officer called for the most rigorous examination and I experienced this at the hands of Frank Cousins shortly after his election as General Secretary when he presided over the examination for the appointment of a new Regional Secretary for the Midlands.

It was not, by any means, a one-horse race – men, older in the movement than I, were in the running – but I secured the appointment. At the comparatively young age of forty-three I became the leader of nearly 150,000 members. The chairman of the Regional Committee, Jock Murray, told me afterwards: 'I didn't support you but by God you won the examination fair and square!'

Bevin, who devised the union structure, once described the Regional Secretaries as the 'General Secretaries of their areas'. A union of the size of the TGWU cannot operate effectively if it is too centralized, so much of the business of the union is dealt with in the regions. As the chief officer I had the responsibility of overlooking all the financial and staff arrangements. The full-time officers were responsible to me on a daily basis and any issues requiring an executive decision had to be chanelled through me. In turn I was in regular contact with the General Secretary. The job is a key one. Maintaining contact with officers and branches; overseeing the unions properties; stepping into industrial disputes when they had reached a crisis: these were just a few of my new duties.

My predecessor, Joe Blewitt, had been brought up in the old school. I admired him for the tight control he exercised over union expenditure, but some of the curbs he had applied began to burst when I took over. Members of the clerical staff objected to feeding coke into the anti-quated boiler; people asked for tea to be supplied (Joe had told them that there was plenty of water available). Little easements had to be made and bigger problems tackled.

Within a short time I was to face a major débâcle. Events at the newly created British Motor Corporation brought trouble to my door. I was attending a meeting of the Light Metal Trades Committee in Glasgow when press and TV people sought me out to tell me that the Corporation had made six thousand workers redundant. I ascertained that the six thousand at the Birmingham and Oxford plants had simply been told they must go, and been given a week's basic wage in lieu of notice. I realized that unless some action was taken immediately the already weak trade union organization at Longbridge (the BMC's biggest factory) and at Oxford would be destroyed. I knew that the shop stewards would want some action. Frank Cousins was away from the office that day and could not be contacted. I told our officers in the Midlands by telephone that we must do all we could to organize resistance. Then I transmitted the same message in interviews on television and radio.

The large number involved made it big news, but I was the only senior trade union official prepared to make a statement. TV, radio and newspaper reporters lapped it up. I told them that the TGWU would back strike action and urged all BMC workers to oppose the redundancies and demand the reinstatement of those discharged. The Corporation's action was inhuman, and I said so with great force. My view was shared by Frank Cousins, of course, but also by much of the media and, more surprisingly, the Minister of Labour in the Conservative Government, Ian Macleod.

Returning to Birmingham as quickly as I could I set the wheels in motion to try to ensure an effective strike. My confidence in Frank Cousins was not misplaced and he readily agreed to support the strike financially. I think it was the quickest response to such an approach in the history of the union. But that was not the main problem. Checking the position I found that the TGWU had only about a thousand members at the Longbridge factory, and the AEU not many more. In total, there were not more than three or four thousand trade unionists out of the many thousands employed. But this did not deter us, indeed I saw it as an opportunity to prove the worth of trade unionism. Dick Etheridge, the senior AEU steward, and other local leaders of the craft trades, saw it the same way. The active members of the unions developed an admirable unity.

Leaflets were rushed out, posters prepared, pickets organized – acting together we organized a big movement. The first week of the strike was strenuous, with headaches galore. Not all the workers responded to our call and we began to develop mass picketing to increase our appeals for solidarity. It is commonplace today but was almost unknown then.

Within the TGWU we made desperate efforts to stop the transport of materials and parts. We were only partially effective. The National

Secretary of the Road Transport Group of the union came down but had little impact in his meetings with transport drivers in the cafés normally used by them. We tried physically to stop vehicles going into the plant. I lay down on the road and encouraged others to do the same. Some of us were hurt in the process, but not seriously. The police were not helpful and did not assist our efforts to hold conversations with the drivers. The one piece of good news which came through was a message from Liverpool and London dockers that they would stop the export of BMC cars.

It could have been a long and costly fight but the two-week annual holiday intervened, avoiding the prospect of some of the weaker brethren returning to work and enabling us to exploit the *threat* of action at the docks and elsewhere. With the help of the Ministry of Labour, negotiations took place during this breathing space. I think the Corporation were conscious of our weakness, and we did not win the dispute hands down. Nevertheless we made a breakthrough, the Corporation agreeing to withdraw some redundancies and providing extra payment in other cases. An assurance was given that longer periods of notice would be given in future and that negotiations would take place on compensation and the scope of future consultations.

Public opinion had had some effect on the thinking of the Company. The Ministry of Labour officials had been anxious to help and Ian MacLeod had told Parliament that he had been profoundly shocked by the overnight sackings. All this prepared the ground for a more humane approach to mass discharges of workers. But in the summer of 1956 we were still some years away from the Redundancy Payments Act and the generous compensation often paid to workers made redundant today.

When the workers returned everyone felt that the action had been vindicated. Enough progress had been made for them to sense that a new era had begun. With officials, shop stewards and branches through-out the plants, we planned a massive recruiting drive. New members joined in large numbers and confidence in trade unionism grew apace.

Strikes are not indulged in by workers or trade union officials for pleasure. Industrial relations in the Birmingham area in the 1950s were so chaotic that often strikes could not be avoided. Managers in the motor industry were notoriously bloody-minded, not only in their relations with employees but among themselves. It was not unusual for top men to be fired in that rough, tough industry. In turn managers tried to reduce the labour force, intensify production, drive hard bargains. Resistance was bound to come as our efforts intensified. From many quarters there was growing support for a new approach in industry. Macleod himself began to express this view. I tried to capitalize on this more sympathetic outlook throughout the Midlands.

It was this development which later led me to seek an interview with George Harriman of the BMC. I suggested that it was about time we reached some understanding about shop stewards. His management treated the stewards as enemies and applied restrictions that made it almost impossible for them to function. I urged a more consiliatory approach, pointing out that if stewards and active members were driven underground it could be more damaging to the Corporation.

Harriman was no pushover, he was thick-skinned and sarcastic, but he listened when I turned the discussion to the need for shop stewards' education and training. My argument was that it was no use his complaining about the conduct of stewards if he was not prepared to help in training them. It had to be done during working hours, I said, because stewards who were married were not inclined to spend a weekend away from home at one of our union schools. Moreover, I felt that it would raise the status of the stewards if they were allowed time-off from work, with the management paying their wages for the periods concerned.

I knew that Harriman would not swallow the idea of the union alone doing the training so I proposed that the tuition should be paid for by the union but undertaken by the extramural department of Birmingham University. Harriman was suspicious but I pressed the point. 'After all,' I said, 'the chief man in the extramural department of the University is Mr Parker, who is a friend of the Royal Family, so you can be sure of his impartiality.' He pricked up his ears at that. I think he made some enquiries; anyway, in the end he agreed.

From little acorns big oaks grow; from that first agreement grew the whole process of shop stewards training in works' time throughout the Midlands, and the whole country for that matter.

Chapter Fifteen

What the hammer? What the chain?
In what furnace was thy brain?
What the anvil?

WILLIAM BLAKE

Jack Scamp became Britain's most prominent industrial 'trouble-shooter' in the 1960s. A warm and friendly character, he inspired confidence in both sides of industry but when I first got to know him he was in the doghouse. He had been employed as a personnel officer at Rugby Portland Cement, after a short spell with the Rover Co., and had agreed to apply increases in pay to the lorry drivers in the Rugby works in line with a national agreement covering lorry drivers. The General Manager was away on holiday and when he got back he instructed Scamp to repudiate the agreement. Scamp refused and resigned. His attitude meant that he stood little chance of obtaining a similar job with other cement companies, for the General Manager was Halford-Reddish, who had already established a reputation as an opponent of unions and collective bargaining. Scamp had my respect and sympathy, and in his subsequent career I remained friendly with him. He went on to work for Plessey and from there became Director of Labour Relations, or some such title, with Massey Ferguson who had decided to seek a national agreement covering their various works. One day Jack Scamp came into my office and asked for my co-operation in constructing the agreement. Being invited in at the pioneering stage provided a unique opportunity, and a very satisfactory agreement was concluded.

Life was not always so easy, but I was surprised one day to hear an American voice over the telephone telling me: 'Mr Jones, you've been elected!' It was a call from the General Manager of the 3 Ms (Minnesota Mining and Manufacturing Company), an American firm with a factory in Birmingham. Without my knowledge the management had conducted a ballot of the workforce, asking them whether they wished to continue with their American-style works council or to be represented by a trade union, and if so which one. Most had opted for a trade union and had stipulated the TGWU, although it turned out we had only three members employed at the works. Over the previous month or so we had distributed recruiting leaflets at the 3 Ms and adjacent factories but had little hope of a response from the relatively well-paid American factory. The approach was a bonus, and I happily joined in the negotiation of an agreement which began a long period of good relations with the firm.

Just off the centre of Birmingham lay the big factory of Bird's Custard, part of the large General Foods Corporation of America. Here too a works council operated and the employees were not in a trade union. We launched a campaign of leaflets and meetings and were especially aided by lorry drivers, who were members of the union, and went in and out of the factory. Eventually the Works Director, Mr Smith, agreed to see me. Our discussion was prolonged but it was clear that his instructions were to refuse any recognition. Eventually I suggested that we both meet the employees and put our views to them, following which a ballot might be held. It was the only way out of a stalemate but I was doubtful of the outcome, especially as the senior staff were conducting a whispering campaign against the union. Mr Smith did not perform well on the platform, he was excited and nervous. I had the best of the argument and we won the day in the ballot. The TGWU moved into an era of co-operation which still exists, to the best of my knowledge, at the newer plant situated in Banbury.

These were interesting but minor successes in our membership drive which added tens of thousands to our strength in the Midlands.

Over the years our union had been the spokesman for the lorry drivers and Ernest Bevin had done much to improve their standards by initiating road haulage wages boards and legislation generally. But wages and conditions in the industry remained poor, largely because of its scattered nature and the low level of union organization. We needed a determined effort to tackle the position. The opportunity presented itself with the appointment of Alan Law as the union organiser of the lorry drivers in the Birmingham area. I had a hand in the appointment, for I knew the need for a different approach, but I realized we were taking a gamble. Law, an ex-commando sergeant, was a tearaway, unpredictable type, and he swept down the haulage companies like a tornado. He led a movement that brought organization among the lorry drivers and car delivery workers to a high level.

In our campaigns to recruit lorry drivers and other workers Alan Law was one of six officers whom I persuaded to use vans rather than the more discreet motor car. The vans advertised the union in bold letters on each side and proved to be a good recruiting medium, but they did not suit the ideas of some of our full-time officials, who felt it to be *infra dig* to proclaim the fact that they were working for the union. A few officers complained, surprisingly, that their neighbours might not like it. Others made the same objection when I asked them to put union stickers on their union-owned cars. The fact that their wages were paid by the members, and that a strong union was needed to advance our cause, seemed to be secondary to maintaining their status among their neighbours.

Our thrusting Midlands Region, with substantial membership increases and exceptionally good financial returns, based on the small number of full-time officers related to membership, evoked admiration from the new General Secretary. We organized large Regional Festivals to bring the active members together, to mix socially, and to provide a platform for Frank Cousins in particular. Frank and I talked extensively about the policies of the union; politically we had much in common, although our industrial experience had been somewhat different. Unilateral nuclear disarmament, opposition to German rearmament, extending public ownership, providing more support for Nye Bevan: these and many other topics were often discussed.

Frank Cousins' election produced a remarkable impact on Labour Party policies and a change in the fortunes of Nye Bevan after he had so long been under attack. Certainly the outlook of the Labour Party establishment towards Nye began to change and it was not long before he was chosen as shadow Foreign Secretary.

In retrospect it is difficult to understand why Bevan moved away from unilateral nuclear disarmament when trade union support for it was growing. Probably he thought the only opportunity he would have to secure the leadership of the Party was to win the centre and this was one way of doing it. Unfortunately when his prospects were at their highest he fell ill and later died. It could be that his critics from the left, whom he himself had nurtured, accelerated the disease that killed him. I did not worship at his feet, so I write without adulation, but I think his leadership would have united the Party in a way Hugh Gaitskell never could have done.

Nye Bevan's problem in the past had been his lack of trade union support, although his public meetings were always packed and enthusiastic. Nye didn't always help himself. He was a distant man who developed an element of grandeur in his style. I stopped him once in Parliament to introduce him to a Yugoslav trade unionist, whom I had taken up to see Parliament from Coventry where he had been on a delegation. Nye could scarcely conceal his impatience. Perhaps it was because I was a TGWU man – it was in Deakin's time. This was not the only occasion I felt he was losing the common touch, but I consoled myself with the thought: 'Politicians are like that'!

The issue of banning the bomb came to the forefront at the 1957 Biennial Delegate Conference of the union. It was Frank's debut as General Secretary and he made a number of able political speeches, especially one on the bomb. The delegates were a little bemused by the issue, which was new to most of them. I discussed the matter with the Midlands delegation and put it to them that it was a question of national priorities. The nation, I said, could not afford 'H' bombs when money was needed for higher pensions for the elderly, more aid for children and big expenditure on housing, education and health. We decided to back the Executive policy and a majority of the other delegates did the same.

Through the years the Midlands Region was the mainstay of the 'ban the bomb' policies, identified with Frank Cousins. When Goerge Brown, who was one of the union MPs, trumpeted his opposition, our delegates ignored him. They acted in an equally disciplined way when, at the 1959 Union Conference in the Isle of Man, Randolph Churchill made a nuisance of himself. He was representing some newspaper or other and went round the hotels making it noisily clear that he was opposed to all this talk of banning the bomb – the Conference and all associated with it were a crowd of reds in his view.

One night Churchill stationed himself in the residents' bar of the Sefton Hotel, at Douglas, where Frank Cousins and a number of us were staying. With a bottle of whisky on the table before him, he sat shouting insulting remarks at passers-by. Anyone who spoke to him got a mouthful of abuse and the staff and management were highly embarrassed. Either he was genuinely drunk or he was trying to provoke a situation which would make news.

I had been helping Frank prepare the arguments he was to use on the nuclear issue at the Conference. After a long session we felt like a drink, but our arrival in the residents' lounge acted like a red flag to a bull. 'You bloody people are letting the country down,' Churchill bellowed. He was almost maudlin in his protestations, and fell about over the chairs beside him. His chin was stuck out like an invitation. I felt like belting him one but was persuaded that it would be better to leave him alone. Had he acted like that in the public bar downstairs, where there were a number of rank-and-file delegates, there would certainly have been a scene which might not have done the union's name any good. He tried to get into the Conference without a press card, and made all sorts of provocative statements, but the delegates voted not to admit him and he was excluded gently but firmly.

In the industrial Midlands I continued to promote more efficiency by the encouragement of high wages related to high productivity. Our union educational activities started to embrace subjects like work study and payment by results. Productivity bargaining, without necessarily using the title, was largely born and nurtured in that setting. The important thing to me was that *all* workers should play a part in improved productivity and *all* benefit by improved earnings. These efforts paid off in our numerous collective bargaining activities.

In the Lucas factories our membership was strong and I got to know the Chairman and Managing Director, A. B. Waring, quite well. We both encouraged the development of the Birmingham Productivity Association and for some time I operated as its Executive Chairman. I wanted to make sure that it was not just a body for the propagation of management views and that both sides of industry should appreciate the full implications of the new technology. With the backing of a number of companies I was able to arrange visits to the Volkswagen, Renault and Phillips factories in Germany, France and Holland. Many shop stewards made their first visit abroad and I made sure they met our trade union counterparts. Productivity can be encouraged by comparison, and international contacts at the grass-roots are good for trade unionism.

Early in 1963 Frank Cousins had been persuaded by Alf Chandler and the Chairman of the Union's Executive Council, Ted Fryer, a jolly and rather worldly-wise busman from Bristol, that he should have extra help in the form of another Assistant Secretary working with him at Transport House. Frank had suffered a heart attack and was clearly affected by the stresses and strains of the job. Harry Nicholas, the Assistant General Secretary, had to step in and carry the extra responsibility from time to time, although he himself was not very fit.

It became generally known in the union that there would be another post at the top. Well before an official decision had been made one or two newspapers began to mention the prospect. As usual names were bandied about, including my own. Frank himself mentioned the matter to me and expressed the hope that I would apply for the post, but I was by no means anxious to go to London. In fact I suggested to a close associate, Harry Urwin, that, if he cared to apply, I would gladly not do so. We both agreed that it would be disastrous if someone got the job who opposed our point of view, the changes in the union could be reversed quite quickly. Most of the full-time officials remained Deakinite in outlook and practice and a number of the new appointments made since Frank Cousins' election had not changed the pattern.

Many friends urged me to apply for the new post and eventually I did so, reluctantly, for I enjoyed my job as Regional Secretary. The appointment was delayed by Frank's illness but finally the examination took place in August. At the end of the proceedings the Finance and General Purposes Committee decided to recommend to the Executive Council that I should be appointed. The Council duly voted me into the post by an overwhelming majority, but not before the 'runner-up' had been given a hearing. The press had no doubt about the significance of the appointment. Next day I was hailed as the 'crown prince' in some newspapers, the 'heir apparent' in others. Naturally I deplored such descriptions and told the press: 'We don't have heirs apparent or crown princes in this union. We are not a one-man band.'

A lot of interest was displayed in my new position and in me personally and I told a press conference that I would be concentrating on building up the membership of the union. We then had about 1.3 million members and I said that, without fixing a firm target, I thought we could achieve a membership of 1.5 million before Frank Cousins retired. Asked about my priorities, I replied that one of my main concerns was the future for labour as automation increased. I was quoted in the *Guardian* as saying:

Managements must be pressed to accept responsibility for the future of displaced labour. I don't think the trade union movement is vigorous enough driving this point home. If managements spend a lot of money on new equipment they must at the same time plan to spend a lot on dealing with the consequent labour problems. . . . Many men would accept industrial change, even at middle life, if they felt they were not going to be pushed down to an unskilled occupation or out of the industry in which they have spent most of their working lives.

I went on to say that people should be able to change their jobs and acquire new skills, and stated firmly:

> We have reached a stage where it is wrong for managements to have the arbitrary authority to dismiss a man. Summary dismissal is not covered by the new Contracts of Employment Bill, yet it is a prime cause of what people like to call wildcat strikes. I don't call them that. There is nothing more likely to bring out a feeling of loyalty and solidarity among working men than the dismissal of one of their colleagues when they feel he has been sacked unfairly.

Moving to London was not easy. Evelyn had been happy in our prefab on the outskirts of Solihull and I knew it was going to be a wrench to leave there. We both had a feeling of apprehension about living in the metropolis, but leaving was easier because our elder son had married and had made his home in Plymouth and our younger son was a student at the Birmingham College of Design and had made it clear that he preferred to have his own digs to living at home.

All through our marriage we had lived in a council house and although the union would have provided a mortgage I was not anxious to take union money for that purpose. I wanted to live close to Transport House, while at the same time finding a place which would suit Evelyn. I was critical of officers who lived long distances from the office, because I felt that their service to the union could be impaired, and I wanted to give an example myself. After some months I was able to get a GLC higher-rented flat in Denmark Hill but before that I tramped around looking at a variety of flats and was almost in a state of despair.

Changing one's home and moving to another town is an upheaval at any time, but trying to find a suitable spot in London is hell's own problem. As soon as my successor as Regional Secretary, Harry Urwin, had settled into his new job I moved to London, but at that stage I had no place to live – except Transport House itself! I had looked round the offices to acquaint myself with the lay-out and found that Frank Cousins had arranged to have a bedroom there. He was then living in Epsom and had felt it would be useful to have a place to change and possibly sleep when he had an engagement in town. Luckily he had not used it and was not likely to, so I persuaded him to let me use it while I was looking for a new home. It was a bit weird being the only person in the large building night after night, but it proved extremely useful for I was able to work late into the night and early in the morning.

Frank was an early bird, usually arriving at the office between 7.30 and 8 a.m. That suited me, since I normally rose at six – a practice which went back to my childhood when I used to get up to cook my father's breakfast before he went to work. Almost as soon as Frank got into his office I would be in there, discussing the problems of the day and the issues facing the union. I wanted to be sure that we were on the same wavelength. We did not always agree and sometimes our discussions continued in Frank's home where Nance, his wife, was always a wonderful hostess.

The responsibilities of my new office had not really been thought out. Despite our friendship I was determined that I was not just going to be an 'assistant'. In a meeting with Frank Cousins, Harry Nicholas and Alf Edwards (the union's administrative officer) I demanded that I should attend all meetings of the Executive and its subcommittees as an Executive Officer with the right to put my own point of view. I felt this to be important if I was to be an effective force in the union.

Full-time officials of the TGWU are appointed after examination by a subcommittee of lay members of the Executive Council, but in each case an Executive Officer leads the questioning. Due to the illness of Frank Cousins and the indifferent health of the Assistant General Secretary, Harry Nicholas, various National Officers had attended the examining committees and the resulting appointments had in some cases caused me concern. I was able to get agreement that I should conduct the examinations, which apart from getting some consistency into the approach, enabled me to visit the regions and find out what was going on.

It was not before time, for I found some of the District Offices to be less than glorious examples of efficiency. On the window of one of them Ernest Bevin's name appeared as General Secretary, and in others the impression was one of Victorian times, the atmosphere dark and uninviting. Above all I found that Regional Secretaries had not been encouraged to discuss their problems and had simply followed old practices. I found myself explaining simple managerial systems to ensure that more attention was paid to recruitment, consolidation of membership and tight methods of finance. I insisted that each full-time officer must be made accountable for his results, for after all, I argued, we were dealing with the workers' money and we had a special obligation to them.

Frank Cousins' health was a worry to everyone. He was still complaining of heart pains and clearly feeling the pressure but he brushed aside suggestions that he should take more rest at home. To my mind what he needed was a good long holiday abroad. I talked with the Chairman of the Executive, Len Forden, and found ready support, and in turn he and I canvassed the members of the Finance and General Purposes Committee. They agreed to leave it in my hands to make the arrangements.

I phoned Andrew Crichton, a shipping industrialist and leader of the port employers, to get his ideas on a cruise for Frank. He suggested a sea trip to Jamaica and a holiday there in the sunshine and between us the arrangements were made. It wasn't cheap, because the trip was arranged on strictly business terms. I was anxious that no one should be able to say that Frank was receiving favours from big business. It certainly did the trick, for Frank, his wife and daughter had a really enjoyable time and Frank returned fighting fit. On his return he told me: 'You have saved my life.'

While he was away I planned and developed a massive organizing campaign, using posters galore and broadsheets setting out union policies. We even tried gimmicks like TGWU beer mats, which had a good response and attracted comment in the newspapers. I moved around the regions, holding meetings of officers and shop stewards, stressing all the time the need for service to the members and laying emphasis on the importance of local negotiations on incentives and better conditions. Repeatedly I made the point: 'This union is not for the benefit of officers, it is a members' union in the full sense of the word or it is nothing. . . .'

A young personal assistant to Frank Cousins was an enthusiastic helper in the campaign; he was Norman Willis, now the General Secretary of the TUC. Norman had started work for the union as an office boy when he left school. Later he had secured a scholarship to Ruskin College, Oxford, and went on from there to the University. When he returned Frank felt it would be useful to have him to help with research. Norman was not overworked and I aroused his interest in a variety of projects needed to make the campaign a success. I think he would agree that he learned more about trade unionism in that period than in all the time he had spent at Oxford.

During this period the TUC produced plans for streamlining the trade union movement. George Woodcock told me it was a 'tidying-up operation', but it involved parts of the TGWU merging with other unions to form industrial unions, for example in the construction industry. The strength of the TGWU would be reduced without regard to the views of our members and I wasn't having any. In meeting after meeting with George Woodcock I emphasized that 'trade union members can't be treated like cattle to be bought and sold at the whim of theorists'. I stood firm and won that one.

A similar situation faced me when I was told that it would be a good idea if we 'swapped members' in certain industries and areas with the General and Municipal Workers Union. It would be nice, it was suggested, if *our* gas workers could join the other union while they transferred their bus workers to us. That might be nice and tidy, I said, but what about the members, how would they feel about it? There was no doubt that our members wanted to remain with the TGWU.

To combat some of these ideas and to present an alternative, I initiated joint talks between the leaders of the three big unions. Although politically and in other ways there were big differences between the Amalgamated Engineering Union, the General and Municipal Workers Union and the TGWU, as represented by their top men at the time, Bill Carron, Jack Cooper and Frank Cousins, I was interested to explore methods which would promote unity on the shop floor and provide better service for all their members.

I knew Carron and Cooper well personally so it wasn't difficult to get them into a discussion with Frank over a meal, together with David Basnett of the GMWU, Jim Conway of the AEU and myself. From this discussion I prepared a document calling for closer relationship between the unions and the examination of ways in which education, research and legal services might be linked or at least rationalized. A joint document was agreed and signed, but maybe the audacity of the first idea on joint educational development led to a halt in our endeavours. I had heard that Cliveden, the one-time home of the Astors, might be leased and it occurred to me that it could be used for residential trade union courses. I suggested we should go to see the place, pointing out that its proximity to London would be a great advantage. The idea was received with some amusement, because of the house's association with the pre-war Cliveden set and the Profumo scandal, but it was agreed to pay it a visit.

The estate is huge and the premises on the same scale. A great deal of work would have been required before it could have been used for trade union educational activity. As Bill Carron, Jack Cooper and Frank wandered round the house and grounds I sensed that they were already imagining themselves country squires. Laughingly they looked in at the massive bedrooms and joked about Christine Keeler and the rest. It was a little difficult to get down to serious discussion, but when we did there was a reluctance to face up to the consequences of joint activity and the joint control required. Finally it was decided that it would be too costly anyway. So the trade union movement lost a big opportunity. From that time onwards the movement for closer liaison between the three unions seemed to grow stale.

My concern with the effects of automation was central to my first speech to the Trades Union Congress at Blackpool in 1964. Moving the union's resolution which called for the introduction of a thirty-five hour week and at least three weeks' paid holiday a year, I explained that the programme served a double purpose, in seeking more leisure for workers and reducing the problem of unemployment as machines replaced workers in industry. Speeches like this call for meticulous preparation. From the information available within the union I was able to give fact after fact about the industrial changes taking place and company forecasts for future development. In many industries, I said 'men will become more and more button pushers; supervisors who watch instrument panels while the work is done for them by machines'.

I poured scorn on the 'amazing moderation of British unions' in not pressing for shorter hours and longer holidays while many other countries had made greater progress, and called for action by all unions. If it was forthcoming we could achieve not only three weeks' holiday a year but quickly go on to four weeks. The motion was carried unanimously and I like to feel that many unions were encouraged to fight harder. Progress was indeed made on the holiday front but we have yet to see decisive moves towards the thirty-five hour week for manual workers.

Harold Wilson gave the fraternal address from the Labour Party at the Blackpool Congress and was well received. He clearly anticipated a Labour victory in the General Election campaign which had just begun. I was impressed by his straight speaking and felt that, if only we could secure a sizeable majority in the election, we would be well on the way to achieving our socialist aims. There were more glamorous figures in the Parliamentary Labour Party but Wilson had a clear-cut approach and expertise on his side.

It was this view of Wilson which led me to support the idea of Frank Cousins joining the Labour Cabinet, when he mentioned the possibility following a discussion with Wilson prior to the election. I thought it was essential to have a strong trade union man in the cabinet. I also felt that Harold Wilson would be under attack from the right wing and would need the sort of support which Frank Cousins could give him. Knowing Frank's short temper I warned him against accepting the post of Minister of Labour. I thought he would worry too much if he took it, and would soon be involved in conflicts which would damage his health. I thought, too, that he would be in difficulty if he became Minister of Transport because of his close involvement with road transport. He seemed to be rather reluctant to accept these suggestions but he cheered up when the Ministry of Technology was put forward as a possibility.

Of course the firm offer of a Government job was not made until after the election. It took place on 15 October 1964, and Wilson offered Frank the position of Minister of Technology on the following day. It was clear that he could not accept the post without the agreement of the union's Executive Council but equally Wilson wanted a quick reply as a number of leading posts had already been announced, including that of George Brown as First Secretary and Minister of Economic Affairs. Immediately he had heard from Wilson, Frank told Harry Nicholas and me and we agreed to convene a special Executive meeting for the 17th. It was a Saturday and we had a fearful time getting our people together at such short notice. Meanwhile we discussed the matter together; there was little disagreement, because the three of us were satisfied that Frank should accept.

At the Executive meeting there was an atmosphere of expectancy on the part of everybody present and of course much pleasure that a Labour Government had been elected. The Labour Party had been out of office for thirteen years and there was great enthusiasm combined with hope for rapid progress. In fact the first thing decided by the meeting, on the suggestion of Frank Cousins, was the adoption of a resolution of congratulations to Harold Wilson, 'with an assurance of the support of the union in the endeavours which would undoubtedly be made to give effect to the policies contained in the General Election manifesto'.

Frank then made a long speech explaining that he had called the meeting to obtain their views on the invitation he had received from Wilson to become a minister in his new Government. It was a wide-ranging address, starting with the economic and other problems facing the new Government, and moving on to the reasons why he should accept the invitation and be granted leave of absence from his post.

This was a difficult one for him to put over, because he had many times insisted that he would stick with the union and that he regarded the General Secretaryship as the most important job in the country.

He presented his views as being the collective opinion of the Executive Officers and this was underlined by Harry Nicholas and me. I stressed the importance of having an authentic trade union voice inside the Cabinet and one we could really trust. There was great faith in Harold Wilson in our circles at that time but that confidence was not extended to most of the other Labour leaders. Roy Jenkins and George Brown (although a TGWU MP) were particularly suspect as right-wingers and in my view potentially disloyal to Wilson. Harold would need strong support if he was to pursue socialist policies and Frank was needed to fill that role, I told the meeting.

Almost to a man the Executive Council members supported Frank's request. One strong voice only was raised against it and that came from Bill Jones, the well-known London busman, a man for whom I had considerable respect. He argued that Frank was needed in the union and could do more to influence the TUC and the Labour Party by remaining at his post. He also feared that being in the Government would weaken Frank, because of the pressures that would be applied. His view looks more convincing in retrospect but it certainly was not accepted then.

With the granting of leave of absence to Frank, Harry Nicholas, the Assistant General Secretary, was appointed Acting General Secretary and I was given a step up and designated Acting Assistant General Secretary. Harry moved into the General Secretary's office but I stayed put in my old office. I was not sure how long the changes were likely to last.

Chapter Sixteen

Oh, the way is hard to go,
And the end is far to see,
And the progress may be slow,
And the body weary be,
Yet something in men's spirits
(What it is who shall reck?)
Keeps them dogged as they plod
On the Great, Great Trek.

'TOMFOOL' (in the
British Worker, May 1926)

The departure of Frank Cousins to the Government meant that he was no longer in regular contact with the union and in effect had no standing in our daily affairs. I much missed our frequent chats and did not establish the same relationships with Harry Nicholas. Harry tended to keep himself to himself.

When the special Executive Committee meeting was over, Frank Cousins walked over to Downing Street and Harry Nicholas left to lead an Executive party on a visit to Romania. The flight was due to depart that afternoon, so he had no time to discuss matters with me. For that immediate period I had sole responsibility for the day-to-day leadership, but I had no worries on that score because I had increasingly taken over major responsibilities from the day I moved into Transport House. I worked always on the principle that you carry out what is necessary, you don't wait to be asked. Sometimes that meant intervening in what others thought to be their business and I became aware of an undercurrent of resentment.

One of the difficulties which I faced was that a number of the National Officers (and some of our other full-time officials) still tended to side with the employers rather than our members. Equally, I had heard others define their role as being 'half-way between the members and the management' – which seemed to me in the end to create more problems than it solved. A trade union officer can be neither a policeman nor a middleman – he represents his members or he represents nothing. It was that outlook I adopted in the docks crisis which was facing the union at the moment Frank joined the Government. With Frank and Harry Nicholas away I became acting Chairman of the National Joint Council for the Port Transport Industry – the negotiating body at the centre of the crisis.

With my old loyalties to dockland very much in mind, I insisted on being involved. There was strong pressure from the members for a 25 shillings a week increase and Frank Cousins and Tim O'Leary (the National Docks Secretary of the union) had been turned down when they had recommended the port employers' offer of 12s 6d to the dockers' conference. What is more, the rank-and-file delegates had pressed for a month's notice to be given of strike action. I had studied the case in detail and was satisfied that the employers could afford more. There was no doubt that the members had strong grievances. An unofficial movement had been active and had fanned the flames of discontent, but I knew the issue was not artificial and that somewhere along the line we had begun to lose the leadership of the men.

A hurried meeting with the port employers, led by Andrew Crichton, was arranged and I confronted them with our intention to call a strike unless our claim was met. I was rough and sharp and my attitude seemed to startle the employers and, to a degree, the trade union party with me. They had been used to a much more conciliatory approach from Tim O'Leary, who had been an officer in the union from 1935 and believed in 'sweet reason', an attitude which was not always respected by the dockers. I knew him to be a conscientious worker, but on many things we did not see eye to eye.

Our brush with Crichton and his friends brought no change of heart, so off we went to meet Ray Gunter, who was then Minister of Labour. The meeting was at his request, made as soon as he had heard of the deadlock. I laid it on pretty thick, telling the Minister of the deep feelings in dockland and of our intention to go ahead with the strike. The outcome was a decision by the Minister to set up a Committee of Inquiry under Lord Devlin to establish the cause of the present dispute and to consider the problems of casual labour and other causes of dissension in the industry. While in some ways this development was welcome, because casual employment still bedevilled the industry, it did not help us with our current problem. I told Gunter that the strike would go ahead unless he could suggest something better and finally he promised me that the Devlin Committee would meet urgently and issue a quick interim report with a recommendation on the wage claim. It is amazing how rapidly things can happen under pressure!

The Committee was set up on 30 October 1964 and issued its interim report on 18 November. The recommendation was for an increase of 19s 2d per week and 5 per cent on piece-rates. Within days it was accepted and put into operation. It was a decided improvement on the employers' offer and the members welcomed it as a step forward.

A little earlier I had gone up to Liverpool with Frank Cousins and Tim O'Leary to a mass meeting of dockers held in the Stadium, Liverpool. Our reception was far from friendly. Mates I had known in the old days told me they were 'fed up' with the TGWU, and I was astounded to learn of the number of men who had joined the 'blue' union (the National Amalgamated Stevedores and Dockers Union). This had operated entirely in the London area until differences during Arthur Deakin's time led to a split. It was later expelled from the TUC for poaching TGWU members in the Northern ports. A number of the men who had deserted us I had known personally when I worked on the docks myself. When I tried to reason with them and pointed to my own record, their response was 'One swallow doesn't make a summer' and, 'Don't forget, Jack, you've been away from the docks for years.'

I determined to do all I could to repair the damage and made many visits to Merseyside, touring dockland, talking to members on the job and meeting our full-time officials and the lay committees. Apathy was widespread and we were under continuous attack from 'Blue' union activists, who had no responsibility so could afford to be irresponsible. The division between the two unions had led to a considerable number of dockers becoming non-unionists. I could have wept, for even in the difficult days I had known we had kept people in the union. We had taught them that the only way forward was to try to make the union better. Now I was faced by a shambles. The most amazing feature in the whole business, to me, was that few people in the higher echelons of the union seemed to know or care.

It was a slow road back. Some changes among the full-time officials were effected. I sought the co-operation of officials and active members in negotiating extra payments and bonuses here and there. The arrangements for dealing with disputes were decentralized. This last was of great importance, because many issues had been dealt with behind the backs of the membership by the District Secretary, who had followed an outmoded practice. Had we gone on that way we would have had no union left at all.

Most NAS&D members in London were solid trade unionists and that was true of its General Secretary, Dickie Barrett. As sharp as quicksilver, he was a cockney through and through. In the summer he would leave his office and go hop-picking down in Kent with friends and their families. He had fallen out with Arthur Deakin, which was not difficult, and on certain points the two unions had been at daggers drawn. I felt that only the port employers gained by our division and I had a number of chats with Dick Barrett and his mates to see what was needed to mend our fences. We did not solve any problems in the early stages, but simply by getting to know each other we removed a lot of suspicion.

The Devlin Committee was proceeding with its examination of decasualization and other matters, but few thought the outcome of the Inquiry would be important. Union officials and rank-and-file dockers alike were saying: 'It will be just another load of whitewash!' I was not directly involved; I did, however, know two members of the Committee quite well, Jack Scamp and Hugh Clegg, an Oxford academic who specialized in labour relations – and I made my views on the industry known to them. According to union protocol I should not have involved myself at all, yet I knew that what I saw as the overwhelming case for a system of shop stewards throughout the ports would not be put by our official spokesmen. The idea that shop stewards were disruptive, which was around in Arthur Deakin's time, still prevailed in some circles and I was afraid it might be accepted by the Inquiry.

I explained my position to Jack Scamp and had a number of discussions with him, reminding him of our joint experiences with shop stewards over the years. I quoted instances where urgent grievances on the job had been resolved, without a stoppage of work, with the aid of the shop steward.

The submission from the TGWU to the Inquiry was, it was said, contained on half a sheet of notepaper. Of course verbal evidence was given, and for the rest the Committee members themselves visited dockland to make their own observations. Its Report and recommendations were far-reaching, even revolutionary, and much of it I welcomed with open arms. I said so quickly and in public, so that no carping criticism should mar the implementation of what was good in it.

I worked might and main to make sure that the dockers themselves would know what was in the Report and that they should be consulted in the ensuing negotiations. It required a campaign, and I did all that was possible to engender a campaigning spirit, trying to put life into officials who had lost heart or had become complacent. The prize as I saw it would be a major improvement in the conditions in dockland and the restoration of our union's standing.

The Devlin Report gave me good reason to contact Dick Barrett of the 'Blue' union once again, and this time I brought in Bill Lindley, the General Secretary of the Watermen, Lightermen, Tugmen and Bargemen's Union, to act as a sort of unofficial referee. I was on friendly terms with Bill and I knew he would help our discussions along. He too is very much a cockney character, not unlike one of W. W. Jacobs' well-known waterfront types. Our good-humoured discussion laid the keel for trade union peace in dockland. Dick Barrett agreed that the 'blues' would cease recruiting members in the Northern ports and we promised to help them secure a place on a new negotiating body to represent their London members.

Around this period I seemed to be perpetually dashing round to staunch the loss of membership or helping to retrieve it. The water-front was still the scene of much trouble, with loss of membership in the fishing industry adding to our difficulties among the dockers. Our trawler-fishing membership had dwindled to almost nothing in Grimsby and a new union had been formed under the direction of a rather aristocratic retired skipper, Charles Chapple. It was going great guns and seemed likely to spread to other ports. I realized the gap had to be closed quickly and dashed to Grimsby. My enquiries brought a bleak response from our officers on the spot and the few members we had left in the industry, so I bearded the lion in his den and walked in to confront Mr Chapple. I found a friendly old chap, who was well into his seventies, ready to talk about anything and only concerned to help the trawlermen. I believe that he was struck by my sincerity for I was as anxious as he was to get the trawlermen a better deal. Conditions were scandalous to say the least. 'Look, my boy,' he said, 'if you can really help I won't stand in the way. I'm spending my own money trying to get this thing off the ground and I can ill afford it but I felt something must be done. . . .' From that time onwards we got on well and finally the United Fishermen's Union merged with the TGWU.

I had never formed a high opinion of Joint Industrial Councils, which all too often had seemed to me to be talking shops from which only meagre concessions were obtained. The NJIC for the Trawler Fishing Industry was like that, and our leadership had suffered through a long period of inattention by the National Officer. Admittedly it was not easy to arouse the interest and support of the trawlermen in their own cause. Short periods ashore between trips encouraged heavy drinking and it was almost impossible to get the men together to discuss their problems. I was sure that what was required was representatives, the equivalent of shop stewards, aboard the trawlers, but the idea was anathema to the owners.

A short holiday Evelyn and I had around this time in Guernsey helped to strengthen the union's position in the fishing industry. It was our first visit to the Channel Islands and we enjoyed it immensely. The weather was ideal and each day Dave Shenton, the TGWU officer on the island, came to the boarding house where we were staying and took us out to one of the beaches. There Evelyn and I would pass the day, eating our sandwiches and buying tea and an occasional glass of brandy from a convenient stall. The sun shone marvellously and we had fun in and out of the sea.

The evenings we spent walking around Peter Port and visiting the local pubs with friends from the union. The atmosphere was jovial, with lively discussions about union experiences and other matters. During our stay I got to know Dave Shenton very well and, with Evelyn, visited his family in their home. It became clear to me that he was top officer material. He had an attractive personality and possessed solid ability. Prior to taking up his job in Guernsey he had spent some time at sea and then for a period had earned his living as a bus driver. On an island where drink was cheap and plentiful he had remained a modest drinker. What impressed me most was his continuing interest in maritime affairs; for example he was a member of the Guernsey lifeboat crew. I recalled his qualities when a vacancy occurred for the Regional Secretaryship covering Hull and the East Coast Region. I urged him to apply for the post, because I felt that a man of his ability should at least be considered. Other able people applied but in the examination he was outstanding, and he was duly appointed. His untimely death some years later robbed the union of a splendid leader.

Regional Secretaries in the TGWU are highly influential people. Men like Dave Shenton in Hull and Grimsby and Raymond Macdonald in Scotland made their presence felt in the major fishing areas. The union increasingly became recognized as the 'voice of the fishermen' and membership grew apace. With this increasing strength I was able to articulate the anxieties of the men and their communities over their low standard of living, the health hazards and the terrible impact of trawler losses at sea.

At the Annual Conference of the Labour Party in December 1964 I was elected to the National Executive Committee. The conference had been delayed because of the General Election and, of course, there was a great deal of enthusiasm. We were all expecting great things from Harold Wilson and the new Labour Government and his speech to the conference confirmed him, in my mind, as an able leader. When he stood for the leadership of the Party, following Gaitskell's death, I had done all I could to gain support from parliamentarians for his nomination, despite the fact that George Brown, his main opponent, was a TGWU-sponsored MP and his constituency was in my region. The fact was that I differed sharply with George on most matters affecting the Party and I felt, especially, that he had been disloyal to the union and Frank Cousins over our 'H' bomb policy. So I had applauded Wilson's election as leader, and eagerly looked forward to the prospect of his Government.

The first meetings of the National Executive Committee did not impress me much. With the exception of the trade union section nearly all the members held Government office. Harold Wilson made it clear that he did not expect members of the Government to oppose him, and they did not. They appeared to wish to impress Wilson almost to the point of obeisance. There was a clear desire to avoid discussions on policy and to get the meetings over as quickly as possible. As soon as it was apparent that the essential business had been disposed of, the Ministers would trip out. I thought that this was treating the NEC as a cipher, but when I protested I was put in my place by the built-in majority of establishment members.

Early on in my membership of the NEC I was approached by Ray Gunter and Len Williams (the General Secretary of the Labour Party), who invited me to have a drink with them and then in a friendly fashion told me that 'the trade union section always vote together, Jack', and 'we hope you will follow the same pattern'. I told them that if that meant I would be expected always to vote with the top of the table, it was not on. My reaction surprised them a little but they were obviously anxious to avoid an argument.

From then on I was given little encouragement. The method adopted for election to the major subcommittees was a little peculiar. Members were circulated with a list of the subcommittees and invited to indicate which they wished to serve on. The General Secretary then made the selection. Although I asked to serve on the Overseas Subcommittee, in view of its relevance to the work of the TGWU and the fact that my colleague Harry Nicholas (whom I was in effect replacing) had previously been a member, I was kept off. It was a rebuke to me for daring to challenge the accepted order of things. However, I secured membership of the Home Policy Subcommittee. I guess they felt that the TGWU nominee could hardly be prevented from playing a part on the subcommittee which dealt with economic affairs. Perhaps it was this which led that subcommittee to appointing me Labour Party representative on the Economic Committee of the TUC.

During the whole of 1965 and 1966 I was thus able to acquaint myself with the work of a principal committee of the TUC. I was welcomed by George Woodcock, who encouraged me to speak in the committee from time to time, although the tradition was for the Labour Party representative to 'see all and say nowt'. Some TUC General Council members regarded George as a colourless 'desiccated calculating machine', fitting the description Bevan once applied to Gaitskell. In this they may have been partly right, but George had great ability and underneath the surface had a warm and friendly nature. He was very different from most of the members of the Economic Committee and appeared to treat them with disdain.

For some reason George Woodcock joined forces with George Brown, First Secretary of the new Department of Economic Affairs, in promoting a Joint Statement of Intent on 'productivity, prices and incomes', shortly after the formation of the new Labour Government. The TUC signed the statement, together with the CBI and the Government. It was hurriedly constructed and highly generalized and I saw it as a gimmick designed to conceal the introduction of a statutory incomes policy. It was launched in theatrical fashion at a ceremony in Lancaster House with George Brown performing an evangelical role, over-selling the benefits of an incomes policy. What a smooth-tongued operator he was – a man who could have sold pork from a stall in Israel!

Perhaps the hurry in issuing the Joint Statement was due to the pressure on the pound, but the iron fist soon replaced the velvet glove with the setting-up of a Prices and Incomes Board. George Woodcock and George Brown had been at great pains to stress the voluntary nature of the policy, but the wage restraint aspect could not be disguised and the TGWU voted against it at the Special Conference of the TUC. George Brown seemed to be obsessed with incomes policy. Running into him in the House of Commons I told him: 'The trouble with you, George, is that you're miles away from the shop floor. The norms you are talking about will mean a bad deal for the low-paid workers and you know it. You are doing the employers' job for them.' He did not like sharp criticism of this kind and his response was to bluster and bully. I strongly resented the fact that economic controls and planning were missing in the Government's policies. Brown, who had manipulated himself into the role of guru of the Government's economic affairs, was, I thought, making a half-baked approach to the crisis. I could not stomach the idea of pushing wages down while Brown and others were attempting to justify big increases in the salaries of MPs. The situation was made worse when the Government decided to defer increases in old-age pensions. I told George Brown in rough terms that this was totally unacceptable. His response was that I was a carping critic.

My relationship with Brown had been strained for many years, dating back to an occasion in the East Midlands. It was an annual dinner at which many union members and their wives were present. He was the MP for the area and I was the Regional Secretary. When it came to the speeches George was called upon first and in a drawling and supercilious manner launched an attack on the TGWU's 'H' bomb policy. Although it was a social occasion I hit back, accusing Brown of disloyalty to the union. I contrasted his efforts with those of Frank Cousins and suggested that Brown's life had been cushioned by the help given to him by the union. 'You owe everything to the union, yet you are doing everything you can to undermine the leadership,' I said. After the function concluded the argument went on. About a dozen shop stewards got into a corner with Brown and myself. As the drink flowed, Brown at first adopted an apologetic tone, almost ingratiating. Before long, however, we were involved in a raging argument, with George at his most blustering. Finally, looking a greenish white and clearly having had too much to drink, he was persuaded to leave. Many similar incidents occurred in subsequent years.

The person I most respected in the NEC was Peggy Herbison, a miner's daughter and very much a woman of her local community. She fought like a tiger for the pensioners. She was straight and true and we got on like a house on fire. Bessie Braddock, on the other hand, appeared severe and aloof. I had known her in Liverpool as a fighting left-winger but now she had embraced the establishment. At times she seemed to doubt Harold Wilson and implied that he was being too soft with the Left. In years past she had gone overboard in supporting Hugh Gaitskell and attacked any criticism of him as being communist inspired. She was highly critical of Nye Bevan, although she softened towards him at the end. Bevan was undoubtedly enigmatic and an individualist, but so was Bessie. In other respects they were very different indeed.

On the NEC I determined to secure what benefits I could for union members, to emphasize the practical, and not to be too disturbed by the foibles of politicians.

Chapter Seventeen

Where are those who will come to
serve the people – not utilize them
for their own ambitions?

PETER KROPOTKIN

Problems within the union involved me in much travelling throughout the country. This inevitably meant that home life suffered, imposing great strain on Evelyn. When I was in London I would invariably arrive home late, due to crisis meetings or preparation for important conferences. At other times I would be away for days on end, too often including weekends. But always Evelyn would be at home when I returned, smiling, encouraging, interested in my work; she gave me strength when I felt too tired even for conversation.

Activity with the local Labour Party and as magistrate occupied a lot of Evelyn's time. Through the Labour Party and residents' committee work she made contact with many folk in our block of flats and arranged Labour Party discussion meetings in the living-room of our small flat. Attendances were assured by the celebrities she brought in as speakers – Konni Zilliacus, Michael Foot, Ian Mikardo and others. The meetings were packed and always animated. Sometimes when I arrived home late, the meetings would still be going full blast (aided by plentiful supplies of Evelyn's coffee). I would be in no mood to get myself involved, so would slip off to bed.

On my travels I built up a picture of industrial Britain. Everywhere I met union officials and shop stewards and became closely involved in local problems. I felt then and feel now that being part of the working community – actively linked with ordinary people – is essential for any trade union leader worth his salt. My knowledge of local industry and links with trade unionists in the district certainly helped during the Nuneaton by-election fought by Frank Cousins in January 1965. One old trade union man asked me: 'What do you think about this fellow Cousins, Jack? He's not going to be a fly-by-night is he?' I

171

sought to reassure the man, and stressed the value of having a trade union voice in the Government. Nevertheless the question revealed an underlying anxiety I detected among many whom I met during the election campaign.

In November 1964 I led a TGWU delegation to the USSR. I hadn't been to Russia before and was pleased that the opportunity had fallen to me. Those accompanying me were all rank-and-file members of the union's Executive: Bill Jones, the London busman; Alf Allen, our shop stewards' convenor at the big Longbridge motor-car plant – both old friends – together with Cynog Jones and George Cook, a chemical plant operator and an electrical power worker respectively. We were a good team and conscientious in our efforts to find out as much as possible about that most interesting country and its people.

We were the guests of the Motor Transport Union, which enabled us to visit many factories in Moscow, Leningrad, Odessa and Kiev. Our practical experience meant that we could appreciate what was good and what was bad. Despite the language barrier we felt a sense of camaraderie; that sort of immediate understanding cannot be disguised. Of course we saw the sights and met many important political and trade union leaders, but our overwhelming impression was of a people struggling against a difficult past, painfully but successfully. From then on I thought it would be a good thing for working people from both countries to get to know each other by two-way exchanges. Barriers could be broken down in a way diplomats were unlikely to achieve.

I did not have close contact with Frank Cousins in his new Ministry and never heard him speak in the House of Commons, but when I did see him I noticed he kept to his old eating habits. On one occasion that I had to see him I went over to the House of Commons about lunch-time. After transacting our business he said: 'We'd better have something to eat.' I thought, 'Hello! Frank's going to take me to the dining-room for a slap-up meal,' but not on your life. We went to the quick-service cafeteria and I stood in the queue with the Minister of Technology and a bevy of staff workers. There were no MPs about. When Frank got to the counter he demanded three pieces of fish – two for him and one for me – with some bread and butter. He seemed reluctant to pay but eventually forked out. I was quite hungry and could have managed another piece of fish, but thought I had best leave well alone. On our occasional meetings I kept him informed about developments at the TGWU, because I realized he was missing the union atmosphere, the cut and thrust and the comradeship. Frank was especially sensitive to any criticism which implied that he had let the members down by going into the Government. He need not have been, for it was very much a minority view. The members generally had a high regard for him and the reassurance I was able to give him on that point gave him some comfort. Nonetheless there were one or two senior officers at Transport House who encouraged the idea that Frank should resign. It seemed to me that they yearned for a return to the comfortable days of Arthur Deakin. Their efforts gained little support, although a few left-wing members backed them on the grounds that pressure for Cousins' resignation might force him to return to the General Secretaryship.

When this got to Frank Cousins' ears, it disturbed him so much that he decided to pay an unannounced visit to the union's Biennial Conference at Portsmouth in July 1965. He received an enthusiastic welcome and was left in no doubt about the overwhelming goodwill the delegates felt towards him. While in Portsmouth, he told me about the arguments that were taking place inside the Cabinet and of his determination to fight against a statutory incomes policy.

I had every confidence in Frank as a man who would fight his corner anywhere, but from his own account and information which reached me from other sources (it's amazing how well informed pressmen are in such matters) I realized he was conducting a lone battle. He started out thinking that Harold Wilson was a friend with whom he would work in close harmony and who would respond favourably to his guidance, but soon became bitterly disappointed and increasingly critical. For the rest of the Cabinet he appeared to feel total disdain. He had no one around him with whom to share confidences and work out a strategy. Nor, as far as I could see, was he disposed to seek allies, even weak ones.

Enthusiasm for his work as Minister of Technology kept Frank from resigning until July 1966, although he frequently mentioned the possibility. On incomes policy especially there was a growing division between trade union opinion and the Government, and Frank found his position in the Cabinet less and less tolerable. His experience strengthened my view that there should have been more people with manual working experience in the Cabinet and in Parliament. Had there been others with him who had endured the rough and tumble of the workers' side of industrial life, his stand would have been more effective. Intellectuals and career politicians have an overweening sense of 'knowing it all', and it was their dominance in Government that swamped Frank's lone efforts.

Within the NEC of the Labour Party I was continually pressing for stronger policies on industrial democracy which would involve workers directly. One opportunity which presented itself was the setting-up of a special study group on the docks industry by the Home Policy Sub-committee of the NEC. It was a hard-working group and brought to-gether among others an industrialist, Michael Montague, and Tam Dalyell and Ian Mikardo, the Labour MPs. Mikardo acted as chairman. I was the only member with dock-working experience. We pushed along at a great pace, visiting ports, taking evidence and reading innumerable papers. Mikardo impressed me by his clarity of mind and eye for detail. He was a splendid chairman. I also experienced much support from Tam Dalyell. 'Jack, is it really like that?' he would ask when we came across some special aspect of dockland. He always wanted to get the facts and examine them in a sensitive and sympathetic manner. Unfortunately some of the union officers who gave evidence were a disappointment and gave the impression of lacking confidence in their own class. On one visit as our party was about to walk the quays I ran into the docks union official on his way home . . . at four o'clock in the afternoon!

Our examination established beyond doubt (at least to my mind) that the industry suffered from the lack of a national framework for planning investment and development, and that development and modernization was being held back by fragmentation of responsibilities and the existence of a large number of separate employers. This was the main reason for the survival of casual employment and the bad labour relations which arose from it. The report of the study group recommended a fundamental reorganization of the port transport industry, involving national planning based on a major extension of public ownership. We called for a single public employer with a sub-stantial degree of worker participation in management; the report went on: '. . . At dock level there should be a Group Operating Com-mittee – which will be the main organ of de-centralized dock operation. The Dock Manager and his principal officers would be members. Other members would be directly elected by local workers through union machinery.'

I had succeeded in establishing my view to a limited extent and made sure that some of the principles were written into the General Election manifesto when it came before the NEC prior to the election in April 1966. But promises are not always kept, and although George Brown on behalf of the leadership publicly accepted the conclusions of the report, Labour ministers showed a less than keen interest in implementing our ideas.

On the NEC criticism of the Government came mainly from Ian Mikardo, Tom Driberg and myself, with occasional support from Danny McGarvey of the Boilermakers Union. Some of the Ministers shared our disquiet but they were muted in debate and never risked voting against the Government. All of them were friendly to me, no doubt due to my TGWU connection. Dick Crossman went out of his way to establish contact and opened his heart about the faults of the Party machine, as he saw them. He was critical of Len Williams, the General Secretary, accusing him of being heavy-handed and insensitive. He felt that Len was neither a good administrator nor a good politician, and should be replaced by someone who would be the political leader in the field and virtually deputy to the leader.

I had known Dick since his adoption meeting for the Coventry Parliamentary seat many years previously. He had always been careful to avoid interference in trade union matters. I admired him for that and we got on reasonably well together, although he typified for me the academic who, in working-class parlance, 'didn't know his arse from his elbow'. His speeches were difficult to follow and often he appeared to contradict himself, although I am sure he must have been very clever. I invited him on one occasion to meet the General Executive Council of the TGWU in order to explain his proposals for a National Superannuation Scheme. I can still see the wonder on the faces of those rank-and-file workers. They could hardly understand a word of it and I was almost as confused as they were.

Discontent with the absence of liaison between the Ministers and the NEC finally led to a joint meeting at Chequers early in 1966. Talk of a General Election was in the air and Harold Wilson wanted to generate as much goodwill as possible. Despite the complaints made during previous NEC meetings, it was only Mikardo and I who made critical speeches. I made a strong attack on the idea of statutory sanctions related to incomes policy which George Brown was pushing, and urged the development of an alternative policy based on increased productivity, with joint committees of management and union representatives at the workplace. My theme was 'trust the workers' and, 'instead of penalizing them – involve them!' I was met with smiles and friendly comment from George Brown, who was careful not to antagonize me, but gave no assurances. The same thing happened to Ian Mikardo, who pressed for selective investment to build up our industrial base.

It was the first time that I had been to Chequers and I was intrigued by the sense of history that prevailed throughout the house. It really ought to be opened up to the general public; for youngsters especially it would bring back to life important moments of our history. The great benefit of holding a conference there is the opportunity it provides for informal conversations. Wilson buttonholed each one of us in turn and, in the process, told me in a very confidential manner of the difficulties he was having getting our point of view across to the Americans. There was no doubt, he said, that he would have much more influence with President Johnson on Vietnam if we could send in a token force. It would only need to be small, maybe thirty men or so, and they could be virtually non-combatant. Their presence would be enough. Did I not agree? And would I use my influence to get the idea across? I made it clear that I would not be party to such an idea and that for him or anyone else to press it would split the movement.

When the manifesto for the General Election was drawn up there was a remarkable mix-up of activity. Different people were involved in drafting and I moved in at every opportunity to ensure that a trade union point of view came through. One point I remember pressing was: 'We shall . . . recognize the right to trade union representation and ensure proper safeguards against arbitrary dismissal.' I was well placed to participate since the Labour Party offices were housed in Transport House, our headquarters. When important things were being decided I tried to put my spoke in. To counteract the moanings of Ray Gunter and George Brown about 'unofficial strikes' (they seemed to be obsessed with their wrongness without trying to understand their causes) I was able to insert: 'To supplement voluntary collective bargaining by substantially increasing the voluntary industrial arbitration and conciliation machinery,' including 'on the spot investigations'. It was an advantage to have had more experience of the industrial scene than the others. George Brown and I had a tussle over his strong desire for a statutory incomes policy, 'a policy with teeth' as he frequently demanded. He badly wanted a manifesto commitment, but with a bit of effort I was able to circumvent his wishes. There were no references to early warnings, sanctions and penalties. Although he went ahead with these later, it was not with the backing of a strict commitment in the election manifesto.

The NEC included a lot of ambitious people, busy whispering, manipulating, trying to gain the limelight. In the light of subsequent events it may be of interest to mention that Tony Benn, at that time, stood aside from the manoeuvring. He was a thoughtful, competent young man, who appeared to me a little colourless.

Altogether I was reasonably satisfied with my efforts on the manifesto. In addition to gaining a commitment to public ownership of the docks industry, a commitment had been given for an extension of industrial democracy through the setting-up of 'pay and productivity committees'. But of course it is results that matter, and although the policies were good, and the 1966 General Election result very much better than I expected, when it came to action the new Government was a disappointment.

I was invited to serve on the IRC (Industrial Reorganization Corporation) under Frank Kearton. I turned it down, as I had done previously an invitation to serve as a Governor of the BBC, because I wanted to devote maximum time to my work in the union. One invitation I could not refuse, though, was from the NEC itself, to chair a working party on 'Industrial Democracy'. Despite all the fine speeches the leadership suddenly realized they were short of practical ideas. It was a well-balanced and able committee and we produced a report within a short space of time. It stimulated a lot of thinking in the movement, opening up new approaches to the problem including the emphasis (with which I was especially concerned) on having one channel for worker representation – i.e. the shop steward and the trade union movement – whether in consultation, negotiation or on policy-making boards. The report was well received and its proposals were approved by the Party Conference. Barbara Castle picked up a number of points to sugar the pill of her 'In Place of Strife' proposals and Harold Wilson took a chunk from the report and put it into a major speech as though it was his own. He wrote to me afterwards in acknowledgement. So that, I thought, is how speeches are written!

Readers may wonder what I did in my spare time. Well, the fact is I hardly had any. I was reading Labour Party documents and TUC papers in bed or on the train or plane, and whenever I could I was studying books and papers on the technicalities of port and road transport. My main enjoyment was having a few drinks with the lads, the active members of the union, wherever this was possible. If I visited a factory or docks I would finish up in a local pub, thrashing out ideas with shop stewards and local officials. When my home life began to suffer, I arranged for Evelyn to accompany me on visits whenever possible. Women shop stewards particularly welcomed this, because she was able to draw on her own industrial experience in giving advice and help or sympathetically listening to the troubles of the workshop. The example we tried to set, of a man and a woman acting as partners, each with their own point of view, was a great success with the women, whether they were activists or wives attending social functions. The men too reacted favourably to Evelyn, for she was as good a trade unionist as anyone.

The vague ideas I had held in 1966 about a 'social contract' were quickly dashed by the events which followed the General Election. The only thing the Government seemed determined to push through was the prices and incomes policy. They were overwhelmed by economic events and they floundered. The Government used a hammer to crack a nut when it brought in the Emergency Powers Act to smash the seamen's strike. Then they introduced statutory enforcement powers into the Prices and Incomes Act, which led to the resignation of Frank Cousins from the Government.

I wrote at the time:

> The legislation will further tilt the balance in favour of . . . employers and worsen industrial relations at a time when there is a pressing need to tackle the problem of low productivity and inefficiency. The trouble is that the authors of these policies are out of touch with day-to-day industrial life and are unfitted to solve its problems. If they had their way we would have an emasculated trade union movement with little or no influence to bring to bear on behalf of its members. In my view weak or tame trade unionism is a positive danger under a Labour or any other Government. . . .

George Brown and other ministers seemed to be operating in a different world. Frank Cousins made this point in his speech to the House of Commons following his resignation. He said that in the 1964 and 1966 General Elections and at Party Conferences the policy put to the electorate had been based on the planned growth of the economy. This included wages. But the new approach simply turned on restraining wages. Our worst fears were realized when shortly afterwards Harold Wilson told Parliament there would be a six-month standstill on wages and salaries, followed by a further six months of severe restraint.

I was a frequent visitor to the House of Commons during this period and was approached by a number of left-wing MPs who asked me to press Frank to become 'the leader of the Left'. I explained that he had a job to do back in the union now that he was out of the Government but, at the behest of Eric Heffer, I did urge Frank to sign a Tribune Group motion condemning the Government's policy and putting forward an alternative strategy. On one of these visits I was involved in a bitter altercation with George Brown. I was having a drink in the small bar at the House of Commons, with two or three MPs including Ray Gunter. We were having an amicable discussion on some of the industrial problems of the day when Brown walked in. He was clearly under the influence and proceeded to pick a quarrel with me. He accused me of arranging Frank's resignation and of being 'a bloody red'. Shouting in an hysterical fashion, he then accused the union of 'messing up the works', and said that he wouldn't have it and he would take on Frank, me, and anyone else that opposed him. Gunter and the others were very embarrassed and eventually shuffled George out of the bar.

At about 7.30 the following morning I was phoned by Harry Nicholas to say that George Brown would like to see us both at his residence in Carlton Gardens, if possible in an hour's time. I agreed and we went along, to be met by a sheepish and conciliatory George. He apologized profusely, saying that he had had a busy day and the job was punishing in its demands upon him. Having got that over, he insisted we joined him in a large gin and tonic. I thought it odd to start drinking at that hour, but to be friendly Harry and I accepted. Over the drinks his mood appeared to change, there were signs of squalls ahead, the pouting lip was appearing and he became more irritable, so I suggested we leave.

Frank Cousins' return to the union caused problems at Transport House. Frank was inclined to treat Harry Nicholas rather roughly while Harry resented losing his office and was concerned about his salary and his car. I did my best to act as a peacemaker. Finally we recommended that the Union's Executive Council should increase Frank's salary by £500, whilst maintaining the status quo in the case of Harry's salary and my own. This avoided any reduction in salary and ensured a £500 differential. The resulting salaries were:

General Secretary (Frank)	£3,750
Assistant General Secretary (Harry)	£3,250
Assistant Executive Secretary (me)	£2,750

We were hardly being overpaid and Frank Cousins' resignation from the Government meant a big financial sacrifice for him. One problem arising from the change concerned motor cars. Harry maintained his status with a new Vauxhall Viscount Power-glide, while Frank got a Rover. I kept my Ford Zephyr.

More trouble arose when the subject of nominations for the TUC General Council cropped up. Frank naturally expected to go back on the Council but Harry (who had served on the General Council in place of Cousins during the latter's period in Government) wanted to keep his place. The other TGWU member of the Council was Len Forden, the lay Chairman of the Executive and a Manchester busman. I consulted him on the problem and he cheerfully offered to stand down and allow both Cousins and Nicholas to go forward. It was a tremendous act of self-sacrifice, because he was close (in terms of seniority) to becoming the TUC Chairman. But that was typical of Len, a man whose character was a good example to the rest of us.

One issue remained unsettled for some weeks following Frank Cousins' resignation. To my own surprise I found that he expected to remain in Parliament while resuming his duties as General Secretary. His Labour supporters in Nuneaton wanted it, and so did he. I accompanied him to a meeting in the constituency after the union Executive had made it clear that Frank must resign as an MP. It fell to me to explain the Executive's position and I had a difficult time. I pointed out that both jobs carried full-time responsibilities and it would be physically impossible to carry them out satisfactorily. This view was reluctantly accepted.

I went on fighting the union's corner as tenaciously as I could on the NEC. At nearly every meeting I was urging changes in government policy on incomes, on Vietnam and on unemployment. On incomes policy the leadership got its way. I could only attract support from Mikardo and Driberg, with some sympathetic noises from Willy Simpson of the Foundryworkers. I won a little more sympathy over Vietnam and on two emergency motions from the TGWU, one expressing concern over the sharp rise in unemployment and calling for short-time working as an alternative to redundancy dismissals; the other demanding cuts in defence expenditure and the abandonment of East of Suez commitments. Barbara Castle tried to help on these motions and earned Wilson's displeasure. Although I had reason to fall out with her on various occasions, I have always admired her courage and ability. At the Party Conference of October 1966 our two emergency motions were carried, although we were heavily defeated over incomes policy. Frank had an enthusiastic response from the Conference floor and our success with the unemployment resolution was greatly welcomed by a lobby of motor-car workers from the Midlands. Frank and I went out of the Conference to see them and amongst the crowd I recognized many old friends from Coventry.

I was again elected to the NEC but 1967 was to be my last year. Harry Nicholas was not re-nominated for the TUC General Council, his place being taken by Bill Jones, the London busman, who was not so self-effacing as Len Forden. Harry was clearly upset by this and I offered to stand down from the NEC so that he could take that position. I was out in the cold from the counsels of the movement but it was no skin off my nose, I had plenty of work to do on the industrial front.

Chapter Eighteen

Early in 1966 a crisis came in the Hull docks. There had been many unofficial actions over rates of pay and conditions on the job and sharp differences existed between the men and the full-time officers of the union. Membership had dwindled. With Tim O'Leary, I visited the port. After talking to the officials I insisted that we go on to the docks for an on-the-spot chat with the dockers.

As we moved around the quays and on the ships we were cat-called and hostility was shown by many of the men. Eventually I persuaded some of them to talk to me and they poured out their complaints. Time after time, they claimed, they had been let down by their officers. Details were given and I asked: 'Why haven't you raised these issues at the branch meetings?' 'We have done,' they replied, 'but the officers hardly ever attend the meetings.' I told them I would send an officer up from London to try to put things right and that there would be a full investigation. Many of the dockers did not believe me but I established a rapport with the unofficial leader of the men, Harry Spavin, a straightforward and decent man, who I could see was inclined to accept my word. He and others persuaded the dockers to give us a chance to correct the position.

I was able to persuade a very efficient docks officer operating in the Port of London, Tom Cronin, to spend some months in Hull. He quickly got to grips with the situation, negotiating improvements in timework and piecework rates and working arrangements together with the introduction of a shop stewards system. The atmosphere in the port changed in our favour despite obstruction from the three full-time officers. One hundred and thirty-seven members were regained for the union. It was clear, however, that action had to be taken against the three officers and a full-scale Executive Inquiry took place under my leadership. This resulted in the dismissal of the officers concerned.

Throughout the union the impact of the dismissals was considerable. Hitherto it had hardly been heard of for officials to get the sack except for embezzlement and in the political dismissals of 1949. It certainly had a salutory effect on some full-time officials, who were not known for energetic activity. It established, too, that although officers are appointed by the Executive of the TGWU (except the General Secretary, who is elected by a ballot of the general membership) rather than by election as in a number of other unions, there is a degree of democratic control. Not that I was satisfied. The Hull experience only sharpened my determination to bring about more democracy in the union, with every official responsible to an elected committee within his area of operation.

I had thought for some time that opposition to wage restraint on the part of the union was in itself not enough. We needed to develop a policy which would unite the union, develop constructive discussion and help to raise the standard of living of the low-paid workers. We should come forward with a positive, alternative policy.

In opposing the Government's prices and incomes policy the TGWU had been in a minority at both the 1966 Trades Union Congress and the Labour Party Conference and Frank and Harry were edgy on the point. I prepared a paper setting out a detailed case for £15 as a minimum wage and proposing that an attempt should be made to set up negotiations between the TUC and the newly constituted Confederation of British Industry (CBI). This, I argued, would put the spotlight on low wages. Other issues could be the forty-hour week, leading to a thirty-five hour week, and a minimum of three weeks' holiday with pay. Of course I knew that these targets looked unrealistic at first sight but my idea was to arouse the movement to a united campaign.

In our early-morning meetings at Transport House, which had been resumed following Frank's return to the General Secretaryship, I was able to persuade him my idea was a runner. We agreed to push the proposals forward at the union Executive and the TUC, and generally to start a campaign. Speakers' notes were produced and meetings arranged. I organized a launch meeting with the support of my friends in the London and Home Counties Region of the union. It was held at Central Hall, Westminster, and we filled the place with shop stewards, local committeemen and officials. 'At last, Jack, we've got something to sell!' said Bert Fry, the Regional Secretary.

In retrospect I think our efforts were puny. We should have risked the expense of sophisticated publicity, using TV and large newspaper advertisements and big posters on the hoardings. The union was big enough to afford it and it would have put the policy on the map. The fact is that none of us in the TGWU dared to think in that fashion at the time. True, our ideas were accepted in a routine kind of way by the TUC General Council, and adopted at the following Congress, and were seen as good points for discussion, but there was no effort by the TUC to win public support. The Communist Party and the Left in general were not happy about the policy, but the real reason for lack of action was the overwhelming inertia of most union leaders. They tended to oppose change and in any case were afraid of upsetting the Government.

One aspect of our policy was the emphasis on productivity agreements. I addressed dozens of conferences and wrote articles on the theme for a variety of publications from the *News of the World* to *Tribune*. In my article in the *News of the World* I said:

> Too many disputes in industry . . . seem to arise from inadequate communication, lack of understanding of agreements and lack of consultation. To deal with this situation, trade union officials and shop stewards should surely have the right to hold meetings of their members on works premises, and when necessary during working hours. Given this approach, productivity agreements represent not only the chance to secure bigger pay packets and shorter hours combined with employment security but also the opportunity for workers to have a larger 'say' in industrial decisions which affect their working lives.

As well as writing for *Tribune*, I was asked by Michael Foot to help with the paper's finances, which then as now were in dire straits. I had written pieces for the paper from time to time, at the request of Dick Clements, the editor, and had become friendly with him and Michael. I recognized their basic socialist sincerity as I believe they did mine, although that did not prevent honest disagreement occasionally. We each agreed on the 'right to disagree' as a principle – which is not true of all friends in the Labour movement! One thing I believe I did was to give them a better understanding of the trade union movement. A result of that was their ready agreement to my suggestion that *Tribune* should seek trade union advertising support. I was able to help on this, especially with the TGWU and, for good or ill, the idea ensured the continued existence of *Tribune*.

1967 saw the birth of our fourth grandchild, David. He and his two sisters, Jane and Sally, were living in Plymouth and we were not able to see them very often. Jack, their father, had left the sea to keep more directly in touch with his family. After a spell on a tug he had joined his wife Brenda as a teacher. The phone made up for the lack of direct contact – at least on Evelyn's part. We had a little more contact with Hannah, our other granddaughter, because for some years she lived in London with Eileen, her mother, and Mick our younger son. Mick had been trained as an industrial designer, including a spell at the Royal College of Art, but he was determined to concentrate more on the fine arts and mural painting, which meant making a living not a little precarious. He broke away on one occasion to make a trip as a seaman to South Africa and came back a more determined critic of apartheid than ever. He was highly critical of the seamen's conditions, much to the displeasure of Bill Hogarth, the leader of the National Union of Seamen at the time. Evelyn and I felt we had reason to be proud of our family, despite the occasional heartache.

Harold Wilson's Government had been living through a rough period. Initially they had tried to introduce some social welfare increases and import surcharges. A run on sterling had resulted. Then they had imposed wage-rise ceilings, but taken a less harsh attitude to profits and dividends. A number of strikes took place, but instead of trying to find their causes, Ray Gunter, the Minister of Labour, seemed to find Communist-Trotskyist agitators under the bed of every striker. I was as concerned as anyone to prevent strikes but I knew that each case must be looked at on its merits and that some disputes were due to frustration or a sense of injustice.

At the end of September 1967 the Devlin Inquiry recommendations on decasualization were introduced throughout the docks. Men were supposed to be allocated to individual employers on a permanent basis and there were changes in certain working practices. Strikes broke out in London, Hull, Manchester and Liverpool. Issues were straightened out in some ports but in London four thousand men continued on strike against changes in the 'continuity rule' (e.g. men moving cargo on or off a ship should be allowed to work on the job until completion) and in Liverpool the whole port was stopped. During the Labour Party

Conference at Scarborough a deputation of Liverpool dockers came seeking support. I knew some of the men and talked with them at length. They admitted that the membership position in the port was a shambles and that there was general dissatisfaction with the TGWU. To their satisfaction I said that if I could get the agreement of Frank Cousins, I would go to Liverpool and spend some time there. I told Frank it was a last opportunity to clear up the problems in the port. If we allowed the position to drift we could say goodbye to docks membership on the Mersey. He agreed that I should go and I left immediately.

Our officers were not talking to the unofficial strike committee, and although they had made various efforts to secure a resumption of work the men were out, solid. I caused some consternation by announcing that I would hold talks with the unofficial committee. The chairman was a 'blue' union man, Jim Benbow, who had formerly been in the TGWU and was all the more suspicious because of that. I met them in a smoky meeting-room and invited them to put their cards on the table and tell me what they saw as the main problems. I took voluminous notes and promised to talk with the employers. The men on the committee, I was sure, realized that I was taking their case seriously and would do my damnedest to make progress.

The employers offered to reconsider the points in the new scheme to which the men took exception but only if there was a full resumption of work. This offer was put to a mass meeting and rejected, although the unofficial committee and I had recommended it. Other efforts to secure a return to work failed and the strike remained solid. The local *Liverpool Daily Post* called the men 'sheeplike' and 'selfish and short-sighted'. The port employers expressed their impatience with the union. Ray Gunter, the Minister of Labour, went further; he denounced the strikes as a 'red plot . . . an unholy alliance of communists and trotskyists to ruin the social democratic movement'. He also declared that 'the unions have lost control of their members'.

Frank Cousins and I went to see Gunter and the Prime Minister. It was necessary to remove a number of preconceived notions from their minds and it was hard work persuading them that the Merseyside dockers had a case. I suggested that the only way to break the deadlock would be through high-powered conciliation and an inquiry. When we considered names it was not difficult to gain agreement for Jack Scamp. After all, he had become the best known industrial relations investigator and he had served as a member of the Devlin Inquiry Committee into the Ports Industry.

Returning to Liverpool, I prepared our officials for the Inquiry and got them working on the sort of details Jack Scamp would require. I also met the unofficial committee and told them I would seek to gain their admission to the Inquiry and that we should work together. They agreed to my leadership, readily accepting that it would be foolish to have too many spokesmen. I explained that I would call certain of the men to give evidence, to support the case I would be putting. Shortly after Jack Scamp's arrival in the city I called on him and outlined how I proposed to proceed. He accepted my approach.

The Inquiry went on for a number of days, and nights! It was held in the august premises of the Liverpool City Council, known as the Municipal Annexe. There were plenty of rooms for side meetings so I was able to keep all the people on our side fully informed of developments. The employers' leaders were not too helpful. They were somewhat irritated by the Inquiry, which was virtually forced upon them. In fact at the start they were reluctant to participate at all. I had to spend a lot of time with them, persuading, pressing, and cajoling. Management seemed ready to fight to the finish, despite the unsatisfactory conditions under which men had to work on the Mersey, and the length of the stoppage.

Unsatisfactory the conditions really were. Our case was based mainly on the information I had gleaned from the twenty-two men on the unofficial committee. Earnings in the port were 10 per cent below the national average in the docks industry – and this meagre result was only achieved by an excessive level of overtime. Many men were paid only the basic time rate. There was no provision of protective clothing, despite previous management promises. Men were expected to work in the rain and under most difficult circumstances without extra pay. The sanitary conditions were almost Victorian, certainly no better than when I had worked on the docks as a young man.

I got to know a number of the men very well and I could see natural leaders emerging from this group, if only we were allowed to develop an effective shop steward system. Jimmy Symes, who later became the full-time Docks District Secretary, and Denis Kelly, who years later was the full-time convenor of shop stewards in the port, particularly impressed me among the throng of bitter and anxious men who made up the committee. Yes, some were communists and Trotskyists, and our sessions were sometimes explosive, but most of the criticisms, it seemed to me, were based on genuine grievances.

The Inquiry proceeded and day after day I brought in evidence and challenged the employers. But the hard work was done behind the scenes with Jack Scamp, trying with his help to persuade the management to make concessions. I knew I had convinced him but it was much more difficult to secure a change in outlook on the part of the employers' leaders.

With the unofficial committee I had arranged a mass meeting in Liverpool Stadium for the Saturday morning so that I could present a report of the proceedings. Somehow or other, I thought, we must get results for that meeting. It became my deadline. By Friday evening the open Inquiry procedures were finished but Jack Scamp remained in the building, as did the employers' leaders and myself. In one of the rooms the unofficial committee was housed and its members stayed there through the night (bringing in fish and chips and beer to keep themselves going) while I was busy with Jack Scamp, trying to work out a formula and, between us, to sell it to the employers.

Jack and I worked out what I regarded as the minimum necessary. I was going to and from the lads, managing to get a quick pint of beer and a few chips which was more than Jack Scamp could secure, but above all gaining their understanding and agreement. The problem, and it was a big one, was that the employers would not budge. It was a breakdown . . . or was it?

I had one card up my sleeve. Earlier in the evening I had been contacted by Harold Wilson, the Prime Minister, who told me that he would be at the Adelphie Hotel throughout the night and I was to keep in touch with him. He would be ready to help in any way. Harold was a Liverpool MP and therefore had a direct interest in the outcome of the strike, apart from his national responsibility. At about 5 a.m. deadlock was reached and I phoned the Prime Minister as promised. He agreed that I should invite the employers and Scamp to accompany me to the Adelphie for a discussion with him. I told him what was involved, so that he could be ready to put whatever pressure he could on the employers. I then went back and told them: 'The Prime Minister is anxious that we should keep talking and he wishes to see us right away.' Well, even at 5 o'clock in the morning you don't say 'no' to the Prime Minister, so off we went. After giving us all a drink, Wilson spelled out the dire consequences of a breakdown, and managed to persuade the employers to think again.

Back we went to the Municipal Annexe and after more detailed discussion we reached agreement at about 9 a.m. I then had a long argument with the strike committee, because a few of the men did not want to make a recommendation to the meeting. Finally we got unanimous agreement to recommend. Shortly afterwards I faced a tense and packed meeting, every seat taken and people standing up all over the place. The chairman, one of the committee, and the District Secretary, each made a contribution, in the main praising me for my efforts. I then gave a detailed report, so that there should be no room for misunderstanding about the terms. At the end of my report there was prolonged applause. I turned to Benbow, the chairman, and said: 'Put it to the vote now, Jim.' To my surprise he turned to the vast audience and said: 'Thanks, Brother Jones, for that good report. Now we've got to think about it. We've got to sleep on it. There'll be another meeting next week. This meeting is closed.' There were shouts but most of the people there were stunned, and the meeting broke up. I appealed to Denis Kelly who was near me. 'It's OK,' he said. 'Don't worry – they'll go back next week.' I insisted that all the committee should go back to the TGWU office and most did. There, after an intense argument, they agreed that a mass meeting would be called at the Pier Head early in the week and they would urge a return. 'Will you get the employers to sign the terms of an agreement?' they asked. 'We don't trust them.' I knew they were anxious to save face and I agreed to arrange this formality. Jack Scamp was angry and felt let down, but I satisfied him that it would work out. It did and the men resumed work on 30 October. They walked tall, for real advances, long overdue, had been made.

The written agreement, signed by Lindsay Alexander (Chairman of the Port of Liverpool Employers) and myself on 26 October, provided for an increase of £4 a week for most men, which meant a guaranteed wage of £17 a week when working normal hours. This put the dockers well ahead of most workers in the city. Undertakings were given on sick pay, protective clothing, improved payment schemes for crane-drivers and checkers, and a revision of the port working rule book. With regard to the vexed question of 'continuity', it was agreed that 'continuity as *previously operated* in the port *will be maintained* with the exception of men or gangs on transfer or on loan. Such instances will be the subject of consultation with the shop stewards.' Finally the principle of 'no redundancy arising from the decasualization scheme' was reaffirmed. Few outside the docks on Merseyside could realize the tremendous strides we had made – but the men knew.

Harold Wilson said in a speech at Worthing in May 1972:

I remember the disastrous strike in Liverpool in 1967. . . . I was struggling at six in the morning to settle it, with Jack Jones commending a tentative agreement to the ultra left-wing unofficial leadership who also accepted it, and a few hours later the unofficial leadership was thrown over by the rank and file. We got the agreement in the end, but only because it was human problems we were dealing with, fears, misunderstandings, trying to reconcile, not to inflame.

That, I suppose, is how history gets written, but life is not so simple. The day after the return to work I was in Liverpool arranging with a reluctant management for the election of shop stewards and for their training. We had won major improvements but there were obligations on our side too. For some years it had been traditional in the port for men to 'spell' away from the job periodically, a practice known as the 'welt'. The system had got out of hand. We agreed measures to bring the 'welt' to an end, and this was achieved, but within less than three weeks a local management leader, Jim Leggate, was publicly complaining that productivity had not improved and showing the same antagonistic attitude as had prevailed for years in management circles in the port. Painstaking efforts eventually brought about an improvement in attitudes, and I was grateful to leaders of the employers like Bill Tongue and Lindsay Alexander for occasionally pouring oil on troubled waters.

Back in London, the dock strike was continuing, led by Jack Dash and his Liaison Committee. In that situation, however, I was mainly a bystander. Frank Cousins was back in town and I had other problems to deal with.

Chapter Nineteen

My work compelled me more and more to study the intricacies of
various industries which were part of the TGWU structure. None
commanded my sympathies more than the trawler-fishing industry.
I was continually reminding myself of those words of Sir Walter Scott:
'It's no fish you're eating – it's men's lives.' I had been astounded at
the atrocious conditions under which men (and boys) were expected
to work and tried hard to gain improvements. Three disasters early in
1968, involving the total loss of the *Rose Cleveland*, *Kingston Peridot*
and *St Romanus*, with the death of the three crews in freezing seas,
shook the fishing world. I demanded a meeting with the ministers
concerned, Fred Peart, the Minister of Agriculture and Fisheries, and
J. P. W. Mallalieu, the Minister of State (Fishing), Board of Trade.
The meeting was arranged within days, for I was in no mood for delay
and played hell with Fred Peart and the civil servants until a date was
fixed.

In meeting ministers I usually felt a sense of complacency on their
part. It was shaken a bit that day. With me were some trawlermen and
about half a dozen outspoken trawlermen's wives. They warmed up
the surroundings considerably and, in an atmosphere almost of drama,
I was able to say that I spoke for the families and the fishing community
generally as well as for the men in insisting upon immediate action.
We wanted to see justice for the relations of those who had perished,
and action to ensure that there was no repetition.

At the end of our talks the two ministers agreed to set up an independent Inquiry into the safety of deep-sea trawling. Meantime they

would instruct the owners that regular ship-to-shore communication must be established for all vessels; that there must be an immediate report of any loss of contact; that there must be safety checks on all ships leaving port; and that there would be a ban on fishing off the North Cape of Iceland whilst the present severe conditions lasted. I was able to say: 'We have achieved more today than has been done in sixty years. We've got action – the wheels are in motion.' The others agreed. I was especially pleased for the wives, for they had fought a noble campaign.

I presented the case for the union to the Inquiry (presided over by an admiral – Labour ministers are invariably impressed by title and position). I told the Inquiry that the cost of fish had been high in terms of Government subsidies (to the owners) 'but in terms of deaths, accidents and tragedies for the fishermen and their families, the price has been far too high, for far too long.' 'At present,' I went on, 'the life of the fisherman is one of casual labour, long dangerous hours and low security of work and earnings. Skippers, upon whose decisions so much rests, know that both their immediate income and their future employment depend upon their success in maintaining large catches, no matter what the weather.'

We made progress. The report was a good one – so far as it related to safety. But as I made clear at the time, improved safety standards alone would not bring safety at sea to the extent required. The whole system of employment and pay needed to be called into question. Short periods of rest ashore, after three weeks or more at sea involving up to eighteen-hour stretches of continuous work even for teenagers on their first trip, aggravated the natural hazards of the job. I drew up a Fisherman's Charter and discussed it at meeting after meeting of trawlermen. We campaigned for it and negotiated where we could, bringing about some reforms but not enough. In many ways the Cod War killed the industry. Iceland had a strong case but British trawler-owners and respective Governments failed to negotiate satisfactorily. Too many in high places thought we could browbeat little Iceland. In talks with Icelandic trade union leaders, I became convinced that a deal could have been struck which would have safeguarded our fishing fleets and employment in the industry. But it was not to be.

One person who was never complacent was Barbara Castle. As soon as she was appointed Minister of Transport she moved like lightning. New experts were brought in, ideas and schemes tossed around, meetings called here, there, and everywhere. Small as she was, she could command attention from the most reluctant audience. She proved herself a bundle of energy with a capacity beyond the normal to master a brief. Proposals and plans of the most detailed kind presented no problem to her. She would read and absorb them and, if acceptable, make them her own property, for which she would fight in any way she thought fit.

During her days at the Ministry of Transport I was present at meetings with her in her cottage (Hell Corner Farm) in Buckinghamshire, her flat in London, her office and in the Commons. However fierce the debate she would stick to her guns. I pay this tribute to her although I was often on the other side. Sometimes our differences were deep but I never doubted her ability. If civil servants or anyone else stood in her way she would do everything possible to outwit them, but she always sought agreement with her allies. I recall spending most of a Sunday at her cottage talking about transport plans along with Chris Foster, an expert she had brought in from Oxford, Stephen Swingler and John Morris who were then junior ministers, and the late Professor Balogh. The latter was a favourite of hers and lived in the vicinity. 'Tommy' she called him, and when he entered he took possession of the room, insisting on squatting near the fire. He immediately launched into a diatribe against car parking on both sides of London streets, based apparently on his experiences in Hampstead where he had his London home. I was not very polite to 'Tommy', which upset Barbara.

After spending some time discussing transport integration and the plans for regional transport authorities, we turned to my views on industrial democracy and how they might fit into the machinery Barbara and her friends had in mind. The discussion was inconclusive, for Barbara thought my ideas 'way out', 'syndicalist', even 'anarchist'. I found her reaction incomprehensible, for I was simply urging that when she came to set up regional transport authorities, working people in the employment of the authority, such as busmen, should be appointed to serve on the board. She conceded that it would be useful to have people on the authorities with practical experience, but did not agree that they should *represent* the workers. Neither did she agree that employees should serve on the authority in which they worked. Her ideas prevailed in subsequent legislation.

In my many dealings with Barbara Castle I found her anxious to do things *for* the workers but not *with* them. Her outlook was not all that unusual in politicians of the Left. On many occasions I have had to listen to politicians telling me what to do, although their practical experience of the subject was negligible. I found myself often feeling like a schoolboy when dealing with Barbara. She was indignant with me on one occasion because she thought I was trying to scotch her plans. A meeting had been arranged between her and the TGWU group of MPs to discuss amendments to the Transport Bill which I had persuaded the group to put forward. They all dealt with the subject of workers' representatives on the proposed regional organization in the passenger transport industry. When she arrived at the meeting she found me there among the MPs and much to her consternation I took a major role in the discussion. I took the view that we were all comrades and there was no harm in my action, but Barbara resented it just the same.

Her fears about my ideas were confirmed, for I was advocating that work-people should be elected, through the trade union machinery, to the policy-making authority and the executive board. 'This is the way to secure the wholehearted co-operation of the workforce,' I argued. 'Busmen, for example, are aware of the grumbles of the passengers, the technical faults of particular vehicles, difficulties over loading and routes. A man with trade union experience would be able to bring his knowledge into management thinking.' Barbara's response was hostile. My ideas, she said, were unrealistic. She did promise to have the civil servants look into the details, but I knew from her manner that we would not make much progress.

That evening I was also made aware of the shortcomings of the TGWU parliamentary group. Some of the members worked hard at putting the union's view; most, however, seemed to lack energy and interest. The original idea of supporting a group of MPs was that they should advance the union's views in the House of Commons and provide a means of access to Ministers and Government departments. The concept was splendid, but over the years too many members had forgotten their obligations to the union once a safe seat had been secured. I am sure that greater efforts should be made in the training of younger workers, so that they can play a useful role in Parliament. People with experience of being shop stewards could do a very effective job in the House.

Political action was a minor part of my activities. I was heavily involved in talks with a variety of union leaders about the prospects of merging their unions with the TGWU. I was especially pleased to bring the National Association of Operative Plasterers into the TGWU fold. This was a craft union which had played a great part in the history of the building industry and I felt that its recruitment would not only strengthen the TGWU's involvement in the industry but would also open the way to further advances among the various kinds of craftsmen. Other smaller unions responded to my approach, from the Cardiff, Penarth and Barry Coal Trimmers to the Scottish Slaters, Tilers, Roofers and Cement Workers. In this work I found out about aspects of trade unionism hitherto unknown to me. I felt pride in working people, my class, whose story was interwoven with the endeavours of the people who had built those unions.

It was not enough for me to look to unions outside the ranks of the TGWU. I was not satisfied with our own structure. I had heard George Woodcock say, at the 1962 TUC, 'Structure . . . in the trade union movement, is a function of purpose', and yet within the TGWU we had overlapping organizations. Two groups especially, the North of England Commercial Section and the Power Group, were not fully amalgamated; the *purpose* of united organization was being neglected by the loose arrangements to which Ernest Bevin, in his time, had given his blessing. Each of the groups mentioned had its own rules, some of which were in conflict with those of the principal union. Almost they were unions within a union. Differences came to a head when I learned of meetings between Bill Tudor, the National Secretary of the Power Group, and the leaders of the Electrical Trade Union. It appeared that prospects for a merger between the Group and the ETU were being aired, and there were real dangers of a substantial part of the TGWU's membership defecting to another union.

Bill Tudor had been a buddy of mine in my Liverpool days. We had both developed over a similar period from shop stewards to national leaders. I could not understand his attitude and asked him why he was creating these difficulties. His answer was evasive, but I insisted on meeting members of his committee and eventually terms for full amalgamation were agreed. It was evident to me that similar action had to be taken with the other group, the North of England Commercial Section. This required a series of meetings with hard-headed Lancashire lorry drivers in Bolton before agreement could be reached. Working people naturally want to retain their traditional practices. I knew that, and when mergers were being discussed I tried to put myself in the position of the other party. That I believe was the reason for such progress as we made. I genuinely wanted to make the TGWU a better, more effective and democratic union and my intentions usually evoked a sympathetic response.

Meanwhile the pay freeze and the operations of the Prices and

Incomes Board had provoked considerable ill feeling in the ranks. Rancorous meetings were taking place, and not least with employers and ministers over the freezing of a wage agreement for municipal busmen. A £1 a week increase had been agreed after proper negotiations, but one way and another it was held up for twelve months. There were overtime bans and local action, but a total strike was avoided as a result of our lawyers' advice that the agreement would have to be honoured in the end. We advised our members throughout the country to keep a record of all hours worked. Eventually many municipal undertakings had to pay out big sums in back pay. What a lot of nonsense it was! To make things worse, a Prices and Incomes Board recommendation for the payment of a 10 shillings a week bonus to busmen who moved into one-man operation of buses, was also held up for many months. In other words, productivity deals were frozen as well as wages. It was a real case of the Government cutting off its nose to spite its face.

Hugh Scanlon's election as President of the Engineers Union at the end of 1967 opened the way to a closer relationship between his union and the TGWU in opposing the Government's policy on pay restraint. I had known Hugh for many years. Occasionally we had clashed over inter-union problems – Hughie, like the rest of his colleagues, strongly disliked the TGWU's strength in the engineering industry – but we shared a similar outlook on many issues. This new-found unity did nothing to help George Woodcock's efforts, as General Secretary of the TUC, to gain approval from the unions for a voluntary incomes policy. At a special Conference of Trade Union Executives held at Croydon early in 1968 the General Council policy, advocated by George, was barely adopted, the voting being 4,620,000 for the policy and 4,084,000 against. The majority was so small that it gave the Government an excuse for continuing – and indeed trying to tighten – its statutory policy. George Woodcock was a very disappointed man.

Despite the division between the Government and the union, we were still on speaking terms with members of the Government. At a small, informal gathering Harold Wilson happily informed me of Ray Gunter's departure and of his appointment of Barbara Castle as Secretary of State for Employment and Productivity, a new title for what was intended to be a more important job. I thought it was great news and congratulated Barbara. She disagreed with Ray Gunter as I did but for different reasons. We both objected to Ray's fanatical opposition to the Left, but I also felt that his attitude to industrial relations was short-sighted and stemmed from his limited experience within the cushioned confines of railway white-collar staff. Mistakenly, I assumed that Barbara would work more closely with the unions than her predecessor, and would have more sympathy with the shop floor. In retrospect I cannot understand why I should have felt so elated, for I had already begun to learn how difficult it was to talk in practical terms to politicians once they had been elevated to Government office.

There was no reason for me to be complacent. Shortly afterwards, in the wake of Enoch Powell's infamous speech about immigration, I was shocked by the march of a couple of hundred dockers from the East End to express support for Powell. A couple of hundred out of over 21,000 registered dockers in the Port of London was not much, but it was a straw in the wind. On top of that I had heard influential trade union leaders expressing sympathy for Powell's views. In the ranks of trade unionism racial feelings were ablaze, fanned by the winds of ignorance and prejudice. Personally I felt that such feelings were repugnant, and for many years I had fought strongly against racial discrimination. In the union that had meant addressing many stormy meetings, to protect the right of immigrants to a job or to promotion where it was justified. Sometimes the fault was on the side of our members, on others of management, but in either case racialist attitudes had to be fought, even if this meant unpopularity.

My feelings were well-known in Government circles and throughout the unions and that was probably why Harold Wilson bypassed the TUC and invited me to serve on the National Committee for Commonwealth Immigrants when it was formed in 1965. I was not then a member of the General Council and my appointment ruffled the feathers of the International Committee of the TUC. They kicked up a fuss, because they regarded themselves as the custodians of TUC policy on race relations. Serving on Government committees was not for lesser mortals like me. George Woodcock told me about this and spoke in derogatory terms of the General Council members concerned – 'pompous asses' he called them. To appease their dignity, it was agreed to appoint an additional member and George Smith of UCATT joined me as the direct nominee of the TUC.

From the start the Committee was a disappointment. Maybe the benign somnolence of the Archbishop of Canterbury, Michael Ramsey, in the chair affected the atmosphere, for there was little sense of urgency. There was a 'do-gooder' approach to the problems. An ever increasing staff failed effectively to grasp the nettle. I felt overwhelmed by the dominance of academic and professional people on the Committee and irritated by its inability to come to grips with discrimination. 'Surely,' I said, 'the main problems are in employment and housing. There should be people on this committee with direct experience – working people.' I think we got one black working man out of three black people on the Committee, the others being a teacher and a doctor. And they were in any case very much of a minority.

I did not like the TUC attitude to race relations. Senior staff including Vic Feather and Alan Hargreaves opposed the Government's Bill to extend the 1965 legislation (forbidding racial discrimination in public places) to cover employment and housing. Their insistence on 'voluntary' action seemed to me to be mealy-mouthed, and I told Vic Feather so. Vic was Assistant General Secretary of the TUC at the time. His views were close to those of Bob Mellish, MP. 'Education, Jack, that's what's needed. We don't want the law in on this,' they said to me. I thought that meant using a feather duster to combat the evil of racist discrimination.

Although I wanted to see legislation introduced I realized that everything possible must be done to stir public opinion against racialism. In my view a campaign had to be conducted against discrimination in the case of both race and sex. This led me to insist, when later I served on the TUC General Council, that a TUC Equal Rights Committee should be established. I had great hopes that the dithering and double talk which had characterized TUC attitudes in these matters for many years would be brought to an end.

I felt a lack of confidence in the Labour Party Head Office. My colleague, Harry Nicholas, had been elected General Secretary of the Party. The pushing and shuffling that went into securing his appointment had disgusted me. I particularly resented George Brown's involvement. It seemed to be a deliberate campaign to prevent a younger man, with more liberal views, getting the post. Anthony Greenwood, the other leading candidate, was no great shakes as a leader but he would have represented progress. I had no personal antipathy to Harry but I thought his age would prejudice any prospect of change at a time when it was badly needed.

1968 saw the TUC celebrating its centenary with a big song-and-dance act at Belle Vue, Manchester. A pageant and carnival were arranged and I saw this as an opportunity to publicize the TGWU. At the time I was devoting a lot of energy to a campaign to achieve a target of $1\frac{1}{2}$ million members, a figure we in fact reached in 1969. I helped to design our union's exhibit in the pageant, a rocket bearing the words 'The Union of the Future'. It was expressing a deeply held and passionate view of mine, that the TGWU could be made a more progressive and democratic union than any other.

The Royal Commission on Trade Unions and Employers Associations under Lord Donovan reported in this period. I had been part of the TGWU team which gave evidence to the Commission and I looked forward to its findings. They were more favourable to my way of thinking than I had dared to hope. Support was expressed for company and plant agreements. The report urged that collective bargaining should be encouraged and was generally favourable to trade union organization. The role of the shop steward received support. If there were some aspects which were not so acceptable they were offset by the report's firm rejection of legal sanctions, compulsory strike ballots and 'cooling-off periods'.

The Commission recommended the reform of collective bargaining procedures to deal with unofficial strikes. This clearly implied that the engineering industry should put its house in order and reform its procedure for 'avoiding disputes', a view I had long held because of the number of local disputes caused by irritating delays in dealing with grievances. Shortly after the report was issued I was invited to address a special seminar of the Engineering Employers Federation in London. I readily accepted. The chief points I made were:

> The reforms proposed by the Donovan Commission can make an immediate contribution to industrial peace, higher productivity, and higher living standards in the engineering industry, if employers will give the lead.
>
> The Commission's recommendation for a change in emphasis in favour of local rather than national agreements has been widely welcomed. But it simply cannot work unless it is accepted that the procedure for settling disputes is going to have to end at factory or company level – with a provision for voluntary arbitration at local level if an official dispute is to be avoided.
>
> The truth is that a system devised nearly fifty years ago, and imposed at a time when trade union organization was weak, is irrelevant where you have strong unions, and an industry where tens of thousands of workers can be put out of work because a dispute involving a dozen or so men or women had not been resolved.

Often the procedure is used to delay settlements which can and should be made at factory level. But, even without ill-will or intentional holding back, settlements can take a long time. The result is that workers are reluctant to let a dispute go into the machinery when they find that a local strike will bring a speedy settlement.

I have quoted my views at length because they represented in part my reaction to Barbara Castle's White Paper, *In Place of Strife* – a document which was to occupy quite a bit of my time. In fact the engineering employers *did* take notice of Donovan and changed their procedures, yet Barbara went in a different direction.

In 1968 the first Rules Conference since I took up executive office occurred. Impelled by a desire to achieve what I regarded as necessary reforms, I drafted a series of proposals for the Executive Council. They included new Trade Group structures, and provided for District Committees as part of a decentralization process. One change I considered necessary related to discriminatory rules which precluded members of the Communist and Fascist parties from holding office. It was a form of discrimination and I felt it to be contrary to good trade union principles. Such discrimination was brought to an end as a result of my proposals, which ensured that members were to be treated on an equal footing but with continued safeguards against disruptive action from any quarter.

A pleasant feature of the rule changes was the creation of an All-Wales Region of the union. I had worked out this proposal with an old friend, Tom Jones, of the North Wales Region (which was now to merge with South Wales). We both knew that once established it would be easy to proceed to the next step – the formation of a Wales TUC. For Tom, a proud Celt, that meant the achievement of a dream.

Later that year I led a delegation to the USA. Three members of the union's Executive Council accompanied me and we saw much of the American motor-manufacturing industry. We got to know members and leaders in the United Automobile Workers' Union, walking the plants, attending meetings and visiting homes. Our other host was the Amalgamated Transit Union, which had its headquarters in Washington and mainly embraced bus and coach workers employed by municipalities and in the well-known Greyhound services.

Our impression of these two unions were very favourable, and we enjoyed the exchanges of information and the sociable gatherings of members. Unfortunately we also witnessed a lot of racial discrimination. Riots had taken place in Washington and some union members were outspokenly racist. In the Ford River Rouge plant at Detroit we noticed that black and white workers were friendly enough on the line and that there was integration within the union. But in the nearest town to the Ford plant, Dearborn, not one black person was allowed to live.

While in the USA I went down to New Orleans to see my brother Wilf, a ship's engineer, who had emigrated to America in 1929 and had been an American citizen for many years. At the time of my visit he was the Port Engineer-surveyor. I had not seen him for thirty-two years and then only on a fleeting visit he made to Liverpool. In the years that had passed his ideas had changed. They were distinctly racist and we differed sharply. I remember his wife referring to a black man walking beside a white girl as 'black trash'. I could not let this pass, and my brother looked uncomfortable as I upbraided her. The air was a little tense when I left.

From New Orleans I went on to meet leaders of the Teamsters. Although the relationship between our two unions had never been close, there had been a virtual freeze since Jimmy Hoffa had been put in gaol and it was felt by Frank Cousins and others that some contact should be established. I'm afraid I was not impressed. Although some of the leaders appeared friendly and straightforward, others struck me as slick business types. One instance may make my point. I met a district leader of the Teamsters in Los Angeles. Having discussed comparative conditions in the haulage trade, and met some of his colleagues, I was taken to dinner in a luxurious restaurant. It was plush in every way and the food was of the highest quality. During the meal the Teamsters man turned to me and asked: 'What do you think of this place?' 'Splendid,' I replied, 'it must be one of the best around.' 'It sure is – I own it and it makes eleven dollars to the invested dollar!' was his amazing response. He was a long way down the list from Hoffa but he could still own a place like that.

I came home from the USA more determined than ever to resist 'business unionism' in the UK and to eliminate any tendency towards corruption. Strict financial disciplines were necessary. The result was not pleasant, for more than one national official left the service of the union in a hurry. One officer claimed expenses for an engagement in Dublin. Since I knew he had no business there I challenged him, only to be told lamely that 'he'd been on a secret mission'.

Chapter Twenty

Learn the simplest things. For you
whose time has already come
it is never too late!
Learn your A.B.C's, it is not enough,
But learn them! Do not let it discourage you,
begin! You must know everything!
You must take over the leadership!

BERTOLT BRECHT

The White Paper *In Place of Strife* caused much division and bitterness. It shook the Labour movement. Yet through it all, there was no desertion from the ranks. I was the Executive Officer of the union (or to give the job its full title – Assistant Executive Secretary) but my standing had been enhanced by the overwhelming majority I had received in the ballot for election as General Secretary. The vote had been concluded in December 1968 but Frank Cousins was not due to retire until September 1969, so I was still in the designate stage. I had, however, been elected to the General Council of the TUC in September 1968 and this enabled me to play a leading role in the debate on the White Paper.

The twofold nature of the Government's proposals put the General Council in a dilemma. Some proposals were favourable, but they appeared to me sugar coating on a very bitter pill. The Government was determined to apply legal sanctions. It had tried it with the prices and incomes legislation and had failed, now it sought to control the trade unions by other means. This approach, the TUC declared, would 'worsen rather than improve industrial relations'.

A great deal of press speculation occurred and leaks suggesting early legislation began to appear. The General Council responded to pressure from Frank Cousins, myself and others to seek a meeting with the Prime Minister. Meantime shop stewards were upset at what appeared to be a direct attack on them. Those of us on the General Council who had lived through the rough and tumble of life on the shop floor knew there would be real trouble if coercive measures were applied.

The meeting with the Prime Minister took place on 11 April 1969. He was accompanied by Barbara Castle. We told them that (except in wartime) there had been no criminal law in industrial relations for over a hundred years, and that we would not co-operate with the operation of legal sanctions. At this and later meetings Harold Wilson and Barbara Castle held stoutly to their views. Their criticism of unofficial and inter-union (demarcation) strikes was scathing, although to my mind they revealed a lack of understanding of working conditions.

The gap between the Government and most of the members of the General Council sharpened considerably, and there were rumblings among parliamentarians and on the NEC. Jack Cooper of the Municipal Workers and George Lowthian of the Bricklayers, however, were half-hearted in their opposition. George Woodcock, too, had not been outspoken and was quickly recruited to the chairmanship of the Commission on Industrial Relations. Vic Feather (who was Acting General Secretary of the TUC pending his election as General Secretary the following September) was bobbing about among all the camps. The movement was restive, but Harold and Barbara stuck to their guns, frequently maintaining that legislation on industrial relations would be a vote winner.

Roy Jenkins was thought to support the projected legislation. Although he had held a membership card in the TGWU since Arthur Deakin's day, it was a card of convenience and he showed little sympathy for trade union views. Roy Hattersley, then a Parliamentary Under-Secretary, waxed lyrical; he declared in a *Sunday Times* article that the Government had to make judgements 'unclouded by sentiment and unprejudiced by history'. This meant, to me, ignoring the qualities which had inspired the trade union and labour movement.

Towards the end of May Evelyn and I went on a holiday to Israel. Parliament was in recess so no meetings with ministers were likely and no industrial crisis was on the horizon. It was our first visit to Israel and we had a great time. The hotel we stayed at had a beautiful swimming pool, the Mediterranean was close and the sunshine marvellous. We had just returned from a trip to Jerusalem when a phone call came through from Vic Feather. He wanted me to attend a meeting with the Prime Minister at Chequers on Sunday, 1 June. He and Hugh Scanlon would be present. It was to be a personal meeting with the Prime Minister, stressed Vic, and absolutely secret. Fine, I said, but 'will the queer one be present?', making it clear that I thought it should be a meeting with Wilson alone. Vic in response gave me a firm assurance that Barbara Castle ('the queer one') would not be there. That pleased me because we all thought (maybe mistakenly in the light of diaries published since) that Barbara had made the issue her personal property and Wilson was the less hard of the two.

On Sunday afternoon I drove to Chequers. Vic Feather met me at the door and his first words were: 'She's here. Don't be difficult!' He went on to explain that it was a complete surprise to him. 'She got to hear of the meeting through civil servants and insisted on being present,' he said.

Harold had laid on a good meal and the atmosphere was friendly enough though a little tense. I was still fuming about Barbara's presence because I felt it would inhibit the chances of getting an understanding. The niceties were soon over and we moved into the argument. I suppose we all felt that the fate of the Labour movement was at stake, so the atmosphere was pretty serious. Barbara was rather shrewish, trying to put Hughie and me in our place. We were told once again that 'The public is looking for action against unofficial strikers. Action must be taken by the Government; you've had your chance, boys!' The nearest thing to a conciliatory tone was adopted when they explained their attitude to 'criminal sanctions', as we called them. 'No,' said Barbara, 'people will not go to prison. Fines could be imposed but they would be collected as civil debts.' It was going over old ground but sometimes the argument was heated. I reminded Barbara that the idea of making procedure agreements legally enforceable had been around the Ministry of Labour for years and it had been put forward by the Department – not the Government – to the Donovan Commission in 1965. 'Why,' I asked, 'should a Labour Government peddle the anti-trade union ideas of top civil servants?' Hughie and I went on to outline the problems created by long-drawn-out procedure agreements and the need to revise them by negotiations rather than introducing laws to enforce them.

Wilson and Castle were basically academics and it was difficult to persuade them to see things from a shop-floor angle. Hughie and I tried to explain why the idea of applying attachment orders on the earnings of workers not observing a 'conciliation pause' before some antiquated procedure was exhausted, seemed so ludicrous. It was simply not feasible for each worker to have his personal circumstances examined. Such action would lead to further strikes and probably violence. I drew attention to the experience of the wartime arbitration orders and subsequent legislation and the need to provide extensive conciliation services, especially at local level. This would be a far better approach than legal sanctions. Barbara, however, was in no mood to change her mind. She poured scorn on any ideas that did not involve legal enforcement. I have seen reports of the Chequers meeting by people who were not there which suggested that Hughie and I were intransigent and arrogant. Such reports were a long way from the truth. We just tried to put alternatives and warn of the dangers in the Government's policy.

I left early the following morning to get to grips with the work which had piled up at Transport House while I had been away on holiday. Later I spoke to Vic Feather on the phone and stressed how important I felt the Special Congress of the TUC, which was to be held on 5 June at Croydon, would be in providing a 'face-saver' for the Government while at the same time preserving our stand against legal sanctions. Vic agreed with me, but I was rapidly coming to the conclusion that he tended to agree with all men. I had learned that he had had frequent private meetings with the Prime Minister and Barbara Castle and that for some reason they thought he was on their side. We might have made more progress had he presented our case strongly, as though it was his own, in his many contacts with ministers. I could not help liking Vic but I got very irritated when he acted as a messenger rather than an advocate. Equally, he was often upset by my bluntness.

Shortly afterwards the Special Trades Union Congress took place. I had been active in pressing for it so that the movement would act together. Ostensibly the main purpose was to discuss the General Council's proposals on the TUC response to the Donovan Commission, but everyone knew that the critical issue was the Government's declared intention to introduce, in the current session of Parliament, their Industrial Relations Bill containing penal clauses. Congress declared itself totally opposed to 'statutory penalties on workpeople or trade unions in connection either with industrial disputes or with the compulsory registration by trade unions of their rules'. At the same time it took a constructive approach to the General Council's involvement in inter-union disputes and any 'unconstitutional stoppage of work which involves directly or indirectly large bodies of workers or which, if protracted, may have serious consequences'.

Armed by this backing from the whole movement, talks were resumed with the Prime Minister. In all there were eight meetings with

Harold Wilson, either with the full General Council in attendance or a negotiating subcommittee. The subcommittee was appointed to get down to details in a way that a large body like the General Council could not. Hugh Scanlon and I were elected to it, although we were junior members of the Council; the other members were well-established figures in TUC circles: Alf Allen, Sid Greene and Fred Hayday. In this smaller body it was possible to spell out some aspects of trade union life which Wilson and Castle seemed not to understand. I found it necessary to explain how differences between unions over membership, for example, had been successfully dealt with by the TUC and that we were proposing to move along the same lines in dealing with demarcation and other strikes. It was this approach which finally prevailed, although Wilson and Castle were insisting, almost to the end, that if they withdrew their proposed legal sanctions the TUC must draw up rigid rules, apply harsh discipline and take measures which might well have destroyed the organization altogether.

As it was, the declaration which we in the TUC proposed to make did not satisfy the Prime Minister until the words 'solemn and binding' were added. At the final meeting the General Council hung around most of the day and there was much toing and froing, but I was satisfied the battle was over before the meeting started. A victory had been scored in defence of the right to strike without fear of legal sanctions, but the TUC took aboard some big new responsibilities. Contrary to the belief of many critics, including some Labour politicians, we meant what we said. Many strikes were avoided in consequence. Demarcation problems have been thrashed out and settled on the spot, with the help of TUC representatives. In fact there have been few inter-union strikes since that time.

When I could I walked to work from our flat in Denmark Hill. Occasionally I cycled, but I found the exhaust from vehicles a little too much; by walking I could dodge into side-streets and avoid the worst of the fumes. I often wished that some of the top people I knew in industry and politics would traverse the same streets with me and witness the many old houses, decayed, dirty and ill-kept, where families lived together in multi-occupation. The streets were cluttered with rubbish including broken-down cars. I knew how difficult it must have been for kids brought up in these conditions to do their homework. How could anyone talk of equality of opportunity while children had no place to read and write in comfort in their homes? They had no chance of acquiring a decent education any more than I had, in my childhood, in the mean streets of Liverpool.

Walking the streets induced in me a tendency to speculate. I frequently wondered why so many politicians who had reached the top in the Labour Party were opposed to trade union thinking; people like Roy Jenkins, Denis Healey and Dick Crossman. Barbara Castle was the same and she claimed to be a left-wing socialist. 'Why on earth is she so bitter against our people?' I often asked myself during our differences over *In Place of Strife*, and even more during the Ford strike which started in February 1969. There were times when I almost thought she was a company spokeswoman.

I was brought in to the middle of the Ford troubles by the members. A few Ford shop stewards whom I knew burst into my office and demanded: 'For God's sake do something for us, Jack! Our union is going to be smashed unless you can stop what is happening.' My enquiries confirmed the need for quick action. New terms were being forced on Ford employees without the agreement of the membership, and in the case of the TGWU in contradiction to the decisions of an officially called delegate conference of members' representatives. It was claimed that the National Engineering Group Secretary of the union, Les Kealey, had failed to carry out the wishes of the conference. The shop steward convenors in the plants had met and had recommended an all-out stoppage. Some people were already on strike and the Executive Council of the Amalgamated Engineering Union had been urged to sanction strike action.

I was in a position to exercise executive authority; although Frank was still General Secretary he left it to me to deal with most industrial matters. A cursory examination of the alleged 'agreement' showed me that it was unacceptable. It was closely in line with the Government's White Paper on cooling-off periods and penalty clauses, which the union strongly opposed. By stipulating twenty-one days' notice before strike action, a 'cooling-off' period was implied, and the penalty clauses could be used by the company to apply sanctions against justifiable protest. Acceptance could not be reconciled with our opposition to *In Place of Strife* and in any case Kealey's promise to consult with the 'lay' (rank-and-file) representatives had not taken place. Les Kealey was clearly unhappy but he claimed that an agreement had been reached by the trade union side of the negotiating committee by a vote of seven to five. He then told me that he had abstained from voting, at which I exploded: 'You did not vote, yet we are the largest union!' I insisted that we should ask for a re-examination of the so-called agreement, since if both the Engineers and ourselves were against it, it could not possibly operate.

Kealey made it clear he would not co-operate and I was obliged to make my own decision. Should I let the position drift, with large-scale unofficial strike action inevitably round the corner? Common sense and my own disposition dictated that everything should be done quickly to find a peaceful solution. I contacted Hugh Scanlon and we both agreed that we should ask for fresh discussions with the company. A meeting of Ford TGWU shop stewards left me in no doubt that this was the right decision. At the delegate conference on 30 January it had been decided unanimously 'that before any agreement with the company was concluded a re-convened delegate conference would take place'. The stewards said that Kealey had been present and had agreed to this resolution. He had also been instructed to 'reject any agreement that introduces penal clauses'. But the decisions of the conference had, apparently, meant nothing to him although, as the spokesman for the largest union by far at Ford's, he could have prevented the agreement being reached.

The company refused to withdraw the penal clauses or to have new negotiations. Kealey took no part in this approach and later resigned when told by the General Executive Council of the union that they took a serious view of his actions. Both the TGWU and the AEF gave official support to the members on strike, who were a majority of the workforce. Ford's reacted immediately by seeking an *ex-parte* injunction restraining the two unions from 'attempting to procure a variation in the agreement' and 'procuring an unconstitutional stoppage of work'. Their request was granted until 3 March, when the company applied for a mandatory injunction ordering the two unions to revoke their official support of the strike. The court hearing lasted three days. Although I was named in the company's submissions, I took no part in the proceedings and did not attend the hearing. I had other things to do. I knew if I was gaoled it would be worse for the company than for me, so I was not worried personally, although I was deeply concerned that the company should not be able to establish a legal precedent. To my delight, and that of the members generally, Ford's lost their case. Our lawyers successfully argued that there was no agreement (because the union executives had not ratified it), and that even if there was one, it was not legally binding.

Vic Feather came to see me and we agreed that he should try to get the parties together but no progress was made in the ensuing discussions. Then Barbara Castle intervened. She was clearly worried by the strike and seemed anxious to placate the management. At no time did she appear sympathetic to the work-people, who, over the years, had had a rough deal from Ford's. That was the problem with her incomes policy, it placed her on the owners' side. In bringing us together she wanted to be a conciliator, but her conciliatory role was severely limited.

Barbara had made up her mind and she used every possible means of pressure. For four days there were almost non-stop talks. Barbara sat in her office, talking to one side and then the other, while her officials acted as go-betweens. Most progress was made when we talked directly to company spokesmen without the presence of government people. Hugh Scanlon and I were joined, without invitation on our part, by Leslie Cannon, the President of the Electrical Trades Union, who insisted that he had a right to be present at any discussions. Les was notorious in the trade union movement as a former ultra-Stalinist who had broken with his former comrades. Les had publicly attacked Scanlon and myself for our opposition to the Ford agreement and claimed to support the idea of penal clauses. At the start our talks with him were bitter and I thought we would get nowhere, but eventually he joined forces with us, though with reservations.

Inch by inch we negotiated out the worst features of the penal clauses, but the involvement of Castle and Cannon, even more than Ford's representatives, made it impossible to eliminate every element without risking a total breakdown. Division in the unions spelt danger, so clearly we had to make the best of a bad job. A major breakthrough was the removal of the provisions for twenty-one-day strike notice and the agreement to reconstitute the National Joint Negotiating Council on a more representative basis. Improved holiday pay and lay-off pay were secured and made our efforts worthwhile, but I remained un-happy that an element of penalties still remained. I fought like hell to get them out but I could not achieve all I wanted. Reluctantly I joined forces with Hugh and Les Cannon and recommended the new terms.

Barbara Castle was all for an immediate return to work but I was insistent that the work people must have the proposals explained to them and be allowed to vote at mass meetings. None of the others shared my view and Barbara thought it 'outrageous', but I was deter-mined that the members should decide. They voted overwhelmingly for the deal and a full resumption of work took place, with the exception of one plant, Basildon, which stuck out a little longer.

Readers may begin to think that I was always in favour of strike action. That certainly would not be true. Most of my time was spent trying to find solutions to industrial difficulties while keeping people at work. I knew that efficient officers, a strong union and good agreements were the best recipe for industrial peace. An opportunity came to strengthen my arm when a new Assistant General Secretary was needed after the departure of Harry Nicholas to the Labour Party. I spent some time persuading Harry Urwin to apply for the position, because I knew that our views on trade unionism and industrial relations were very much the same. I was satisfied that if he was appointed we would be able to trust each other to act as the other would wish although operating independently. I enjoyed a similar relationship with Frank Cousins, but with Harry Urwin there was a closer affinity based on a long experience of working together in the Midlands. Harry was reluctant to apply, because he enjoyed the job he was doing as Regional Secretary in the Midlands, but he eventually agreed and, as easily the most able candidate to appear before the Executive, secured the appointment.

Life at the time was full of new experiences. One such was meeting Richard Nixon, the President of the USA. Vic Feather rang me up one day and said: 'I want you to come with me to meet Nixon; he's anxious to talk with one or two trade union leaders.' Vic had also invited Les Cannon, so the three of us met the President. It was in a private room at Claridges but apart from the location there was nothing of the luxury usually associated with the hotel. We had coffee and an intense couple of hours' discussion. Dr Henry Kissinger accompanied Nixon and was equally involved. I tried to put the President right on our industrial situation, explaining that it was infinitely more peaceful than the USA's. I also said that in my opinion British people wanted to see him improve America's relationship with the USSR and China (China was the No. 1 'hate' of the Americans then). I suggested he should visit countries like Romania. It was wrong to think that our countries lived in separate worlds. I was impressed by Nixon's keenness and clarity of mind.

My activities increased with the publication of a Government White Paper on the Reorganization of the Ports. I had been Deputy Chairman of the National Ports Council for some time, appointed by Barbara Castle when she was Minister of Transport. The White Paper was a disappointment because it excluded from public ownership a number of the smaller but growing ports like Felixstowe. Moreover the principle of workers' participation was inadequately dealt with, a sore point for me since I had expected a substantial advance in the direction of industrial democracy. A lot of detailed work was involved in trying to secure changes: deputations from our Docks Group, meetings with the Union's MPs. I discovered more about drafting parliamentary bills than I had ever known before. On these occasions I was in and out of Parliament almost as much as the average MP. Even the police greeted me like an old friend.

Our union's Conference that year was held in July in the Isle of Man. It was my first Biennial Delegate Conference since I had been elected as General Secretary, and Frank Cousins' last as retiring General Secretary. For Evelyn and me they were busy but happy days. We saw quite a bit of the island and, as in our previous visits, liked what we saw. For me there were nostalgic memories of the one holiday I had in my childhood.

It was wonderful to meet the delegates and their families. Evelyn and I felt a real sense of family, talking over with them their experiences, their problems and aspirations, having a drink and a laugh. These rank and file representatives are the salt of the earth, in our eyes.

At the Conference itself, future policy was being made. On the vital issues of minimum wages, industrial democracy and, not least, penal sanctions in industrial relations, I made major speeches on behalf of the Executive Council. I wanted to make clear where I thought our union should go on these issues and I got overwhelming support. With an eye to the future I declared: 'Shop stewards are the greatest instruments of democracy, and the system should be nurtured, refined, and extended.' The most important aspect of the Conference for me personally was establishing the principle of members having control over the agreements which affected them. 'Penal clauses,' I said, 'should be avoided like the plague,' and 'if employers want agreements to be honoured, then they will have to adopt a system that allows for agreements to be fully explained to and knowingly accepted by workers'. Negotiations increasingly dealt with new methods of work, technological changes, flexibility, job evaluation . . . and, 'No negotiator has the moral right to change a worker's life without asking him first.' There was much fluttering in the dovecotes among some officials who had thought that they had a divine prerogative to decide things *for* the members and not *with* them.

The Conference ended with a warm show of appreciation for Frank on his retirement. I felt exuberant as we finished the proceedings because of the enthusiasm which had prevailed throughout. Evelyn had had a good week too. The sun had shone and together with wives of other officers she had sunbathed and gossiped through the week. Perhaps the nicest occasion was when Frank Cousins' grandchildren accompanied Evelyn and me on a walk along the promenade. I cleaned out some limpet shells and dropped cut pieces of limpet into the sea. Out came crabs and small fish to grab the limpet. The children were thrilled and their laughter lightened our hearts. It was a trick I had learned playing with my own children and later grandchildren on the sea shore.

Chapter Twenty-One

Throughout my career I have always tried to swap ideas and experiences with other trade unionists I thought it would be a good idea, for example, to exchange views with our friends of the United Automobile Workers Union of the USA, so we invited a group of its leaders over and spent a fruitful week at the Royal Agricultural College at Cirencester. Leaders of the AEF joined us in a three-way exchange of views. In our team I made sure there were two lay members so that we kept close to the shop floor in our deliberations. Leonard Woodcock, the President of the American union, and Doug Fraser who became his successor (both of whom had been born in Britain and spent their childhood here) intrigued us all by their presentation of the scene in the American car industry. We learned a lot and found many similarities in our problems – certainly more than we had previously realized existed. This was the first of many similar exchanges and enabled me to encourage the participation of rank-and-file members in international meetings both here and abroad. With the UAW group a friendship developed, extending over many years, not only with union representatives but with their wives as well. While discussions were taking place in the college the American wives were enthusiastically brass-rubbing in Cirencester church or touring the Cotswolds. Evelyn acted as car driver and guide. She had been driving since 1932 and was very competent, which was a great benefit to me since on most of our long journeys she was at the wheel. Although a magistrate, she did not always observe the speed limit. . . .

In the last months of 1969 I was able to announce the achievement of a target. The membership of the union passed the 1.5 million mark; only just – by 1531 members – but enough to celebrate. I determined to do my best to see that we would never fall below that line and thought that our aim should be two million. The news was applauded throughout the union and Frank Cousins, at his retirement dinner, said that I had given him the finest possible birthday present. The dinner was a grand affair at the Grosvenor House Hotel, organized by Alf Edwards, the meticulous Administrative Officer of the union; a galaxy of industrialists and union men and women swirled around the place as though they were at a debutantes' ball.

Two of the guests, whom I had invited, brought an international dimension to the speakers' list. They were my good friend Vic Reuther, International Director of the UAW, and Harold Gibbons, one of the few leaders of the Teamsters with progressive views and generally regarded as 'clean'. I tried to get Vic to throw light on the disappearance of the socialist movement in the States. Why, why, why? I asked. Vic made soothing noises but the question remained unanswered and I am still perplexed.

One of the first big public occasions I attended after I took over as General Secretary was a conference of the Institute of Personnel Management at Harrogate. Employers, management and personnel experts, about thirteen hundred of them, packed into the big conference hall, among other things to scrutinize the new bloke at the head of the TGWU. Jack Lee, the IPM President, had invited me and told me to be as controversial as I liked. We had known each other since 1939, when we had met at a negotiating session at the Rootes (Humber Hillman) factory in Coventry. Lee was a young trainee then, but he later moved to an important position at Shell where I came into contact with him from time to time. Of the Harrogate conference he had said: 'It will be a major national platform for you, Jack. Start as you mean to go on.' And I did.

The huge audience was a mixture of sophisticated management and young personnel officers. The main thrust of my appeal was to the latter. I wanted to gain their support for changes in negotiating arrangements and fuller acceptance of the shop stewards system. But I especially wanted to change attitudes over wages. 'Low wages degrade the standing of the firms that pay them,' I said. 'High wages lift output and encourage efficiency – that is why you will find the lowest unit costs among those industries that are best organized by the unions and which pay the highest wages.' Low wages could not be justified on the grounds that the company would not otherwise survive – 'If it cannot pay decent wages, it should not survive.' I warned of the dangers of ignoring the growing mood of rebellion among groups in both private industry and public services who traditionally got low wages: 'Either we react to that in time, or we face the consequences in terms of industrial disruption.' I'm afraid my declaration fell on deaf ears, although there was a better response to the case I made out for industrial agreements to be settled at the work place and for more conciliation and local arbitration. I felt a bit like John the Baptist crying in the wilderness, but my speech created a great deal of interest and became a talking point in some industrial circles.

Vic Feather, by now General Secretary of the TUC, was attracted to establishment figures like a moth to a candle, and possibly with an eye to the future, he began to cultivate Ted Heath, then the Leader of the Opposition. Occasionally he would let it be known that 'Ted Heath is not a bad fellow, you know!' At one of the meetings of the National Economic Development Council (shortly after I had been appointed to that august body, to succeed Frank Cousins) he invited the trade union members to join him in an informal chat with 'Ted'. Arrangements were made and at Heath's invitation we joined him for dinner in his flat in Albany, off Piccadilly, the oldest block of flats in England and probably the most exclusive. 'We' were Vic, Alf Allen, Sid Greene, Jack Cooper and myself. The others were pillars of the TUC establishment, who set out to impress our host with their responsible attitude on all matters industrial. I tried to bend Ted's ear to the need for better pensions for the elderly, and industrial training for our young people. There is no doubting Ted Heath's sympathy for people and we quickly established a feeling of camaraderie. It was a pleasant evening, with Heath talking of his yacht and musical interests. At one stage he showed us a new piano he had bought and at our invitation played one or two short pieces. Then Vic Feather called out, 'Play the "Red Flag" for Jack,' and the leader of the Tory Party cheerfully played Labour's national anthem. It put the seal on a jolly evening, although I must say that Ted did not play the "Red Flag" very well.

Early in 1970 I went with a TUC team to Gibraltar. I already knew the position there and had pressed the General Council to send a delegation to meet trade unionists on the 'Rock'. General Franco had closed the border between Spain and Gibraltar and was applying pressure to get Britain to cede Gibraltar. The TGWU was the largest trade union there although, at that time, by no means as strong as I thought it should be. I had established a good relationship with the active members and was popular with them because of the interest I took in their working conditions and my opposition to the Franco regime.

I confess I resented the light-hearted way Alan Hargreaves, the TUC departmental head for international affairs, treated the visit, which was also true to some extent of the other members of the team, Fred Hayday and Vic Feather. They seemed to feel that the place was so small as to be insignificant. Our local members certainly got that impression and were strongly critical. What I intended to be a fillip to Gibraltar's morale turned out a flop. It rained heavily throughout the visit and maybe it was that which dampened the spirits of my colleagues.

There was one lighter moment when Vic Feather told Evelyn and me of a crisis in his hotel room. He had turned the bath on and had then got absorbed in some papers. Water came seeping under the door of his room as the bath overflowed. When Vic noticed the seepage he ran in panic to the bathroom, turned the tap off and began mopping up as best he could. He was engaged in this when a surprised lady from the hotel staff arrived. Vic's defence was to call out: 'Mucha rain, mucha rain!' His explanation was not accepted.

We had our differences, Vic Feather and I, but on one thing we were agreed – to make the TUC more efficient. Although it was expected to have an expert opinion on the problems of industry, in day-to-day affairs it was far removed from the unions and the shop floor. I advocated the setting-up of industrial committees, which would bring together the unions concerned in each industry within the framework of the TUC. Once I knew that Vic was receptive to the idea I submitted detailed plans for a range of industrial committees which would replace existing trade union federations and also provide the means for co-ordination in areas where nothing yet existed.

My proposals caused endless argument. The building and construction industry unions, for example, were wedded to the National Federation of Construction Unions and the leaders were loath to change, although they could see the advantage of closer links with the TUC. 'There would be no point in having a TUC committee if you also have a federation,' I told them. They gave way, and many other industries followed suit. The principal exceptions were the engineering and shipbuilding trades where the confederation lingers on, at considerable cost to the unions.

I thought the TUC industrial committees would be helpful in coordinating policy at a time when collective bargaining was expanding at company and plant level. They would provide a forum for exchanging information and occasionally give a lead in the negotiation of shorter working hours and basic wages, or in productivity bargaining. 'How do these ideas square with your decentralization policies?' asked Vic Feather. I explained that I had been consistent in advocating national co-ordination in the trade union movement at the same time as expanding the role of local bargaining and shop stewards' committees. Vic gave his blessing and helped some of the changes along, but he remained suspicious of shop stewards' committees and my suggestions for widening their role were lost in the machine.

In three areas opportunities occurred for me to press ahead on industrial democracy: in Leylands, on the docks, and in London Transport. Tony Benn, the Minister of Technology, told me of his efforts to secure a merger of BMC (British Motor Corporation) and Leyland. It was an encouraging move and I welcomed his efforts to ensure a substantial British motor-car industry. Donald Stokes, the chairman of the new company, quickly got to work. Many of his moves in improving management were welcome but he tended to be abrasive in his attitude to the unions. In many cases, I had no doubt, management had tried to deflect his criticisms of them by placing the blame on the shoulders of the shop stewards. He responded by making bitter public attacks on the latter, talking of 'chaos and anarchy' and 'planned and deliberate disruption by unofficial action'. It was the same old story. I felt like making allegations, just as sensational, against management, but did not. Instead Hugh Scanlon and I asked for a meeting with him and he agreed to meet us privately at his flat in St James's.

After we had been received by Donald, Les Cannon (the leader of the electricians' union) moved out from a corner of the room. He was very much at home and within minutes seemed to take over the role of host, inviting us to take a cigar from a huge box of Cuban cigars (part of a Leyland deal with Castro, I learned later). I refused because I don't smoke but Hughie took one 'for an old friend', he said. It was clear that Cannon was no stranger to the Stokes abode but he took little part in the discussion which ensued. Hughie and I set out to convince Stokes that we wanted Leyland to be a model of industrial efficiency and of our willingness to co-operate in any way we could. We argued that there were many justified grievances and a need for swifter methods for resolving industrial disputes.

The upshot was an agreement that the union leaders should meet shop stewards from all the Leyland undertakings in order to get to grips with problems on the shop floor and make proposals for improvement. I presided over the conference, which proved to be most constructive. The only doubt I had was that we might sacrifice local identities and bargaining arrangements in the move to develop the overall negotiations which the company and most of the union leaders had in mind. From the start I was opposed to new payment systems which sought to eliminate locally negotiated piecework. The direct incentives involved in such schemes meant high productivity and in the long run it would have been better for management to seek union co-operation in ironing out difficulties in that system rather than adopting a more centralized approach.

In the docks reorganization was also in the air. The Labour Government produced a Bill which would have nationalized the larger ports but left out the small ports. All sorts of technical reasons were advanced for this less-than-total nationalization, but I was terribly disappointed. From my experience of dockland I was convinced that the efficient use of our port resources was only possible with full public ownership (a view, incidentally, that was shared by the leader of the port employers, Bill Tonge). With the support of two MPs, John Ellis and Roy Hughes, I fought hard and long to extend the area of public ownership and to establish the representation of dock-workers on the policy-making boards of the proposed new Ports Authority. We made some progress in that direction and dockers' representation was the central feature of a delegate conference to which the union invited the Minister of Transport and the chairman-designate of the proposed Authority, Peter Parker.

Peter Parker is a born diplomat. The docks delegates gave him a great reception, although almost all he did was smile at them. Years later I learned that he had done quite a bit of amateur acting and it certainly carried him through that day. Fred Mulley, the Minister of Transport, told the conference: 'For the first time in any Bill, workers' participation is assured.' I decided not to tell the conference what hard work it had been to get the Minister to that stage! Parker thought it was marvellous; he told me that 'workers' participation will be the flashpoint for the success of the industry'. All seemed set fair, but then the General Election came along and the Bill perished with no prospect of being revived under the incoming Conservative Government.

Results were somewhat better with the London Transport Executive. We established good relations with the new chairman of the

Executive, Sir Richard Way, and with the Central Bus Committee (the lay negotiating body for London busmen). I was able to encourage the development of joint union/management committees to enable rank-and-file representatives to participate more fully in decisions affecting London's buses. More could have been achieved in the direction of industrial democracy but for the restrictive views of the leaders of other unions who were reluctant to break with tradition.

Of the many visitors to Transport House at this time none impressed me more than the leader of the American farm-workers, Cesar Chavez. Totally different to any other US trade union leader I had met, he came shyly and nonchalantly into my office. He expressed simple thanks for the efforts of our members in thwarting attempts to dump boycotted US grapes on the British market. From an illiterate Mexican labourer he had become a gifted labour leader and had campaigned brilliantly for the downtrodden farm-workers in the US who, in many areas, were still suffering conditions reminiscent of Steinbeck's *The Grapes of Wrath*. While in London he had preached at Westminster Cathedral and had appealed for a bell, to ring out a message of hope across America. His message brought a response from the owner of London's Whitechapel Bell Foundry, who decided to donate a quarter-ton church bell to the United Farm Workers Organizing Committee. Chavez invited my help in shipping the bell to the USA and I agreed that our union would make the arrangements and bear the cost. He told me that when the bell arrived in New York it would be transported across the country in an open freight car, stopping at town after town to raise funds.

Not long after the visit of Chavez, the news came through of the death in an air crash of Walter Reuther and his wife. It was a sharp blow, for Walter too was a wonderful man who had stood for decent standards in the unions and in industry against a background of corruption and thuggery. I felt his death deeply and sent a cable to his brother Victor, saying: 'The inspiration he gave will live on, and we will play our part with you in serving more strongly than ever the ideals and principles for which he fought so valiantly.'

The General Secretary of the TGWU, if he works hard, can have a lot of influence both inside and outside the union. Ernie Bevin had seen to that when he had devised the constitution of the union. Innovations which I had thought should be made over the years, but which had been thwarted by the dead hand of 'custom and practice', could now be attempted.

I got busy with the creation of a union newspaper. We had a monthly magazine called the *TGWU Record*, which mainly consisted of articles and reports on union functions. It fulfilled its purpose of making leadership activities known to the members, but it had little impact on the shop floor, a fact well known to the shrewd old trade unionist who was the editor. When I looked at costs I found that the printing charges for the magazine had been enormous; this alone was a good reason for change. I called in Ken Sprague, a freelance lay-out artist and a good friend with plenty of ideas, Bob Rolfe, the editor, and Norman Willis as researcher, to thrash out ideas. I first of all explained my aim: to create a lively monthly newspaper that members would want to read. It had to be a tabloid and to put the main emphasis on union achievements in the localities. 'Every week,' I said, 'our members are making progress on some issue or other which should be brought to life in story form so that others might emulate their success.' Events moved at a brisk pace and for some years the new *TGWU Record* led the way in trade union journalism. Even Vic Feather expressed pleasure. Certainly it shook up the staid and self-satisfied officials when members asked, 'Why can't we try to get what such-and-such a firm has agreed to?' But much more should have been done and I blame myself for not carrying the initiative further and spending more money and effort on making the paper essential reading on the shop floor.

The new publication had hardly got into its stride before Harold Wilson decided to go to the country in 1970, so it played no significant part in conveying to the membership the union's support of the Labour Party. I looked to a new innovation to help achieve this end. I called together the full-time officers, six hundred of them, from all parts of the United Kingdom. We had troubles enough with the Labour Government. Nevertheless, I knew that the prospects for working people would be worse under a Conservative Government and when Harold Wilson made his decision I told him I would do all I could to help the Party remain in office.

When I invited Wilson to speak to the officers' conference there was no great enthusiasm in his acceptance. I explained its importance in terms of making contact with shop stewards and union branches and the possibility of the officers setting up joint TGWU–Labour Party committees in the localities. His response was enigmatic – not at all 'Let's talk about what should we do to win the election.' His attitude was much the same when he spoke to the conference. He said little or nothing about the future and displayed as much fervour as a cold fish. I could feel the disappointment among the audience. Even Vic Feather, who also spoke, appeared less cheerful than his usual self.

Maybe Harold Wilson felt that the record of his Government was enough to win the General Election, but that wasn't the view of many active Party workers to whom I spoke up and down the country. There was no doubt that Ted Heath's campaign over prices was having some effect, and in our own ranks there was some dismay about rushing the election through in June. Anyway, Labour lost the election. Some time afterwards, I took a trade union friend from New Zealand into the House of Commons and introduced him to Wilson. I left them together for a chat. Afterwards my friend said: 'I asked Harold why he thought he had lost the election, and would you believe it, he told me in his opinion it was due to England losing in the World Cup!' I knew that Wilson was not as naïve as that, but the argument saved him from having to give more laborious explanations which might have reflected upon himself.

Ted Heath's success evoked a Vicar of Bray response in the TUC. Vic Feather, with the support of some of the TUC old guard, could hardly wait to assure the new Government that the TUC would welcome consultation with it and even offered to provide advice, despite the grumbles of a few of us that the first consideration should be an assurance that the law courts and the police would be kept out of industrial relations.

Within weeks of the election I was involved in a national dock strike, the first since 1926. Normally the General Secretary of the TGWU is not involved in day-to-day industrial negotiations, but when a major strike is on the horizon he is obliged to move in because the interests of the whole union are involved. This is especially the case in the docks industry, where he is nominally the chairman of the trade union side of the national negotiating body. For quite a long time the docks section had been pressing for an increase on basic rates, but the employers, led by my friendly adversary in the Liverpool dispute, Bill Tonge, would not budge. Six weeks' notice of strike action had been given, with the support of the union executive, in the hope of breaking the deadlock, but without avail.

As the clock ticked ominously towards the deadline I tried hard to persuade Mr Tonge to talk. I was convinced that he and the other employers had been panicked into believing their own propaganda that the union's demands meant a fabulous 50 per cent increase in dockers' earnings. I had worked out that the wage bill would go up by only 7 or 8 per cent if our claim was met. I sought to explain this to Tonge, but he would hear none of it.

In some ways we could not have been dealing with a nicer bloke. He seemed more like a Victorian clergyman than the managing director of Hays Wharf and leader of all the port employers. Behind his smiles and courtesy, it was difficult to sense the stubborn nature of his character. On the docks the lads joked about him riding about in an ancient taxicab and living in Budleigh Salterton, but his style concealed an iron fist. He himself joked about the support being given to the employers; he told a meeting: 'I've had a letter from the South-East England Ratepayers Association at Worthing. You'll be glad to know that they are with us all the way.' But he was determined to take on the union, with some encouragement from the Government.

The deadline for the strike was 14 July. It was only shortly beforehand that the Government dropped its feigned indifference and Robert Carr, the new Secretary of State for Employment and Productivity, called the parties together. He maintained his ostrich-like attitude throughout a long meeting but at least it enabled me once more to try to dent the employers' armoury. They did in fact make an across-the-board offer, but only on condition that I would call off the strike. The offer was not a satisfactory one, but it opened the prospect of negotiations. I had said repeatedly that if the employers would negotiate I was sure a basis of settlement could be found.

I explained that I personally could not halt the strike but said that if the employers would maintain their offer I would go on television and appeal to our members to hold their hand and convene a delegate conference. The employers agreed and I made the attempt, although the cards were stacked against me. It was a calculated risk which Vic Feather described as 'courageous', although I felt later that it was a little foolish. A number of the ports had already stopped work when the delegate conference assembled, and my appeal for the employers' offer to be accepted as a basis for negotiation was rejected by forty-three votes to thirty-nine.

Once in action I was anxious to maintain unity among the men. The withdrawal of labour was complete. It was the effectiveness of the strike which led Robert Carr to set up a court of inquiry. It was a climb-down by the Government, which had been taking an abrasive attitude towards the unions, and it meant that our claims could be examined while the strike continued. The response of the court, under the chairmanship of Lord Pearson, was to grant substantially what we had been asking for. Of course it was a compromise, but one which the employers could have had by negotiation and without a strike. As it was the economy had suffered, the union had spent £500,000 in strike pay, and the employers had lost considerable business.

Work was resumed on 3 August. Although the Emergency Powers Act had ostensibly been brought in early on in the strike, it had not been put into operation. Reggie Maudling, the Home Secretary, had called me to his office to tell me he proposed to introduce the EPA. I told him it would not be necessary and that if troops were used in the docks it would only increase tension. I knew that our men would act in a disciplined way and we would be able to deal with any special difficulties. Our attitude was vindicated when our members ensured food supplies for the offshore islands and handled emergency medical supplies and perishable cargoes. We insisted that any profits or wages should go to an agreed charity.

The Pearson Inquiry saw their award as a step in the modernization process which was already under way. Some results were remarkable. In London, as one example, our members achieved a $31\frac{1}{4}$-hour week in a semi-shift system with a level of guaranteed wages unheard of in the previous history of dockland. As Lord Pearson and his committee saw the proposition:

> The port transport industry is in the course of making a major, far-reaching and vitally important transition from the old-fashioned and relatively inefficient methods of working and an archaic, complex and not wholly rational pay structure to new and more productive methods of working and a simplified and rational pay structure.

Their assessment proved to be optimistic.

Although I had spent a large part of my life in the motor industry, problems in the ports increasingly loomed on my agenda. I knew, and felt the impact in my very being, of the container revolution: Ro-Ro, gantry cranes, straddle carriers, side-loaders, packaged timber, fork-lift trucks, and all the other revolutionary changes in the loading and discharge of ships. On the ships and the quays the dockers sensed trouble, and so did I, because all the forecasts coming before the National Ports Council pointed to massive cutbacks in labour requirements. The development of inland container bases caused deep suspicion because of the threat to jobs entailed. Growth in the smaller ports, which were not involved in the dock-labour scheme, was also seen as a threat to employment and the generally higher wages and conditions we had achieved.

Perhaps the worst feature about the many changes in dockland was the way containers were being increasingly used to bypass the registered dock labour force. Small firms, which our people called 'cowboy operators', were engaging in 'stuffing' (loading) and 'unstuffing' (unloading) containers all over the place, using any type of labour, often casual. Despite all the promises of permanent employment for registered dockers, job insecurity increased. Sectional trouble intensified and in 1972 I was confronted once again with the challenge of a national dock strike.

Before that occurred, however, the TUC had to face up to the gruelling challenge of the Conservative Government's Industrial Relations Bill.

Chapter Twenty-Two

Question not, but live and labour
Till yon goal be won,
Helping every feeble neighbour,
Seeking help from none;
Life is mostly froth and bubble,
Two things stand like stone,
Kindness in another's trouble,
Courage in your own.

ADAM LINDSAY GORDON

(Often quoted by my mother when I was a youngster.)

Nothing arouses my anger more than the attitudes adopted by petty bureaucrats. At the Labour Party Conference in 1970 I had my fill of them. Acting for the union, I wanted to submit an emergency motion to the Conference on pensions. I was told that there were already one or two motions on the agenda from constituency Labour parties dealing with pensions but that the Conference Arrangements Committee had decided that pensions would not be debated that year. I considered the issue was crucial. To my mind the pensioners were getting a rough deal. It was hell's own job convincing the officials and then the members of the Conference Arrangements Committee, but we won in the end and a debate was allowed.

My feelings on this subject were such that, early on in my speech, I banged the rostrum so hard that a cardboard placard bearing the slogan 'Britain needs a Labour lead' fell off into the auditorium. I had made two other major speeches to the Conference, one on industrial relations and pay policies and the other on community democracy, which attracted a lot of support, but I felt even more passionately about the situation of the elderly. My emotional appeal must have touched a raw nerve amongst the delegates. In pressing for a 'massive campaign', I said that the union itself would produce a million broadsheets within a week. That brought a tremendous roar of approval from the floor.

My promise rather shocked the Labour Party shell-backs and some of my colleagues at Transport House. They doubted whether it could be done and a considerable effort had to be mounted to prove them wrong. With the help of Norman Willis and Ken Sprague, plus a willing printer, the job was finished in time. It gave a lead to the rest of the movement and the response was heart-warming. From the Party organization in the past I had all too often found a tendency to be long on words and short on action, but on this occasion action was quick and strong. A huge demonstration was organized in the Albert Hall for 12 December. Celebrities from the stage and screen – Miriam Karlin, Clive Dunn and others joined Vic Feather, Shirley Williams and myself in identifying with the thousands of senior citizens present. I addressed similar rallies in Liverpool and Edinburgh and then led a lobby of Parliament. It was the start of a continuous campaign.

The approval I had received from the Conference delegates for my views on pay policies was certainly not reflected on the platform. Jim Callaghan, Barbara Castle and Roy Jenkins in their various ways revealed their continued support for a statutory incomes policy. I'm afraid I shouted out my objections rather vociferously when Jim Callaghan was speaking, and I regretted it afterwards. It was a wrong thing to do, especially as Jim went out of his way to be friendly. In a way I was more disturbed by articles written at the time by Lord Balogh and Harold Lever, which took a hard line on incomes policy. I was worried that these two men would exert influence on Harold Wilson and his colleagues.

The *Observer*, *The Times* and the *Guardian* were critical of my conduct that week. *The Times*, for example, talked of my 'blustering use of the card vote'. I replied by pointing out that the union's vote was not mine to use. It was determined by the TGWU delegation. The delegates were almost entirely lay union members, who came from their jobs at the bench, or in offices, garages, building sites and docks. Their decisions were based on the decisions of the thousand-strong lay conference of the union, which again consisted entirely of people working in the country's industries and services. Every one of the votes that we had cast was in line with the democratically determined decisions of the union.

I invited my accusers to say where our votes had been out of step with the members' wishes. By voting against wage restrictions we had drawn attention to the fact that there was powerful pressure for higher wages and salaries. It was not just a union conspiracy, it was a fact.

Yes, I said, we had taken the initiative in pressing for a debate on the Common Market. That could hardly be called undemocratic. And we had pressed for a campaign on behalf of the old-age pensioners.

But the issue which had aroused most ire in the press was my plea for a new approach to community participation in national and local government. I had said that there should be community councils through which MPs and local councillors could find out what ordinary people were thinking. I did not think that the views I had advanced were all that revolutionary, and I knew that they reflected rank-and-file opinion, but I used the phrase 'shop stewards in the streets', and had talked of industrial democracy and a 'people's democracy, for all the people'. Some journalists made it appear that I was advocating revolution. I explained my view by quoting the words of Thomas Jefferson:

> Where every man is a sharer in the direction of his ward repub-
> lic, or of some higher one, and feels that he is a participator in
> the government of affairs, not merely at an election one day in
> a year, but every day; when there shall not be a man in the State
> who will not be a member of some one of its councils, great or
> small, he will let the heart be torn out of his body sooner than
> his power be wrested from him by a Caesar or a Bonaparte.

Bevin scorned journalists. For my part I tried to be as open and available as possible, not because I particularly liked the press but since I hoped the union would get fair treatment in it. 'You don't accept our invitations for a meal,' said one journalist. 'Well, I'm very busy,' I replied, 'and in any case I prefer Evelyn's cooking.' That wasn't the whole truth – I simply had not the time to waste. I never found any takers from the press lads when I offered to share my sandwiches with them! In fairness, I found most industrial journalists with whom I dealt to be straightforward and helpful. It was the exceptions who were the problem!

The new Conservative Government announced their plans for industrial relations legislation early in October. They were as bad as we had expected. The effect was to bring about a surprising degree of unity on right, left and centre of the TUC General Council. Of course there were differences of emphasis. Some members of the Council wanted to talk to the Government and others did not. A few would have conceded without a battle. But all were agreed that the unions were in real danger.

It was clear to be that the Government was in no mood to conciliate. They were determined to 'tame the unions' one way or another. On the economic front harsh anti-inflation measures were adopted. The Chancellor, Anthony Barber, applied public-spending cuts; arbitration awards were repudiated and unemployment increased rapidly. Even conciliation facilities were refused by the Department of Employment to the unions catering for local authority workers, unless they accepted pre-conditions laid down by Robert Carr. Union leaders whose policy was 'peace at any price' began to realize that they were faced with a policy of confrontation which had not been experienced since the 1930s.

I thought it would be a waste of time trying to negotiate with the Government on their consultative document dealing with industrial relations legislation, although some members of the General Council still wanted to do so. At a special meeting of the Council Tom Jackson of the postal workers said that we should try to negotiate the best possible agreement with the Government. He was supported by Jack Peel of the Dyers Union. They advanced the pessimistic view that, if we denounced the Government and campaigned against it, we should be 'weakened enormously' if the Act was finally passed. Peel suggested that 'a public campaign might get out of hand'. I was very pleased when their defeatist line was rejected.

The General Council included a number of middle-aged union leaders who disliked their comfortable existence being disturbed. They thought it deplorable that this new Government seemed to be departing drastically from the tradition of previous Tory administrations by not wishing to play 'footsy' with the union leaders. There was little room for manoeuvre because the Government had told Vic Feather that under no circumstances would they change the main planks of their platform. Some furious thinking had to be done to grapple with this challenge. The majority rapidly came round to the view that we had to persuade our members and the public in general to oppose the Government's policy.

Quite a few voices, including my own, demanded that the TUC should display no weakness in dealing with the situation. For me the greatest danger lay in the threat to use the law against workshop trade union organization. Others saw it as the hamstringing of union leadership and the destruction of the authority of union conferences. The reason that Jackson and Peel got short shrift was that even the respectable old guard on the Council knew that it would not do the movement any good to crawl to the Government, especially when it was already known that the cupboard was bare.

There were understandable doubts about how far we should go. Some said that public opinion was not very sympathetic to the unions at the time. We had to face the fact that many people did not see us as we saw ourselves. There had been a lot of criticism, and indeed hostility, although unions had continued to grow at a remarkable rate. From my own experience I had found that people might accept that a trade union was good for them, but at the same time condemn as irresponsible a group of workers taking action elsewhere. They might respect their own shop steward, yet regard shop stewards in general as troublemakers. They might recognize the need for collective strength in their own work place, yet still talk about 'the unions having too much power these days'.

I recall it being said at the time that something like 80 per cent of the people believed that 'some people in Britain are getting too much money for the amount of work they do'. This sort of resentment rubbed off on the unions. Maybe it was our own fault in not explaining our role to the public over the years. All too often trade unions officials when asked questions about strikes or difficult industrial situations have said, 'No comment', or even worse, 'It's none of your business!'

Such considerations weighed heavily on the General Council as we thrashed out what was to be done. We all agreed that there should be a big publicity campaign but only after some argument was agreement reached on a national day of protest, involving work-place meetings all over the country and culminating in a major rally in the Albert Hall. This eventually took place on 12 January 1971. I and others knew that we had to keep the pressure up before the proposed Bill became an Act of Parliament, so we pressed for a massive demonstration to march from Hyde Park to Trafalgar Square with members from all over the country taking part. I urged that this should take place in February, but I encountered a variety of doubts. 'It will be too cold then'; 'We'll look daft if the members don't turn out'; and from George Lowthian of the Bricklayers Union: 'You know very well, Jack, people won't take part in that sort of thing unless they're paid to do it.'

The doubting Thomases were undone. The great march on Sunday 21 February 1971 exceeded all our expectations. It was truly a remarkable day. People came from all parts of the United Kingdom and all industries. They marched proudly behind bands and banners that provided marvellous sound and colour to a serious and determined assembly of working people. Seven miles of marchers were cheered on by members of the general public, among whom were many elderly and disabled who would have liked to march but physically were not up to it.

It was the largest demonstration of the century. As the TUC said at the time: 'It was the biggest demonstration since the Chartists moved working men to demand the right to vote, 130 years earlier.' Estimates put the number of participants between 140,000 and 200,000, but whatever the precise figure it was tremendously impressive. There was a total absence of cranks and rowdyism, no arrests and no scuffles – although Trafalgar Square and its surrounds were not large enough to hold the crowd and many marched on to another meeting on the Embankment.

All were united around one simple message – 'We say NO to the Bill.' The newspapers could not hide their admiration and the police commented favourably on the order which had been attained. Our purpose of showing the world the strength of trade union opinion had been achieved. Vic Feather was justifiably proud and I felt much personal satisfaction at the part I had played in moving the TUC 'back to Trafalgar Square'. Some critics called it posturing, but it proved the prelude to a long and effective campaign of non-co-operation.

That was the key to the discussions at the Special Trades Union Congress held in March at Croydon. Hugh Scanlon and I failed to gain a majority for industrial action against the Bill and for uncompromising resistance to registration, but a framework was agreed which enabled the unions most opposed to the Industrial Relations Act to render it ineffective.

Surprisingly, little enthusiasm was shown by employers for the Government's plans and it proved relatively easy to persuade them to add a clause to collective agreements which read 'This is not a legally enforceable agreement' (a phrase whose acronym – TINA LEA – became part of industrial relations jargon). By that action they struck a blow against one of the main tenets of the policy, which was that all collective agreements should be deemed legally enforceable. Our adviser on this, and indeed all other matters related to the proposed legislation, was Professor Bill Wedderburn (a law professor at the LSE, later to become a Labour peer). I had consulted him at an early stage and was busy advising officials and shop stewards on what action to take before the TUC had even looked at the matter. With the Special Congress decision calling upon all unions to exclude legal enforcement from collective agreements, the approach became universal.

Dashing up and down the country, addressing rallies, marches, stewards' meetings, factory meetings, I knew there was considerable support from the shop floor. Wherever possible I tried also to rustle up support from managers, MPs and media people. An old friend, Maurice Edelman, the Labour MP for Coventry North, who despite his politics mixed often with wealthy and influential people, wrote in the *Daily Express* after a chat we had together: 'I am opposed to the Industrial Relations Bill. Co-operation, not the courts, is the way to peace in the factories. Because of that, I want the Labour movement to fight the Bill by every legal, constitutional, and democratic means. . . . I want to see such a build-up of opinion in the pubs and clubs and buses and trains that eventually the Tory Government, like the Labour Government with its White Paper *In Place of Strife* . . . is obliged to give way.'

Most unions followed the policy of withdrawing from the register when the Act came into force. (Registration under the new Act meant that the content and operation of a union's rules would be subject to surveillance by a Government official, the Registrar, and ultimate control by the National Industrial Relations Court. Refusal to register was seen as a major act of defiance against the Government's labour legislation.) As the numbers taking this action increased, so the pressure on the more reluctant unions grew. The Government's plan to use registration as a means of disciplining unions was shattered. By sheer persistence the unions which chose to remain on the register were isolated (despite the substantial taxation concessions given to those which did so). One renegade was the National Union of Seamen, which no doubt pleased the Government and the shipowners. Its decision did not surprise me, because for some time I had been keeping an eye on the leaders of the union and knew how much they were influenced by the owners.

Hugh Scanlon and I were put in the dock by the newspapers. We were made to appear terrible ogres and some extremists even threatened me, Hugh, and Clive Jenkins with assassination. Menacing phone calls were made to us at home and at our offices. Frankly I thought it was a joke and treated it as such; when I was questioned I said: 'It's a lot of nonsense and I'm taking no notice.' I made no contact with the police and they none with me. Clive Jenkins thought it was the activity of 'cranks', but he was still accompanied by a Special

Branch guard when he flew north to a conference. Hugh Scanlon said on TV: 'It is upsetting, but I must say without divulging too much that the unobtrusive protection and feeling of security which I have received during these trying times speaks well of the police.' Anyway, nothing came of it.

I concentrated on trying to present the positive side of trade unionism in a series of meetings I addressed at that period. One, organized by the Industrial Society, was presided over by the Duke of Edinburgh, who seemed somewhat impressed in an amused sort of way. In general, I was advocating a new, completely independent and impartial conciliation service to help keep industrial peace. A new way had to be found to encourage both sides in any dispute to keep talking and reach agreement where possible. 'The Government's conciliation service used to do this,' I argued, 'but the Government is now suspect because it appears to be always on the side of the employer.' If the Government could not meet the need, then employers and unions must be prepared to set up their own service. We, the trade unions, did not want strikes if they could be avoided, nor did the rest of the community, but the Industrial Relations Bill would aggravate strikes. In more than 90 per cent of the companies with which the TGWU had agreements there were never any strikes, but that fact was ignored when a strike occurred, whatever the reason.

One of the most urgent problems that confronted us was the need to raise the level of the union's negotiating abilities. That is why I encouraged John Hughes, the Vice-Principal of Ruskin College, with his idea of a Trade Union Research Unit based on the College. In my talks with him I suggested that the team he was assembling should first concentrate on preparing the union's case for the Ford negotiations which were to start shortly afterwards. They would work closely with our own union officers, and if it worked out we would help to finance the new unit. I had in mind similar projects for ICI and local government negotiations which were due to take place in the ensuing months.

There emerged from this approach a brilliant presentation of our case, about which Peter Wilsher wrote with some enthusiasm in the *Sunday Times*. He said it marked 'a clear stage in the growing-up of British trade union negotiation', and appeared to be setting new standards in the normally rather tedious pay debate. Basically it was a case for parity with the wages paid in the Midlands motor car industry. We made sure that our case, printed in pamphlet form, was widely distributed on the shop floor and it was debated and highly appreciated by the rank and file.

Our presentation convinced the Ford membership that their demands were just and fair, and they were all the more astounded when the management made a very small offer and stuck to it. The two sides were deadlocked and eventually an official strike took place, backed by all the unions with membership at Fords. The strike continued for nine weeks. It was a punishing period for the men, many of whom were experiencing strike action for the first time. There were signs of weakness on our side and the strike was having a sharp effect on the firm too.

In the ninth week I was contacted (as the leader of the union with the largest membership in the firm; we had more than 20,000 members out of the 47,000 employed) by the chairman of Ford-Europe, Mr Gillan, asking if I would agree to have an informal meeting with him. I said yes, provided Mr Scanlon could come too, which was agreed. Hughie in turn concurred. (He was, of course, the leader of the other major union in the company.) Although we were both subjected to criticism from some on the trade union side I did not see how we could refuse such an invitation since a few weeks previously I had made a public offer to meet Henry Ford II, during his three-day visit to Britain. My offer had been refused but no criticism of my initiative was voiced at the time.

The meeting, which took place in a London hotel, was a long one, and although intended to be exploratory it quickly turned into a negotiating session. Hughie and I were experienced negotiators and we vied with each other to make maximum progress. In the end we secured a substantial offer averaging $16\frac{1}{2}$ per cent in the first stage and two further increases over seventeen months which would nearly double the initial advance, plus equal pay for the female workers. Gillan had urged as a condition of his final offer that we would take the responsibility of accepting it. We said we could not do that, but we would recommend it to the National Negotiating Committee for submission to the membership. He then insisted that a ballot should take place on the offer, and that is what happened following a quickly called meeting of the Negotiating Committee. It was difficult, with twenty-eight plants and eighteen different unions involved, but finally the members made their own decision and voted overwhelmingly for the offer.

'Let the grass grow over the plants!' was the view of Reg Birch,

233

secretary of the trade union side, who favoured a prolonged strike. I did not share his idea; had I done so trade unionism at Ford's could have been weakened beyond repair. In fact from that time onwards there was a substantial expansion in membership at the firm, with increased shop-floor participation, and I lent my weight to a total reform of the negotiating committee in favour of the shop stewards and rank-and-file involvement.

Leonard Woodcock, the President of the American auto-workers' union, came over during the strike for an international meeting, and at his request I arranged a meeting with Ted Heath, the Prime Minister. We wanted to discuss the threats made by Henry Ford II during his visit about the possible withdrawal of investment from Britain. I had expected a hostile meeting but Heath greeted us in a most friendly fashion and gave us a courteous hearing. It was not just a formality with him, he followed closely the arguments put forward by Woodcock, Scanlon and myself, commented freely and indicated some sympathy. There was none of the woodenness that seemed to come over him on television; indeed I noticed then, and on many other occasions since, that with working-class people he appeared to have no inhibitions and mixed easily. Possibly this was because of his own background, but I have to confess I found it was easier to chat with him than with some Labour friends like Roy Jenkins.

We told Ted Heath that Ford workers objected to Henry Ford's threats which appeared to be a repetition of those made in the past as far back as 1924. The firm had promised the Government in 1961 that they would expand the company in Britain and they should be held to their promise. Ford were trying to play one country off against another and their attack on wages paid in Britain was a form of blackmail. We reminded the PM that high purchase tax, high interest rates and hire purchase restrictions were also factors which firms like Ford's would take into account in considering investment plans. For good measure we took the opportunity of lodging our views on the Industrial Relations Bill, and Woodcock neatly registered the point that even in the USA, with all their legal restrictions in the industrial relations field, they did not make collective agreements legally binding.

My industrial involvement was normally concerned with preventing a strike rather than arising out of one. In the event of a breakdown in negotiations in a major industry I would often be asked to intervene, especially where the TGWU had the sole or a major interest. Although there was a considerable measure of autonomy in the union we tried as much as possible to pursue a unified strategy. This meant I was familiar with the top men in British industry in undertakings as diverse as Courtaulds, ICI, National Freight Corporation, London Transport, Esso and the other oil companies, British Leyland, Chrysler, and of course the ports and waterways, plus the major engineering and electrical companies. There were and are many common elements and I sought to develop these by emphasizing the value of local bargaining, particularly in the area of productivity and incentives. I was often under fire for my advocacy of industrial democracy. I recall being invited to talk with Roland Wright when he was chairman of ICI about my insistence that collective agreements must be reported to and agreed by the shop-floor membership. Not only he and his management, but the leaders of the General and Municipal Workers Union, the other major union in the company, were critical of this approach. I was able to explain how successfully it had operated elsewhere and 'Surely,' I said, 'if people are to be expected to honour agreements which affect them they should have some say in approving them.'

Pensioners had no union to fight for them, but the campaign launched at the 1970 Labour Party Conference was having some impact. The Government had promised to increase pensions by £1 a week in the autumn of 1971; not enough but a decided improvement. Like Oliver Twist I wanted more, and the National Council of Labour, an almost moribund outfit, consisting of leaders of the Labour Party, TUC and the co-operative movement, was resurrected as part of our campaign. What should have been a meeting of common minds turned into a sparring match between Roy Jenkins, then deputy leader of the Labour Party, and myself. In answer to the constant question 'Where is the money to come from?' I mentioned, in passing, the case for levying a wealth tax. Quoting from a ministerial reply in the House of Commons, I claimed that a 5 per cent tax on those with a total income of £50,000 a year or more would raise as much as £600 million. Jenkins immediately retorted that the suggestion was 'irresponsible'; he later withdrew the word when I protested but said, nevertheless, in his opinion it was 'ill-considered'. After a lengthy debate the National Council issued a declaration calling for the doubling of the Government's planned £1 pension increase, a further substantial increase to be made the following year, and an annual review to protect pensioners from inflation. I had had to work hard to get that result, and the experience convinced me that some other body was needed to bring the unions and Labour more closely together.

With the politicians it was for the most part a contest with intellectual snobbery or languid indifference. Idealism, hope and courage always had a greater hold on trade unionists: to right a wrong, to live and breathe brotherhood, to hold out a helping hand to the worker in difficulty. Yet the trade unions needed the Labour Party just as the Party needed the working-class vote. For Labour to regain power there had to be a new confidence between both sections of the movement. The 1964–70 Labour Government had blown its chances by placing the burden of its inherited economic crisis on the backs of the workers. Instead of going for growth its deflationary tactics had allowed the rich to get richer while it deeply offended the workers. Could the lessons be learned and a new approach applied in time?

From the moment of Labour's defeat in 1970 much thought had been given as to how the fortunes of our defeated, and somewhat disillusioned party were to be restored. At a Labour Party meeting I addressed in Newport, and often elsewhere, I urged the need for a liaison body which would work out a clear programme, but Labour's leadership did not respond. The pace of my thinking accelerated as the new Government showed its bias against workers' interests. When I received an invitation to address the Fabian Society's tea meeting at the 1971 Labour Party Conference I accepted it immediately because I thought it might provide an opportunity to gain the support of the intellectuals. With most of my major speeches I arranged for a press release to be issued beforehand, but on this occasion I decided to make it informal, in the hope that it might start the thinkers thinking.

The meetings of the Fabian Society attract few trade union delegates and this one was no exception. Most of those present were staid, middle-class members of the Party. Shirley Williams, whom I always felt was a 'jolly hockey sticks' type of woman, was much in evidence and greeted me in a friendly way. But I was under no illusions – I felt I was in suspicious if not hostile territory. At the end of my speech I received an enthusiastic round of applause, but the important thing for me was the conversation which followed. I knew then that I had hit the target.

The theme was not new, I had been banging the same drum in trade union circles for a while, but I wanted to get a response from leaders like Shirley Williams with whom we were not normally in touch. The Party Conference itself started to provide the answer. I had called for 'an end to the stress and strain between the trade union and intellectual wings of the Party' and astoundingly Roy Jenkins spoke up for talks between the Party leaders and the unions. 'None of us wants a return to the past,' he said.

During the conference I talked to everyone I could about the need for a joint body which would bring Parliamentary leaders as well as the NEC together with the TUC, in regular sessions. I said to Harold Wilson: 'Surely to God, we can knock out essentials on which we can all agree, the bedrock minimum which will get the support of the public. And then let's campaign for it.' I made clear that we would all have to sacrifice some of our old ideas to get agreement. I put the same view repeatedly to Vic Feather – who was 100 per cent politician, indeed more of a politician than Harold Wilson.

In January 1972 the TUC–Labour Party Liaison Committee was set up, with six members of the shadow cabinet, six of the NEC and six of the TUC General Council. That makes it sound easy, but it took a devil of a lot of pressure to overcome the objections of the NEC to the Parliamentary Labour Party having direct representatives on the Committee. To most of us at the TUC it would have been a waste of time if they had not been there. We wanted commitments, especially on the repeal of the Industrial Relations Act, and only the leaders of the Party could deliver these. I had in mind too that if it worked it would be a means of ensuring regular consultation with a Labour Government when it was in office.

We set to work, and the spirit of goodwill was maintained, by and large, until Labour's victory in 1974 and for some time after that. What was later called the 'social contract' grew out of the early meetings. This was what I wanted, because I knew that Labour would not win again without our unity. Of course I wanted priority to be given to certain essentials: a better deal for the pensioners, rehabilitating the national health service, a massive housing programme, measures to eliminate low pay, support for industrial democracy, the repeal of the Industrial Relations Act. I knew that Labour leaders like Denis Healey and Barbara Castle would want to talk about incomes policy, and we did. I told them that the key to union co-operation lay in keeping down retail prices, rents and rates. Hard-hitting discussions went on for a long time, culminating in the document 'Economic Policy and the Cost of Living'.

Unity was not in evidence on everything and certainly not on Britain's entry into the EEC. It was a controversial issue at the 1971

237

Trade Union Congress which was held in Blackpool. The occasion remains literally a painful memory. Shortly before the Congress Evelyn and I had snatched a short holiday down in Devon. We stayed in our eldest son's caravan and in fact were looking after his three children while he and his wife (both teachers at that time) took a break away from their family. The weather was good and it was wonderful to be with the children. Then one morning at breakfast I turned to hand some toast to our grandson. Suddenly I felt a sharp pain and was almost unable to move. Friends on the camp site tried to help, one rubbed my back and applied various measures which he was sure would put me right, but the trouble remained.

With the Congress on my mind I persuaded Evelyn to run me to the station and managed to get on the train to London. She meanwhile phoned the union's driver to meet me at the station and then, through my secretary, arranged that I should be seen by doctors at Manor House hospital. I thought some magic would clear the problem but I was wrong. The doctors said I must stay in hospital, flat on my back. After three days I insisted on leaving, although the doctors thought I should stay for another ten days. It was foolish of me for my back was very painful. I got little benefit from the treatment but the doctors arranged for a special corset to be fitted to help me on my way. Evelyn drove me to Blackpool, while I lay flat on the floor. It was agonizing but we made it. Each day at the Conference was a trial and I felt like an old man as I moved around, especially when getting up and down to the rostrum.

I suppose I could say it was worth the trouble. I successfully proposed a motion which read: 'This Congress opposes the present proposal for Britain to join the Common Market on the terms now known, and believes that a General Election should be held before any decision on entry is taken by Parliament. Congress therefore calls upon the General Council to launch a public campaign in support of this policy.' My satisfaction was even greater when Congress adopted our proposals on pensions, which signalled a long-term involvement by the TUC in the movement to improve the lot of retired people.

The Industrial Relations Act was not our only worry. Economic measures adopted by the new Government had accelerated the upward swing in unemployment. Vic Feather told me that a big West Midlands rally against unemployment was being organized by the TUC at Coventry: 'That's your old stamping ground, Jack. Will you speak there for the General Council?' Of course I said yes. When I arrived at the meeting place it was a pleasure to meet old friends again, but the story they told me was a sad one. In an area I had known for many years and which had seen full employment, high wages and high levels of productivity over a long period, unemployment, the great scourge, had raised its head. When I addressed the thousands who had assembled I said that working people were being caught in a vicious squeeze, with new technology and new methods cutting jobs on one hand while lack of expansion failed to provide jobs on the other. It was a story which was to haunt the nation for years ahead.

Chapter Twenty-Three

You cannot be a union man
no matter how you try
Unless you think in
terms of 'we'
And not in terms
of 'I'.

A piece of union doggerel
from the thirties.

It was in the little town of Wirksworth, in Derbyshire. Evelyn and I had travelled up for the annual branch dinner. The room was full and we had enjoyed meeting old friends and greeting new ones. Most of the men present were lorry drivers, others were factory workers as were many of the wives. After a few drinks there were smiles everywhere. Evelyn and I were at home among our own people. That sounds a little extravagant, but those who know trade unionism at the roots will recognize the feeling. For the dinner we sat at long, narrow tables. The first course was soup. Tomato soup, I remember it well, because after my first couple of spoonfuls I pulled the plate towards me and it overturned into my lap. I could not have felt more embarrassed. I looked around quickly but no one seemed to notice except Evelyn who was sitting alongside me. I took her serviette and mine and moved quickly to the cloakroom. Once inside I stripped and, using serviettes, singlet and underpants, wiped off the soup. I slipped my underclothes into my overcoat pocket in the cloakroom and resumed my place at table as discreetly as I could. Most people probably assumed that I had been taken short. It wasn't long before the meal ended and I was on my feet, exchanging views with the members, the crisis nearly forgotten. As we moved around and the evening grew warmer I wondered if any of the members noticed that I kept my jacket buttoned up, so that the top part of my trousers was well concealed. It was there that the soup had really made its mark. It was just one of many evenings with the union family, but it certainly stuck in my mind!

240

Critics used to say that my advocacy of increased rank-and-file influence in the affairs of the TGWU meant that I belittled the role of the full-time official. This was never true. I had been long enough in the service of the union to realize the value of the good, efficient and conscientious officer. But I was determined not to tolerate 'bad eggs'. I was continually emphasizing that the job of the official had changed and we needed to face up to it. Rank-and-file members were claiming and winning a larger role in the formulation of demands and the conduct of negotiations. Final agreements were increasingly being made subject to their approval. The emphasis moved back to the place of work, encouraged by some of us who saw the process as a widening of industrial democracy.

Naturally all this had implications for our officials. They were regarded as part of a team, alongside the shop stewards, rather than as a one-man band. They became co-ordinators, trouble-shooters, and were judged according to their abilities rather than their status. I had these thoughts in mind when I went to the ICI annual lunch for trade union officials and local managers at the Park Lane Hotel. They came from all the different ICI locations in the country, which meant that many of those present were two or three days away from their work. The company must have felt it was good public relations but I confess I thought it a waste of money.

As the General Secretary of the TGWU, the union with the largest membership in ICI, I was expected to attend and to join the chairman of the company at the top table. After lunch I had to 'say a few words' and, after paying a justified tribute to the good relations enjoyed between the company and the unions, I referred to the way union representatives had been involved in work study and job evaluation schemes within ICI. Looking round the ranks of officials and managers I remarked: 'I'm sure if all of us here were subjected to a job evaluation exercise there would be some wonderful results . . .' The lads got the point all right. There was an abundance of wry smiles as I moved around the assembly afterwards.

In January 1972 we celebrated the fiftieth anniversary of the formation of the TGWU, with a big rally in the Royal Festival Hall. I managed to persuade a number of leading employers to join with the union to set up an 'Ernest Bevin International Group Study Scheme'. Included among the projected activities were short educational visits by shop stewards (and foremen in some cases) to international institutes such as the International Labour Organization at Geneva. Lord

Watkinson (of Cadbury Schweppes) and others were enthusiastic but the chairman of one company rather sourly refused to help shop stewards go on 'overseas jaunts'. I knew that Bevin himself would have appreciated the idea of the shop floor getting to know more about international labour relations, but even more he would have applauded the spectacular growth in membership the union was achieving fifty years after its formation.

By the end of 1972 membership of the TGWU stood at $1\frac{3}{4}$ million; 1,746,234 to be precise. A quarter of a million members had been added in just three years. The previous quarter of a million had taken twenty-three. A sense of crusade prevailed throughout the union and non-unionists were responding to our recruiting appeals in large numbers. A further fillip to our progress came from mergers with other unions, which established our position as a truly multi-industrial union. Since its inception in 1922 the union had been described as 'general' or 'unskilled'. I detested these descriptions which inaccurately presented a picture of a union based on defined industrial groups, increasingly organizing large numbers of skilled craftsmen and technicians. I devoted a great deal of effort to persuading key trade unions to join us in industries where we had a major interest.

After prolonged negotiations I was able to welcome the Scottish Commercial Motormen's Union into our ranks, which gave extra punch to the Commercial Transport Group of the union. Alex Kitson, the General Secretary of the Scottish union, became Executive Officer of the TGWU. Another old friend, Bob Edwards, MP, led the Chemical Workers Union into amalgamation. At the same time the Watermen, Lightermen, Tugmen and Bargemen's Union, led by my cockney friend Bill Lindley, 'uncrowned king of the River Thames', together with the Glasgow dockers' union, the Scottish TGWU, merged with us, thus laying the basis for unity throughout dockland.

But the major merger of that year was with the National Union of Vehicle Builders, which consolidated the new Vehicle Building and Automotive Group of the TGWU. This merger not only confirmed the union as the leading organization in motor manufacturing and allied industries, but brought in a further large number of skilled tradesmen. The event was one of the most significant in the history of trade unionism but it nearly didn't happen. After months of detailed negotiations and meetings all over Britain and Ireland, we were about to enter a period of balloting by the NUVB membership when the General Secretary of the NUVB, Alf Roberts, with whom I had conducted most of the negotiations, died unexpectedly. He had entered hospital for a comparatively minor operation and I was shocked when, at nearly midnight on a Sunday evening, the telephone rang and Grenville Hawley, the assistant secretary of the NUVB, told me that Alf was dead. He went on: 'This means that there must be an election for a new General Secretary . . . and of course, Jack, the merger will have to be looked at again.' I was distressed at the passing of a good friend and concerned that the work we had done together might go down the drain. Eventually I was able to persuade Grenville to convene a meeting of his Executive Committee so that I could talk with them about the new circumstances. When the meeting took place I put forward some amended proposals which were accepted and saved the day. The ballot proceeded and the merger was approved.

The trade unions needed all the unity they could achieve. The Conservative Government under Ted Heath lost no time in seeking to curb the unions by legislation and harsh economic measures. Unemployment soared and a number of firms collapsed, even Rolls-Royce was only saved at the last minute by a remarkable U-turn in which the Government nationalized it. While the post office workers, led courageously by Tom Jackson, were defeated after a seven-week strike, the Government was less successful in disputes affecting electricity supply workers, refuse collectors and railwaymen. At the beginning of 1972, however, it was the miners' strike which occupied the headlines.

Following prolonged negotiations the miners had struck and the Government seemed determined to pull out all the stops to defeat them. The NUM began to organize mass picketing, a comparatively new phenomenon in British industrial relations. Joe Gormley and the other leaders of the NUM were well aware of the burning resentment of the miners at their falling standard of living and the fact that they had not benefited from the massive run-down of the industry (over the previous ten years the number of miners employed had fallen by over 400,000). Faced with an unsympathetic Government which seemed hell-bent on defeating the miners, the NUM simply had to fight.

The miners stopped to a man but it was clear that something more was necessary to bring a favourable result. Ray Buckton of ASLEF and I were determined to do all that we could to offer the support of our two unions. I told Joe Gormley: 'If you want to stop oil going into the power stations you'll have to get your men to picket them. We'll do all we can to persuade our men not to cross those picket lines – we want the NUM to win.' Joe seemed surprised, I think he felt that a simple appeal from people like me would do the trick without pickets, but his members learned quickly. For my part I arranged considerable publicity for our support of the miners and called for picket lines to be respected. In some cases I went down with other officers to gain the support of tanker drivers. This helped to ensure that our members knew where we stood. That the General Secretary was personally involved had a good effect. It pleased me to know that oil tanker drivers in particular were responding to the call and turning back their vehicles when they came to the picket lines.

Oil company managements, in some cases, threatened their drivers with dismissal or other disciplinary action for refusing to take their vehicles through the picket lines. I knew we had to make a vigorous response, otherwise our support might collapse. I made it clear that any action against the men would result in a total stoppage of drivers in that company. That did the trick. Unfortunately we were not always so successful with coal and coke-tipper drivers who, in a number of cases, were non-union. A case in point was the huge Saltley Depot in Birmingham where something like 100,000 tons of coke were stacked. Many of our members refused to go in but there were too many non-unionists moving in and out for comfort. A mass demonstration was arranged outside the gates, with our members and those of other unions from the Birmingham factories joining forces with miners' pickets. The action was so strong that the police closed the gates and Saltley was a danger no longer. Arthur Scargill gained national prominence over this action and many of the 140 or so miners he brought down from Yorkshire to participate were given accommodation for the night at the TGWU premises in Birmingham.

After seven weeks' strike the NUM notched up a decisive victory. They had started out with a ballot which strongly favoured action. The support of the TGWU and the railwaymen had been decisive. I received messages of thanks from all over the minefields. The miners had a special place in the heart of trade unionists; the nature of their work, their solid sense of community, and the debt owed to them for their betrayal by the TUC leadership in 1926, all combined to create in people like myself a strong desire for their strike to succeed. Their victory was all the more sweet because of the blow it struck at the Government's Industrial Relations Act. In speeches and articles I was urging what I regarded as a constructive alternative to the Government's punitive legislation, the creation of an independent conciliation and arbitration system.

Over the Christmas holiday I drafted a few pieces for the union's journal, one of which, because of its length, I decided to shape into an article for the *New Statesman*. Dick Crossman was the editor at the time and I wondered how he would react to it. Surprisingly he was enthusiastic and the article was published in February 1972. In it I set out my views on a conciliation service and on methods of making progress on low pay and industrial democracy. I wanted the article to be published in the *New Statesman* because I knew that it was more likely to be read by Labour's leaders than any 'paper' submitted through the TUC or Labour Party research departments. I also hoped that my friends in those research departments would read the article, because I wanted them to know that it was the blueprint I would be sticking to in policy discussions within the Liaison Committee. All too often, in TUC and Labour Party discussions, academic researchers prepared papers on policy and committee members gave their instant reactions. I thought this was a hit and miss approach to policy-making. I was determined to fight my corner and the *New Statesman* piece was part of that. In fact the eventual setting up of ACAS and certain aspects of the Employment Protection legislation of the 1974 Labour Government were initiated in that article.

Ever since returning from Spain I had kept in contact with the illegal trade union movement there. Union members there risked a great deal running illicit printing presses, organizing meetings, keeping freedom's flag flying. Some were caught and sentenced to long periods in prison. I gave what help I could, for I had never relinquished my fervent opposition to Fascism and Franco.

Although I had strong links with the Spanish trade unions (UGT) and Socialist Party in exile, operating as they did from Toulouse and Paris, I knew that their leaders had grown old and a little too complacent. It was like a shot in the arm to see occasionally younger people from inside Spain: men like Felipe Gonzalez and trade unionists fresh from the factories. I knew that the future lay with them. I applauded Felipe's election as leader of the Socialist Party, but I was saddened by the divisions between trade union groups which began to develop in the long years of illegality. In the Spanish Democrats Defence Committee (of which I was treasurer and occasionally chairman) we drew no distinctions and helped to provide defence in the courts for those under attack from the regime, irrespective of whether they were from the socialist, communist or anarchist groups.

The Basque trade unionists had their own centre in Bayonne. Outside it looked like a wealthy merchant's mansion and it was located in a prosperous area of the town, but inside it was totally different. Printing presses, duplicators, typewriters, were all going hell for leather. Contact with their people across the border was close and continuous. On one of my visits I met the daughter of José Aquirre, the much respected leader of the Basque Republic during the Civil War. She was obviously playing a leading part. In nearby Biarritz on one occasion the Basque community expressed its appreciation for the help being given by a happy party with much folk-singing and dancing. Charles Blythe and I had brought aid from the International Transportworkers and Basque seamen in exile. The atmosphere was wonderful, the community feeling of the Basques embraced us. The evening ended with us being presented with Basque sword-sticks. My involvement in the Civil War and in the struggle of the Spanish and Basque people in exile was specially mentioned and drew warm applause. But what were we to do with the sword-sticks? Charles and I worried all the way to Paris, but we had no doubt that we must take them home as mementoes. We decided not to declare them to the customs and to take the risk of being discovered with what might be regarded as offensive weapons. To our relief no challenge was made.

Such diversions from my main responsibilities were few and far between. On and around the docks big problems were emerging, with the blacking of container traffic by dockers in a desperate attempt to retain jobs in face of the container revolution. Two haulage firms, Heaton's and Craddock's, decided to use the new legislation against the union. They sought to take the union to the National Industrial Relations Court, on the grounds that we were responsible for the actions of Liverpool dockers in blacking their lorries. I myself was opposed to the blacking activities. Lorry drivers and warehousemen were also concerned about their jobs, and I recognized that their point of view would have to be taken into account. I applied all the pressure I could to get negotiations going and to persuade our members to cool down. 'Dividing the membership is no solution,' I told the docks officers, and I personally made appeals by telephone to shop stewards in the Liverpool docks. They listened to my views and in response told me that the dockers were at boiling point; the work was moving away from dockland 'like butter melting in the sun'. It was also made clear to me that the strongest advocates of the blacking were members of the 'blue' union over whom we had no influence.

Despite my efforts to achieve a negotiated settlement, Heaton's Transport went to the National Industrial Relations Court (NIRC). They did this without prior discussion with or notice to the union. They got an interim order against the union to end the blacking at Liverpool docks. In a letter to the court I explained that the union would not be attending the hearing in line with TUC policy. When the court order was conveyed to me I arranged for our members in Liverpool to be informed and urged them to suspend the blacking so that discussions could take place. I was told that our members would probably respond to this advice but before we could take the matter further the firm rushed off to the NIRC again and a fine of £5000 was imposed on the union for 'contempt of court'. Sir John Donaldson, president of the court, said it was 'contempt almost without precedent'.

The fine provoked a strong response from the Liverpool dockers. Mass meetings unanimously decided to continue to black container lorries belonging to Heaton's and two other firms. Within days the union was fined a further £50,000 for contempt and a warning was given by Sir John Donaldson that if defiance of the court continued the whole of the TGWU's assets might be seized.

The union was caught between the devil and the deep blue sea. From the dockers there were increasing calls for a national strike; on the other hand the threat of sequestration posed a challenge to the very existence of the TGWU. No one had known what measures the NIRC would take to enforce its decisions. Many people had thought in terms of arrests and gaol sentences. It was feared that, as General Secretary of the union, I might be subpoenaed and I had taken a decision, backed by the union's executive, to refuse to accept a subpoena and, if necessary, to face arrest and gaol. But the NIRC had been too clever to follow that course. Instead, it had worked out a line of attack which would mean taking over the union's bank balances and lifting out the £55,000 in fines and £100,000 or more in damages. Because of its size the TGWU was very vulnerable, but I was still convinced that a collective response by the whole trade union movement could defeat the challenge.

'All we need is the full backing of the TUC, and no half measures, and we'll continue to refuse to pay the fines or recognize the NIRC,' I told Vic Feather, who came rushing over to Transport House as soon as he heard of the court's decision. He had been inclined to make a joke about sequestration at the £5000 stage, but he was in a very

"All right, driver — now you stick 'em up!"

Daily Telegraph, 5 May 1972

serious mood as he reviewed the implications of the latest judgement. One point he had not understood was that the union was being held responsible for the actions of non-members as well as those of members acting unofficially. I insisted that while we would continue to tell the dockers not to black container traffic, we would under no circumstances act as informers against working people. Vic said that there should be an urgent discussion at the General Council and I agreed to that.

In the event, when the General Council had had spelled out to it the need to back the TGWU with all the consequences that might follow defiance of the court, some of the members – according to one commentator – 'ran like rabbits frightened by gunfire'. A motion I proposed – 'that the TGWU be advised to continue the policy of non-co-operation with the National Industrial Relations Court; that any financial penalty involved is accepted as the responsibility of the TUC; and that a fund be organized for this purpose' – was ruled out of order by the chairman. At a later meeting a similar motion by Dick Briginshaw was shelved. The majority on the General Council decided to hedge its bets; the TGWU was advised to pay the fines and it was decided that unions should have the right to be represented at the NIRC, without prior consultation with the General Council, 'where offensive actions were taken against unions or their members'. To sugar the pill it was also agreed that, in the case of the TGWU, 'a measure of financial responsibility should be accepted by the TUC'. In fact, when it came to the point, a paltry £20,000 was paid to the TGWU. It was offered reluctantly and I accepted it as a token rather than engaging in a dutch auction with Vic Feather. I felt let down. I realized then how weak an instrument the General Council was, and tried to get approval for the calling of a special congress so that the whole movement could determine its position. I said there was a need to re-establish unity against the Industrial Relations Act and to adopt positive policies which would show that the movement meant what it said. Although I was supported by Hugh Scanlon and others, we were defeated by fifteen votes to eleven.

If the Government thought that their legislation would reduce industrial disputes they were badly mistaken. They failed on the railways and troubles in dockland intensified. The Executive Council of the union, a body of thirty-eight rank-and-file representatives, nearly threw out the TUC recommendation to pay the £55,000 fine, and it was only my appeal to them to remain within the TUC and continue our fight from there that persuaded them, by a narrow majority, to accept the TUC advice 'with the utmost reluctance'. Within days, the docks delegate conference, with my approval, decided to tender twenty-eight days' notice to the port employers of a national docks strike over the employment situation in the industry.

It wasn't much use talking to the employers, who were still led by Bill Tonge; their response had been totally negative and they seemed unable to think their way out of the havoc being created by the technological revolution. But in quick time John Peyton, the Minister for Transport, asked me to meet him together with Maurice Macmillan, the Secretary of State for Employment. They were both obviously concerned about the crisis in the ports. Peyton was very much a Tory of the old school, a 'man of the world' with a twinkle in his eye; Macmillan, sallow in complexion, appeared dour and somewhat shy. As I looked at them, I thought that there was an opportunity for a breakthrough. I explained that invariably, in the past, when there had been major difficulties in dockland, the Government of the day had appointed Lord Devlin or some other legal or academic luminary to conduct an inquiry. I told them that that sort of approach would not do now. Past inquiries had left too many problems unsolved; and although the Devlin Inquiry had made a number of good recommendations, the failure to keep its promise of permanent employment for all registered dockers was the kernel of the current troubles. I persuaded them to adopt the idea of a joint committee of people from the industry; but not the run-of-the-mill port employers, I urged – 'Why not include the chairman from each of the major port authorities?' This was agreed, while at the same time they left the selection of the dockers' representatives to me. Along with Tim O'Leary and other dockers' leaders, I made sure there would be two rank-and-file dockers.

We talked of an independent chairman for this new Special Committee and finally came to the conclusion that it would be a good idea to have joint chairmen. 'If Lord Aldington, Chairman of the Port of London Authority, will agree to be one, will you be the other?' they asked, and I agreed. I was able to get agreement on another suggestion, that the back-up work for the new committee should be performed by the National Ports Council. From my experience as Deputy Chairman of the Ports Council I knew we had a good body of experts well versed in the background of the industry.

Of course I was aware that Lord Aldington had been a prominent Conservative politician and minister and I wondered how I would get on with him. I felt that if I could influence him it would have considerable impact on the committee, and became more and more convinced of this as I got to know him. He was brisk, clear and capable and got to the point quickly. Evidence was taken from all quarters concerned with the ports, but I had a tussle with my own side when I suggested a hearing for the unofficial shop stewards' committee, which included men like Bernie Steers of the 'blue' union, and Vic Turner, a TGWU steward, who were involved with the blacking campaign. It was agreed that they should attend but instead of putting a strong case which would have helped the trade unionists on the committee, they treated us to a dose of rhetoric.

Good progress was in fact being made, and I was able to get the strike threat deferred while we continued our work. Our efforts were nearly destroyed however by the unofficial picketing and blacking campaign, which had now switched to the London area, and the inept over-reaction of the NIRC. Chobham Farm, a new container depot in London, had insisted on using non-registered labour and was being heavily picketed. The firm took a case to the NIRC against a number of men rather than the union, the Appeal Court having ruled that the TGWU was not responsible for the local blacking and picketing. Sir John Donaldson told three men, Bernie Steers, Vic Turner and Alan Williams, that they must cease the blacking or be committed to prison.

The result of this threat was an unofficial strike of 35,000 dockers throughout the country and a huge build-up of pickets outside Chobham Farm. All expected the court tipstaff to turn up and take the three men off to prison. Indeed the three men had prepared themselves for martyrdom. But the law did not appear. The fact that he was not arrested led Vic Turner to declare, 'It's a diabolical liberty.' Presumably he was referring to the actions of the Official Solicitor (of whom hardly anybody had previously heard) who briefed Peter Pain, QC, to make representations to the Appeal Court. The three men knew nothing about this . . . but I did. Peter Pain frequently acted for the union and kept me in touch with events. The Appeal Court, under Lord Denning, overturned the order for contempt and the employers realized that conventional negotiations were the better course. In very quick time we were able to achieve an agreement which provided for registered dockers to be employed at the depot. Some said I had pulled off a great coup, I simply thought it helped industrial peace. But Sir John Donaldson and his NIRC were not finished.

The Midland Cold Store at Hackney, one of the Vestey companies, went to the NIRC over the picketing of their store, and once again men were named. On this occasion five men were arrested and taken to Pentonville Prison. Immediately all hell was let loose. Dockers in all the ports stopped work and workers in many other sections of industry, including the newspapers, joined them. Even the lorry drivers who had been at odds with the dockers came out in sympathy with the arrested men, as well as the members of another union (USDAW), who had been working at Midland Cold Store. The TUC General Council had an emergency meeting with Ted Heath, who said he could do nothing – 'The law must be obeyed.' In face of this the General Council decided to call a one-day General Strike. Supported by Hugh Scanlon, I had pressed for this; the one thing a free trade union movement cannot tolerate is the imprisonment of its people, even if they are out of step.

The General Strike was not necessary, for almost immediately the five men were set free. The House of Lords moved hurriedly to overturn the Appeal Court's ruling and announced that the union was legally accountable for the actions of shop stewards, after all. This provided a convenient excuse for the men's release. It was treated as a great victory throughout dockland. The emotion generated by these events spilled over to the next day, when we had arranged a national dockers conference. The decision to hold a national dock strike on the employment question had been held over until that meeting, and in the meantime considerable progress had been made on the Special Committee. A report on progress was laid before the conference. It got short shrift, the delegates were in no mood to discuss details. One simple view prevailed: 'If action can spring five of our mates from prison, we can get all we want by having a national strike.' The strike was on!

Under normal circumstances the interim report of the Special Committee (known in dockland as the Jones/Aldington Committee) would have been accepted and approval given for further negotiations, because we had achieved a great deal of the programme laid down by the dockers' own committee. The reason for the rejection of what amounted to a peace package was the Industrial Relations Act and the imprisonment of the five dockers. It was just one of the things that determined me to get the next Labour Party Conference to insist that the immediate repeal of the Industrial Relations Act must be a major item in the Labour Party's manifesto for the next election.

Three weeks later the national docks delegate conference voted fifty-three to thirty to end the dock strike and accept the recommendation of the Special Committee. I was proud that we had brought to an end the 'temporary unattached register', which meant that a large number of men, although registered dockers, were treated as unemployed. They were now to be given permanent employment and attached to a permanent employer. Instead of £20 a week they would be receiving £50 plus. Among the many other points were a commitment that there would be no compulsory redundancy and the provision of a voluntary severance scheme offering up to £4000 to older dockers who wished to leave the industry. It was the best voluntary redundancy scheme in any industry at the time.

Going into the conference that morning I was met by a number of men, of whom Bernie Steers was the most prominent, who clearly wanted the strike to go on. I asked Bernie: 'Why don't you go to your own union and put your case; better still, tell them to reach agreement with us and you could be a delegate at these conferences!' He would not listen, instead he made a great fuss about a number of policemen who were at the edge of the crowd. I invited him to come with me to ask the policemen to go away, because I certainly hadn't invited them. 'This is a private difference between some of our people and we can handle it ourselves,' I told them. I'm bound to say it was not as easy as all that. I avoid disparaging working people, but on this occasion my attitude was tested to the limit. Many in the crowd were vociferous, bordering on hysteria. A few men talked to me in a reasonable way. They told me that some of the slogan shouters were not dockers, they didn't know where the hell they had come from! Having seen some of the publications of the ultra-Left I had a good idea.

The conference had been peaceful in its approach but as soon as the decision was taken to call off the strike a large number of men burst in and swept through the hall. I became the centre of attention, with a miscellany of epithets directed at me: bastard, traitor, leper, scab. A metal ash-can was hurled at my head; it missed but nearly caught Tim O'Leary who was standing by my side. As soon as I could make myself heard I said I would talk to the crowd outside the building. I was pushed and punched, but was determined not to lose my temper, because I knew that many of the men were genuinely angry and had come a long way. There were so many interruptions that I gave up my attempts to report to the mass of people milling around Smith Square and instead invited them to send a deputation to put their case inside a committee room. Thirty or forty men came in, but before we could settle down a much larger number invaded the room and forced a few pressmen who were there to leave. A young man screaming insults picked up a water jug and proceeded to chuck the water at me.

Some, who genuinely wanted to talk, although critical, seemed intimidated by the fists and threats. I'd been in the thick of many confrontations before but always on the side of working people, and I was not going to run away from this. I shouted, 'Let those who want to talk put their case, and I'll listen as long as you let me put my case too.' Eventually I got a bit of order. I persuaded one of the unofficial committee, Ollie Williams, to take the chair and to each question I gave a detailed answer. It was clear that most had little idea of the Jones/Aldington Committee's agreements and some of the men at least began to realize the measure of our efforts. Others went out muttering abuse. I had spent over two hours in rough argument. It might not have been necessary if only more of the rank-and-file members had participated in union activities.

As I left Transport House that day one of the shop stewards from the London docks came up to me. He was holding his little son by the hand. 'What about my future?' he asked. 'You've got a permanent job as a result of this agreement,' I replied. 'Ah,' he said, 'but what about the boy?'

Chapter Twenty-Four

Having the vexed question of wage adjustments to deal
with, we submitted a proposal to the Government that they
should control prices. That, in itself, would prevent any
panic action upon the question of wages, and we suggested
that the difference in cost should be met by the Exchequer.

ERNEST BEVIN

The terrace at Chequers is a nice place to be on a summer's evening,
but I was there on serious business. My two companions were Ted
Heath and Lord Aldington, and we had met to discuss the financing
of the big increases in severance pay for dockers which had been
recommended by the Special Committee on the Ports. The employers
and the port authorities had been persuaded to support the case but
pleaded that they did not have the money. Lord Aldington and I
undertook to urge the Government to meet the bill and we had gone
right to the top.

Life in dockland, the sweat and strain, were a far cry from Chequers,
and yet I detected warm sympathy as I put the case. After all, we were
dealing with the problems of the over fifty-fives, who had given their
lives to the industry and whose pension prospects were poor indeed,
and the unfit, whose problems arose mainly from the harsh nature of
the industry. Aldington was on my side and he was a close friend of
Heath. Inch by inch we edged forward, details were gone over, the
cost estimated (eventually it came to over £30 million). Ted Heath
agreed the principle. There was one last point. 'It would be wrong to
treat the people in some ports worse than the others,' I said. 'The
offer should apply to all ports even those where there isn't a surplus of
labour.' The Prime Minister agreed to that too. It was a very important
element in ensuring goodwill throughout the industry.

A lot of the older men took up the new offer. £4000 was a big sum
in 1972; some men managed to buy a house; others, in the tradition
of dockland, enjoyed being 'millionaires' for a month or so. It was a
tonic to see them smoking their cigars, treating their mates to drinks,
and enjoying a holiday.

Although I had known that Heath was not unsympathetic to labour, from the days when I had met him as Minister of Labour, the exchange at Chequers strengthened my conviction that he genuinely wanted to get on with working people. There was a marked change in his attitude towards the unions following the early abrasive months of his Government. He was always ready to meet TUC representatives and on a number of occasions himself invited them, probably with some prompting from Vic Feather, who seemed to fancy himself as un-official ambassador for the TUC and special adviser to Ted Heath.

In April 1972 the TUC was invited to meet the Prime Minister to discuss the economic situation. Before this was reported to the General Council Vic Feather had a word with me in a heavily confidential way. At that stage I was opposed to such a meeting and I quizzed Vic, saying: 'Why do you keep having these private meetings? They may give the impression that we're weak, when its the Government that's taking a battering!' His reply was: 'We've got to talk. Ted's coming our way.' He knew he was on an easy wicket with a majority of the General Council, who at that time were opposed to confrontation with the Government. (A motion objecting to the talks was defeated by 21 votes to 9.)

At the April meeting and subsequently Heath and his ministers wanted to concentrate on economic co-operation, with an eye to wages restraint, despite the Government's earlier protestations of opposition to the idea. We for our part were determined to make the Industrial Relations Act the major issue. Our approach was constructive, trying to gain acceptance of improved conciliation and arbitration procedures as an *alternative* to the Act. I made much play with Ted Heath's own statement on TV: 'We have to find a more sensible way of settling our differences.' It was perhaps too much to expect for him to do an about turn-on his legislation, yet had he been able to it would have trans-formed his relationship with the trade unions and his future in the Tory Party.

Should we talk to the Government, if they want to talk to us? That question became an issue the General Council debated over many months. I became convinced that it was in our members' interests not to miss an opportunity of changing the Government's mind. Unem-ployment was growing rapidly, and inflation was rising, our attitude on these developments needed to be put strongly, as did our concern over low-paid workers and the pensioners. Vic Feather had a sneaking idea that some agreement could be reached on wages and prices. 'Tell them that we'll get nowhere without getting rid of the Industrial Relations Act,' I urged him. His reply was: 'We've got to listen to them, Jack.'

In the event the industrial membership of the National Economic Council (the TUC and the CBI had six members each) was called in for the joint discussions Ted Heath seemingly wanted. Examination in detail of the problems of low-paid workers and of prices was on the agenda. We could not say 'no' to that, and we were soon into a series of meetings at Downing Street or Chequers. The talks were a little abrasive at times, but always Heath was at his most courteous with the TUC representatives. This led me to reflect on those lines from *Alice in Wonderland*:

> 'How cheerfully he seems to grin,
> How neatly spreads his claws,
> And welcomes little fishes in
> With gently smiling jaws.'

I for one was not willing to be swallowed up, and that went for Hugh Scanlon too. We continued to press the trade union case doggedly. For the most part the TUC team were united, but at times Alf Allen and Jack Cooper were at pains to emphasize their differences from the 'terrible twins'. Repeatedly I pressed for control of food and other retail prices but Allen and Cooper joined in ridiculing the idea. Allen bemoaned the reduced profits for the distributive trade that control of prices would mean. The CBI spokesman gleefully exploited the occasional division in our ranks. Of all the people around the table, Hughie and I were in the most difficult position, because in both our unions there was strong opposition to our participation. In Scanlon's case his union decided he must withdraw from the second round of talks.

Whenever I could, I tried to widen the area of discussion to include the pensioners. The fact that the Government, under pressure, had agreed to an annual review of pensions, had encouraged me to look for further concessions. Heath refused the major increases in pensions I was seeking, which would have lifted the retirement pension to £10 a week for a single person and £16 for a married couple, but he did seem attracted to a view I expressed that some gesture should be made annually to the elderly.

I mentioned to him that, in the TGWU, I had introduced a Christmas bonus to our retired officers and staff. 'You would be surprised at

With Hugh Scanlon of the AEU –
the 'terrible twins' . . .

With Harold Wilson in 1974.

On a visit to Romania with Vic Feather and George Smith of UCATT.

Upstaged by a lamb at Llanberis in North Wales.

the pleasure it has given them – it would be a wonderful thing to do nationally,' I told him. Sir William Armstrong, Secretary to the Cabinet and head of the Civil Service, smiled sympathetically. Someone had told me that his parents had held office in the Salvation Army and I used that knowledge when I pursued the matter with him. During a break in the discussions I buttonholed him and said: 'Look, William, your father and mother would be ashamed if they thought you weren't using your influence to get the old people a little extra at Christmastime.' Shortly afterwards Ted Heath announced the introduction of a £10 Christmas bonus for the nation's pensioners. It was a good positive step and it is a pity that the bonus has not been adjusted over the years to maintain its purchasing power. The Labour Government dropped the bonus for a year when they had given a sizeable increase in the weekly pension; many pensioners couldn't believe that Labour would do that to them. I used all the influence I possessed to get the bonus restored, and succeeded. It was almost a one-man battle but I knew it was worth fighting. 'Some of them don't need it, Jack,' said Barbara Castle when I was putting the case to her. 'My Ted just spends his on whisky.' The deputation of pensioners I was leading was aghast. 'Does that mean you want a means test?' I asked. Under an avalanche of criticism from the pensioners she withdrew and agreed to help get it restored. Most of the time, however, our meetings with Ted Heath were taken up in argument about prices in the shops. During one heated discussion over food prices Vic Feather, who was sitting opposite the Prime Minister, fell asleep while still smoking a big cigar. I looked at Heath who smiled understandingly. After a few minutes Vic woke up, appeared to shake himself, and then picked up the thread of the discussion as though he had been awake all the time.

Proposals and counter-proposals were argued over the table. The TUC and the Government spokesmen did most of the talking, the CBI contribution was very limited. Then, after countless hours of meetings, there was an abrupt ending. To the surprise of the trade union side, Ted Heath declared that certain important items we had been emphasising – pensions, rents, the impact of EEC membership, the Industrial Relations Act – were outside the scope of negotiation. Such matters, we were told, were for the House of Commons to determine. A rigid posture was suddenly adopted by the Government; even to this day I am unable to understand why.

No one could have been more disappointed than Vic Feather. He had been a firm supporter of the talks throughout and had taken at face value the Government's claim that it was prepared to enter into a real partnership with both sides of industry in the management of the economy. He felt that Ted Heath had thrown away a golden opportunity. And yet he himself may have been responsible for the disappointment, by misleading Heath and Armstrong into thinking the Government could get agreement on wages and prices without commitment on the wider issues we had raised, while at the same time encouraging me and others to feel that agreement was possible on those very issues.

In place of talks we had confrontation. A ninety-day standstill on wages, prices, rents and dividends was announced by the Government, but most of us at the TUC thought 'standstill' was a misnomer and that the new legislation was weak in key areas such as food prices and rents. So we were back at Downing Street, but as protesters, not as potential partners. The 'standstill' was followed by a second and third phase of incomes policy and limited restrictions on prices and dividends. Industrial disputes increased and the General Council refused to put representatives on the Pay Board and Price Commission which the Government had set up.

In 1973 there were almost as many meetings between the TUC and the Government as in the previous year, but without the presence of the CBI and Hugh Scanlon. The TUC team consisted of five – Feather, Green, Allen, Cooper and myself. Presumably Heath talked to the CBI separately, but the media no longer wrote of 'tripartism' or 'corporate states'. A battle for public support was in progress. Although I became increasingly despondent about the possibility of changing the Government's policies, I was convinced that we had to put our point of view at every opportunity. If the spotlight shone on Downing Street then we should be there, otherwise our members would feel we were not doing our job. At the TGWU Biennial Delegates Conference in July 1973 I was under strong pressure to oppose talks with the Government. In reply I told the Conference: 'The Union should not place itself in the position of being blamed for not talking when our people expect it of us. . . . You do not pay me to sit dumb. You pay me to speak, to act, to help, to advise, and part of the process is publicly to present our case. . . .'

Our difficulties in establishing our case with Ted Heath and his ministers served to strengthen my efforts in the TUC/Labour Party Liaison Committee. The programme we had been urging on the Prime Minister, I believed, should become Labour's policy. Getting this accepted did not prove easy; I found myself having to argue as strongly with the Labour leaders as I had done with Heath and his colleagues over the control of retail prices, for example.

No Prime Minister, either before or since, could compare with Ted Heath in the efforts he made to establish a spirit of camaraderie with trade union leaders and to offer an attractive package which might satisfy large numbers of work-people. That was the case with his 'stage three'. He and his advisers offered a deal permitting limited free collective bargaining on top of threshold agreements to help the low paid and compensate for increases in the cost of living.

Attractive as this was, it meant the continuation of the Industrial Relations Act and a failure to meet our social programme. Statutory control over wage increases hit workers in the public sector most of all. This was especially the case with the miners who had a strong case for much more than the Government schemes would allow. The miners wanted direct negotiations with the Coal Board, although informal talks had taken place between Ted Heath and Joe Gormley during the overtime ban imposed by the union. The Government responded to the ban by imposing a three-day-week throughout industry, which willy-nilly led to the involvement of the TUC. The Government regarded the miners' action as a challenge to their strategy and were determined to make a stand against them.

The Government was beset with problems; balance of payments, devaluation of the pound, highest interest rates ever, Middle East oil dispute, combined with the results of a period of wild financial speculation and a property boom. Against this background it was difficult to understand why Ted Heath and his Government should wish to take on the miners. Yet they clearly did. 'The miners are being made to carry the can and we should do all we can to support them,' I told the TUC General Council.

Len Murray, the new General Secretary of the TUC, advised the General Council once again to seek meetings with the Prime Minister through the NEDC group. 'The Government must be given a chance to get off the hook,' said Len. Well, they certainly didn't want the chance – or not at our price. A number of meetings took place, some at our request, some at the invitation of Heath, or of Anthony Barber, the Chancellor of the Exchequer, or Willie Whitelaw, the new Secretary of State for Employment. Whitelaw especially tried to apply the maximum degree of sugar, and indeed he got on exceptionally well with most of us on the trade union side. But the talks led nowhere.

The miners' attitude was the result of pent-up demands that had been denied over a long period. Any doubts in my mind were removed by my colleague Harry Urwin, whose family background was in the mining industry. He explained to me how miners were far less favourably treated in payments for shift-work and other items than workers in other industries with which we were familiar. It was perhaps a reflection on the negotiating abilities of the miners' leadership over many years but they had a strong case for better treatment.

The Government spokesmen made it clear that they would not allow their phase three counter-inflationary policy to be undermined. They resisted all efforts to establish that the miners had an exceptional case. The TUC General Council told the Government that it accepted

> ... there is a distinctive and exceptional situation in the mining industry. If the Government are prepared to give an assurance that they will make possible a settlement between the miners and the National Coal Board, other unions will not use this as argument in negotiations in their own settlements.

I was personally active in promoting this view, which was endorsed at a conference of chief officers of the unions affiliated to the TUC. The most active opponent of the approach was Frank Chapple of the electrical workers' union; he did not accept that a miners' settlement should not be cited in other negotiations. His attitude was ignored or discounted by most people in TUC circles, although it obviously didn't help in our efforts to persuade the Government to change its mind.

It was a genuine attempt but all our efforts were negated. Ted Heath told us that $4\frac{1}{2}$ million workers had settled under his new policy and that it would be letting them down if the miners were allowed to negotiate an unrestricted settlement. An examination of the NUM case by the Pay Board was offered, but of course that did not satisfy the NUM.

On 5 February 1974 the NUM leadership announced that 81 per cent of their members had voted for strike action in a pit-head ballot and it was their intention to call an all-out strike in the coalfields. The nation was moving into chaos. Next day a joint meeting of the TUC and CBI took place. An attempt was made to achieve a common approach but without success. I proposed that 'The Secretary of State for Employment accompanied by the Director-General CBI and the General Secretary TUC meet NUM representatives on 7 February, to explore the possibility of a monetary advance on the present offer – pending a long-term examination as already promised by the Government.' My proposal was rejected. Michael Clapham and Campbell Adamson, the two leaders of the CBI, were less inclined to move than industrial leaders like Frank Kearton of Courtaulds, with whom I had been in touch separately.

I knew Frank well. An astute and able employer, he was very conscious of the economic dangers. I told him of our approach and said: 'Look Frank, we mean it. If the miners are allowed to negotiate directly with the Coal Board, whatever they get will not be quoted by us or used as a lever to get a similar increase.' Kearton knew I was a man of my word, as did other industrialists like Jack Callard of ICI. I asked them to make representations to the Government and I believe they did, but it was too late to change the Government's attitude.

At mid-day on 7 February, not long after our meeting with the CBI, Ted Heath announced that he was calling a General Election. The die was cast and yet during that very afternoon Willie Whitelaw, the Employment Secretary, took a new direction by asking the Pay Board to undertake an examination of the case for the miners securing a larger increase than 'stage three' from 1 March. This implied that the miners *did* have an exceptional case and there was a need for urgency in dealing with it. It was a remarkable move which might have averted the strike had it been made earlier.

I believe that Ted Heath made a wrong decision. With a little more patience then he might still be leader of the Tory Party today. The TUC case for the miners to be treated as a special case could have been met, and relations with the unions improved by dropping the Industrial Relations Act. The legislation had few friends. Campbell Adamson, Director-General of the CBI, had privately and later publicly denounced the Act and his view that it had 'sullied every relationship at national level between unions and employers' was to be made much of during the General Election campaign. The TUC had suspended and effectively muzzled those unions which remained on the register, and the Government itself, whatever its brave words, had in practice abandoned the use of the Act.

So why did Ted Heath go to the country when he was close to reaching an accommodation with the unions? Those of us who had got to know him well felt keen disappointment when he lost the leadership of his party. At the outset I thought he represented the hard face of the Tory Party, but over the years he revealed a human face of Toryism, at least to the union leaders who met him frequently. It is doubtful whether the public gained that view of him, partly because, as he himself admitted at one of the Downing Street meetings, he was a bad communicator. Amazingly, he gained more personal respect from union leaders than they seemed to have for Harold Wilson or even Jim Callaghan.

My chief criticism of the Conservative Government, apart from its suppression of free collective bargaining, was its basic neglect of low-paid workers (I told the 1973 Trades Union Congress that $3\frac{1}{2}$ million heads of families were earning less than £25 a week) and its failure to substantially raise the level of pensions. I pushed the 1973 Trades Union Congress at Blackpool into an unprecedented decision to lead industrial protest action as part of the campaign to win higher pensions. My message to the Congress was that, for most pensioners, to be old in Britain meant to be poor. 'The scandal of that poverty must be wiped out. We can delay no more. If industrial action is necessary to secure justice then action should be taken,' I said. The demands of the pensioners should be met no later than the following spring, otherwise days of strike action should follow. The motion was carried unanimously.

It was a shot across the bows of the Heath Government. In my speech I also delivered a message to the Labour Party, which was later taken up by them: 'We have got to move to a pattern that links pensions not just with prices but with wages.' My commitment to the elderly was firm, and I knew that the trade union movement had the capacity and will to take strike action in its furtherance. But the action proved unnecessary with the coming of the General Election and Labour's victory, for I had made sure that the Party would meet the pensioners' demands in the first financial measure put through Parliament.

Action on behalf of the pensioners featured in a film about me – 'A Day in the Life of Jack Jones' – which had been shown on TV earlier in the year. Although it was a typically full day, the film showed that I had time to take part in meetings and marches supporting the pensioners' case. The programme started just after seven in the morning, with Evelyn cooking my breakfast. About half a dozen of the TV crew crowded into our small kitchen. No housewife could be at her best in those circumstances but Evelyn shone through it all. For the benefit of the feminists I should say that Evelyn did not stay in the kitchen; she was with me at the pensioners' meetings later in the day, talking to them and encouraging them in the campaign.

The programme gave me an opportunity of explaining to the public something of the day-to-day management of a large trade union. There were discussions with national trade group officials, and then a review of the union's finances with the financial secretary. Important decisions on legal claims on industrial compensation were reached with the legal secretary of the union. During my varied activities I managed to fit in a chat with a group of ICI shop stewards; like the rest of the programme it was not arranged, it was genuinely a normal day for me and the meeting with the stewards demonstrated my commitment to shop-floor democracy.

That busy day was just part of a busy year for me. An overriding feature had been the fight to retain jobs. In the steel industry I was caught up in a campaign against the threatened closure of plants and I well recall the occupation by many of our members of the Triumph motor-cycle factory at Meriden. In such instances I had no doubts I was on the side of the workers. The question that had to be tackled, however, was how they could succeed.

Since I had visited Bristol, to see Concorde and its engines being constructed, our members there naturally turned to me when production was under threat, and I became much involved in urging continuation of the programme. It was not easy, because the costs were enormous, but equally, we argued, the social costs of putting whole communities out of work was considerable and it would cost the nation, in more ways than one, much more to stop production than to continue it. I told Michael Heseltine and other ministers involved that it was better to go on, and the campaign in the areas affected gave strong point to this argument. One way or another the Government was persuaded to continue with the 'massive white elephant' – a phrase frequently used in Whitehall to describe the venture.

Loss of trade and the sharp threat to long-term employment continued to haunt the major ports in the docks industry. The promised survey of the smaller, non-scheme, ports, occupied a lot of my attention. The National Ports Council conducted the survey, and as deputy chairman I made sure that I was on the spot at all the key moments, including visits to some of the ports.

The survey recommended that casual labour for cargo handling on a 'normal and relatively constant basis' should be eliminated. It also called for rates of pay and conditions to be raised to the level agreed by the negotiating body for the industry. It provided me with arguments for the extension of the Dock Labour Scheme and for the public ownership of the industry. In pursuit of those arguments I often came into conflict with Philip Chappell, the chairman of the Ports Council, who was essentially a City man and had obviously been appointed by the Tory Government because of his commitment to a free market philosophy. He was supported by the shipowning and business elements which dominated the Council, and I tended to be one man against the rest.

John Peyton, the Minister of Transport, was surprisingly sympathetic on some issues and he helped forward the idea that there should be one employer in each of the major ports. Lord Aldington was also especially helpful on that. Peyton, incidentally, was, I think, the only Tory Minister of Transport who found his way into Transport House. I invited him in to meet some of our docks officials and stewards and much to his delight presented him with a copy of the original mace carried by the dockers in the 1889 dock strike. Peyton appointed Les Reynolds, a former Talley clerk, to the National Ports Council. At the time Les was working as a lecturer on Port Transport at Thurrock Technical College, and had established contacts with many European ports. He organized visits of dockers and other port workers to such ports as Dunkirk, Rotterdam and Antwerp, where revolutionary developments in technology were taking place. This certainly increased the understanding of the rank and file about competitive developments abroad. Les and I had the advantage of having had practical working experience of dock work, which was useful in some of our detailed discussions. We did not always agree, but I appreciated his appointment as a slight opening of the door towards industrial democracy.

I knew that a much stronger push would have to await the election of a Labour Government. It was an issue on which I was personally determined to make progress.

Chapter Twenty-Five

The strongest bond of human sympathy outside the family relationship should be one uniting all working people of all nations and tongues and kindreds.

ABRAHAM LINCOLN

Internationalism is part of the life-blood of the trade unions and from my earliest days in the movement I had taken a keen interest in the conditions of working people in other countries. Early in 1973 I was able to persuade dockers in various ports to act in support of black seamen from South Africa. In one company our solidarity action resulted in the wages of black seamen being raised from £38 a month to £87. A letter of thanks from the International Transport Workers Federation gave me pleasure, but the important aspect for me was the way our members demonstrated their understanding of the needs of brother workers of a different colour and country who were being exploited by a British employer.

Some months before, I had been elected chairman of the International Committee of the TUC. The pressure for me to stand had come from Danny McGarvey, the tough leader of the Boilermakers Union, and I had been supported by men like Richard Briginshaw of the printers and Hugh Scanlon, but a vote in my favour from Cyril Plant, one of the longer serving members of the Committee, caused trouble for him. Cyril was General Secretary of the Inland Revenue Staffs Federation and considered one of the TUC establishment, a group of old hands on the Council who tended to support each other for senior posts. Alf Allen of USDAW was supported by this group and confidently expected to get elected. In the event Cyril Plant's vote ensured my election. Allen was annoyed and Cyril Plant told me they played hell with him. For the leader of a small trade union like Plant's it was worrying because it could mean that nominations for important positions might be withheld from him. In years past threats of this kind had been used by Arthur Deakin to enforce his views on the Council, but the balance of power had changed and Plant was in no danger.

In my new role I led many deputations to the Foreign Secretary and to various embassies. The jailing of ten trade unionists in Spain in December 1972 was the subject of a visit by Vic Feather and myself to the Spanish Embassy. We were received by senior Embassy officials (the Ambassador, we were told, was away in Madrid). The officials seemed anxious to placate us but Vic was clearly apprehensive that I would go over the top. I certainly felt strongly about the case and spoke with much emotion, because I had known a couple of the men personally and was anxious that there might be a threat to their lives.

We had a special right to make the protest, I explained, because four of the men were employees of British firms: Babcock and Wilcox, Rolls-Royce, Lucas and Massey Ferguson. 'British trade unionists are not going to stand idly by while their employers connive with your Government to put trade union men in jail!' Vic kept putting his hand on my shoulder as though to hold me back. We were politely shooed out of the Embassy but not before we were assured that our view would be transmitted to the Franco Government. I made clear that we would follow up our representations, and we did, but the men remained incarcerated for a long time.

The 'Carabanchel ten' as they were called were in my mind when I addressed the founding conference of the European Trade Union Confederation. This body initially united trade unions in the areas covered by EFTA and the EEC, and was associated with the International Confederation of Free Trade Unions, although the intention was to spread out to take in the so-called Christian trade unions and big national confederations like the CGIL of Italy and the CGT of France which were regarded as being under communist influence. Speaking as the President of the EFTA Trade Union Committee I referred to Spain, Portugal and Greece (three totalitarian countries at that time) and said: 'We have a responsibility to use our combined influence to assist in the development of independent and genuine trade unionism in those countries and prevent economic privileges being extended to their Governments until trade unionism is allowed to operate freely.'

The creation of the European TUC owed a great deal to Vic Feather and during many difficult negotiations I was proud to be at his side. The Scandinavian trade union leaders were the most enthusiastic and Heinz Vetter, the gentle and capable leader of the German trade union centre, DGB, gave considerable support. We made no secret of the TUC's desire for 'trade union unity – a single voice, a single purpose, for trade unionists in Western Europe', but many of the leaders from other countries would not go that far.

An early snag in our discussions was the name of the proposed new organization. Bergeron, the leader of the French *Force Ouvrière*, wanted the word 'free' in the title with the object of keeping out the CGT and the CGIL because, in his view, their communist connections meant they were not free organizations. There was almost a stalemate but it was overcome when I mentioned that the East German Trade Union centre contained the word 'free' in its title, so the magic talisman evidently didn't work very well.

Differences over the entry of the French CGT were bitter, and were never resolved. The *Force Ouvrière* was composed mainly of non-communists who had split away from the CGT. Political differences seemed to be the main reason for division. Leon Jouhaux, the old and heroic leader of the original CGT, had led the split but later, before his death, recognized that it would have been better to stay in and fight. I mentioned this view to our French colleagues but it was brushed aside. They even opposed for some time the entry into the ETUC of the former Christian and mainly socialist French trade union centre, the CFDT.

Feather and I were elected to the Executive Board of the new ETUC, Vic being the first president, and we both used our influence to achieve unity and to encourage co-operation. Progress was not easy. It was almost as difficult to get the socialist trade unions of Belgium and Holland to accept their Christian counterparts as it was to persuade the German DGB to agree that the communist/socialist coalition, the CGIL of Italy, might join us. We argued that, in dealing with the big new institutions in Europe and in face of the growth of multinational companies, there was a need for united action on the part of workers' representatives.

Opposition to our ideas of overcoming the divisions between the 'Christian' and 'communist' trade unions was very strong in the ICFTU (International Confederation of Free Trade Unions). I was an executive member of this, together with Vic Feather. It had been formed as a result of a split in the World Federation of Trade Unions, which had been established just after the Second World War. The fear of disunity and in-fighting was understandable, but our experience within the TUC had shown that unity could be achieved. New developments affecting working people in Europe justified a new approach, and Vic and I were determined to forge ahead.

We went even further than the *Ostpolitik* practised by the German Social Democrat Party, under the leadership of Willi Brandt. Support was given to the idea of an all-European trade union conference, straddling East and West European trade unions, to be held under the auspices of the ILO in Geneva. The purpose was not to create one organization but to have periodic exchanges of views on social and industrial matters across the political boundaries. Preparatory meetings were held in Helsinki, Vienna and Geneva between representatives of the German, Hungarian, British, Swedish and Soviet trade union centres. Here the key figure was Heinz Vetter of the German DGB; his cautious approach made sure that mistakes were avoided and a series of useful conferences took place.

Vetter could not be regarded as a communist sympathiser by any stretch of the imagination, but his activities were the subject of a bitter attack from George Meany, the president of the AFL/CIO, the main trade union organization in the USA. For a long time Meany would not speak to Vetter and seemed to regard him as a communist stooge. Vic Feather and I had to listen to the sharp end of Meany's tongue, when, together with George Lowthian of the Building Workers and Terry Parry of the Fire Brigades, we went to Miami to meet the Executive Board of the AFL/CIO. Surprisingly the blast came at the end of a series of amicable meetings. We were invited to attend a press conference to be addressed by Meany. The old boy laughed and joked with the media people and then, looking sharply at us, lurched into a real anti-red tirade. He talked of the red danger in European trade unionism and suggested that it came from the 'Berlin-Moscow-London' axis.

The TUC group was astounded. I had had a friendly argument with Jay Lovestone, the former communist leader in the US who was in charge of the international department of the AFL/CIO and had become a strong, almost fanatical, opponent of the communists, but otherwise we had been treated like long-lost brothers. Vic had delighted George Meany with a present of a big box of cigars. They were Cuban cigars, from which the labels had been removed, and they had been placed in a Jamaican cigar box. We got the impression that Meany had not been deceived; after smoking one he smiled and said: 'This is just like a Cuban cigar, the Jamaicans are making a good job of it.' Interesting and enjoyable as the trip had been, our departure was frosty, I was annoyed that Vic Feather had not protested to Meany about his unreasonable behaviour. He had said he would do this privately, but he never did.

During our stay we were housed in the same hotel as the Americans, a luxurious place with its own swimming pool. One morning we were walking around the pool with Teddy Gleason, the leader of the East Coast dockers' union, when a young man approached us with a press camera. He said: 'Have you seen some English guys around. I'm looking to take a shot of them – they're labour union men from England. A paper from over there called the *Express* thought I might find them in the pool.' 'I haven't seen those guys,' replied Teddy, and we nodded our heads. So a story about Vic and I living it up in Miami was denied to the *Daily Express*. The real story would have been more interesting, for we were trying to stop a boycott of British ships in the East Coast ports, which the American union was threatening in protest against British policies in Northern Ireland.

Meany was a typical American tycoon, surrounded by too many sycophants. Luckily there were some who were different, like Ike Abel of the steelworkers with whom I had useful exchanges on the problems of automation and technical change. It was important to find out as much as possible about developments in American industry because often what happened there was and is repeated in the UK.

The search for information led to more contacts with the East European countries too. One country we visited was Poland. A small TUC group went, consisting of Dan McGarvey, Cyril Plant, Vic Feather and myself. We spent some time at a relatively new motor-car factory in Warsaw which was making cars of Fiat design (the Polski-Fiat). It was explained to us that, though the production line was designed by Fiat, the factory was owned by the Polish Government. The vehicles were starting to be sold in Western Europe as well as Poland while engines were sold to the Italian Fiat concern.

In the light of the highly publicized events of later years, it may be of interest to mention that we found trade union representatives functioning at the workplace but not very vigorously. I put this down to the newness of the plant and the preponderance of inexperienced labour. Conditions on the shop floor compared favourably with many of our own factories. With the aid of an interpreter we discussed levels of earnings. Comparisons were difficult because of the low cost of housing, transport and other services in Poland. Taking an active part in the exchanges was the 'party representative', a commanding personality who appeared to be influential.

The most lively trip was to a large steel works just outside Cracow. There we met a group of men who had served with the RAF during the war. We ended our visit with a jolly get together. Most could speak a little English, so we did not require the interpreters' services. We were old friends in no time and joined in singing 'Pack up your troubles in your old kitbag', and 'Tipperary', just like a crowd of Tommies from the First World War.

On the way to Cracow Vic Feather behaved with surprising childishness. I was recovering from a heavy cold and pulled out a packet of mints, whereupon Vic asked me where I had got them. I told him that McGarvey had given them to me. In a flash Vic whipped them out of my hand and threw them from the car window. 'That bloody man's a fool!' he said. I felt aggrieved at being denied a little comfort because of his dislike of Danny. Differences between the two men had come to a head that morning, when Danny had attempted to sit next to the president of the Polish trade unions at breakfast. Vic considered that it was his right to be there and had insisted that Danny should go to the bottom of the table. Bad language was used on both sides and feathers were truly ruffled. It was amusing and revealing – but my mints were lost as a result!

The search for a better understanding between the trade unions of East and West continued with a TUC visit to the USSR in 1973. The structure and purpose of the two movements were very different, but like myself the other members of the TUC team had been to Russia previously and knew something about their trade union movement. Vic Feather, who was due to retire within a couple of months, obviously enjoyed the visit.

In Moscow we met the union leaders. They were inclined to be stiff and stolid although Vic's humour helped to break the ice a little. We were able to knock out a preliminary programme for an all-European trade union conference. It was to be the first of its kind and Vic and I were anxious to avoid any difficulties by ensuring that the agenda would deal with practical matters. In fact we reached quick agreement that the conference should deal with health and safety problems in industry.

The visit was a short one and our hosts tried hard to make it interesting. Vic much favoured a trip to Vladimir, an old town with religious connections not far from Moscow, while I thought we should see something of their industry. We did both. The industrial part was covered during a visit to Minsk, a town which had been substantially destroyed by the war and subsequently rebuilt. During our stay there we looked over a new heavy vehicles plant and had discussions with management, trade union and party representatives.

I noticed that nearly all the personnel were young men and asked the works director about it. 'Most of the work is heavy and not suitable for women,' he replied. I wondered what our feminists would have thought of that. We were told that new factories were being built for lighter production which would employ women. Since it was a newly developed area they had made special efforts to attract people to come and work there. Most were younger men and women and in due course it was expected that they would marry and have children. We were shown plans for housing, community centres, shops, schools and so on.

Our TUC group could not get over the almost clinical way the Russians planned such developments. Perhaps because of this I was especially anxious to explore the human factor. I asked the union men: 'What does the union do for its members in this plant?' and was given a long answer explaining how the union representatives had considerable responsibility in negotiating incentives of various kinds as well as overseeing conditions of work, safety and welfare. 'Ah, but in your system you always have to agree with the manager,' I suggested. The reaction was sharp; no overtime, I was told, could be worked without the agreement of the union committee, and no norms or incentive pay could be altered without their agreement. 'The manager has no right to dismiss a worker without the consent of our committee.' As the spokesman said this, I noticed a wry, almost aggrieved, look on the works director's face.

I was not happy that the working conditions and lay-out of the plant were as good as they might have been, but at least I felt satisfied that a trade union system, not unlike our own, was operating at plant level. The political influence, however, was alien to our British traditions, and we began to realize the difference between the political and industrial systems of our two countries.

This became evident when Vic Feather and others insisted that the undertaking must be making a profit and that therefore the workers were exploited as they were under capitalism. We had a long discussion about this. The party spokesman claimed that there was no question of 'profits', but admitted that the undertaking achieved a 'surplus' as a result of over-fulfilling the plan laid down. This surplus, we were told, was used to support the provision of housing, sports centres, holiday and rest homes and cultural and educational institutions, for use by the people employed in the plant and their families.

On our return to Moscow we resumed talks with the leaders of the All-Union Central Council of Trade Unions in their substantial head-quarters. In the course of our lengthy meetings I raised the question of Jews wishing to emigrate from the Soviet Union, explaining that there was much interest in the subject in Britain. Their president had obviously been fully briefed and provided a lot of information. He said that 97 per cent of applications from Jewish people to emigrate had been granted, but there were reservations over people in possession of secret information or with high scientific or academic qualifications. He went to great pains to assure us that they were not anti-semitic, and that many Jewish people occupied important positions.

There was some sharp questioning and Tom Jackson gave details of a Jewish family which had been refused permission to leave the USSR. He was told that the case would be looked into and on our return home we were informed that the refusal had been rescinded. If for no other reason, this showed that the contact had been worthwhile, but there was still a deep division on this issue, which remains a sharp cause for concern today.

The British Ambassador told me that he had been delighted with our visit and felt sure that it would help to improve relations. A number of high-ranking Soviet trade unionists accepted his invitation to attend a party in the Embassy, including a member of the Politburo. The Ambassador was all smiles, because it had not previously been possible to talk informally with such influential people. Vic Feather was beaming, he seemed to take credit for having achieved more than the conventional diplomats could do.

The treatment of black people in South Africa was the subject of many discussions in the TUC International Committee, including the shooting and imprisonment of black workers involved in industrial struggles. We felt directly involved because of the substantial British investment in South Africa, and it was decided to send out a small delegation to survey the situation and render what help we could to the trade union organization of black workers. This led to my next journey abroad.

Vic Feather had made most of the arrangements for the visit prior to his retirement as TUC General Secretary in September 1973. It was unfortunate that his links had been with TUCSA (Trade Union

Council of South Africa), a white-dominated federation of unions with white and coloured members. It was suspect to black people, and it took us some time to gain the confidence of those who were active in the movement to create black trade unions.

When we went to South Africa we had idealistic ideas about uniting white, coloured and black workers in one trade union movement. It was a naïve view. The South African Government expressly forbade the admission of black workers to registered trade unions of white, coloured, or Asiatic workers. Nor would it permit black trade unions to register, and only if unions are registered do they have access to the industrial council machinery or to the wage boards, both of which are a central feature of collective bargaining in South Africa.

In many cases we found white trade union leaders were willing participants in apartheid, a system which meant lower wages being paid to black workers doing the same work as whites or coloureds and which allowed extensive discrimination against black workers. Surprisingly, many of the employers I talked to were more ready to welcome black trade unions than the white trade union leaders. I became quickly aware of the reason for this as in factory after factory that we visited, we found black workers doing highly skilled work. I was told that over 60 per cent of the labour force was black.

But the employers were not as good as their words to us suggested. Black trade unionists, on a number of occasions, told our group that when their unions made an approach to management, meetings were refused or delayed. Worse still, promises (for example about wage increases) were made and in some cases were not kept. There were even instances of men who were attempting to organize unions being reported by management to the secret police, and this was followed by action to prevent workers taking part in meetings.

Police action had led to banning orders being applied to some of the black trade union leaders, and I was only able to meet them surreptitiously. In one case I wanted a man to meet Vic Feather as well as myself. I arranged for him to see me at a Johannesburg hotel. First I talked to him in the hotel room on my own, then I went out and sent Vic in. It was the only way we could have the meeting without him breaching his banning order, which forbade him to be with more than one other person at a time. This man, and others, poured scorn on the paternalistic ideas of some of the white trade union leaders. He told me: 'We welcome material assistance, with no strings attached. But we are not going to be dominated by the whites.' There was little evidence of white people helping black workers to organize, with a few honourable exceptions. These were principally among the clothing, leather and tobacco workers. In Johannesburg 15,000 black workers, mainly women, were organized in the Clothing Workers Union, which worked jointly with the Garment Workers Union of white and coloured workers. Both unions were housed in the same headquarters and co-operated closely in representations to the official industrial countil. This demonstrated what could be done, in spite of almost insuperable difficulties. It owed much to the heroic work in earlier years of Solly Sachs, the General Secretary of the Garment Workers Union from 1928 to 1952, when he was forced to leave South Africa. I got to know him in the latter part of his life in Britain and was delighted to meet his successor and disciple, Johanna Cornelius, a proud, capable and brave lady. She introduced us to the leaders of the two unions and arranged factory visits and meetings which were like a breath of fresh air after the fetid atmosphere of apartheid which prevailed throughout the country.

We heard the official view of apartheid from ministers and civil servants. At that time they were selling the idea of the 'black home-lands', and it was put to us that every black African would be treated as belonging to a homeland or a tribe. They justified pass laws and housing segregation on these grounds. With some Government people, and a few white trade union leaders too, I got the impression that black people were felt to be sub-human.

Our delegation was regarded as sufficiently important to be received by the Prime Minister, Mr Vorster. There was a little of the Boer farmer about him, he seemed wily yet domineering. He was anxious to impress us and at first adopted a sweetly reasonable approach. 'Job reservation is a measure which protects industrial peace,' he told us, 'and the control of movement by the blacks in the towns is necessary for social and industrial purposes. Many blacks agree with it.' It was news to us!

I asked him why the black trade unions could not be recognized, and allowed, for example, to participate in the industrial councils. Black workers doing the same jobs as whites should receive the same wages. His response was to bluster. There had to be some limit on wages to prevent industrialists from being pushed into excessive mechanization which would cause unemployment. For the rest, he said, the issues we were raising were political in nature and we should not involve our-selves in South African politics. It was the people of South Africa who had to live with the results.

We asked Vorster if we could visit David Kitson, a Briton and member of the Draughtsmen's Union, who was serving a twenty-year prison sentence. 'No, that man is a murderer!' Vorster's manner was almost threatening. At least, I urged, could we see John Hosey, a young man from Britain who was also serving a prison sentence, in his case of five years? I pleaded his youth and the worries of his parents back home. Eventually it was agreed that Feather and I would be permitted to see him in Pretoria gaol.

Both men had been imprisoned for alleged terrorist offences and communication with them had been very difficult for their families and friends. We knew that both were housed in Pretoria prison, and Vic and I worked out a strategy to enable me to talk to Hosey and give him a message for Kitson. We were shown into the Governor's office and the Governor, a small and apparently friendly Afrikaaner, told us he would have Hosey brought into the office. We must talk to him in the Governor's presence. When Hosey came in I sat next to him while Vic engaged the Governor in conversation. He was at his best, telling the Governor funny stories in a loud voice. This enabled me to tell Hosey quietly about the movement back home and the activities of his parents in trying to secure his release. I found that he occasionally saw Kitson and gave him the message to pass on. Never were Vic Feather's abilities as a raconteur put to better use.

In townships across South Africa I met the black dockers, seamen and other transport workers who were beginning to build their own unions, and arranged for some practical aid to be rendered through the International Transport Workers Federation. I got the feeling of a giant rising from a long sleep. Some of our talks were like the pioneering trade unionism of the old days back home. There was great enthusiasm and much hope, and yet the odds against the twenty million or more black people achieving equal rights seemed formidable then. . . .

At Cape Town a group of students had accomplished remarkable work in exposing the exploitation suffered by black workers. They were, however, critical of our visit and put out leaflets suggesting it was just another pro-white approach. I made contact with them, although Vic wanted to ignore them. Their initial hostility turned to friendliness and helpful discussion. This was also true of the many selfless and devoted people associated with training and research projects supporting the black trade unions in Durban and Johannesburg. The most constructive result of our visit was in fact the financial help the TUC agreed to give to these projects.

From time to time during our rushed trip, I had sharp differences with Vic Feather and Alan Hargreaves of the TUC staff, who accompanied us. The two other members of the team, Dan McGarvey and Cyril Plant, invariably supported me. This was the case in our visit to a gold mine in the Transvaal. The barrack-like arrangements for housing the black miners (many of them immigrants, on six-monthly contracts, from other African states) were primitive in the extreme. No wonder there had been revolts in other mines. I argued that we should protest publicly but Vic, supported by Hargreaves, was all for keeping quiet.

At the end of our three week visit Vic suggested that Alan Hargreaves should issue a press statement. 'Not likely!' I said. Vic, rather petulantly, countered, 'You do it then!' and I did. So for a precious hour or so, while the rest of the team had a last look around Johannesburg I wrote the statement. The last couple of paragraphs indicate my feelings:

> The delegation are convinced that apartheid offends against the dignity of man and its continuation cannot be justified. Moreover we are firmly of the opinion that apartheid is having a detrimental effect on the economic development of the country. If non-white people are given free, democratic rights in industry and society South Africa could become the workshop, the banker, the merchant, and a principal influence for true civilization and democracy in the whole of Africa.
>
> Among the first steps needed are the establishment of the right to freedom of association and collective bargaining through trade unions for all workers; a living wage and fair conditions of employment for all workers, including the application of the principle of the rate for the job; repeal of the laws which discriminate against African and other non-white workers; provision of adequate social insurance for African workers, particularly in urban areas; provision of universal free education . . . and provision of trade training opportunities on a massive scale. . . .

While interest was aroused in the trade unions at home when we reported, there was no great rush to action. Our proposal that British investment in South Africa should be opposed unless British firms there, 'show in a practical way that they are encouraging and recognizing genuinely independent trade unions for black workers', met with opposition from the Conservative Government and little response from the Labour Party or the trade unions. The employers to whom we made representations acted like pharisees. Feelings of international solidarity are not easy to arouse and yet they are part of the fibre of trade union principles. We had and have much work to do. . . .

Chapter Twenty-Six

I have no confidence in the superman; the limitations of
supposedly great men are obvious. I have spent my life
among ordinary working people; I am one of them. I have
seen them faced with the most difficult problems; place the
truth before them – the facts, whether they are good or bad
– and they display an understanding, ability and courage
that confounds the wisdom of the so-called great.

ERNEST BEVIN

Harold Wilson was speaking when I got to the eve-of-poll rally in St
George's Hall, Liverpool, the night before the October 1974 General
Election. The crowd was large and enthusiastic and the atmosphere
was typical of Liverpool. I wanted to avoid interrupting Harold, so I
crept in at the back of the platform. He knew that I had been addressing
an election rally at Ellesmere Port and this was the reason for my late
arrival.

Later in his speech he noticed that I was on the platform and he
departed from his script to pay a warm tribute to my efforts. His
reference surprised me, because Harold was not well known for his
appreciation of the work of others. It occurred to me that perhaps he
intended to correct a discourtesy he had done me at the previous
General Election eve-of-poll rally eight months before, also in Liverpool. On that occasion I had been in the middle of a speech when
Harold Wilson walked in, followed by a big group of supporters.
Naturally I cut short my remarks and joined with the crowd in cheer-
ing Wilson. I suggested he should speak right away, which he did.
However I did feel that he might have held back his entry for a
while. . . . .

Not that Wilson had always been well treated by the TGWU. I
recall one occasion when he had come to see me at Transport House.
He was then Leader of the Opposition and wanted to talk to me about
the sit-in at the Fisher-Bendix factory in Liverpool. A lot of his con-
stituents were involved and the TGWU also had a big interest. It was

about six in the evening when he arrived. I rang down to the porter's room and said: 'Mr Harold Wilson is with me, could you make us a nice cup of tea?' Shortly afterwards Ernie, the porter, came bustling in with a couple of big mugs and a huge tin teapot blackened by age. It looked the sort of utensil you would get your tea out of in a ship's galley. Ernie poured out the tea with ill grace. He showed little respect for Wilson. I saw him the next day and said: 'You don't think much of Harold Wilson then?' His reply was to the point: 'He's not much good for us.' Ernie had a strong working-class outlook and was something of a character. Often in the early morning before the office had begun to operate, or in the evening after office hours, we would discuss current events. I appreciated his basic common sense. When I chided him about his blackened teapot, he answered: 'Well, it makes a good cup of tea!' And so it did.

Ernie was certainly no respecter of persons. One of the many occasions he brought his famous teapot into use was when Frank Kearton came to see me unexpectedly. There was a crisis at Courtauld's and Kearton wanted an urgent discussion. It was about seven in the evening and on entering my office he expressed surprise that I had no security men in the building. 'I've come up four floors and I haven't seen a soul,' he said. I told him I didn't worry about things like that and invited him to have a cup of tea. Ernie in due course appeared with his teapot and the mugs. He bustled in, with no knocks and no apologies, and proceeded to pour out good strong tea – whether Kearton liked it or not.

Perhaps I took a secret pleasure in bringing people down to earth. It was in part this feeling which led to my participating in the Liaison Committee of the Labour Party and the TUC. I had been largely responsible for bringing it into being, and I got some satisfaction from knowing that trade unionists with shop-floor experience would be engaged in regular discussion with the political leaders of the Labour Party. In the early days Vic Feather and Harold Wilson appeared to take the lead in the new committee in public, but in fact they played little part in working out the details of its policy statements. In 1971 I put my view to the Labour Party conference: 'There is no reason why a joint policy cannot be worked out, but let us have the closest possible liaison. This is not a matter of brainstorming in the back rooms of Congress House and Transport House just before the next election. In the past we have not had the necessary dialogue. . . .' I wanted to secure a joint programme, to which the Labour Party would be tied when it was next elected and on which both Labour Party and TUC could campaign. It never occurred to me to call it a 'social contract'; at the time I used phrases like 'a blueprint' or an 'agreed platform'.

Of course the first thing we talked about was industrial relations. We agreed a firm commitment to the repeal of the Industrial Relations Act and a plan to set up an independent conciliation and arbitration service. I helped to draft the essentials of what later became the Employment Protection Act. The first public statement issued by the Liaison Committee dealt with these matters and outlined plans to ensure trade union recognition and disclosure of information to trade union representatives. A major feature was our proposals for statutory rights to be given to safety and health representatives in the workplace.

I did not get the impression that all the politicians on the committee were very clear about the industrial relations issues we were pressing. After all, such things as tighter control over unfair dismissals and longer periods of notice from employers were generally outside their experience. That was a good reason for the existence of the committee.

It was not long before the issue of an incomes policy was raised and it was clear that, although the experience of a statutory incomes policy operated by the Labour Government of 1964–70 had been disastrous, some Party leaders still hankered after a wages policy. I warned them against the danger of a split with the TUC if they persisted, and argued that the priority should be control of prices, plus a comprehensive social policy which would command public support. Gradually a social policy was hammered out and found expression in the second main statement of policy from the Committee: 'Economic Policy and the Cost of Living.'

So we hammered out what was later to be called the 'Social Contract'. In many ways it was like negotiating a collective agreement, with the highly experienced political leaders – Denis Healey, Barbara Castle, Shirley Williams, Jim Callaghan and Harold Wilson amongst them – seeking to make sure that they did not give too much away.

One issue on which I succeeded in gaining full agreement was that of pensions. The motions I had proposed at repeated Labour Party and trade union conferences now bore fruit and a commitment was agreed to raise pensions to £10 per week for single retirement pensioners and £16 a week for married couples immediately after the election of a Labour Government.

The General Election of February 1974 was a disappointment. I had campaigned in various parts of the country, mainly in the industrial areas, and had felt that we were on a winner. The failure to secure a majority meant that progress on the Social Contract would be slower than I had hoped. The whole situation was in the balance while Ted Heath made his abortive attempts to work out some sort of coalition with the Liberals. I was glad when that failed and Harold was invited to form a government.

While Wilson was waiting in Ron Hayward's room at Transport House for the call to come from Buckingham Palace, I was able to talk with him. Pressmen were maliciously describing me as 'the *real* Labour leader', but in fact I did not presume to press my personal views except on one point. I told Harold that the trade unions would not stand for Reg Prentice being made Secretary of State for Employment. It was the first time that Labour had been elected on a programme agreed with the TUC, and we needed a man at the Employment post who was sympathetic to our views. We agreed that Michael Foot would be the ideal choice.

Over the years I had come to respect and, indeed, have a great affection for Michael Foot, because of his honesty and sincerity – rare qualities amongst politicians in my experience. In Deakin's day Michael had been regarded as an enemy of the TGWU because of his support for the 'blue' (Stevedores') union. Prentice, who had been the shadow Secretary of State for Employment until the General Election, was a member of the TGWU Parliamentary panel and a former servant of the TGWU (for many years he had been employed in the legal and social affairs department of the union). In contrast to Foot he had increasingly fallen out of step with trade-union thinking.

The crisis caused by the miners' strike and the three-day week in-tensified membership support for the Labour Government in settling the miners' claim and restoring full-time working in industry. I knew that the manifesto of the Labour Party in the General Election had faithfully reflected the policies agreed by the Liaison Committee. Now I was anxious to see results. Achieving a major advance for pensioners was great, but I was continually pressing other parts of the programme too. The manifesto had declared that the Labour Government would 'control prices, attack speculation and set a climate fair enough to work together with the unions'. Where was the action? I asked. The timetable for the repeal of the Industrial Relations Act was another important question.

I realized that the weakness of the Government in Parliament made it difficult to implement quickly the promised public ownership of the ports, shipbuilding and repair, and aircraft manufacture but I saw no reason for delay in ending the incomes controls set up by the Heath Government. I pressed for the speedy development of the promised comprehensive system of voluntary conciliation and arbitration services (ACAS). Altogether I was something of a nuisance to ministers and occasionally upset the equanimity of the TUC old guard.

The Liaison Committee's statement on 'Economic Policy and the Cost of Living' had declared:

> It will be the first task of the Labour Government on taking office, and having due regard to the circumstances at that time, to conclude with the TUC, on the basis of the understanding being reached on the Liaison Committee, a wide-ranging agreement on the policies to be pursued in all these aspects of our economic life and to discuss with them the order of priorities of their fulfilment.

There was a degree of forgetfulness about these words in Government circles. Shortly after the election some of us made sure that the Liaison Committee remained in being, and this proved to be a powerful aid in keeping the Government on its toes. It helped us to make a contribution in the preparation of policies by the Government. On the whole I guess that Harold Wilson, Jim Callaghan and the rest preferred to deal with the Liaison Committee rather than the NEC of the Labour Party.

Contact with Government ministers was not confined to formal meetings. There were many informal get-togethers, as when Michael Foot and Jill, his wife, arranged parties at their home. George Wigg, whom I had known for many years, persuaded me to have a meal with Denis Healey, after telling me what a good chap Healey was and giving a glowing account of his abilities. I had always thought Healey a hard right-winger but Wigg tried hard to change that opinion. So did Denis himself. When we got down to discussion he made clear his intention to tax the wealthy in favour of a socially just programme. But he painted a depressing picture of the economy. Arrangements were made for informal talks to take place between him and Michael Foot on one side, and Len Murray and me on the other. Perhaps that formulation is wrong – we felt we were all on the *one* side. From those initial contacts sprang the TUC policy that wage claims should be kept in line with price increases.

We had so many meetings at that time that I felt glad our flat was relatively close to the centre of London. When meetings finished late at night it was a comfort to know I would be home in twenty minutes. Always Evelyn, my stalwart supporter, would be waiting to give encouragement when things were difficult. Trying to help a Labour Government had its problems.

The industrial relations legislation of the previous Government remained for a period. We still had trouble on the docks and at Heathrow Airport the TGWU was being pursued by a Canadian firm called General Aviation Services for nearly £2 million compensation. The British Airports Authority had granted the firm a concession to provide ground handling services, and because our members feared for their jobs they had taken spontaneous blacking action. The Authority then withdrew the concession and the firm went rushing off to the National Industrial Relations Court. In the last decision it made before it was abolished, Sir John Donaldson's court found that the union was liable. We appealed and the case dragged on until May 1975, when the Court of Appeal decided that the union was *not* liable to pay compensation and awarded us costs. All the time the issue was in the balance it worried me greatly for if there was one thing I had in common with the late Arthur Deakin it was concern to protect the workers' money which constituted the funds of the union.

Hugh Scanlon was also in trouble. In a prolonged dispute with Con Mech (Engineering) Ltd the AUEW had been fined £75,000 for contempt by the NIRC, and this had been taken out of the union's assets by sequestration. Later, while the Heath Government's industrial relations laws were being dismantled, the NIRC ordered costs of £65,000 to be paid by the union. The consequence of this was that not only the AUEW was in difficulty; the Labour Government and the nation itself faced industrial chaos, with a threatened strike in the engineering industry. Out of the blue a prominent engineering employer contacted me in confidence, and asked 'What can we do to help Hughie?' 'Well, if anyone wants to pay the money the court will accept it,' I told him. 'It doesn't *have* to be the AUEW.' 'I think we can do something,' he said. Shortly afterwards the money was paid.

The relationship with Harold Wilson and other Government leaders was very different to the days of *In Place of Strife*. He was clearly looking upon the trade unions as a partner and anxious to make progress together. In meetings with the General Council he opened his heart and explained the difficulties presented by his not having an effective majority. It would be necessary to apply priorities, he said, and he suggested that the first priority, in the industrial relations field, should be the repeal of the Industrial Relations Act. This was chosen because Liberal and nationalist MPs were not likely to oppose the repeal.

The so-called 'counter-inflation' legislation of the previous Government was a different matter in Wilson's view. Much as the trade unions opposed the legislation, there was a majority in favour of statutory incomes control in the House of Commons. If the Government was to take risks, he suggested, they should be taken later. 'Let us concentrate on getting rid of the Industrial Relations Act first.' I pointed out that, when the repeal of the counter-inflation Act was being put through, we would want definite legislation on prices. Success in that direction, I reminded the Prime Minister, was vital if the Government wanted to influence unions into making more moderate pay claims.

Michael Foot had the ball in his court in preparing to revise employment law. He was a worried and often flustered man, who genuinely wanted to help the trade unions but found he was sinking into a morass of complex problems. Bill Wedderburn had helped us by drafting the legal framework for the changes the TUC wanted, but it was another matter to get it through the Department of Employment and to deal with the Parliamentary draftsmen. Michael Foot had wanted Bill to become a temporary civil servant and to work in the Department, so that he could see it through, but Bill refused. It would have meant giving up his chair at the LSE and restricted his wider efforts in the field of trade union rights. He continued to give as much aid as possible and his expertise helped the TUC a great deal.

The achievements of the Wilson Government between 28 February and the General Election in October 1974 were considerable, despite its minority position. One significant step forward was the setting-up of the Advisory Conciliation and Arbitration Service. In a sense it was my baby, and I was glad when Michael Foot consulted me about the chairmanship. We agreed that Jim Mortimer (a trade unionist who had become Personnel Director of London Transport) would be a suitable choice, although it was made clear to me that the position was mine if I wanted it. I had no wish to leave my post, however, and my interest in the success of the Service was met by my membership of the ACAS Council as one of the three TUC representatives.

Yet another big advance was the passing of the Health and Safety at Work Act, the most comprehensive legislation ever drafted covering people at work. In my life I have had many bitter experiences arising from death and injury at work. Nothing is so traumatic as having to meet the widow and dependants of a man killed or severely injured in an industrial mishap. I more than welcomed the legislation; it had started under the Heath Government, but Labour added a number of strengthening clauses. One of them provided for the introduction of trade union safety delegates, but this evoked the anger of the CBI and opposition in the House of Lords. I felt this keenly because considerable delay followed. My friend Terry Parry, of the Fire Brigades Union, was the main TUC spokesman dealing with the question and I rather fell out with him because I felt he should be doing more. I realized afterwards that it was unfair to blame him for the activities of members of the House of Lords.

About this time I paid a visit to the scene of the terrible explosion at the Nyprox UK Ltd plant at Flixborough, where many had lost their lives. Such disasters reinforced my concern for stronger efforts over health and safety. In pressing for a public inquiry into the disaster I was in touch with Harold Wilson, Michael Foot, Roy Jenkins and other ministers and I expressed my views in the strongest terms. I wished the Lords and others who had delayed progress on the health and safety legislation could have been with me to witness the devastation at Flixborough.

We were in for some disappointments. 'Oh, yes, there will be a wealth tax,' Denis Healey assured me in the early months when he was wooing the trade unions, but it never came. But we were thankful that progress was being made in many directions. Pension increases and the repeal of the Industrial Relations Act provided red-letter days. Bills were being drafted on Employment Protection (which I had said would be a 'shop stewards' charter') and on the nationalization of aircraft production and shipbuilding. The Health and Safety Act had been put on the statute book, and Concorde was saved. Not least, ACAS had been established.

And what about the trade union side of the Social Contract? I had said publicly that the Government was entitled to look for a response. That did not look so good as retail prices rose by 17 per cent and wage increases averaged 25 per cent. Harold Wilson and Jim Callaghan said some soothing words at the 1974 Trades Union Congress. Harold Wilson declared: 'Recent comment, some of it, if I may say so, a little illiterate, has sought to narrow the Social Contract as though it concerned only the area of wage claims and wage settlements. This is not what the Social Contract is about.' He went on: 'I believe that an essential part of the Social Contract is pressing on with productivity agreements.' This I regarded as most important, because I had been an advocate of productivity agreements from the beginning and saw in them opportunities for widening the area of collective bargaining as well as bringing about increased earnings. My advocacy of the idea over the years had led to differences with some union leaders, both on the right and on the left, who were inclined to dismiss such deals as 'phoney'. I suspect they felt too much local bargaining would upset their way of working. Lord Cooper and Lord Allen were particularly vocal critics. Sometimes I thought that their attitude was unduly petty, with an element of jealousy about it. Perhaps I was over-sensitive, but they seemed to me to be typical of the old guard of the TUC, who took no initiatives themselves but were happy to criticize.

Jim Callaghan also made a good speech to the Congress. Jim is a wily customer and sensed the mood of the delegates when he paid tribute to the work done by the Liaison Committee and the part played in it by the TUC. 'Why was the Labour Government able to swing into action within days of taking office and act so effectively?' he asked. 'The answer lies in the agreement reached by the Liaison Committee.'

Sitting beside me on the platform Jim whispered: 'You've performed miracles. You should be with us in the Government. You could go into the Lords and be with us in no time.' I whispered back: 'I don't want to go to the Lords and I don't want to be in the Government, but I'll help it all I can.' I knew that he and Wilson were above all anxious for the election of a Labour Government with a substantial majority, and so was I. I had concluded a speech to the Congress calling for support of Labour in the coming General Election, with the words: 'Help Labour to win for Britain and begin the job of building the new Jerusalem.' Maybe I was starry-eyed, maybe I always have been.

Wage restraint was the big issue of the Trades Union Congress, according to the newspapers. They made the most of any sign of division, and when the Amalgamated Union of Engineering Workers at a meeting on the Saturday before the Congress decided to vote against the Social Contract it became big headlines. As always the reports were highly personalized: 'Jack Jones appealed to Scanlon to be more realistic, to think again,' or 'On Wednesday, Scanlon dramatically capitulated, and the Social Contract was voted through Congress with virtual unanimity.' In fact it wasn't quite like that.

To be honest I could not imagine how any delegation could vote against the motion to be moved by Lawrence Daly of the miners. It was a simple affirmation of support for efforts being made 'by the TUC and the Government towards solving the economic problems facing Britain'. It went on: 'Congress believes in free collective bargaining that will give all workers a fair living wage and a decent standard of life.' It opposed a compulsory incomes policy and 'endorsed the guidance given by the General Council'.

The opponents of the Social Contract were led by Ken Gill of TASS, a section of the AUEW (which remained very much a loose federation), and Bill Ronksley of ASLEF. They urged eight specific pre-conditions before co-operation could be assured. Since the eight specifics were contained within the objectives of the Social Contract Len Murray gave assurances about them, but could not make them pre-conditions. This became the crux of a discursive and somewhat chaotic debate, with opinion clearly on the side of the Labour Government. The danger of losing the advantages we had already received, let alone prospects for further advance, if Labour lost the Election, concentrated the minds of a lot of people including Hugh Scanlon. He asked Ken Gill to withdraw his resolution. So strong was the desire for unity in the Congress that Gill agreed, against what he said was his better judgement. Next day he was condemned by the *Morning Star*, which declared: 'The Social Contract is a re-vamped version of Phase Three wage restraint . . . it was wrong to withdraw the resolution under the erroneous conception of unity.'

TUC support for the Government was important but it had to be translated into action. I wanted to do everything possible to support Labour's campaign, both within the union and by meetings and can-vassing. That meant meetings at factory gates, such as one at the big Longbridge car plant, and in industrial areas throughout the country. It was exhausting but exhilarating, because industrial workers seemed to be responding with an enthusiasm we had not witnessed for a long time.

At Garston, South Liverpool, I took a trip down memory lane. Canvassing for the TGWU-sponsored Labour candidate, Eddie Loyden, I went to where I had lived as a youngster, and was able to renew friendships from those earlier days. Sentiment gave way to anger as I realized that too many of the slum houses I had known as a kid were still around, including the two-up-two-down in which I was born. I told a meeting: 'One of the things I'm looking forward to under a new Labour Government is that they will make an attack on slums as part of the Social Contract and build a lot more council houses at reasonable rents so that these folk can be rehoused quickly in decent conditions.'

Labour won the General Election but its majority was small, and the economic crisis intensified. Just after the election I went up to Scotland to make some factory visits and attend the Scottish Conference of the TGWU. My principal speech reflected my growing fears:

> The growth of unemployment is the main danger and we in the unions must play our part in fighting it. It is simply no use pressing for actions which lead to the closure of the firms we work for. A wonderful wage agreement is no value if the firm with whom we have negotiated the agreement doesn't employ people any more.
>
> If there is a failure to agree with an employer I urge shop stewards and officials not to hesitate to involve the new Conciliation and Arbitration Service. We should all give it a fair wind in order to reduce the number of disputes. . . .'

My words were quietly received by the delegates but there were wide repercussions. I was attacked in various areas but I knew that if I did not make a stand no one would. We could easily have had a 'winter of discontent' just as severe as that of 1978/79, but we fought it successfully with the weapon of the Social Contract.

One item in Labour's General Election programme had been the promise of a referendum on membership of the European Economic Community. I had campaigned with Tony Benn for many months to commit the Party and the TUC to the proposition that either a General Election or a referendum should decide whether we should continue in the EEC or not. The Party had opted for a referendum. I was firmly opposed to EEC membership and made my position clear at every opportunity, strengthened by repeated decisions of the TGWU policy-making bodies. This led to sharp differences of opinions with a number of Labour leaders.

I shared anti-Market platforms with Tony Benn, Peter Shore and Michael Foot in the 'Get Britain Out' Campaign, but I was stunned when George Wigg suggested I should speak alongside Enoch Powell and himself at a big rally in Pudsey, Yorkshire. At first I was against the idea but George persuaded me that the combination would attract

With Les Dawson, Jim Callaghan and Mike Yarwood at my 'retirement rally' at the Royal Festival Hall in February 1978.

With Evelyn on the sands at Blackpool during a break from the TUC in 1977.

Three generations of Joneses at my retirement 'do'.

Leading the May Day march at Cleveland with Neil Kinnock, 1984.

Lobbying Parliament with the pensioners, March 1981.

a big audience and give a fillip to the campaign. I opened my speech by saying that the platform represented the unity of opposites, and explained that on most things I profoundly disagreed with Powell as I knew he did with me. He made a brilliant speech, and I wondered whether I had done the right thing when I noticed that members of the TGWU staff were eagerly queuing up for his autograph.

Opposition to the EEC was popular among many sections of TGWU membership for practical reasons – the threat to employment and further increases in the cost of living. Lorry drivers especially were worried about the prospect of having to submit to EEC regulations, so I got a cheer from a group of them in the meeting when I said:

> Let me give you one example of the costs which Brussels control will impose on us: by the beginning of 1976, Britain's lorries – 700,000 of them – are required to fit tachographs, the 'spy in the cab'; it will cost the industry something like eighty million pounds initially. All of it will be passed on to the consumer. The idea is a bureaucrat's monstrosity. It is not needed in Britain and both the transport employers and the union are totally against it. We are paying in to a club to impose penalties like this on us!

Although my opposition to the EEC has never diminished, I accepted the result of the referendum and the TUC's decision to participate in EEC institutions. I was thus able to use my influence within the EEC substantially to delay the introduction of the 'spy in the cab' into Britain during my period of office as General Secretary. The much-feared instrument did not in fact become operative in Britain until five years later, on 31 December 1981.

Chapter Twenty-Seven

To be, or not to be : that is the question ;
Whether 'tis nobler in the mind to suffer
The slings and arrows of outrageous fortune,
Or to take arms against a sea of troubles, . . .

And where the offence is let
the great axe fall. . . .

WILLIAM SHAKESPEARE

The military coup in Chile in 1973, followed by the Pinochet dictatorship, had shocked the world of Labour. Many people thought the
situation was similar to that in Spain in 1936. As in Nazi Germany and
Franco Spain the trade union movement in Chile had been the subject
of severe attack. Numerous trade unionists had been put in prison.
Many were missing and some had been executed. In September 1974
the International Transport Workers Federation organized a forty-
eight hour boycott of Chilean transport; at the same time I had proposed, in the Executive of the ITF, that a delegation should proceed
to Chile to protest at the attacks on trade unionists and to explore ways
of giving aid to their wives and children. Three of the delegation went
out from London on a British Caledonian flight; they were a leader of
the Norwegian seamen, Harold Lewis, the General Secretary of the
ITF, and myself.

As we approached Santiago airport a voice boomed out over the
plane's intercom: 'Señor Jack Jones and the Transport Federation
group must remain on board.' I thought, 'Hello, they're going to
send us back without landing,' but shortly after the plane had ground-
ed, air force officers entered and told me that the Minister of Labour,
an army general, was waiting to receive us. It was not an invitation we
could accept or refuse. The officers escorted us across the tarmac and
into a small reception room just under the area where spectators were
watching the aeroplanes. As I moved towards the room I heard a call
from above, 'Jack Jones!', and a note came floating down. It was from

one of the British Embassy officials, giving his name, telephone number and an address and saying he would keep in touch.

Our passports were checked by the air force men and our bags brought in. It was still not clear what was going to happen, but after a while we were hustled into a limousine. With air force officers in the car with us and escorts in the front and the rear, I realized that we were well under control!

Eventually the car stopped. We were taken into a rather forbidding building and put into an ante-room to wait for the Minister. A middle-aged, rather diffident Chilean came into the room and told me he would be acting as the interpreter. I gathered he was some sort of Government clerk and he seemed anxious to ingratiate himself with us. It quickly became apparent that his English was not a lot better than my Spanish, which was very basic. Communication wasn't easy when we finally met the Minister, but we made do.

Dressed in a general's uniform, the Minister conveyed his irritation at our visit. He asked why we had come, and when I tried to explain he said it was interference. I asked that we should be allowed to see the Transport Union men in prison and started to read out their names from a list that I had with me. He replied: 'No, not now! We are busy preparing for the visit of the ILO mission.' Then he became placatory. 'You will be welcome to come again later, some time next year,' he said, 'and we will arrange for you to visit the prisons. You will be our guests.' I brushed his proposal aside. Surely, I said, he could give us some information about the men, what prisons they were at and whether they were alive. I mentioned the names of two men whom I understood had been killed. He became angry. 'You can accept our invitation if you wish, but you cannot stay.' When I persisted, he replied: 'Later, later, next time you come, not now!' The atmosphere became heated towards the end and his final words were that we must leave on the next plane.

We thought we were going to be rushed back to the airport, but outside the Minister's office our erstwhile interpreter told us that the next plane out would not be for about two days. We would at least be able to try to make more enquiries. We were allowed to go to our hotel, although the interpreter insisted on accompanying us and only after some time were we able to get rid of him. Finally he departed, no doubt to report to the secret service all he had got to know about us.

At our hotel the Canadian delegate joined us, but Teddy Gleason, leader of the US East Coast longshoremen, who had been expected, failed to arrive. He was a close friend of George Meany and his absence symbolized the lack of support from the AFL/CIO and was consistent with the failure of most US transport unions to support the ITF boycott. It confirmed our suspicion that the American State Department, whose views the AFL/CIO invariably reflected in international affairs, did not favour too much criticism of the Pinochet regime.

Santiago is an impressive capital and in the centre there were signs of affluence, but such was not the case in the slums, where stark poverty abounded. With the aid of the British Embassy official who had tried to make contact on our arrival, we made out way to the centre run by the interdenominational Peace Committee which enjoyed the sympathy of Cardinal Archbishop Silva Henriquez. Much good work was being done there to feed the wives and children of the dead, missing or imprisoned trade unionists and political opponents of the regime. Help was also provided in organizing employment for many of the women, making articles of clothing and cheap jewellery. The centre was directed by Christian Precht, a young, able and determined priest. His devotion and courage impressed us deeply.

Apart from the humanitarian aspect of caring for the women and children, what was being done indirectly helped to sustain their menfolk in prison. As a result of our visit we decided to recommend that financial support should be given to the Peace Committee by the trade union movement internationally. As I talked to those women I was filled with emotion, and decided to do all I could to share my feelings with the world. We talked to lawyers and others and established sources of information which proved useful. Some contact was made with people active in the transport unions, despite the restrictions which were being imposed on them by the regime, and other illicit contacts were made with opponents of Pinochet.

Our group did not return directly to Britain but first went to Lima, Peru, where we gave evidence to an ILO inquiry mission which was assembling there prior to visiting Chile. We also met trade union leaders who had contacts inside Chile. On our return to London I addressed the Labour Party Conference and a series of trade union meetings, reporting on our visit and pushing for aid to the Chilean trade unionists and their families.

A year later I was responsible for an eventful nine-hour descent on Santiago by the leaders of the International Confederation of Free Trade Unions World Congress, who were then meeting in Mexico. I insisted that the Congress must publicly demonstrate its solidarity with the trade union opposition to Pinochet and with those who were trying to relieve the suffering of the wives and children. The Congress wished me to lead a six-man commission but I insisted that the General Secretary of the ICFTU, Otto Kersten, should lead the party. I would accompany him. After a five-thousand-mile flight we made for the centre of the Peace Committee, where I renewed my acquaintance with Christian Precht and his friends. We talked with the relatives of the detainees, and then moved on to a meeting with Cardinal Silva Henriquez. It was a serious yet happy occasion, and I was proud to pin the badge of the trade union International on his robe. He was an outspoken critic of the regime and had done much to help its victims. We learned a lot about the thousands of known political and trade union prisoners, and of the many who were missing. The latter were men who had been taken away yet the regime denied any knowledge of them.

We were under close observation during the whole of our day in Santiago but that did not stop us passing and receiving messages to or from brave people who were operating illicitly and who were encouraged by our visit. In addition we met some political leaders, whose movements were restricted but who were still not under arrest. It was at the airport, when we were going to catch our return flight, that the secret police showed their hand. We passed through the Customs, and then our group was suddenly surrounded by armed security men who pushed us into a side room. They opened and searched every bag and demanded to know whom we had visited. They separated me from the others, whom they allowed to go, purported to read some of my papers, then grabbed the rest of them.

At this stage it was not clear whether they were going to arrest me. Outside, my colleagues were shouting, 'Let that man go,' and a Canadian diplomat, who had come to see off one of our group, apparently started to make representations on my behalf. I was very indignant about the theft of my documents and insisted that they were my personal property and they had no right to take them. I was told they would not be returned. I asked for a receipt but that was also refused. I was then pushed to the departure door with the police all around me. I shouted to the crowd: 'This is what the Fascists do to a visitor from a friendly country. They are thieves. They have taken my property!' The police seemed embarrassed by the commotion and glad to get rid of me.

My papers included material issued by the Chilean Peace Committee and printed pamphlets about the Chilean situation, together with notes for speeches I intended to make at the ICFTU Congress on Industrial Democracy and the situation in South Africa. There was nothing of any value to the DINA (the secret police set up by the Pinochet dictatorship with the help of ex-Nazi SS officers) but despite demands by the British Ambassador that the documents should be returned, the Chilean Foreign Ministry made no move to hand them back for some time. It was nearly three months before I was able to reclaim them from our Foreign Office.

'Man's inhumanity to man' could be seen at home too. This struck me sharply when a London bus conductor, Ronald Jones, was killed while on duty, in a mindless incident over a 2p bus fare for a dog. Two men were later charged with action which led to his death. He was the first London busman to die while carrying out his duties and revulsion at his killing was widespread, coming as it did in a period of increasing violence on the buses. So strong was the feeling that it led to a one-day strike on London Transport buses.

Ronald was a Jamaican who had travelled thousands of miles from his homeland to earn a living. In his funeral procession I marched at the head of hundreds of London Transport employees, black and white together, from Clapham Common to the African Methodist Chapel at Wandsworth. If ever an occasion epitomised unity in adversity, that was it. It was a moving ceremony, in a packed chapel and with large crowds outside to whom the service was relayed. I was called upon to address the gathering. My final words were: 'We mourn our brother and we shall remember him as a symbol of the need to bring about a better world.' As I looked out from the pulpit to the ranks of black faces, with a sprinkling of white here and there, emotion overcame me. 'Here are my brothers and sisters,' I thought. 'We must learn to live together. It is not good enough to oppose apartheid in far-away South Africa and do little about the divisions between black and white in London.'

'I felt like a parson in that pulpit,' I told Jim, the TGWU driver, as I came out from the chapel. 'You looked like one!' he said.

I again thundered from a pulpit at a chapel in Llanberis, Snowdonia, to commemorate the centenary of the Slate Quarrymen's Union, now part of the TGWU. Afterwards we walked in procession from the chapel to a rock on the hillside outside the town, known as the 'rock of the union'. It was there that the quarrymen used to gather secretly to organize their union and defend themselves against the oppression of Lord Penrhyn and the other quarry-owners. A memorial had been placed on the rock and it was my duty to unveil it. As I began a white lamb appeared, just above the memorial stone – it stole the show. While I was speaking the lamb 'baa baa'd' just like a political heckler, to the delight of the gathering on the hillside.

By early in 1975 the Social Contract was under severe attack. Harold Wilson and Denis Healey did not seem happy at the co-operation they were receiving from the trade unions and there was strong criticism of the Government in our ranks because of their inability to stem the rapidly rising tide of unemployment and inflation. I never doubted the value of the Social Contract, which I saw as a major step towards economic equality and better conditions for working people, and used every democratic means to gain the co-operation of fellow trade unionists. Sometimes I felt that political leaders did not appreciate the hard work involved in influencing rank-and-file opinion.

Carping criticism of trade union activities by Harold Wilson and Denis Healey had not helped, and at a meeting of the Liaison Committee I appealed to them to appreciate the constructive work being done. Len Murray was constrained to say that wage restraint was not the 'be all and end all', and presented the TUC case for more emphasis on investment and productivity in solving the economic problems of the country. At the same meeting Hugh Scanlon appeared to be coming round to supporting the TUC guidelines, which encouraged me quite a bit. But what struck me most was Harold Wilson's warning of the Conservative Party's growing commitment to a strong monetarist policy – which promised a grim future for the workers if the Tories regained power.

The Annual Congress of the Scottish TUC took place at Aberdeen in April 1975. I broke away from docks problems in London to speak to the Scottish trade union leaders. In the course of my speech I said: 'My appeal is to respect the Social Contract, and to support it. To do this would mean advancing the interests of our members and keeping a Labour Government in power. Can we really afford to let this Government be thrown out? The Labour Government, for all its limitations, is two hundred times better than a Tory Government.' I added that the Social Contract was one means of laying down the policy on which the Government would move. 'How else but with unity between the trade unions and the Labour Government are we going to fight rising unemployment and the redundancies that are taking place?'

There was no doubt the nation was in a serious state. The Chancellor of the Exchequer (Denis Healey) was uttering dire warnings and in the background were threats to use legal powers on pay once again. He was like an old-time reactionary crying, 'Bring back the cat!' Prices in the shops rose week by week and this upset the budgets of working people, who were constrained to seek wage increases to correct *their* economic position. Contrary to 'expert' opinion, I do not accept that wage increases are the root cause of inflation; they are a reaction to rising prices and, therefore, feed inflationary trends.

I knew someting had to be done. Should I take an initiative or wait for the TUC economic departmental staff to produce yet another paper? I decided to act. At a union rally in Bournemouth early in May 1975 I called for a new approach to be made, 'to provide for wage increases to be on a flat-rate basis. The figure should be directly related to the cost of living. The one figure should then apply to all people at work – MPs, judges, civil servants and other workers.'

I explained then, and in more detail in a series of articles I wrote for the popular dailies, the benefits of the flat-rate scheme. Flat-rate increases would mean that *everyone*, irrespective of occupation or position, would get the same amount of money in the next pay round. All would be required to make sacrifices. The lower the income, the smaller the sacrifice. They would be simple to apply and straightforward in effect. No one could get round them by plausible interpretation. *They would be seen to be fair.*

The idea had a generally favourable reception. Jim Callaghan stated that my proposal was something to be looked at seriously but jibbed at the idea of a prices freeze. Harold Wilson made encouraging noises and Denis Healey regarded my approach as promising. Michael Foot reacted favourably, and one 'high Whitehall source' quoted in the *Financial Times* said it would be 'very encouraging if all workers and employers could accept Jack Jones' formula'. There were some doubts on the part of the TUC economic staff, who at one stage proposed a return to the ill-fated 'wage-vetting' machinery operated by the TUC in the 1965/66 period. They were also critical of the flat-rate idea because of its effect on differentials. These objections were eventually abandoned, however, and Len Murray expressed support for a flat rate at the June 1975 meeting of the General Council. In fact overwhelming support was expressed for the idea, subject to agreement on a figure and the Government's adoption of a price target for the following twelve months. Only Hugh Scanlon put forward serious doubts; he said that the TUC could not deliver.

My own faith in the policy grew with the support I received at a variety of conferences, from the Lancashire Miners and the Hosiery Workers Union, to the tinplate workers at Swansea and the Automotive Workers' national conference at Blackpool. These, and dozens of other meetings gave me encouragement, but I knew that the real test would come at the Biennial Delegate Conference of the TGWU, which was held from 30 June to 4 July at Blackpool.

The centre of attention during the proceedings was the debate over the Social Contract, which occupied nearly a full day of conference time. The democratic nature of the conference was exemplified by the participation of nearly a thousand delegates, all of them lay members. The presiding chairman was himself a rank-and-file busman, Len Forden. Thirty-four delegates made speeches in the debate. As the General Secretary I presented the Executive Council's point of view, but I was the only full-time official allowed to speak in the debate.

The interest was intense. I did not have an easy task, for the opposition to any understanding about incomes was considerable. Statutory controls and the Social Contract were damned as one and the same thing. But this view did not prevail, and when the vote came support for the Social Contract was overwhelming, including for the proposed flat rate, to apply for the next twelve months.

The whole project then almost foundered. There was a fall in the value of the pound and Healey panicked. He made an emergency statement to the House of Commons, proposing a 10 per cent limit on wage increases, the introduction of cash limits in the public sector to cover wage negotiations, and other similar measures. No one warned me; the Conference only knew what came to us by the media.

There was consternation. Some delegates felt cheated. Confidence in my leadership was shaken. I thought, myself, that Denis had been ham-fisted, to say the least. The delegates who opposed the Social Contract demanded a fresh debate and submitted an emergency motion. It was opposed and defeated, but the spirit of the Conference had been upset.

It was an amazing period. With the exception of Michael Foot, who was always sympathetic, I found it impossible to have a man-to-man discussion with any top minister. It was difficult to detect the difference between a minister's point of view and the attitude of his Department. We would have made a lot more progress if Denis Healey, for example, had not rushed to make speeches immediately the Treasury had persuaded him on some issue. Having made a public statement it was difficult for him to move away from it. Time and time again during the 1975 crisis it was all too apparent that Government leaders, and even the staff of the TUC and the Labour Party, had no conception that the support of rank-and-file members had to be won, and their confidence sustained.

The TGWU Conference decision cleared the ground for an agreed policy in discussions between the Government and the TUC. However the Treasury preferred a percentage for wage increases and only grudgingly gave way to a flat-rate approach. Healey, who was putting the Treasury arguments, then stuck at £5, while I had been pressing for £7 to £8. It became a hard negotiating session. I came down to £6, reluctantly but in order to get an agreement. We then pressed for the increase to apply only to wages and salaries under £7000 a year. Healey insisted the figure ought to be £10,000 and we finally settled on £8500, which indicates the haggling that went on.

The £6 policy was accepted by the General Council at its meeting in July but only narrowly, nineteen votes to thirteen. I urged those who opposed the policy not to push the Government to the point where it might fall. If they did so, we would lose the Employment Protection Act, the Industry Act and the new nationalization measures. But the Government was not its own best friend. The switch of Tony Benn from Secretary of State for Industry to Secretary of State for Energy had not helped matters, and the talk of a Reserve Powers Bill to enforce a pay policy created indignation in our ranks.

I knew that Michael Foot and Tony Benn were ready to resign at the drop of a hat, but urged them to remain in the Government. We had been promised higher food subsidies, increased grants to keep council house rents down and other action on prices, as well as measures to reduce unemployment, and it was essential to keep friends in the Cabinet to see that such promises were kept. Wilson and Healey seemed over-anxious to satisfy forces outside Britain that, if necessary, they would be tough with the trade unions. Their measures bringing sanctions against employers who gave wage increases above the permitted limit, came near to statutory policy. I faced a similar dilemma to Michael Foot's. Was I to be responsible for bringing down the Government and, as I saw it, doing a disservice to trade unionists and the nation? I decided to see it through.

Once the TUC General Council made its decision I worked within the union to gain acceptance for the £6 policy. For many lower-paid workers the policy offered an increase in pay they would not normally have expected. The task was to maximize the benefit for the low-paid and to use the opportunity to organize the large number who were not in any trade union. I put this view to all officers of the union. For many there would be an element of sacrifice, I admitted. 'No one is claiming that this is the ideal solution, but it is the best we can achieve at the present time. It is fair and socially just in its application.'

Whatever happened in other trade unions the spotlight would be on the TGWU. This I knew, and I spared no effort to win the support of our members. The justice of the approach seemed to touch officers and members alike, and considerable goodwill was demonstrated. Since that time I have noted that two or three officers of the union have said they did not agree with the policy. I have been amazed at this because all of them, individually and collectively, expressed their support at the time.

At the September 1975 Trades Union Congress I moved the motion supporting the £6 policy and outlining the many measures the TUC hoped to achieve through co-operation with the Government. It was a good-humoured but hard-hitting debate, and the result was as expected, an overwhelming vote in support of the policy. Len Murray and I got a lot of credit for our contributions, but I knew that it would require much hard work to make it meaningful.

When we got to the Labour Party Conference a month afterwards there appeared to be more acrimony than unity. I had called for more government action to deal with unemployment and had expressed dissatisfaction at our failure to make progress on selective import controls, but any criticism I made was designed, as I put it at the time, 'to gee up the Treasury, and Trade and Industry Departments'. 'We have a right to expect action,' I said, 'because we are playing our part in solving the nation's economic problems as never before.' At the same meeting I called upon the Government to make employment for young people a first priority. When Michael Foot and Harold Wilson spoke, my worries were eased. I thought they were on the right lines. Denis Healey too got a good reception, although I had the impression that he was accepting the Treasury line too readily.

Whatever my misgivings I was determined to back the Government, 'warts and all'. Not least because Harold Wilson, Barbara Castle and others had told me that there were members of the Government who were looking for a break-up, and were ready to move towards a coalition.

I had warned of this possibility at the TGWU Conference in July when I said:

The circumstances, including the betrayal, of 1931 could happen again. Do we want it to happen? The Macdonalds, the Snowdens, the Jimmy Thomases, are lurking around, their names do not need to be spelt out. Some of them, including a few in high places, are ready to stick a dagger in the heart of the Labour Government. . . .

These threats from the Right worried me, but I wasn't surprised. On the other hand I was shocked to learn from Barbara Castle that Ian Mikardo was going to make a savage attack on me and the General Council at the *Tribune* Rally in the middle of the Conference. I could hardly believe it because my relations with Mik were friendly. Bob Harrison, the Education Secretary of the union, obtained a copy of the advance press release of Mikardo's speech and there it was. Barbara's story was confirmed, except that the attack was a collective one against the General Council, and did not mention me personally.

I felt indignant that a man I regarded as a friend and colleague could plan so meticulously to attack the Government and the General Council, suggesting in effect that the latter had sold the workers down the river. This was no spontaneous attack, it was designed to get the maximum publicity. Mik was a member of the NEC of the Labour Party and represented them on the Economic Committee of the TUC. Why had he not made his attacks there?

What troubled me most was the prospect of Mik's references to the TUC going through without challenge and the media getting the impression that the *Tribune* rally unanimously backed his statement. I was at the Tailors and Garment Workers Union reception when I read the press release, just before the rally was due to start, and I decided to protest at the point where Mik referred to the General Council. I stood at the back of the meeting, then moved forward swiftly to the platform when the moment came. All eyes were on me. When I reached the platform I shouted to the chairman: 'I object to these attacks on the trade unions and the TUC. We want unity, not splitting attacks like this!' I was not near the microphone so that only those around the platform could hear me clearly, but quite a cheer went up at my intervention. I had not intended to speak, only to make my protest, and I was about to leave when the chairman (Dick Clements, then editor of *Tribune*) persuaded me to stay on the platform. A little later he asked if I wanted to speak. I declined, saying that I would leave it to Michael Foot, who was also on the platform. I thought I had done enough for that evening.

Sunday Times, 5 October 1975

I dislike disorder, but even when my temper had cooled I remained convinced that I had done the right thing. A challenge had to be made to a calculated attack on a collective body genuinely trying to keep a Labour Government in power and to serve the best interests of its members. My difference with Ian Mikardo did not reduce my appreciation of his considerable abilities. He would have made a most effective Secretary of State for Trade or for Industry. I'm sure he would have served the movement better as a minister than as a critic, and I often wondered whether he had rebuffed an invitation from Wilson as rumour said.

There were many, less spectacular incidents in the campaign for the £6 policy, but to the consternation of some people both on the Right and on the Left, it succeeded. We proved that the trade union movement *could* deliver, and not one instance of a breach of the policy from the trade union side was reported. Within the twelve months of operation which had been stipulated, inflation fell by more than half, from 25 per cent to 12 per cent.

An egalitarian approach to the solution of economic problems had been attempted, but before the effects of the £6 policy could be assessed demands went up to maintain the sacred principle of 'differentials'. In the main the cry came from academics, politicians, and some

301

white-collar unions. The overwhelming majority of people in industry had accepted the £6 solution, but forces, in the main not directly connected with industry, were determined that favourable lessons should not be drawn from that.

Chapter Twenty-Eight

If, of all words of tongue and pen,
The saddest are, 'It might have been',
More sad are these we daily see:
'It is, but hadn't ought to be!'

FRANCIS BRETT HART

At the end of 1975, Chrysler, the American car-making corporation (which had previously acquired Rootes), threatened to close their British factories unless the Government wrote off its debts and provided further financial help. Unemployment was the big worry when the crisis burst. Harold Lever played a big part in the negotiations and like others realized the consequences of a closure would be dire. The Government decided to rescue the American company at great cost. We all wanted to see the 37,000 jobs saved, and the Chrysler directors knew this and managed to secure a good bargain without the sort of guarantee that the trade unions wanted. Personally I would have preferred to see a link between the Chrysler factories and British Leyland, with joint development as a totally British undertaking. I thought Eric Varley (Secretary of State for Industry) and Michael Foot shared that view, but it was not to be.

In the course of the Chrysler talks I had spoken with Harold Wilson, both at Chequers and at the House of Commons. I thought he looked tired and worried but I did not anticipate the events of 16 March. Fairly early in the morning of that day Len Murray phoned me and said, 'Harold wants to see you and me urgently.' We both thought it must be about some new development in the economic crisis, but Harold soon made it clear he was resigning as Prime Minister. 'I wanted you two to know before the world knows,' he said. 'I've put my resignation in to the Queen. In fact I told her I would do this months ago.'

He warmly thanked Len and me for the help we had given him. He said he wanted to give others a chance in leadership and made it clear that he expected Jim Callaghan to succeed him. He was not leaving a sinking ship, he insisted; he thought the prospects were good. I reflected that the Government had been defeated in the Commons a week before on the issue of public expenditure cuts and on the following day had won a vote of confidence with a majority of seventeen only with the help of Liberal votes. Dependence on Liberal support was anathema to Wilson. Deep down I had the feeling that he thought he might be called back at some stage, but he did not say anything to us about it. Sagacious and shrewd as Harold was, I found it hard to comprehend the reasons behind his Resignation Honours list, particularly the promotions to the Lords. On one occasion when he had mooted the possibility of my going to the Lords – an idea I quickly turned down – he had poured scorn on the numerous people who had sought his favour in order to get a peerage. His opinion of some folk who were in already was not very high. And yet . . .

The attacks from the *Tribune* Group of Labour MPs over public expenditure cuts may have had some influence on Harold's decision. I felt as strongly as the MPs about the cuts, but keeping the Government in office was still more important. In a press interview on the day of the resignation I said: 'The main thing now is to close the ranks and make the transition to a new leader as quickly as possible. Nothing should be allowed to weaken the close relationship of the Government and the trade union movement and the determination of both to reduce unemployment and get inflation under control.'

The day before Harold announced his decision I had persuaded Hugh Scanlon and David Basnett to join me in issuing a call for united support for the Government. We were the chief officers of the three largest unions affiliated both to the Labour Party and the TUC, and we agreed that the three of us acting together would influence the rest of the movement. Scanlon was now very much part of the team, following a reversal of policy by the AUEW National Committee.

Our statement warned that 'the forces opposing Labour are capitalizing on recent divisions and the dire economic difficulties facing the country'. We declared that 'trade unionists want to ensure that the gains secured for workers by the present Government will not be eroded. Of course there are genuine differences of view as to how the crisis should be handled but personal spleen does not help in resolving these differences. It is certainly not our purpose to apportion blame . . . the real question is, on what basis can unity be ensured to maintain the continuance of Labour government?'

When Jim Callaghan succeeded Harold Wilson in 1976, he readily conceded that trade union support provided a backbone for the Government throughout that period. Sometimes, however, I wondered whether this was fully appreciated by others. Denis Healey seemed to be attempting to bludgeon the unions by means of public statements which aroused considerable indignation in the ranks. His colleague at the Treasury, Joel Barnett, a chirpy little man, was impervious to trade union comment and appeared to be hypercritical of our efforts. Despite this we swallowed our irritation and acted as defence counsel for the Government.

At the eve-of-poll meeting in a crucial by-election at Coventry I said: 'Some public spending has to be restrained to help convert our candy-floss economy into a thriving industrial society. The key battle is not about public expenditure – it is the battle for the very industrial heart and life of Britain. Are we to have jobs – to make things on which we can survive – or will we continue to drift into a phoney super-salesman's Britain where there are no jobs for working men and women but plenty of secret bank accounts in Switzerland . . . or the Cayman Islands?'

Labour won the by-election in Coventry because of the solid strength of the trade union movement and the fact that we had a good candidate in Geoffrey Robinson. Any satisfaction we had from the result was, however, soon dissipated by Denis Healey's pressure for a 3 per cent pay limit to follow the £6 policy. It was then that he started to advocate his 'tax-pay' proposal, that is to say that tax concessions should be linked with low pay increases. It was an ingenious approach, and to Healey's credit it was also the first time that the tax elements of a budget had been the subject of previous public debate.

I was not convinced of the need for a further year of restraint. We had carried out our part of the bargain and had achieved a big cut in the inflation rate. My criticism of Healey and Co was that they were taking the trade union movement for granted. It took many meetings before I was convinced that we should try to persuade our members to co-operate for a further year. Michael Foot used his persuasive powers. I suppose we were both convinced that it really was in the best interests of working people to keep the Government in, but we had no illusions about the lack of socialist outlook on the part of many of his colleagues.

The Treasury proposal advanced by Healey was for £1000 million tax concessions to come into operation when agreement was reached with the TUC, back-dated to Budget day. The Treasury published information to back up the proposal, which showed that a man with

305

The Observer, 11 April 1976

a wife and two children on average earnings of £66 a week would benefit to the extent of £7 a week, a married couple without children by £5.40 and a single man by £4.50. It was a clever approach and put the TUC team on the spot. But in spite of its attractions, I knew that a 3 per cent wage increase would not be enough. We had frequent discussions with Denis Healey and other ministers, both at the Treasury and over a meal at 11 Downing Street, and the exchanges were often abrasive.

Dire warnings were issued as to what might happen if we strayed from the strict 3 per cent laid down by the Treasury. I wanted to stick with a flat rate, which I felt would be more acceptable if there was to be one further year of sacrifice, but I was assailed on all sides about the terrible problems caused by a squeezing of differentials.

In our meetings with Healey and other ministers and Treasury officials, we failed to make any real progress. We talked not only about wages but about the need to strengthen the price code because of its importance to the housewife. The case for a bigger and earlier pensions increase was put forward. With unemployment very much in the minds of the TUC, we urged action to increase industrial investment including increased control over the export of capital. We were rebuffed on every point. Denis Healey seemed to us intransigent. I sweated at the thought of what it might mean if we had to walk out with no agreement.

Obviously Healey had been keeping the Prime Minister informed and, almost at the last minute, a request came through for us to meet Jim Callaghan in the Cabinet room. The ground was covered once again. Some of us expressed bitter feelings. Jim, who had a greater understanding than most ministers of the difficulties facing trade union officials, began to encourage a slight movement on the Government side. Little by little we edged upwards, but the most we could achieve was a reluctant agreement to 5 per cent, with a minimum increase of £2.50 and a top figure of £4 plus the income tax concessions which had been offered us.

It was after 2.30 a.m. and everyone was very tired when we agreed to recommend the agreement. I felt terribly dissatisfied because I knew the figures were inadequate. A further flat-rate increase would, in my opinion, have been more satisfactory. But in the end I felt we should not to take the risk of a catastrophic run on the pound and a General Election. That is what a breakdown would almost certainly have meant, and the others in the trade union team took the same view. Nevertheless, we knew that the end of the marathon session for us was only the beginning in trying to gain the support of the membership.

A special Trades Union Congress was called to consider our discussions, but before it was held I convened a special meeting of the union's General Executive Council. After a lively debate it was unanimously decided to accept the approach. There was some opposition to the policy but the consensus was that the TUC General Council had sought to get the best arrangement possible and that their efforts should be supported. This decision was taken in the knowledge that the TUC would be pressing for selective import controls, the maintenance of price and dividend controls and improvements for pensioners. It would also use its influence to secure further reductions in the level of unemployment and to expand the training and job creation programme. The special Trades Union Congress held on 16 June 1976 decisively approved the terms we had hammered out in Downing Street by a vote of 9,262,000 votes to 531,000.

But I was in no doubt that our agreement with the Government was wearing thin. I told both Jim Callaghan and Denis Healey: 'We will have to get back to normal collective bargaining. The most you can expect from us is an attempt to organize an orderly return with emphasis on some priorities.' Denis acted as though he didn't believe it.

The Government's industrial policy was supposed to reduce unemployment, but their measures, in financial terms, were never quite enough. Tony Benn's daring ideas failed to win the acceptance of his Cabinet colleagues. Harold Lever and other champions of expansion were restricted by the semi-monetarist policies being pursued by Denis Healey and Joel Barnett, who always seemed to have the International Monetary Fund breathing down their necks.

Among the victims of the stringent policies was the Meriden (Triumph) motor-cycle co-operative. I had the job of putting the trade union case to Harold Lever. A major rescue operation was needed to modernize the plant. Had that been done, and good marketing provided, the Meriden co-operative could be in existence today, and a genuinely British motor cycle industry would have been preserved. A splendid body of men was involved, who were prepared to make considerable sacrifices and put in amazing efforts to make the project a success. Many of the men were friends of mine from the old Coventry days, and it grieved me to see their experiment brought to disaster.

On one occasion, putting the case for Meriden, I went to Harold Lever's home at Eaton Square. It was like Aladdin's palace, full of the most marvellous works of art. 'It's like a museum, Evelyn would love to see this place!' I exclaimed. But Evelyn did not get an invite. She had spent a number of years in Manchester, the Lever homeland, and had told me of Harold Lever's early leanings towards socialism, but I found little of it left in his millionaire's mansion.

The record of the Government in industry fell far short of its promises. The intention to introduce planning agreements, to ensure that big companies would be accountable and that Government aid would be conditional on agreements embracing investment, employment, exports, etc., was virtually abandoned. I urged the setting-up of an Investment Board, which had been Labour Party policy for years, but the idea was shoved aside by the Treasury, as was my advocacy of an Oil Fund, to be based on North Sea oil revenues, intended to ensure that the oil 'miracle' would be used for industrial investment and a new deal for pensioners.

It was not all bad. For a time the National Enterprise Board looked like being a success. When it was set up, it was mooted that I should be chairman and, when I had made clear that was not possible, it was suggested that I should at least be a member. Instead I proposed Harry Urwin, then Deputy General Secretary of the TGWU. Hugh Scanlon and Dave Basnett were also invited and agreed to serve and the three of them worked hard to make the NEB a success. The trouble was it operated in a vacuum, so that the trade union movement was never directly involved in its problems and government financing, the key to its power, was always inadequate. But the conception was good, and I have little doubt that something of the sort will be reintroduced when the next Labour Government is elected.

The National Economic Development Council, on which I served, was never more than a useful talking shop, but it was drawn into the act when the new industrial strategy was launched at another Chequers meeting in February 1976. Much emphasis was placed on the setting-up of 'sector working parties' within the framework of the NEDC. It looked to me like something which would involve paperwork, talking, and more work for academics. I'm afraid I made myself unpopular by opposing the idea from the start, on the grounds that I could see little relevance to the shop floor.

Our disappointments did not lead to a parting of the ways. Even though, try as we might, we could not change the Government's outlook, we were not prepared to do anything that might threaten its existence. The majority of the TUC General Council were more loyal to the Government than some of its own ministers.

When Jim Callaghan became Prime Minister he gave me an assurance that he wanted to unite all the principal interests within the Parliamentary Labour Party and to ensure that the Government worked closely with the unions. More approachable than Harold Wilson, he had a friendly attitude that broke down barriers. On the whole he was well liked by most of us in the unions, even though I personally had hoped that Michael Foot would win the leadership contest. Foot did win a substantial vote, however, which meant he became Deputy Leader. I was glad about that but disappointed that he would no longer be Secretary of State for Employment. I told him that the unions had lost the best ally they had had in Government since the war. Self-effacing as usual, he replied: 'Albert Booth [the new Secretary of State] will do a better job than me.' But things were not the same.

On the TUC–Labour Party Liaison Committee a new joint statement was agreed; it was entitled 'The next three years and the problems of priorities'. In fact it was drawn up in response to the call I, Hugh Scanlon and David Basnett had made earlier in the year. The statement laid down a series of important priorities, including such things as the massive expansion of training, a wealth tax, selective import controls, food and fuel subsidies, industrial democracy legislation and expansion of planning agreements, pensions to be raised to 50 per cent of average earnings for a married couple and a third for a single person. It also included the extension of public works schemes to relieve unemployment, the introduction of a national transport planning authority and other important measures. Some of these were achieved despite the economic crisis and the Government's difficulties, which increased when its majority went down to a single vote.

One measure, dear to my own heart, the Dock Work Regulation Bill, was emasculated because of the Government's weakness and the hostile reaction of the House of Lords. I had worked patiently to achieve an extension of the Dock Labour Scheme so as to mitigate the effects of containerization and the unrestrained growth of the non-scheme ports. It was a battle against the reintroduction of casual employment and the threat of port closures. The Bill was the logical outcome of the Jones/Aldington Committee. The Lords put forward wrecking amendments, and when the Government attempted to reverse the amendments in the Commons two Labour MPs withdrew their support. The loss of important elements of the Bill almost led to a major stoppage in the ports, something only averted by the strenuous efforts of union officers and committees.

A little of the background was filled in for me years later when a Ruskin College student wrote to me, saying that he and another student at Ruskin had attended an informal politics seminar headed by David Butler at Nuffield College in February 1982. The guest speaker, a Parliamentary lobbyist, spoke of his involvement in defeating the Dock Work Regulation Bill. At the time, the speaker explained, he was employed by the Inland Cold Storage Employers' Federation, including the Vesteys. He had contacted Vic Feather and they had dinner together. Feather 'not only told him how to go about the task, but himself set about mobilizing opposition within the trade unions and the Labour Party. On the evening of the vote it was arranged that two members would leave the Chamber of the House of Commons (they were John Macintosh, now deceased, and Brian Walden of TV fame) thereby causing the defeat of the Bill'. It was known beforehand exactly how the Bill would fail.

The truth will out, although I was sorry to learn that Vic Feather, whom I had helped a lot in the TUC, should have acted in this way.

The big question was whether Jim Callaghan and his Government should remain in office, dependent as they were on the support of Liberal MPs. I took the view that, as long as the Government remained in office, I would back them to the best of my ability, while joining with the TUC in pressing for stronger action in some priorities. The failure of the Government to keep down prices and unemployment were two great anxieties, but against the failures had to be measured considerable achievements in labour relations.

Unemployment was still growing rapidly and unions were at their wits' end to stem the tide of redundancies. The most crucial spot in the uneasy peace of dockland was the port of Preston, which was threatened with closure, due in part to the silting up of the River Ribble. It was the first time a port within the docks scheme had faced such a threat and I knew it was the spark which could set alight a huge flame. Strenuous activity by councillors, MPs and the union succeeded in keeping the port open. Our joint efforts eased tension throughout the waterfront, but it was not a permanent victory since some years afterwards it was found impossible to keep the port functioning. Similar situations in other industries were being reported to me daily, and efforts to keep open factories and other workplaces became my main preoccupation.

In 1976 the Congress of the European Trade Union Confederation was held in London and I made it my business to force the issue of unemployment onto the agenda. With the aid of John Hughes and his research unit at Ruskin College, Oxford, I had prepared a detailed paper on the case for a thirty-five hour week. Copies were issued to all the delegates and when the debate took place I was able to secure a commitment to press the claim throughout Europe's industries. Although action was slow, some successes were secured and the battle goes on. British employers can no longer say that they are being singled out. German trade unionists came to me and said: 'We agree with you, Jack, and we must all fight very hard.' They did so too, in fact they made a greater effort than the British trade unions.

European institutions were used as a platform to advance other forms of action against unemployment. When, following the referendum over membership of the EEC, the TUC took up its eight seats on the Economic and Social Committee of the EEC, I urged that measures to deal with the recession and unemployment should find a place high on the committee's agenda. We soon found, however, that the committee was impotent. It could pass opinions to the Council of Ministers, but the Council could take note of them or not, as they saw fit.

I well recall our first meeting in Brussels after a boycott lasting almost three years. Our plane from London had been delayed, so three of us, David Basnett, Terry Parry and myself, got places on a Romanian plane, while Len Murray and the rest of the party came on afterwards. They missed the first day's business, but we were only an hour late. I spoke for the TUC soon after arriving and received polite applause when I declared: 'We have come as friends and are looking forward to making friends in this assembly; if we find anything to criticize we will do it in a friendly way.' The atmosphere was colder when I laid emphasis on the TUC's commitment to be intolerant of inaction, bureaucratic complacency or red tape.

The question asked by many who study events in the EEC is whether all the speeches, papers, and conferences are worthwhile. Len Murray and David Basnett made unwearying efforts to persuade governments and EEC institutions to tackle unemployment, but the effect was like water on a duck's back. As to bureaucracy, the endless meetings, all handsomely paid for by the Commission, seemed meaningless and terribly costly. I challenged Roy Jenkins, then President of the Commission, on this and he had no answer. In his drawling way he said he would arrange for a study of the question to be made, but it was hard to see any changes as a result.

Part of the Social Contract which was repeated in the Labour Party's manifesto of 1974 was a commitment to an Industrial Democracy Act 'to increase the control of industry by the people'. Closer contact with Europe through the EEC and the European trade union movement increased our interest in the subject. It meant a lot to me personally. From my youthful days I had been associated with the extension of collective bargaining. Now I saw the possibility of elected shop stewards taking their place in the boardrooms of private companies and publicly-owned industries.

I wanted to avoid at all costs the sort of fiasco which occurred when Harold Wilson's Government of 1966–70 experimented with industrial democracy in the steel industry. When the idea was first considered I personally urged on Barbara Castle and Dick Marsh, the two ministers involved, the need to ensure that the worker directors should be elected and accountable to the shop stewards, and through them to the workforce. Their reaction was that my idea was 'syndicalist', if not 'anarchist', and could not be entertained. In fact, as it worked out, the procedure became meaningless and patronizing. The men who were appointed had to give up any active connection with their union. Indeed, in the early stages it was decided that the 'worker directors' should not operate in their own industrial group – as if a bus driver was appointed a director for the docks industry. As a result the 'worker directors' were virtually unknown to most of the workforce.

From the days of the Labour Party working party on industrial democracy in 1967, over which I had presided, practical policies had been worked out in the TUC and the Labour Party. I had anticipated quick legislation but it was not to be. Peter Shore, the Secretary of State for Trade, dragged his feet, eventually agreeing to set up a committee of inquiry. I felt let down by the attitude of many members of the Cabinet, who seemed anxious to avoid a clear commitment.

A private members' Bill introduced into the House of Commons by Giles Radice speeded up Government thinking. The Bill was roughly in line with TUC policy for 50 per cent worker representation on boards of directors, having been largely drafted, at Giles's request, by Bill Wedderburn and David Lea of the TUC. David, an assistant general secretary of the TUC, was an able and devoted advocate of industrial democracy.

There began months of in-fighting, as leading members of the Government sought to evade action on the Radice Bill. Michael Foot and I fought hard to get the Government to legislate without delay, but our efforts were deflected by the Cabinet setting up a committee of inquiry. 'Whose side are they on?' I asked Michael. His reply was a mumbling defence of his colleagues, for there was none more loyal than he.

The battle was not over even then, as Len Murray, David Lea and I sought to secure terms of reference for the Committee of Inquiry which would be helpful to our cause. It seemed as though influential members of the Government, all of whom had benefited from the Social Contract, were doing their damnedest to circumvent the whole idea. An attempt was made to put terms of reference to Parliament without the agreement of the TUC and seemingly designed to weaken our approach. It took a direct appeal to Jim Callaghan before we could get agreement. Instead of pushing at an open door we experienced opposition as hard as any we would have expected from the Tories.

The TUC nominees on the Committee, David Lea, Clive Jenkins and myself, did not expect to secure full agreement, but at the start there appeared to be a surprising degree of sympathy for some of our views from the employer members. One of them, Barrie Heath, then chairman of GKN, enthusiastically backed a visit to Germany to study the operation of supervisory boards. He was not afraid of worker directors, at least of the sort he had on the boards of his German companies.

Jim Callaghan, I think, had similar views. He certainly admired Chancellor Schmidt, who in turn was enthusiastic about the German co-determination system. They were both in Bonn at the time of the Committee's visit and arranged to meet us. Schmidt effectively refuted the idea that foreign investment would dry up if worker directors were introduced into Britain. On the contrary, it was clear to me that he thought the 'old school tie' was inimical to British interests and that worker directors would be a beneficial influence.

The basic difference of view on the Committee was exemplified by Jack Callard, Chairman of ICI, and myself. Jack favoured 'consultation and participation', but workers on the board? oh no, no! I pointed out that non-executive directors sat on the ICI board who had little or no practical knowledge of its workings. Why should they not be replaced by men and women who worked for the company and whose future was bound up with it? Callard muttered about the expertise of the non-executive directors but his answer did not satisfy me. The other idea I advanced, that the worker directors should be shop stewards elected through the trade union system, was met with hostility from him and Barrie Heath to a degree which I could not understand because in both their companies trade-union membership was very high indeed. Maybe they were aghast at my other suggestion that worker directors should be paid the rate for the job they normally did. They certainly did not relish the idea and I'm sure they dismissed it in their own minds as just another 'anarchistic view'.

Alan Bullock, historian and biographer of Ernest Bevin, was the chairman of the Committee. He tried hard to reach a consensus. We could not have had a more impartial chairman, and, despite my well-known doubts about academics, I formed a high opinion of his ability. Undoubtedly too the two professors on the Committee made a considerable contribution. George Bain and Bill Wedderburn were quick to see the value of the proposal that shop stewards should express workers' views to the board of directors and tell the shop floor about the board's discussions.

The majority report of the Committee in my opinion went a long way in seeking to transform the running of industry and to ensure joint agreement with the workforce in its operation. The CBI didn't agree; they were even critical of the minority report of the three employer members of the Committee, who wanted to settle for a small number of worker members on some form of 'supervisory boards' and without any relationship with the trade unions in the workplace.

After the Report of the Committee was issued, the forces of reaction combined to weave a tissue of half-truths and misrepresentation around it. I heard industrialists refer to the Report as the 'bollocks report'. One MP spoke of handing over power to trade unions 'representing only 40 per cent of working people'. Robert Carr, who had been Secretary of State for Employment in the Heath Government, spoke in the House of Lords of the Report 'disenfranchising many millions of workers'. These spokesmen showed not only ignorance of the Report but an abysmal lack of understanding of industrial relations in Britain. For one thing, the proposals only referred to companies employing over two thousand people and evidence was given in the Report to show that in such companies trade union membership was approaching 100 per cent.

Strong attacks on the Report also came from the Left. The *Morning Star* was highly critical and one delegate at the Labour Party Conference described it as 'a sop to workers' control which would smash the unions, destroy their bargaining powers and leave them as puppets of management'. Joe Gormley didn't want anything to do with it either. But my worst disappointment was the way in which Government ministers treated it, playing for time, failing to think it through, and refusing to face the challenge to the old ways of doing things. Albert Booth, the Secretary of State for Employment, fought manfully for the Report, but Edmund Dell, Secretary of State for Trade, was less than enthusiastic. Eventually Shirley Williams, Paymaster General and Secretary of State for Education, was appointed by Jim Callaghan to sort out the position. That killed the main thrust of the Report and eventually a puny White Paper was produced. Even that failed to get to the legislative stage. At the time of my retirement it was 'in the air', and what was left of the Bullock Report sank in the disaster of the winter of discontent.

A trade union leader must get used to attacks in the media. My participation in the Bullock Committee, and a Gallup poll sponsored by the BBC which suggested that I was the 'most powerful man in Britain', sparked off a diatribe from the journalist Paul Johnson. He dubbed me 'Emperor Jones' and said I was as domineering and untouchable as the eighteenth-century Duke of Newcastle. He also compared me to the French King Louis XIV, who coined the phrase 'L'État c'est moi', and likened the power of union bosses to that of the Spanish Inquisition. They were, he said, 'a privileged aristocracy enjoying perks and immunities virtually unknown in Britain since the eighteenth century'. Johnson excelled himself in fantasy but his article made him some money. First published in the *New Statesman* it was later given centre-page treatment in the *Daily Mail*. I reacted by saying: 'I think this is a stunt to sell the *New Statesman*. Would Mr Johnson like to see me and discuss the difference between his style of living and mine?' I received no response, which did not surprise me.

Shortly afterwards Anthony Howard, then editor of the *New Statesman*, came to see me. He was extremely worried because he had published an attack on the TGWU and myself in a letter from the General Secretary of another union. The attack was without foundation and constituted the strongest possible case for a libel action. He explained the tenuous finances of his paper and I told him he had no need to worry. All I wanted was the publication of a letter of correction and apology from the other man, and this was done.

Opinion polls can sometimes create an illusion!

Chapter Twenty-Nine

It is time we outgrew the miserable and petty narrowness that resents criticism, no matter how kindly it is offered.

The nation, the community, the individual that cannot accept and profit by suggestions for betterment of its actions is hopelessly damned.

We need more of sanity and less of vain and ignorant pride . . .

JIM LARKIN

Although General Franco had died in 1975, the Spanish trade union movement was still illegal. In the autumn of 1976 the socialist-led UGT invited the TUC to send a delegation, and although I had misgivings about going to Spain while the Fascist framework remained, the UGT leaders insisted that it would help the advance of trade union forces. So in November I was glad to join Len Murray, Joe Gormley (NUM), and George Smith (UCATT) in paying the visit, which for me was the first since the civil war.

From my underground contacts, which I had maintained over the years, I knew that determined efforts were being made to establish independent and democratic trade unions based upon the place of work and to destroy the official *sindicatos*, the vertical organizations of employers and so-called worker representatives which had been developed under Franco. At our first meeting in Bilbao I strongly denounced the *sindicatos* as a threat to the solidarity of working people and as 'relics of Fascism'. My colleagues looked a little apprehensive, perhaps justifiably so, because my remarks received widespread publicity in the Spanish press. This was probably the reason for Len Murray and I receiving letters containing a threat of action against us if we did not leave Spain pronto. Our Spanish friends told us the threats came from a Fascist organization.

The UGT found it necessary to rearrange the date and place of a meeting because of undue police interest. But the meeting did take place, and together with UGT activists came a group of building trade workers who had been on strike for over five weeks. Strictly the strike was illegal, but employers and police did not know quite what to do in the volatile situation. The men had displayed enormous courage, because there was no strike benefit or other financial assistance.

I embraced each of them and gave them words of encouragement, for this was the spirit I had longed to see on Spanish soil. We experienced an equally strong sense of fraternity at another, and larger meeting, of Basque trade unionists arranged by the STV, the Basque trade union federation. Some of the leaders I knew, and they greeted me warmly. All was not peace and light, however, when Joe Gormley came to speak. Near pandemonium broke out as he told the meeting that he didn't see why there should be a separate Basque trade union and that he did not agree with the idea of a Basque state. He compared the situation with that of Northern Ireland. It was a daft thing to say and I rushed in to calm things down, paying tribute to the history of the Basques and making clear that the TUC wanted to see the Basque trade unions growing strong and joining with other trade union movements in the Iberian peninsular to restore democracy.

Barcelona, a great industrial centre with proud trade union traditions, was bound to form part of our visit. We were not disappointed as we went from meeting to meeting, all of them animated, reviving old memories in my case and impressing us all with the spirit of the young and growing trade union movement. Union posters, banners and leaflets were on display everywhere. Young people predominated and were keenly interested, not just in the message of trade union solidarity brought by the TUC, but in the civil war. They wanted to know about the International Brigade.

The UGT arranged that we should visit the civil war battle areas on the Ebro. We dashed down the 130 miles in fast cars. On the way our UGT friends became apprehensive and said we were being followed. They feared that a police or Fascist group was on our trail, trying to disrupt the visit. I told the driver (who was the most worried) to pull into the next petrol station. As we did so the car which had been following us came alongside – it contained a BBC Television crew!

We made for Grandesa, the town which had been a centre of the bloody Ebro battles. The town was still battle-scarred, with buildings pitted with bullet holes and some still in ruins. The centre was thronged with people attracted by our group. Almost immediately Luis Riella greeted me. It turned out that he had been a captain in the Republican Army and we had both fought together in the same division. He was seventy-four and still working as a bricklayer, weather-beaten and tough, but weeping as he recalled the old days. We were joined by another soldier of the Republic, Miguel Meix, and we reminisced together as we moved into a little wine bar. It was an emotional occasion, as we toasted the memory of those who had been killed fighting for the Republic.

Old enmities were forgotten when Tomas Rabas joined our circle. He was a peasant who had fought on Franco's side, so he told me. He had not joined the Franco forces by choice, he had been drafted in. 'We might have shot at each other,' he said, when I told him I had been wounded on the Ebro and he explained that he had been wounded too. One of my Republican comrades chipped in, saying, 'We are all brothers now,' and there were smiles all round as we drank another toast . . . this time to 'democracy and peace'. The young press men, photographers and broadcasters who had accompanied us were enthralled, and we were pleased that such a gathering could take place without interference from the authorities. Earlier I had made a short speech to a small crowd of local inhabitants, and had been applauded when I spoke of our wish to see reconciliation and the restoration of democracy in Spain.

We travelled the rough roads and saw something of the battle areas I had known. The roads were tortuous and on our way back our driver, who had drunk heavily at midday and may have been affected by the heat, fell asleep and nearly landed us at the bottom of a ravine. We were able to waken him just in time as we ploughed along the edge of the ravine. It was a close shave for Len Murray and me. Had we been killed it would have created a sensation, certainly back home, because of our involvement with the Social Contract which was then going through a crucial phase. Luckily only one journalist was in the vicinity. He was clearly looking for a big story, but Len and I dismissed the whole thing as trivial. 'We are OK, it was nothing, the driver just overshot the road, he was in complete control.' Apart from other considerations, we did not want any reflections cast on our UGT hosts.

The days were exciting as we went from one assembly to another, acquainting ourselves with the rapidly growing democratic forces. Two characters stood out sharply: Nicholas Redondo, leader of the UGT, and Marcelino Camacho, leader of the Workers' Commissions, the former a socialist the other a communist. Each had long records of illegal struggle and their outstanding personalities had inspired large numbers of workers to follow them, in spite of the Franco repression.

Although we had no intention of interfering, the TUC favoured the development of one united trade union movement in Spain, on similar lines to the TUC itself. Deep political divisions prevented a fusion, but the two principal organizations, together with another trade union body, the USO, were increasingly acting together. Just before our arrival a short general strike had taken place, involving about $2\frac{1}{2}$ million workers. It was the first test of workers' strength since the days of the Republic and struck fear into the hearts of employers and the Government then led by Suarez.

Despite promises of opening up towards democracy, the Suarez Government reactivated the repressive apparatus that had been created by Franco. There were numerous dismissals and imprisonments. One of the worst features was the imposition of heavy fines which had to be paid before striking workers could be released from prison. Property which formerly belonged to the old UGT still remained with the official *sindicatos* and other privileges remained in the hands of these Fascists and their sympathizers.

Redondo, who had made prodigious efforts to develop the UGT, told us that our visit had been a morale booster. We in turn were conscious that a number of multinational companies, some of them with British connections, were operating in Spain, and that it was in the interests of British trade unions to give maximum support to the growth of independent and free trade unions there.

In retrospect the visit had a deep effect on me. It was a tremendous relief to know that democracy was on the march. Our hectic schedule took me to Portugal, on the way home. There too there had been a massive political upheaval and Mario Soares, whom I had met during his years in exile, was prominent in the move towards democracy. A new trade union movement was emerging and I had frank talks with the leaders, who leaned towards the Communist Party although they appeared to see the sense of non-alignment. It was not my first visit to Portugal following their revolution, indeed on one occasion when I was visiting the country I was at a meeting with Mario Soares when bombs began to drop on the airport. A counter-revolution was being attempted, but it fizzled out.

My international activities had to be fitted in to the needs of the membership. I insisted that trips should normally last no longer than two or three days and some were made during the Christmas holidays.

Most contacts were with industrial groups which related to sections of the TGWU membership, so I got well acquainted with the problems of transport workers and their working conditions in many countries. On one such visit to Egypt the transport union arranged for me to see President Sadat, who had a special relationship with them because of aid they had rendered when he was in trouble with the British rulers.

It was some years before Sadat took his famous initiative and made his trip to Israel. Evelyn and I were invited to his home and spent nearly two hours in conversation. No interpreter was required, because Sadat spoke very good English. After he had told us of Egypt's economic problems and the devastation suffered during the wars with Israel, he spoke of the pressure from other Arab countries for continued war. In a revealing sentence he said: 'They think that to give money is enough, and they even want a return on that, while my people do the fighting and endure the suffering.' He listened with close attention as I spoke about the desire of Histradut, the Israeli Labour Federation, to develop contacts with the Egyptian trade union movement. I asked him his views on that. His reply was clear cut, he saw no objection and thought that it was good for workers' movements to get to know each other. He may have been over-optimistic then and later but we were highly impressed by his ability and apparent sincerity. The hope he gave was encouraging, for the poverty we had witnessed in Egypt had depressed us greatly.

In pursuit of understanding between the trade unions in the Arab world and those of Israel, Len Murray and I paid a quick visit to Syria. It was a modest effort to reduce the tension in the Middle East, where the explosive atmosphere had within it the potential to produce a third world war. We established from the Syrian trade union leaders, who claimed to be reflecting the views of their government, that Syria, at least, did not seek the destruction of Israel and would accept its existence if Israel would retreat to the pre-1967 borders. As to possible talks with Histradut, the Syrian trade unionists were much less forthcoming than Sadat.

We saw something of the reasons for their feelings when we travelled to the Syrian side of the Golan Heights and witnessed the terrible destruction which had been wrought by the Israeli attacks. In the middle of it all we met a middle-aged English lady who greeted us in an aristocratic Oxford accent. She had been living there for many years and had no intention of leaving the place . . . come what might!

Len Murray was in fine spirits during our short visit and surprised me and our hosts by eating raw liver and other Arab delicacies with gusto and smoking a bubble pipe like a local Arab. I was a little more diffident.

Evelyn and I had few holidays in those years, so when an invitation was received from the Wellington Road Transport Union to spend two weeks in New Zealand we made arrangements for Evelyn to accompany me. It was our first time in the antipodes and it was a wonderful period of fraternal interest and relaxation.

On landing at Wellington Airport we were greeted by a voice out of Liverpool. 'M'name's Pat Kelly. Did you know my late uncle Owen Kelly from Bootle? He worked on the Liverpool docks.' 'You mean "*Oweny*" Kelly,' I said. 'I knew him well.' And I did! The encounter was typical of many that followed as we visited the ports in the North and South Islands. 'Do you know my brother? My cousin?' Some I did know, and one relative I had worked with on the docks. It was like coming home instead of being on the other side of the world.

So much of the trade union movement is like the traditional extended family, and this was very much the case in New Zealand. The Maori trade unionists were especially wonderful people. I felt a pang of regret that the *real* British Commonwealth was fading out, its demise being accelerated by British membership of the Common Market. My opposition to the EEC was well known before my arrival, and I suppose because of this the conference of the New Zealand Federation of Labour gave me a great reception when I addressed them. Many told me of their well-founded fears that New Zealand agriculture and trade would suffer and the links with the 'old country' diminish.

Back home, I took the initiative in an exciting new project. Ernie Bevin had had a vision of a holiday centre for TGWU members on the south coast and I was able to help turn the dream into a reality when, almost by accident, I came across a vacant site on the seafront at Eastbourne. The union's Executive Council had been persuaded that we should construct a combined centre for convalescence, holidays, and union education, and we were lucky that a group of speculators had 'caught a cold' over their plans for a new hotel at Eastbourne. The land concerned was to be sold. A 'For Sale' board caught my eye and we were able to buy the site at a reasonable price.

I wanted the standard to be high, to create a 'palace of labour' where retired members could enjoy holidays at reduced prices and in some cases free, alongside members recovering from illness or accident, while during the season members and their families on holiday would be able to enjoy the facilities of a first-class hotel in the beautiful surroundings of Eastbourne. Throughout the year branch officers and shop stewards would be able to study in the seminar and conference rooms, so that at any time there would be a mix of different age groups and interests.

It was a labour of love to work with the architects and builders to make sure that the high standards we desired would be achieved. The most modern materials were used, designed to stand up to the rigours of seaside winters. New and original ideas influenced the design, which proved to be too modern for many of the staider residents of Eastbourne. The Duke of Devonshire, a principal landowner in the town, told me it was all right, and time seems to have assuaged the feelings of some critics. There were worries too on the part of some of the wealthier retired population about 'rough union people' invading the place, but even they take sly delight in pointing out the unusual features of our building. Occasionally they refer to it as 'The Kremlin'!

Back in London, difficulties arose at Transport House with the expansion of Labour Party headquarters staff and their increasing demands for more space. It was my wish to retain a Labour Party presence at Transport House because I knew the importance of our proximity to Parliament to some officials of the Party. The Party paid an extremely low rent, but that was not the reason for the reluctant decision I had to convey to Ron Hayward, then General Secretary of the Labour Party. 'You can have some but not all the space, Ron,' I said, explaining our own increased needs. The NEC of the Labour Party decided that they wanted all their headquarters staff together and opted for a new building, in the knowledge that the unions, including the TGWU, would largely find the cash. It was a sad break with the past, for the Labour Party had been at Transport House from the beginning. As a young neighbour of mine said at the time: 'It's like the Pope being put out of the Vatican!'

The decision of the Labour Party to move away at least provided me with another opportunity to work with our architects, this time in planning the modernization of the interior of our building. We needed improved facilities for members and staff but could not put the plans into action until the Labour Party finally moved to Walworth Road, and they were not fulfilled until after my retirement.

By 1977 there was a greater awareness than ever before among people generally of the growth in trade union influence. Not only had membership increased substantially but there was growing participation at the grass roots. Collective agreements, although reached within the TUC guidelines, were now the subject of shop-floor ratification. Successes had been scored in our campaign for a £30 minimum wage, and women members were becoming more conscious of their right to equal pay. Trade union recognition was being conceded in many firms. The Employment Protection Act opened up the prospect of time off from work for activists to function effectively on trade union committees and gain the benefits of trade union education. An extended base for trade union freedom and an expansion of collective bargaining had been laid.

The first years of the pay policies agreed under the Social Contract protected the lower paid and helped curb inflation and unemployment. In a capitalist world and with a weak Labour Government our co-operation in voluntary pay policies could only be of limited duration. At an early stage I had warned of the strains which would be created, and had urged the adoption of fiscal measures to deal with income restraint, if this was necessary, including a wealth tax. Above all I had repeatedly called for effective control of prices.

For whatever reason, and membership of the EEC was part of it, The Government's efforts had been limited. The difficulty was that the Government was not master in its own house. Pressure from the Treasury had forced cuts in public expenditure and the introduction of high interest rates, which accelerated the rise in unemployment, then pushing beyond 1,300,000. Callaghan and Healey seemed obsessed with the need to reduce the public sector borrowing requirement as an aid in the negotiations with the IMF for a major loan.

Wide divisions on this approach were revealed in meetings with the Economic Committee of the TUC. We argued forcibly that the best way of improving the balance of payments was by the use of selective import controls rather than cuts in public expenditure. The Economic Committee, however, was too large and diverse in its interests to be effective, and often day-to-day contact with ministers was left to Len Murray and me.

We worked closely together in that period. I appreciated his competence and his commitment, and there was considerable trust between us. He differed from some of his predecessors in that he did not always try to give the impression that he was the leader. S me observers in other parts of the world (Eastern Europe and the USA especially) held the mistaken impression that the TUC was a strong centralist organization and that its General Secretary therefore had enormous power. Len at least did not suffer from that illusion.

At the height of the Government's negotiations with the IMF, Len Murray told an IMF representative: 'If your conditions are too onerous, it will not be a question of phase three of incomes policy, there won't be a phase two; it will collapse. . .'

He was nearly right. It was a struggle to maintain support for the 5 per cent policy but the unions did deliver, as they had done over the £6 policy, notwithstanding that the Government had not been able to keep its promises to us entirely. In September 1976 the TUC meeting at Brighton expressed the view that 'a planned return to free collective bargaining should begin to take place in 1977'. In April 1977 the then Prices Secretary, Roy Hattersley, declared publicly that my call for 'a just and temporary prices freeze' was 'simply not possible'. His response was not helpful to our campaign for an orderly return to normal collective bargaining.

That the situation was sensitive became apparent after I had made a speech saying that no pay norm or ceiling could be fixed for another round. The pound, share prices, and Government stocks all fell in value and the Bank of England was forced to support the pound. I continued to press for moderation in pay claims and the observance of the arrangements we had entered into with the Government, but my efforts and those of Len Murray, Hugh Scanlon, David Basnett and others were not sufficient to stem the tide of disgruntlement against the Government. I became increasingly aware of a massive campaign for a return to free-for-all bargaining.

The mood could not be ignored and I knew that any form of pay policy would take a hammering at the TGWU Biennial Delegate Conference which assembled on the Isle of Man in July that year. The union's Executive Council had tabled a motion which followed the pattern of the TUC decision that I have referred to. In supporting a return to free collective bargaining, the motion also emphasized the need 'to avoid a wages free-for-all which would be injurious to weaker members of the community and could destroy or jeopardize our long term objectives'. The alternative composite motion called for 'a return to unfettered collective bargaining'. It won the support of a clear majority of conference, as I had expected.

The rank-and-file members who spoke for the Executive motion put the case courageously and well, but against them an avalanche of delegates spoke out for the more extreme version. Towards the end of the debate I was asked to speak. I realized that whatever I said would not change the minds of the majority in the hall, and yet I felt that when they returned to their homes many would reflect on my words.

I tried to explain that the words 'free collective bargaining' did not of themselves get rid of inflation, put right thirty years of neglect of our manufacturing industries, or create a million jobs. What was wanted was not slogans but *real* wage increases, employment security, and greater influence in the running of their industries. In the light of subsequent events, including the 'winter of discontent', there is little satisfaction for me in the knowledge that I warned that a mad scramble for larger wage increases would only make our troubles ten times worse in the years to come. 'The benefits of North Sea oil and an improved balance of payments are on the horizon. If this Government fails you will hand these to the party of privilege. You will put back the mighty in their seats and kick the people of low degree in the teeth. That is the danger. . .'

Critics have said that I was defeated by the very democratic spirit in the TGWU I had sought to create. Well, I am still in favour of democracy. When the result of the voting was announced and I rose to comment, the delegates showed that they respected my views although so many had voted against them. I told them that I believed in the acceptance of conference decisions and would do my best to implement this one. 'The Executive will consider how it can implement this in a way that will maintain the unity of our union and still keep a Labour Government in Westminster.' That was easier said than done, yet it is on the record that the TGWU did keep to the TUC recommendation to allow twelve-month intervals between wage settlements and, with one or two justifiable exceptions, accepted the 10 per cent pay increases policy introduced by the Callaghan Government for the following year.

Nothing in life could be quite like the friendship which Evelyn and I experienced at the Isle of Man conference, tempered as it was for me by my sadness at that momentous defeat. It was now only months before my retirement but I did not let up in my endeavours, indeed I had told the conference that I would continue to strive in the years ahead 'as a soldier in the great army of labour'.

At another conference, this time in County Down, Ireland, I became aware of another Jack Jones. A group of our Irish members accompanied John Freeman, the union's Irish Secretary, and me into a pub. They were a little proud of the fact that I was a well-known figure, appearing regularly on TV and so on. I'm sure they thought that everyone would recognize me. John Freeman went over to an old man, sitting in the corner, and pointing to me said: 'We've brought Jack Jones to see you.' 'Ah,' said the old man, 'is that Jack Jones the harbour master at Kilkeel?'

Occasionally I have met very old men who were inclined to confuse me with the redoubtable Jack Jones, MP for Silvertown, a fighting trade union agitator of earlier days, who had been born and bred in Nenagh, Tipperary. His Christian name, like mine, was James.

Towards the end of 1977 I was involved in several controversies. I took issue with the author A. L. Rowse, who had claimed in an article in the *Daily Telegraph* that Ernest Bevin, in his last words, had said of Britain's ordinary people, 'The buggers won't work.' I challenged him to prove this; he dithered and claimed that Bevin had said something of the sort to Lord Boothby, but there was no verification. I did not believe that Ernie Bevin had ever said that of his own people, and said so. Rowse gave his own view of British working people, denouncing 'their brute selfishness and bloody-mindedness, forever striking, like a lot of kids playing about . . .'

I was indignant that what I regarded as anti-worker prejudice should gain publicity and replied in detail, using the *New Statesman* as my platform. I assembled the sort of details that one would prepare in a major negotiation and, after quoting fact after fact, wrote: 'So it would appear we work longer hours, have fewer holidays, and no more strikes than do the rest of our competitors, and we have less malingering.' I quoted evidence from foreign firms in Britain, and high-powered economic institutes to show the real recurring weaknesses in British firms: lack of mechanization, short runs and small batches, poor production planning and control, insufficient standardization, and low investment.

Within the Labour Party some private companies seemed to me to be enjoying growing influence, to the detriment of socialist principles. Public revelations about the operations of the Peachey Property Corporation and some influential members of the Party aroused disgust in the ranks of Labour generally and I articulared the criticism on the eve of the 1977 Labour Party Conference. The purchase of grand country homes and enjoyment of the fruits of property deals by some leaders seemed to me at the very least insensitive to public feeling. 'It's about time leaders set a personal example,' I told a pre-conference meeting. My criticism was picked up by the press. Their headline treatment of the story did not endear me to everyone but the lesson had to be driven home.

At the Conference I proposed the TGWU motion calling for the abolition of the House of Lords. Important pieces of legislation favourable to the workers had been emasculated in the Lords. The bill nationalizing the aircraft and shipbuilding industries, the Dock Work Regulation Bill, the Rent Agriculture Bill, the Education Bill and the Health Services Bill had all been delayed and almost wrecked by an unelected and unrepresentative institution. The motion was carried by 6,248,000 votes for and 91,000 against. The majority was so decisive that the abolition of the Lords should have been included in the 1979 Labour Party election manifesto. It was not, and only Jim Callaghan knows why. It is still, however, Labour Party policy.

In 1977 J. K. Galbraith organized an informal seminar at his farm in Vermont to discuss the problems raised in his TV series 'The Age of Uncertainty'. I accepted his invitation to take part because it was a great opportunity to meet a number of leaders from various parts of the world. It was a weekend of intensive discussion. From the USA Henry Kissinger, Arthur Schlesinger, Katherine Graham (of the *Washington Post*) and Thomas Winship (of the *Boston Globe*) were present. From the USSR came Georgie Arbatov of the Academy of Sciences, and from the Third World, M. R. Kukrit Pramoj, the former Prime Minister of Thailand. A wonderful old character, Professor Hans Selye, represented Canada and from the UK came Ted Heath, Shirley Williams, Ralph Dahrendorf (of the London School of Economics) and myself.

Hans Selye encouraged a few of us to eat flower heads and talk about the philosophy of life, but for the most part we examined economic and political problems and the outlook for the individual in a world of vast organizations. To the forefront were growing mass unemployment and the threat of nuclear war. The issues were debated keenly, brutally on occasion when Heath, Arbatov or Kissinger intervened, yet there was to me encouragement in the very fact that the dialogue took place.

Galbraith had done a great deal to develop understanding with his television series, and he demonstrated the art of the diplomat as well as that of the economic expert in the way he guided the discussions. My own role was less clear. I suppose I was there to ensure that the view of the man and woman in the street and the workplace wasn't overlooked – at least that is how I saw it.

On the way back to Boston Ted Heath and Shirley Williams thought we should have some culture and I was persuaded to join them at a concert given by a famous flautist. When we were having a drink together, then and later, I learned how deeply Ted Heath resented Margaret Thatcher for her conduct towards him and the course she was adopting. For all his Toryism (and he really is very much a traditional Tory – as came out in the Galbraith talks) he commanded my respect by his humanity and integrity. Shirley Williams, on the other hand, appeared to me then, and all the time I had known her, as a pragmatic middle-of-the-roader veering to the right. I liked her for her friendly nature but she was and is far removed from the trade unionist of the workshop floor.

In September 1977 the TGWU reached a membership total of more than two million. It gave me special pleasure, because of my strong personal commitment to the building of the union's strength over many years. It was not for me the magic of numbers but the growing popularity of the union at the workplace which mattered. More and more people were coming to rely on the weapon of trade unionism as represented by the TGWU. The size of the union was important in dealing with the Government and with employers. In providing services for members, it meant we could enjoy the economy of size, keeping our contributions relatively low but expanding essential help.

The real strength of a Union lies in its activists: the shop stewards, collectors, branch secretaries, chairmen and the rest. In the TGWU they had responded enthusiastically, with the officers of the union, in organizing, consolidating, spreading the message. My contribution was to use all my efforts in raising the prestige of the union and in doing so to improve the conditions of the class into which I was born and bred.

Chapter Thirty

Do not go gentle into that good night,
Old age should burn and rave at close of day;
Rage, rage against the dying of the light.

DYLAN THOMAS

The Dimbleby Lecture, held to commemorate the work of that splendid communicator Richard Dimbleby, is an event in the BBC calendar carrying great prestige. In December 1977 the lecture took place in the grand surroundings of the Livery Hall of the Clothworkers Company in the City of London. I had the unique opportunity, for a trade unionist, to deliver the lecture. Since the lecture was televised live, I was conscious that large numbers of people were watching and listening all over the country. It was an awesome thought that I had to try to keep their attention for the best part of fifty minutes.

My chosen subject was 'The Human Face of Labour', and I used the occasion to explain the role of trade unions in defending human values at the place of work. I argued, for the benefit of the Government, that peace in industry was more important than pay restraint and that, 'if strikes are to be avoided industrial justice must be made available easily and speedily'. This, of course, led me on to expound the case for extending the arbitration and conciliation service. My other main theme was to advocate industrial democracy. And of course I could not miss the opportunity to put the case against low wages and for a better deal for the pensioners. It was a statement of my personal credo, including my ideas on trade union leadership: 'Surely true leadership is the leadership of ideas. Justify your arguments. Use your experience and, above all, don't lay down barriers of red tape and pomposity between your members and the decisions that affect them.'

In a gentle sort of way Roger Woddis in the *New Statesman* reminded me of the dangers of 'lecturing people'. In a TGWU shop stewards' handbook I had suggested that they should be courteous in negotiations with management. Roger wrote:

Speak gently to your kindly boss,
     Avoiding sudden rages:
It doesn't help to make him cross
     When seeking higher wages.

He may appear to be perverse,
     If not downright unstable,
But you will only make him worse
     By thumping on the table.

Try emulating Mr Jones,
     However it upsets you:
Negotiate in dulcet tones,
     And then see where it gets you.

Present your case with care and skill,
     Bow low when he refuses,
And show you bear him no ill will,
     Especially if he loses.

He may be suffering from piles,
     His wife may be a warlock;
So win him round with teeth 'n' smiles,
     While tugging at your forelock.

Show him how well you understand,
     Regard him as your neighbour,
And shake him warmly by the hand
     When you withdraw your labour.

Versifying is not just the prerogative of the professional. At an all-Wales TGWU pre-retirement function for me at Caerphilly they had even composed and printed a song about the union to the tune of *Sosfan Bach*. It was a great occasion, and Evelyn and I felt very proud of the tributes paid to us in the warm-hearted way of the Welsh people. In responding I suppose I was more emotional than usual and spoke of my vision of socialism. While I was doing this Jim Callaghan leaned over to Evelyn and said: 'Jack really means what he says!' When telling me about this Evelyn said: 'I felt like saying to Jim, "Don't we all then?" – but I kept quiet.'

331

Towards the end of 1977 retirement pensions went up by 14 per cent and the £10 Christmas bonus was restored. It was an advance but it was still not enough, and I used a lot of my energy in trying to convince everyone with influence that British pensioners were not 'doing all right' – as Jim Callaghan had said to me some time previously. 'Where do you get that idea from, Jim?' I asked. His response was to tell me that he had recently visited a pensioner who had declared that he was doing very well. It turned out that the home he had been to was that of Tom McNally's father (McNally was Jim's personal assistant at the time) and that his occupation before retirement had been a foreman in the steel industry. It was fair to assume that the old man was in receipt of an occupational pension and no doubt some help from Tom McNally too. 'That's not exactly a typical case,' I told Jim.

Generosity and goodwill were evident in our union ranks, and I was touched and encouraged by it. On the other hand I was amazed at the weakness of the pensioners' organizations. At this time I was invited to become a vice-president of Age Concern, an organization for which I had and still have great respect. I accepted the invitation but realized that I must do more than that and I proceeded to launch the idea of linking the various pensioners' movements and charities together with the TUC in one united body. At least, I argued, we should have a common set of claims to put to the Government, and, if possible, we should make joint representations to stop ministers playing one organization off against another.

These views prevailed and eventually we were able to form the National Pensioners' Convention and adopt a Declaration of Intent which set out the most urgent needs of the pensioners. The movement lacked finance, so we turned to the TUC to provide clerical assistance and research. Even with this success I realized that very hard work was required to build the movement at the grass roots. I determined to devote most of my efforts to developing the union's retired members' association, whose president I had become. I hoped to induce retiring trade unionists to recapture the sense of community which most experience at work, within the fellowship of a retirement association. As I write we are still trying to make progress in this direction. At least we can say there is much greater awareness that there is a pensioners' movement than there used to be. Retired people are becoming more conscious of their rights and are beginning to see that the problems of old age are not just for the professionals. Our point of view should be taken into account.

Jim Callaghan's premiership had not been easy but his dependence upon Liberal support did not seem to trouble him unduly. He seemed confident, in his comfortable way, that he could get along with David Steel. We in the unions were more worried about the position than he was, for Liberal involvement meant a loss of trade union influence. He and I occasionally had talks together, and on one occasion at the end of 1977 he returned to the idea that I might join the Lords. When I rejected it as I had done previously, he said: 'I think your work must be recognized. Will you accept a Companionship of Honour? It was set up to take the point of view of people like you into account. It carries no title and no privileges.' Jim went on to explain the background to the honour, making the point that it would be a recognition of the union as well as myself. I agreed to accept it, perhaps somewhat against my better judgement. Many members of the union wrote congratulating me including, surprisingly, a number of left-wing members. They knew it wouldn't affect my fight for the abolition of the House of Lords and against other forces of reaction in society.

Because of the award I had the opportunity of having a private talk with the Queen. I had met her before a number of times and had formed a high respect for her personally. On this occasion she displayed a remarkable awareness of human problems that I thought would be outside her ken. We spoke of working conditions in the motor-car industry and the human problems of assembly-line production and of redundancies. And of course we discussed my interest in the situation of retired people.

Later Evelyn and I, together with Michael Foot and his wife Jill, were guests of the Queen at Windsor. She was quick to remind me that she suffered from industrial troubles too. Shortly before our visit the Castle had expected a delivery of oil, an oil tanker arrived only to turn back because it was 5 p.m. and an overtime ban was in operation. She knew that the tanker drivers were members of the TGWU. Jokingly she told me that 'we had to walk about this big place with our overcoats on to keep warm, thanks to your members'.

Because of our visit a special display of materials dealing with the Tolpuddle martyrs was put out for us to see. The Duke of Edinburgh told us that, at that time, the Home Secretary was Lord Melbourne, and that his papers were part of the Castle's archives. I'm not sure whether the Duke approved of the way trade unionists were dealt with then, but he occasionally smiled at me significantly.

There are some wonderful paintings at Windsor Castle and we

delighted in seeing them and other treasures, but at one stage the Duke was pointing out some smaller paintings, one of which was of the Castle grounds. It looked a little amateurish to me and I said so. 'That's mine!' exclaimed Prince Philip. He had, I gathered, taken up painting as one of his many hobbies. It might have appeased his irritation if I had told him that he was a better painter than me, for that was the case, but I thought it best to say nothing. The *faux pax* had been committed and there it had to stay.

In the last months before my retirement I was still heavily involved in industrial matters, in particular pressing for decasualization schemes in the trawler-fishing and construction industries. The insecurity of employment in both industries was appalling, and I led deputations in the one case to the Prime Minister and in the other to Albert Booth, the Secretary of State for Employment. Only Government action could have effected real changes, but the Government's power had gone; it was in pawn to David Steel and his colleagues. On the National Ports Council the Labour Government had not changed the heavy majority in favour of market forces and shipowners and commercial interests continued to dominate ports policy. From the earliest days of the Council this had caused problems for me, when I advocated social considerations as a primary factor in port development. I argued for instance, that the National Ports Council should force shipowners to use Liverpool or London by preventing developments elsewhere. Little or no support was forthcoming for this view, with the result that we now see the terrible dereliction of the London and Liverpool docklands.

I enjoyed plenty of variety: one day negotiating with the chairman of a large oil company over trade union representation on the oil rigs, on another meeting dockers and Harris tweed weavers on the Isle of Lewis, and then paying my last visit before retirement to Gibraltar. I had taken a special interest in the industrial affairs of the Rock since the days of General Franco and had encouraged the TGWU branch to grow from about 1000 members to over 7000. Whatever the future of Gibraltar may be, trade unionism is firmly established there.

A unique opportunity came my way when I was invited to address five hundred top businessmen from some fifty countries in a European business symposium in Davos, Switzerland. It is a marvellous conference centre, set in the midst of the Swiss Alps – that is probably what attracted so many business people. My contribution was to warn of the crippling weight of bureaucracy in multinational corporations and other large organizations, resulting in a worsening deal for workers. I said that trade unions wanted to stamp out managerial inefficiency and to achieve lower unit costs; giving workers an equal voice in decision-making would help in this. I also put the case for the adoption of a thirty-five hour working week and earlier retirement as a means of reducing unemployment, but my views did not find universal acceptance.

From the city of Coventry where I had spent so many active and happy years came an invitation out of the blue to accept its special Award of Merit. Shortly afterwards another award was extended to me in Coventry, when I received an honorary doctorate from Warwick University. Naturally I felt honoured, yet I got more satisfaction out of the visits I paid to Coventry for the pensioners' movement. Among the many retired people who were becoming active in the campaign were old friends who had held various posts in the trade unions in former days. Men or women who have been active as union officials or shop stewards do not need training to speak up for their fellow pensioners, it is in their bones. I found this to be the case not only in Coventry but all over the country.

In the months before I retired I continued to use trade union influence to push the case for the retired. One day, after presenting the case for a non-statutory body for national transport planning, I raised with Bill Rogers, the Secretary of State for Transport, the need for more concessionary fares for retired, blind and disabled people. Shortly afterwards local authorities were told that it would 'be appropriate for an authority in introducing a concessionary fare scheme to aim to meet about half the cost. . . .' This meant that money would be made available in the Rate Support Grant for this purpose. Some months later a Green Paper was issued announcing the Government's intention to introduce a national scheme for half fares on trains as well as buses for local journeys anywhere in Britain. Unfortunately the promise of a national scheme was lost with the change of Government in 1979.

For many years I held the post of Chairman of the TUC Transport Industries Committee. If there was anything on which all the transport unions were agreed it was on the need for more integration and for the planning of transport operations. From our varied experience we knew that this would be in the public interest. As part of this approach I initiated talks with the Department of Transport and the chairmen of the Railways and Docks boards, the National Bus Company and

Daily Mail, 29 March 1978

the National Freight Corporation. Early talks were encouraging but, again, prospects faded with the change of Government.

Retirement did not come on me suddenly, because I had actively prepared to work in the pensioners' movement. When my official responsibilities came to an end there was I, as busy as ever, speaking, writing and organizing just as I had done for dozens of years in the union cause. But now my appeal was to and for the senior citizens.

There was no sad parting. In fact the final rally, where I was expected to make my retirement speech, turned out to be an hilarious affair. There had been so many retirement functions for me that Jim Callaghan suggested I was being treated like Dame Nellie Melba! The show was dominated by Mike Yarwood, whose impressions of Jim and me had everybody rocking in their seats. Of course the speeches and the messages from all over the world touched me considerably, but the greatest pleasure was to have Evelyn and all our family around me, together with so many of my wider family – activists from the far-flung corners of the union, nearly three thousand of them.

Among the awards I had received, during my life, I cherished none more than the gold medal of the TGWU. It was presented to me by

Stan Pemburton from Liverpool, who was chairman of the union's Executive Council and one of the most able and devoted of the union's shop stewards. In thanking him and the TGWU I urged the need for international solidarity and peace and referred to my life-long belief in socialism. But, I emphasized too the need to continue organizing the unorganized: 'Organize, that's still a magic word, because with organization you can move mountains.'

With deep feeling I told the massive audience: 'It has been a wonderful privilege for me to serve within this great army of labour, and now I am about to retire to the ranks – but I will still remain in the army of labour, even if it's the dad's army section.' It was to this section I asked that my testimonial fund should be devoted, as I passed the cheque back to the chairman.

Without the knowledge of anyone within the union two representatives of the UGT journeyed over from Spain to bring a message from the leadership and a present in the form of wooden carvings of Don Quixote and Sancho Panza. Said one of the men: 'You fought for the workers everywhere, in a practical way . . . not like Don Quixote!' I did not deserve such tributes but at least they encouraged me to continue to strive in support of working people and those, in Walter Reuther's words, who are 'too old to work but too young to die. . . .'

In the years immediately following my retirement as TGWU Secretary, active trade unionism continued to fill some of my time. For one thing I had remained Vice-President of the International Transport Workers Federation, and when opportunities came along for me to visit countries in the South Pacific, the first people I looked for were members of the local unions of transport workers which were linked to the ITF. Most of the countries were former British colonies and their labour laws had a background in our 1906 legislation. This had certainly helped with trade union development, and trade unions were numerous – in some ways too numerous, resulting in financial weakness.

A decision of the Fiji Government to review their labour laws led to the TUC inviting me to go there and participate in discussions with the Government and an ILO representative. The unions have developed impressively in Fiji, except for the reservation I have made about numbers, and the leadership has carefully sought to ensure unity between the Polynesian and Indian communities. It was not difficult to fit in with so many friendly people and a situation not dissimilar to what I knew in Britain.

Evelyn made this trip with me. We agreed that she should not be left out, and by planning our budget economically it did not present too much difficulty. Women were making their way in the Fiji trade unions and Evelyn's presence helped a lot. We stayed in a modest self-catering hotel, which meant that we saw much more of the local life than would have been the case if we had resided in one of the luxurious (and probably foreign-owned) hotels on the outskirts of Suva. Evelyn went daily to the local market to buy our food while I worked at the Fiji TUC office or took part in the many meetings. We were welcomed into the homes of trade unionists and mixed together as good friends.

The absence of a Labour Party surprised me and I sensed that, under the surface, communal divisions existed. Within the unions there were those who would have been described as militants in Britain, and others who favoured the establishment, but in neither case were the traditional politics of the West in evidence. The right to strike without legal restrictions was at the core of our discussions, and it was clearly worrying to a Government subjected to pressure from the growing capitalist-entrepreneurial section of their society. I wondered how long it would be before the political scene took a sharper form.

While in Fiji I was asked to pay a quick visit to Tarawa, the capital of Kiribati (the former Gilbert Islands) to talk with the trade unions there about a prolonged industrial dispute. Virtually the only employer was the Government and most of their employees had been on strike and then dismissed. In a developed country this would have meant calamity, because the workers were without unemployment or strike pay and the union was bankrupt. In Tarawa there was food available for the taking – coconuts, breadfruit, and plenty of fish in the sea. On a sunny coral island, with huts built from the coconut and pandennis trees, life might have been idyllic if there had been no invasion from 'civilization' outside.

The administration at the top was largely in the hands of seconded Britishers who gave no help to my attempts to get talks going. On the contrary, they had been extremely upset by the tactics of the strikers who, when told it was illegal to cut off the electricity supply, restored the electricity but cut off the water instead. The effect of this had been to make life uncomfortable in the Government offices and the houses of the administrators. There was an obvious desire to make no concessions, in the knowledge that there was ample alternative labour in the other islands of Kiribati.

Though I was not successful in breaking the deadlock I was able to help in restoring union morale, in uniting the small but different unions, including the seamen and teachers, and in forging stronger links with the Australian trade unions and the newly formed Commonwealth Trade Union Council, whose director Carl Wright had urged me to make the trip. Our impression of the trade unionists of Kiribati was one of outstanding dignity and innate ability. We were welcomed with friendly affection, in the traditional style of a naturally sincere people. It was the same when we went to the Solomon Islands; workers in these remote areas proved that their trade union spirit was as strong as that of their brothers and sisters in the developed countries. I was satisfied that this was the case when I took part in a meeting between shop stewards and management in the big palm oil project in the Solomon Islands. They spoke in pidgin English, and to my surprise I could not understand a word! I had to ask one of their number to interpret for me, but there was no doubting their ability and determination.

These and other visits confirmed my belief in international solidarity. It would be a mistake to think that people in the Third World are just waiting for hand-outs or to be led like little children. It is the hand of friendship, not paternalism, which is required. Big powers and multinational corporations with special interests and often ulterior motives are a danger to them, but trade unions should see their relationship in the words of Keir Hardie: 'They are of the workers, they are our kin, we are part of them – their battle is our battle. What hurts them hurts us – where they gain we gain.' As I recall trade union leaders wearing a pair of shorts and walking in their bare feet, working in primitive conditions and striving to overcome almost impossible odds, I know they would nod their heads in agreement.

'That will keep you occupied, Jack,' said the chairman of one of the union's regions when presenting me with a marvellous set of painting materials. And I thought it would, for I dearly wanted to spend time painting. But more immediate activities have filled my retirement. It would have been a hard-hearted person who could have ignored the enormous volume of letters which I received from elderly people in all parts of the country, describing their troubles. I wrote to ministers and lobbied Members of Parliament, and if the advances made were few and far between at least nobody slammed the door in my face.

The National Pensioners Convention gained support and became known especially for its annual lobby of Parliament and deputations to party leaders. Our message was that $9\frac{1}{2}$ million citizens should not be ignored. Mrs Thatcher, as Prime Minister, at first was not inclined to see us. When an approach was made we were rebuffed, and it became known that she was lunching somewhere in the City on the day we wanted to meet her. The resulting publicity made sure that she met our deputation in the years which followed. Not that we made much progress. The means test and low pensions remained. Repeatedly we were told: 'It's the wrong time. The burden on the working population and the taxpayers would be too great.' My reply was: 'It is never the wrong time to do justice to the retired.' So the campaign continues and I'll be part of it until our aims are secured.

If the problems of my fellow senior citizens concerned me, neither could I stand aside from the social challenge which was reappearing on a scale as great as any I had known in my youth – unemployment. As a grandfather I worried at the lack of employment prospects for my grandchildren and their generation. I could not rest, and I do not think that any serious-minded person should, while the opportunities for youngsters leaving school are so dismal.

'The economic and social problems of society cannot be ignored when considering how crime should be dealt with,' I told the Royal Commission on Criminal Procedure to which I was appointed by Merlyn Rees, the Labour Home Secretary. Such bodies are supposed to be the preserve of 'the great and the good' but I was neither great nor good; on the other hand I had rather more experience of the life of working people than other members of that august body. The one person on the Commission with whom I closely identified was Wilfred Wood, a black clergyman, now Bishop of Croydon, whose knowledge of the disadvantages suffered by the black working population and the unemployed coincided with my own.

My academic knowledge was negligible although I welcomed the facilities granted to me by the London School of Economics when I was invited to become an Associate Fellow. I used the library, and enjoyed welcome clerical assistance. In return I gave the odd lecture, but the whole thing got me into hot water. I was persuaded to stand against Princess Anne for the Chancellorship of London University. The Chancellorship had never been contested in the 144-year history of the University.

The University authorities were embarrassed at finding that Princess Anne would not be allowed to succeed her grandmother, the

Queen Mother, without a contest. I stood because I did not believe that the appointment should automatically go to the elite and I genuinely thought I could help to bring the University down from the clouds and nearer to the people. Although I finished well behind the Princess, the fact that I received a big vote from graduates justified my standing. Had I been elected I would have sought to bring the university closer to working people and to highlight the need for an increasing role for retired people within the universities and in the educational field generally. Not least I would have tried to put the spotlight on the curse of racialism.

After I had been nominated, a group of graduates put forward the name of Nelson Mandela, the imprisoned leader of the black people of South Africa. Although the nomination was symbolic I had every sympathy with it, and I suggested to my supporters that I should withdraw in his favour. They reacted strongly against the idea, on the grounds that my nomination was a serious challenge to the establishment, and insisted that my name should stand. I reluctantly agreed, although on looking back I am sure it would have been better to withdraw, for it might have given more publicity to Nelson Mandela and the cause he stands for. I would certainly not have wished to harm his cause, for in my retirement I remain a vice-president of the Anti-Apartheid movement.

So one way or another my active life continues with Evelyn, as always, by my side. I remain close to the trade union movement and the TGWU in particular, for trade unionism has been my life. In retrospect I wonder if I could have done more, and yet I have devoted so much of my life and strength to the cause of working people. It was not a sacrifice – it was an honour of the highest degree.

To be the leader of a large union like the TGWU is to fill a position of great responsibility. It means unlimited worry but it provides unique opportunities for helping the interests of working people. It is not an easy job – you need all the assistance you can muster. You need stamina and determination to stand up to the attacks from critics on all sides: not just from the employers, the media, and right-wing politicians but criticism from within the union and the Labour movement.

Justified or not, it is right that criticism should be made, otherwise it would be too easy to become self-satisfied and flabby. In my time I have seen too many union leaders enjoying the fleshpots and seeking perks and favours. There have been too many weak and vacillating leaders. Criticism can be a safeguard against such people, whilst at the same time helping one to learn from one's own mistakes. Open discussion and honest criticism is a vital element in ensuring the strength of trade unionism.

For let it be said – so long as there are employed people there will be a need for strong trade unions, in which the rank-and-file-members are the effective masters. Some would describe this as participating democracy. I am all for it and always have been, from the moment I took trade union membership fifty-six years ago.

Despite its opponents and critics, trade unionism is needed more than ever today to secure equality and justice at work and in society. It is needed to grapple with the problems of technological change and multinational companies. My hope is that it will grow in the spirit of internationalism, helping the poor of the world to rise from their poverty and strengthening the efforts for world peace. Is it a dream? I do not think so.

INDEX

Jones, Hannah (JJ's grandaughter), 185
Jones, Jack (JJ's son): born, 85–6; as child,
  93; in air-raid, 99–101; in nursery, 115;
  falls in canal, 137; goes to sea, 141;
  married, 154; as teacher, 185
Jones, Jack: childhood, 11–20; ill, 18; first
  job, 23–4; early union activities, 24–5;
  and unemployment, 25–6, 36–41; as
  young union activist, 30–31, 45–52; and
  safety conditions, 31–2; and local politics,
  53–4, 57–8; joins International Brigade,
  59–62; wounded, 75–6; marries, 81;
  resumes union activities, 82–6; as
  Coventry District Organizer, 85–98; as
  Engineering Group Secretary for Midlands
  Region, 140–53; appointed to TGWU
  headquarters, 153; organizes recruiting
  drive, 156; as Acting Assistant General
  Secretary, 160; on NEC, 167; leisure
  time, 177–8; stands down from NEC,
  181; and racial discrimination, 197; and
  In Place of Strife, 202–12; as General
  Secretary, 211–336; in Gibraltar, 215–16;
  and pensions, 225–6; injured, 238; travels,
  200–201, 203, 317–23, 227–9; awards,
  330–37; 'The Human Face of Labour',
  330; and passim
Jones, James (JJ's grandfather), 15, 16
Jones, Jane (JJ's granddaughter), 185
Jones, Marsden, 136
Jones, Michael (JJ's son): born, 119; at
  Solihull School, 141; student, 154; as
  artist, 185
Jones, Ronald, 294
Jones, Sally (JJ's granddaughter), 185
Jones, Syd, 19, 80
Jones, Tom, 200
Jones, Wilf, 201
Jones, Winnie (JJ's sister), 12, 43
Jones/Aldington Committee, 252–3
Jouhaux, Leon, 267

Karlin, Miriam, 226
Kealey, Les, 207–8
Kearton, Frank, 177, 261, 279
Keeler, Christine, 158
Kelly, Denis, 187, 189
Kelly, Pat, 322
Kersten, Otto, 293
Kiev, 172
Kingston Peridot (ship), 191
Kiribati, 338–9
Kissinger, Henry, 210, 328
Kitson, Alex, 242
Kitson, David, 275

Labour Party (Coventry), 121

Labour Party: JJ member, 25; and
  unemployment, 36–41; and local Liver-
  pool politics, 54; after 1970 defeat,
  236–7; NEC, 282; discussions in, 245
Labour, Ministry of, 92, 110, 114, 128
Larkin, Jim, 13–14
Law, Alan, 149–50
Lea, David, 313–14
Lee, Jack, 214
Leggate, Jim, 190
Lenin, V. I., 65
Leningrad, 172
Lett, Harry, 142
Lever, Harold, 226, 303, 308
Lewis, Clive, 75, 80
Lewis, Harold, 290
Liberal Party, 40
Lima, 292
Linaria (ship), 56–7
Lindley, Bill, 165, 242
Little, Jack, 69
Liverpool City Mission, 18
Liverpool Daily Post (newspaper), 186
Liverpool Trades Council and Labour
  Party, 24
Liverpool, Bishop of, 80
Logan, David, 53
London Transport Executive, 219
London, 78
Longbottom, Pastor, 53–4
Lord, Leonard, 129
Lord, Mr (Works Manager, Standard Motor
  Company), 134
lorry drivers: organization of, 149–50
Louis XIV, King of France: JJ compared
  to, 316
Lovestone, Jay, 268
Lowthian, George, 203, 229, 268
Loyden, Eddie, 287–8
Lyons, Sir William, 98

MacDonald, James Ramsay, 25, 40, 48
Macdonald, Raymond, 166
Macintosh, John, 311
MacLeod, Ian, 145–7
Macmillan, Maurice, 249
Major Attlee Company, the, 67–8, 70
Mallalieu, J. P. W., 191
Mandela, Nelson, 341
Mann, Tom, 13, 17, 51–2, 62, 70
Marsh, Richard, 313
Marty, André, 70
Marx, Karl, 48
Massey, George, 119
Maudling, Reginald, 223
McGarvey, Dan, 175, 265, 269–70, 276
McGree, Leo, 37

347

349

women: in trade unions, 113; employment in USSR, 271

Wood, Wilfred, Bishop of Croydon, 340

Woodcock, George, 139, 156–7, 168, 195–6, 203

Woodcock, Leonard, 213, 234

Workers' Educational Association, 35

Working Men's Conservative Clubs, 50

World Federation of Trade Unions, 132, 267

World Labour Party, 42

World War I, 12

World War II: old-age pensions after, 51; declared, 93; JJ in Coventry during, 93–120

Wright, Roland, 235

Wyatt, Woodrow, 138

Yarwood, Mike, 336

York, Archbishop of, 40–41

Yugoslavia, 49–50, 137–8

Zilliacus, Konni, 171